Body of Power, Spirit of Resistance

mnemonic
- assisting or intended to assist
memory
- verse; formula

BODY OF POWER SPIRIT OF RESISTANCE

The Culture and History of a South African People

Jean Comaroff

The University of Chicago Press
Chicago and London

The University of Chicago Press, Chicago 60637
The University of Chicago Press, Ltd., London
© 1985 by The University of Chicago
All rights reserved. Published 1985
Printed in the United States of America
03 02 01 00 99 98 97   6 7 8 9

Library of Congress Cataloging in Publication Data

Comaroff, Jean.
  Body of power, spirit of resistance.

  Bibliography: p.
  Includes index.
  1. Rolong (African people)—Ethnic identity.
2. Rolong (African people)—Religion.   3. Rolong
(African people)—Politics and government.   I. Title.
DT764.R65C65   1985   306'.089963   84–24012
ISBN 0-226-11423-6 (pbk.)

∞ The paper used in this publication meets the minimum
requirements of the American National Standard for
Information Sciences—Permanence of Paper for Printed
Library Materials, ANSI Z39.48-1984.

for John

Every household in the fine suburb had several black servants—trusted cooks who were allowed to invite their grandchildren to spend their holidays in the backyard, faithful gardeners from whom the family watch-dog was inseparable, a shifting population of pretty young housemaids whose long red nails and pertness not only asserted the indignity of being undiscovered or out-of-work fashion models but kept hoisted a cocky guerilla pride against servitude to whites: *there are many forms of resistance not recognized in orthodox revolutionary strategy*.

Nadine Gordimer, *Something Out There*
(emphasis added)

Contents

Illustrations

Map

Figures

Plates

Preface

A book, says Foucault, is an emerging object within a "group of multiple relations"—relations that are both material and conceptual. More than that, the connection between text and context is largely one of "silent development," and the conventional acknowledgments of authors tell us little about the actual formation of any intellectual product. Mindful of this, I yet offer a brief account of the tangible foundations of a project long in the making. In a sense, this study is itself the outcome of the colonial process that is its explicit focus. For those of us raised on the margins of the First and Third Worlds, the interplay of center and periphery gives predominant shape to the actual and the possible, whether we realize it or not. A few, born to privilege, have been permitted the luxury of contemplating the forces that, for the majority, especially in modern South Africa, are an immediate, coercive reality. This book is the product of that privilege, and in conveying something of the logic and subtle creativity of those whose discourse remains stifled, it must, at best, be inadequate.

My study draws upon two periods of fieldwork, one among the Tshidi Barolong of the Mafeking District of South Africa, carried out in 1969–70, and a second among the Barolong of southeastern Botswana in 1974–75. My research was supported, at various stages, by the Social Science Research Council (U.K.) and the Esperanza Trust, and the preparation of this volume was made possible by a fellowship from the Bunting Institute of Radcliffe College, Harvard University, and by a grant from the Lichtstern Fund of the Department of Anthropology, University of Chicago.

It was Monica Wilson who first taught me that the anthropology of southern Africa was about the "Reaction to Conquest," and that social relations were a matter of history as well as structure, of ritual as well as pragmatics. My training under her was followed by graduate work at the London School of Economics under Isaac Schapera, the doyen of Tswana studies. The LSE was a heady place in the late 1960s, especially for those of us who came from the colonial fringe, and it left a permanent mark upon our moral sensibilities as social scientists. Subsequent work at the Universities of Manchester and Chicago served to sharpen my emerging concern with social transformation, and with the reciprocal determination of material forces and cultural forms.

The Tshidi Barolong among whom I worked showed tolerance and even enthusiasm for an enterprise which they had every right to reject as a self-indulgent intrusion. My colleagues at the University of Chicago continue to provide a uniquely challenging environment, and the many students with whom I have had contact there have also taught me a great deal. Raymond Smith read an earlier draft of this manuscript and commented on it with care and acuity; so too did Nancy Munn and Terence Turner, whose creative insight into the symbolism of the body, space, and time have left a definitive mark upon my thinking. My children, Josh and Jane, for whom "work" and "book" have long been four-letter words, have shown forbearance, faith, and healthy resistance. And John Comaroff, who has shared this journey from its early South African beginnings, has been a constant support. He has tempered my unruly imagination with analytic rigor and it is hardly possible for me to separate his authorship definitively from my own. If there is any merit in this study, it is as much his as mine.

1

Introduction

This study examines the relationship of social practice, historical process, and cultural mediation in an African society, that of the Barolong boo Ratshidi (Tshidi) of the South Africa-Botswana borderland. Within the span of one hundred and fifty years, this independent Tswana chiefdom has become a part of the rural periphery of the South African state, its predicament being a typical instance of the contradictory relationship between the First and Third Worlds aptly termed "neocolonialism." My concern is with the social and cultural logic of this relationship, with Tshidi history as a dialectical process in a double sense: the product of the interplay between human action and structural constraint, and between the dominant and the subordinate in the colonial encounter. I set out to explore the role of the Tshidi as determined, yet determining, in their own history; as human beings who, in their everyday production of goods and meanings, acquiesce yet protest, reproduce yet seek to transform their predicament.

The Tshidi of the late twentieth century occupy a position in southern Africa similar to that of other peripheral peoples in the underdeveloped world. While they have been drawn systematically into the labor market over the past eighty years, they are compelled to remain dependent upon nonmonetarized agricultural production, a condition referred to by Parson (1980) as that of the "peasantariat" (see also Palmer and Parsons 1977; Amselle 1976; Meillassoux 1975). A century and a half ago, Christian missionaries served as the vanguard of colonialism among the peoples of the southern African interior, introducing a mode of thought and practice which became engaged with indigenous social systems, triggering internal transformations in productive and power relations, and an-

1

ticipating the more pervasive structural changes that were soon to
follow. [The innovations of the mission not only exacerbated internal
contradictions within the Tshidi system itself, they also instituted a set of
categories through which such tensions could be objectified and acted
upon.] But these categories bore with them the imprint of the indus-
trializing society that had given them birth: evangelical Methodism was
to prove an efficient teacher of the values and predispositions of the industrial workplace. Indeed, Christian symbols provided the *lingua franca*
through which the hierarchical articulation of colonizer and colonized
was accomplished. At the same time, however, the interchange of Protestantism and proletarianization also concretized an awareness of inequality, creating a new basis for challenge and resistance. Where state
coercion stifled manifest political expression, the polysemic metaphors
of the Old and New Testaments offered a haven for the critical imagination. As has occurred elsewhere in the Third World, the submission to
authority celebrated by the Christian faith was transformed into a biblically validated defiance (cf. Ileto 1979 on the Philippines and Post 1978
on Jamaica). Yet such defiance had, of necessity, to remain concealed and
coded; and a central concern of this study is to arrive at an understanding
of its cultural logic and its long-term historical significance.

Of course, there are certain parallels here with the cultural changes
that accompanied the industrial revolution in Europe; for, in an important sense, the colonial process involved the making of an African working class (Marks and Rathbone 1982). Yet, as the ethnographic record
shows, the extension of capitalism into the Third World was by no
means a replay of the history of the modern West. The transformation of
preexisting modes of production has seldom been a smooth, unidirectional process (Meillassoux 1972); and, far from sweeping all before it,
and replacing indigenous cultural forms with its own social and ideological structures, the advancing capitalist system has clearly been determined, in significant respects, by the local systems it has sought to engulf
(Foster-Carter 1978; Marks and Rathbone 1982).

The modern Tshidi are living embodiments of such contradictory processes of articulation.[1] Most participate in the labor market to a greater or
lesser degree, and are acutely aware of their unequivocal role as black
workers in a repressive, racist regime. Yet they also engage in productive
and exchange relations that perpetuate significant features of the precolonial social system, one in which human relations were not pervasively mediated by commodities and dominant symbols unified man,
spirit, and nature in a mutually effective, continuous order of being.
Such a sociocultural order stands in contrast with the mode of production of industrial South Africa, its dominant ideology, and its underlying

semantic design—a world in which social and cultural continuities appear to be fractured and individuals, abruptly wrenched from their human and spiritual contexts, are no longer able to recognize or realize themselves. I shall examine the ways in which persons thus decentered strive to reconstruct themselves and their universe. But I shall also show that the movement from nonmarket to market-dominated relations is not an all-or-none, unidirectional process; it entails a complex oscillation whose cultural dynamics still challenge our understanding (Mauss 1966; cf. Phimister and van Onselen 1979:43 on the South African case).

General Analytic Issues

The focus of this study places it within the purview of several key concerns in modern social theory. At the most general level, it speaks of the essential interdependence of anthropology and history in the study of social systems, and attempts to span a series of stubborn dichotomies in the legacy of modern social analysis—the division between global and local perspectives; between materialist and semantic interpretations; between structuralist and processual models; and between subjectivist and normative methodologies. My account, in short, is an exploration of the viability of a dialectical approach to the life of a single social system over time. It sets out to examine the reciprocal interplay of human practice, social structure, and symbolic mediation, an interplay contained within the process of articulation between a peripheral community and a set of encompassing sociocultural forces.

Central to my project is the perennial problem of identifying the appropriate unit of analysis. The social field here is the product of the continuous and changing relationship between the "system" under observation and the "external" world (J. L. Comaroff 1982). Its scope, then, is not an a-priori assumption of this research; to wit, at each step I encountered difficulties in defining the widening universe that might be thought to have constructed the "Tshidi context." What is more, the dynamics of this universe were themselves in question. In Africa, as elsewhere in the Third World, the relationship between local social orders and the agencies of the world system shows clearly the inadequacy of synchronic models that presuppose the "perpetuation" or "reproduction" of existing sociocultural structures. But they also belie the assumptions of teleological models of transformation (whether of "modernization" or "dependency") which beg all the key questions about the nature and direction of historical processes. Both local and global systems are at once systematic and contradictory; and they became engaged with one another in relations characterized by symbiosis as well as struggle. It is the specific configuration of such forms and forces in the Tshidi case—its particular motivation—that concerns me here; and, inevitably, this has features both unique and more general.

Motivation, in turn, is to be conceptualized at two distinct levels with respect to such historical processes: the first concerns the determining force of sociocultural structures upon those processes; the second, the transformative practice of human actors. Both levels are entailed in an adequate conception of historical agency, and indeed, their principled interconnection is an important problem for modern social analysis in general. At issue here is the very constitution of social practice itself—and, with it, the connection of context, consciousness, and intentionality, an order of relations often treated within the more general debate on the nature of "ideology." One aspect of that debate bears directly upon my treatment of historical motivation in the Tshidi case.

Where he dealt explicitly with the concept of ideology in his own writing, Marx related it to the exercise of specific group interests, thereby laying the basis for its association with "discourse," or the conscious management of ideation (Marx and Engels 1970:64ff.). Yet, especially in his later work—on the notion of commodity fetishism, for instance—he envisaged consciousness as taking shape in the representations implicit in "lived experience" (Marx 1967:71ff.; cf. Giddens 1979:183). These two dimensions of ideology—"theory" and practical consciousness—are seldom brought into satisfactory relationship in the work of subsequent writers in the critical tradition. Thus Williams (1977:55ff.) treats ideology and its role in human practice as a matter of "belief," of the "conscious imagination" which rationally mediates all action upon the world. Consciousness, from this perspective, resides in contemplative rather than practical understanding.

Foucault (1980[a]:58) has noted that this stress upon a rationalizing consciousness implies a particular vision of the motivation of historical processes: "what troubles me with [those] analyses which prioritize ideology is that there is always presupposed a human subject on the lines of the model provided by classical philosophy, endowed with a consciousness which power is then thought to seize on." Furthermore, the stress upon ideology as discourse also entails an essentialist theory of meaning, in terms of which ideas are either "true" or "distorted" representations of the real world; and these representations, in turn, are seen as concepts, their content to be determined by just so many specific interests. They are not understood as signs which, as elements in *systems* of signification, might have a meaningful logic of their own and hence can serve as the meeting ground of two distinct orders of determination—one material, the other semantic.

A contrasting thesis holds that consciousness is embedded in the practical constitution of everyday life, part and parcel of the process whereby the subject is constructed by external sociocultural forms (Althusser 1971; Bourdieu 1977; Foucault 1980[a] and [b]). "Ideology" here is the *Ideology* coercive dimension of society and culture, the medium through which particular relations of domination become inscribed in the taken-for-granted shape of the world—in definitions of the body, personhood, productivity, space, and time. Bourdieu exemplifies this approach in his notion of socialization as a dialectic between human experience and a conventionally coded context; a dialectic in which the world "appropriates" the person as social being by playing upon the physical organism as an order of signs, investing it with a preexisting repertoire of meanings and "presuppositions." This process, he suggests, involves an apprenticeship never "attaining the level of discourse" (1977:87), for ideology is most effective when it remains interred in habit, and hence "has no need of words" (p. 188): "The principles embodied in this way are placed beyond the grasp of consciousness, and hence cannot be touched by voluntary, deliberate transformation, cannot even be made explicit" (p. 94). For all its cogency, this formulation leads us so far into the domain of implicit meaning that the role of consciousness is almost totally eclipsed. In his effort to correct what he perceives to be a subjectivist bias in prevailing views of human practice, Bourdieu goes so far in the other direction that his actors seem doomed to reproduce their world mindlessly, without its contradictions leaving any mark on their awareness—at least, until a crisis (in the form of "culture contact" or the emergence of class division) initiates a process of overt struggle (p. 168f.). For this model, it is only with disenchantment, when the world loses its character as "natural phenomenon," that its social constitution can be contested.

In the account that follows, I attempt to rethink the relationship between ideology as explicit discourse and as lived experience; to be sure, this is unavoidable in the Tshidi case. I examine their reactions to their changing context as a problem of symbolic mediation, tracing in detail the effects of the fracture of a precolonial cosmos, itself devoid neither of struggle nor of change. In the face of growing estrangement, the Tshidi sought to reestablish the coherence of their lived world and to render controllable its processes of reproduction; this process must be understood primarily in terms of signifying practice, which was only partially subject to explicit reflection. In order to make sense of these developments, therefore, I have focused primarily upon social action as communicative process, in which the pragmatic and semantic dimensions are fused. It is in practice that the principles governing objective orders of power relations take cultural form, playing upon the capacity of signs— their polysemic quality, for instance, and the meaning they acquire through their positioning in relation to each other in sequences or texts.

But this process of construction is never totally witting or unwitting. It involves the reciprocal interaction of subjects and their objective context; and it may serve both to consolidate existing hegemonies (ruling definitions of the "natural") and to give shape to resistance or reform.

This analysis, then, is an effort to do more than reexamine the relationship between idealist synchronic analysis and pragmatic determinism. It explores the interplay of subject and object as this occurs in the course of "signifying practice,"[2] that is, the process through which persons, acting upon an external environment, construct themselves as social beings. But this process is not locked in a cycle of mere tautological reinforcement. On the contrary, it is motivated by dynamic tensions which are inherent in a particular historical constitution of the world, which force themselves upon human experience and require reconciliation, thereby making of practice more than mere habitual repetition. Thus the dialectics of subject and object in *all* social contexts—whether of "simple" or more complex systems—generate both reinforcement *and* tension, reproduction *and* transformation (see Sahlins 1981); and such dynamic processes need not be reduced to the stuff of "consciousness" or "crisis" alone.

Nonetheless, as Sahlins (1981:68) has suggested, the simultaneous reproduction and transformation of historical systems becomes especially marked in their conjuncture with other social orders. In such circumstances, change and resistance themselves often become overt facts, for there tends to occur a process of argumentation between the bearers of distinct cultural forms. In the account that follows, I shall examine the continuities and discontinuities of the Tshidi system, from the "stifled debate" (Parkin 1978) of the precolonial epoch to the long and sometimes overt dispute of the colonial encounter. Throughout my empirical inquiry, however, the major focus of attention remains the realm of signifying practice itself, supplemented, wherever possible, by documentary and ethnographic evidence of Tshidi consciousness and reflection.

Bodies Social and Natural
The Constitution of "Signifying Practice"

The relationship between the human body and the social collectivity is a critical dimension of consciousness in all societies. Indeed, it is a truism that the body is the tangible frame of selfhood in individual and collective experience, providing a constellation of physical signs with the potential for signifying the relations of persons to their contexts. The body mediates all action upon the world and simultaneously constitutes both the

self and the universe of social and natural relations of which it is part. //
Although the process is not reflected upon, the logic of that universe is
itself written into the "natural" symbols that the body affords.

This insight is, of course, not novel. Both Marx and Durkheim argued, if in somewhat different terms, for the continuing dialectic between "social" and "natural" classification, a dialectic routed through
the forms of human experience, within which collective constructs appear both natural and ineffable (Marx 1967; Durkheim and Mauss 1963).
In an extension of this insight, the human body has repeatedly been
viewed as providing the primary "raw material," the presocial "base,"
upon which collective categories and values are engraved (van Gennep
1960; Turner 1967:93f.; Douglas 1970; Mauss 1973; Bourdieu 1977;
Turner n.d.[a]). Through socialization, the "person" is constituted in the
social image, tuned, in practice, to the coherent system of meanings that
lies silently within the objects and conventions of a given world. In this
view, once they have taken root in the body, acquired a "natural" alibi,
such meanings assume the appearance of transcendent truth (Barthes
1973). The physical contours of experience thus come to resonate with
the external forms of an "objective" reality.

In their concern to demonstrate the sociocultural construction of body
and person, scholars have frequently treated the human physical form as
a tabula rasa (van Gennep 1960; Mauss 1973; and, arguably, Bourdieu *tabula,*
1977); or, in a more determinedly structuralist view, as a repertoire of *rasa*
contrasts of largely arbitrary social implication (Needham 1973; Douglas
1966, 1970). The body is thus portrayed as the "simple piece of wood
each has cut and trimmed to suit him" (van Gennep 1960:72); alter-
natively, it is depicted as "good to think" with because it provides a set
of homologies of the social world, typically understood in terms of unidimensional oppositions (Needham 1973) and mediating anomalies
(Douglas 1966). The ethnographic record, however, suggests that the
effect of physical form upon cultural logic is more complex and pervasive than is allowed by either of these perspectives (cf. Ellen 1977;
McDougall 1977). In an analogous domain, Sahlins (1977:166) has noted
that the physiological facts of color discrimination have challenged both
the arbitrariness of the sign and the sui generis character of culture. That
these facts enter into the determination of culturally elaborated color categories is underscored by the universal tendency, in natural languages,
for their lexical markers to follow a natural-perceptual logic. Yet, as Sahlins goes on to stress, such categories are themselves just one of a series
of available cultural "implements"; whether they will be selected and
how they will be used in a given cultural scheme is clearly a function of
semantic rather than "natural" considerations. He thus concludes that it

is only through the dialectic of natural facts and semantic projects that we can account for "the presence in culture of universal structures that are nevertheless not universally present" (1977:179).

Much the same may be said of the constraints imposed by physical facts upon the perception and cultural construction of the human body. Of course, the latter subsumes a highly complex constellation of elements, relations, and processes. Apart from all else, stable organic structures coexist with, and occur within, the temporal processes of the biological life-span. The former describes paradigmatic relations of contrast (left/right; front/back; head/foot; inside/outside; male/female) and combination (the taxonomies that order such contrasts into hierarchical series); and it is this aspect that has been the primary concern of anthropological analyses of the relationship between body metaphors and social categories (Griaule 1965; Ellen 1977). Much less attention has been paid to the relation, within the human organism, of synchrony and diachrony; to the embeddedness of categories and taxonomies, for example, in transformative bodily processes—in alimentation, in gestation and birth, in aging, and in death.

Taken together, these aspects of the "natural" constitution of human bodily form give it enormous potential for symbolic elaboration and representation—of structures in space, of processes in time, and, most significantly, of the interrelationship of the two. But the body is not merely capable of generating multiple perceptions; it also gives rise to contradictory ones. Thus, within corporeal confines, physical stability coexists with physical transience, stasis with disease and degeneration. It is hardly surprising, then, that, as biological metaphors come to represent sociocultural realities, they signify not merely relations and categories but also contradictions in everyday experience; it is very common, for example, for sociocultural conflicts to be apprehended in terms of the archetypical metaphor of contradiction, physical disease (Sontag 1977; Turner 1967:359ff.). It makes sense, therefore, that the effort to allay the debilitating effects of social disorder tends to involve exertions to treat and repair the physical body, and vice versa; the body social and the body personal always exist in a mutually constitutive relationship.

This study of Tshidi transformations centers on the contrast between two focal ritual complexes, each an objectification of the social system at a particular historical point. Both the precolonial initiation rites and the Zionist cult practice which I examine below seek to produce a "new man": the first, by making the child into an adult formed in the image of a hegemonic order; the second, by reconstructing the adult as metonym, *pars pro toto,* of the universe that encompasses him. Both work on the body so as to prize apart and refashion the continuity between social, natural, and personal being. But, where the initiation rites set out to redress experiential paradox in conformity with established social arrangements, Zionist practice is an effort to reformulate the constitution of the everyday world, to deal with conflicts inadequately addressed in prevailing ideologies and institutions. Not surprisingly, the metaphors of social contradiction deployed by these cults are often rooted in the notion of the body at war with itself, or with its immediate social and material context; and desired transformations focus upon "healing" as a mode of repairing the tormented body and, through it, the oppressive social order itself. Thus the signs of physical discord are simultaneously the signifiers of an aberrant world.

Ethnographic and Historical Overview

My point of departure is the sociocultural order of the southern Tswana during the first three decades of the nineteenth century; that is, before colonial penetration and articulation with the subcontinental political economy. I develop a model of this order which treats its observable features as the product of the interplay of structural form and everyday practice, a process mediated by a coherent scheme of symbols and values. The precolonial system comprised a set of contradictory organizing principles—"contradiction" here denoting a disjuncture between the elements that constitute a historical system (Giddens 1979:131)—which, in turn, configured the lived-in world and its endemic modes of conflict. Such conflict, the struggle between individuals and groups predicated upon incompatible norms and values (ibid.), realized the surface arrangements of these Tswana polities over space and time. In so doing, it effected a practical reconciliation of the contradictions which underlay Tswana economy and society: the mutually negating tension between political centralization and productive decentralization, agnatic aggregation and individualistic disaggregation. Such surface arrangements were not fixed or invariant, however; nor was their realization a mechanically repetitive process. Apart from all else, they were conditioned by the legacy of past events, and by a range of diverse historical circumstances. Tswana communities did not exist in an ecological and social vacuum; as we shall see, their politico-economic organization stood at odds with their unpredictable and drought-stricken natural environment, and individual chiefdoms were located within a broader constellation of independent states and acephalous groups, lateral relations among which affected internal political processes. During this early period, then, the manifest sociopolitical arrangements of the southern Tswana were subject to transformation. But, by and large, they did not undergo alteration in the principles of their constitution; these were reproduced, and inherent contradictions contained, by prevailing forms of material and symbolic action. This is not to

deny that fundamental structural change could and did occur in the precolonial era, or that different cultural forms might emerge; for hegemonic
processes never control all the conflicts generated in any historical society
(Williams 1977:125). Nonetheless, for reasons which will become clear,
dominant patterns of social, economic, and ritual practice in the *immediate*
precolonial context tended to perpetuate the system in place.

The particular constitution of the Tshidi social order, c.1800–1830,
was formative in important respects of the subsequent conjuncture with
external forces and agencies. With colonial penetration and the rise of the
state of South Africa, the Tswana were relegated to the periphery of a
new structural field; a field dominated by racially indexed relations of
class. Nevertheless, these encompassing structures were not merely imposed upon local systems: they interacted with them to produce reciprocally determined transformations. This is exemplified by the complex
exchanges between the Tshidi and the Methodist church, forerunner of
colonialism among the Tswana. For most of the nineteenth century, the
missionary enterprise was deeply affected by indigenous political processes, this being reflected in the fact that evangelists remained under the
formal jurisdiction of the chiefship, legitimating its status in many respects and serving its interests, both internally and in the emerging colonial arena. But the missionary was himself an imperialist, if ostensibly
only in the realm of the spirit, and soon became locked in struggle with
the chief for control over the signs and practices of ritual authority. This
struggle had many implications: for power relations within the polity;
for the working out of its endemic contradictions; for the revaluation of
the very cultural categories in terms of which the church was understood
and accommodated to the lived-in world of the Tshidi. Above all, it
fostered a growing awareness among the rank and file of the discrepancy
between their position and that of the elite, the monopolistic guardians of
a now objectified "tradition." For the ideological forms of nineteenth-
century Protestantism were derivative of British industrial capitalism,
projecting its values of individualism, spiritual democracy, and rational
self-improvement through labor.

This was also to have fundamental repercussions for the articulation of
the Tshidi into the subcontinental political economy; the intervention of
the church in relations between them and their would-be colonizers—
intervention pursued in the name of liberal humanism and the protection
of the natives—provided the levers of eventual overrule. Not only did
the actions of the missionaries facilitate the extension of a colonial administration to the southern Tswana heartland; but, more pervasively, the
ideology with which they confronted the Tshidi, itself resonant with a
managerial strain in the precolonial cultural order, paved the way for the

process of proletarianization. For this ideology gave divine legitimation to the reified and divided self, the value of private property, and the "free" market in both labor and commodities.

But mission Christianity was to founder on its own inherent contradictions. Most notably, it failed to mitigate the strains of the neocolonial predicament and to account for the manifest inequalities that now dominated the experience of the Tshidi and other black workers. Thus, although the church continued to serve as an accessible source of signs and organizational forms, these became the elements of a syncretistic *bricolage* deployed to carry a message of protest and resistance, and to address the exigencies of a runaway world. While such expressions of resistance, embodied in the rise of independent African denominations, were aimed most directly at the culture and institutions of orthodox Protestantism itself, their subtle metaphors bespoke a rejection of domination in all its aspects. Yet the independent African Christian movement was to replicate its European parent in important respects, generating a tension that found voice in the forms of a second evangelization, this time by emissaries of the urban counterculture of late nineteenth-century America. They bore a message of more radical antipathy to the values and concepts of Protestantism and bourgeois liberalism. Indeed, for many black South Africans, the former had come to stand for the latter; hence the repudiation of church and state, of Protestantism and the spirit of colonial capitalism, went hand in hand. This evangelical onslaught gave rise to the many and varied Zionist sects that pervade the theological landscape of the subcontinent; and it introduced a mode of practice which interacted with indigenous cultural forms to yield a Christianity that stood in vivid contrast to colonial orthodoxy. The emergent religious spectrum—its internal cleavages between mission, independent, and sectarian churches marked out in an elaborate order of signs and oppositions—came not merely to objectify the stark lines of differentiation within the modern context; it also opened up a general discourse about estrangement and reclamation, domination and resistance. Although not always explicit— for example, it never spoke to the issue of class relations per se—this discourse stretched far beyond the domain of ritual itself, penetrating acutely into the experiential fabric of everyday life.

In order to describe and analyze these processes of transformation, of the particular dialectic of structure and practice they represented, I have divided my study into three parts. The first begins with an event history, a chronicle which summarizes the major episodes of the Tshidi past and present, and frames the inquiry to follow. Chapter 3 moves from the level of event to that of structure, providing an account of the precolonial system, its sociocultural order, and political economy. But this account is incomplete, since it does not fully explain the role of cultural mediation and symbolic practice in the realization of social arrangements. Thus I go on, in chapter 4, to examine the indigenous ritual complex, focusing on rites of initiation into adulthood; these being the most inclusive context in which the constitutive principles of the contemporary system are objectified, its contradictions addressed, and its conflicts reconciled in terms of prevailing hegemonies.

The second part, contained in chapter 5, considers the process wherein the precolonial system became engaged with the forms and forces of European industrial capitalism, represented initially by the mission church. Here I show that the interplay between these forces and the dynamics of the indigenous system restructured both orders at the same time that it drew them into a wider field of material and symbolic relations. As this suggests, incorporation into colonial society was not a one-sided process of domination: it was a conjuncture in which existing cultural structures were deployed by Tshidi so as to develop novel modes of practice; practice that expressed resistance to the self-image bred by proletarianization and subordination.

This, in turn, prepares the ground for the third part of the study. Thus chapter 6 traces the emergence of the modern sociocultural order of the Tshidi in the wake of articulation with the South African state. It shows how their contradictory involvement in both the labor market and peasant agricultural production, itself a function of cumulative underdevelopment, resulted in a complex process of reproduction and transformation, reinforcing some features of the precolonial system and undermining others. The Tshidi response to this contradiction, to the discrepancy between a transformed rural domain and the industrial workplace, was not to rebel directly against the neocolonial order. In the main, it was to find expression in resistance at the level of everyday practice, the most cogent form of which occurred within the dissenting discourse of Zionist Christianity. Chapter 7 examines Tshidi Zionist practice in detail, for such practice provides a coherent statement of the conflicts that characterize the world of the peasant-proletarian; and it makes a trenchant protest against the workplace by creative violation of its symbolic order. The rituals of Zion are a *bricolage* whose signs appropriate the power both of colonialism and of an objectified Tshidi "tradition," welding them into a transcendent synthesis; an integrated order of symbols and practices that seeks to reverse estrangement, to reconstitute the divided self.

This mode of ritualized resistance has analogues among other dispossessed populations on the margins of the modern world system. Hence, in the Conclusion, I consider the more general implications of the present analysis, paying particular attention to the interplay of indigenous and external forms in the transformation of precolonial systems and the rise of local movements. As the Tshidi case shows, the significance of such movements lies in the fact that they are *specific* responses to a structural predicament *common* to many peripheral Third World peoples; systematic revaluations, mediated by local symbolic orders, of elements of the increasingly global culture of industrial capitalism. This returns us to the problem of power in the motivation of historical practice itself—power material and symbolic, both concentrated and dispersed in the various domains of social action. For, ultimately, the logic of such sociocultural responses on the part of the oppressed resides in their attempts to impose some form of control or closure on the world. Their efficacy, however, both as efforts to subvert structures of domination and as cryptic but passionate statements of the human spirit, remains a matter of some controversy.

Methodological Considerations

This project raises a clutch of thorny methodological issues. It calls for a wealth of historical material at a number of levels, particularly that of the mundane practice of ordinary people (Prins 1980). Such data are notoriously difficult to rescue from oblivion, even in literate or semiliterate societies (Thompson 1963). The historiography of everyday life in the precolonial era of a people such as the Tshidi would thus seem less than feasible.

Nonetheless, such a venture is essential if we are to understand the continuities and discontinuities of the modern Tshidi world. For reasons already touched upon, the immediate precolonial period yields relatively rich data, the early emissaries of imperialism (traders, missionaries, and travelers) having had ample motivation to make detailed observations of "native life and custom." Hence, apart from a number of travelers' and missionaries' journals[3] dealing with the Tshidi and neighboring Tswana peoples located on the "route to the north," there are useful primary sources, such as the regular dispatches sent by missionaries in the field to the home societies over a span of some fifty years. A few evangelists also published ritual and mythical texts and commentaries in scholarly journals of the day.[4] Like all accounts, these are culturally constituted and thus "partial," although the naked interests at work in most cases provide overt indication of the conceptual framework of their authors. But this study is not a quest for some phantom objectivity. It is as complete a description as is possible of the structures of thought and practice motivating the various actors in the historical drama under scrutiny. Thus I have also relied heavily on available Tshidi ethnohistorical texts,[5] and on ethnographies produced in this century.

These sources offer a wealth of material on the social and symbolic

forms of the Tshidi in the early to middle nineteenth century, and on
their articulation with colonial forces. As I have already noted, my concern focuses largely upon the structures of power and significance inherent in everyday social action; and I have discerned these structures in
information about the minutiae of dress, spatial organization, bodily gesture, and productive technique. Such general description is often provided in great detail by the early accounts, but it gives only limited
insight into prevailing modes of consciousness. Here the documentary
sources have been supplemented by field observations. I am aware, of
course, of the dangers in constructing the past through the grid of the
present, or of reintroducing to a would-be processual account a pre-
sent/past dichotomy. In the field I consulted many older informants,
some of whom had been born prior to overrule and whose parents and
grandparents had lived through the periods and events considered here. I
have placed these ethnohistories alongside local records of the churches,
the "tribal office," and the chiefly court, as well as the many personal
papers collected from Tshidi households. I was also given limited access
to certain South African government files dealing with the affairs of the
Tshidi, and free access to relevant documents in the Botswana national
archives. But, in the final analysis, all historical accounts are themselves
historically situated, and I make no claim to being able to regard Tshidi
society, then or now, with a gaze that is not prestructured. Indeed, the
very purpose of this introduction has been to render my perspectives as
unambiguous as possible.

Part

1

2

Event History
A Chronicle of the Problem

I have noted that the Tshidi, like others on the margins of the expanding world system, became engaged in a process of articulation that both undermined fundamental aspects of the precolonial order and perpetuated its component elements in novel relationship with the forms of industrial capitalism. Tshidi history is the product of two analytically distinguishable but mutually entailed constituents—the internal dynamics of a precolonial system and the developing forms and agencies of capitalism and the state in southern Africa. Their conjuncture here is a matter of particular historical circumstance; but its more pervasive logic lies in the interaction of structures formerly separate, now part of an encompassing political economy.

In order to understand the transformation of Tshidi economy, society, and culture, therefore, it is necessary to examine the internal dynamics of the precolonial system and its progressive engagement with the southern African political economy. Such an account is, inevitably, a narrative of overrule and domination; but it is also a record of the Tshidi struggle, first, to retain their independence and, later, to develop a mode of viable self-determination in the face of social and cultural displacement.

I approach the study of Tshidi transformations in the first instance through this tangible record, through what Braudel (1980:27f.) has termed the "time of the chronicle and the journalist," or the occurrences of the "short time span." The relationship between the flow of such events and the deeper structure of the "long run" is the very subject of my inquiry: for, while events are the realization of structure, they cannot explain its form or its existence in time. Rather, they are themselves the outcome of social practice, whose motivation is configured by an underlying system of principles ("structure"). The latter shapes human con-

17

sciousness through the mediation of symbols; yet its implications for practice are seldom free from conflict, and practice, in any case, occurs within material circumstances that impose constraints of their own. Social action is thus not merely an "expression" of structural principles, it is an attempt to reconcile contradictions inherent in these principles and in the relationship between them and embracing material realities. Events, as the palpable outcome of such action, may either reinforce the system in place or undermine it. Moreover, they have cumulative consequences, and sometimes give rise to irreversible change in the conditions of practice which are unintended at the level of individual motivation. But events can also have a feedback effect upon human consciousness, forcing upon it the discrepancy between its forms and those of practical circumstance, thereby serving to direct purposive activity. The relationship between these dimensions of the historical process will guide my investigation of the present case. As will become evident, Tshidi culture itself entails a conception of agency, effectiveness, and time—a notion of history that affects practice and undergoes transformation in the long run.

The event history of the Tshidi over the past two centuries, then, catalogues the process of colonial engagement. The perceptible "facts" have been described in a range of accounts of different orders, produced by various categories of participants and observers.[1] My concern here is to outline the major sequence of episodes in relation to which the structural transformations of the Tshidi system may be analyzed.

The Tshidi Polity
Origins and Early History

In terms of conventional linguistic and sociocultural classification, the Barolong are of the southern Tswana peoples, part of the more inclusive Sotho-Tswana category of southern Bantu speakers.[2] The Tswana, who possibly originated in interlacustrine East Africa, are generally thought to have migrated to their central southern African habitat sometime before 1600 (Schapera 1953:15; Wilson and Thompson 1969:134). But genealogical evidence for such southern Tswana peoples as the Barolong and Bafokeng suggests earlier settlement; thus the eponymous Rolong founder, Morolong, and his putative son, Tshipi, who is indigenously held to have lived just north of the present Tshidi domain, may reasonably be dated to the fourteenth century (Legassick 1969:115).

Fragmentation, precipitated by competition for office among polygynous royal houses, was a recurrent feature of Sotho-Tswana history (Schapera 1953:34; J. L. Comaroff 1973). In fact, most chiefdoms owe their origins to such internecine political conflict, the royal lines of the many Tswana communities still recognizing (partially ranked) genealogi-

cal links which date back to their putative membership in parent groupings. Legassick (1969:107) suggests that the period of fission and expansion of the Sotho-Tswana chiefdoms, which began around 1500, gave
way to a process of amalgamation into large "confederations" in the
eighteenth and early nineteenth centuries, although some of these
chiefdoms later divided again. This process, due mainly to the reduced
possibility of establishing viable politico-economic independence in the
wider southern African arena, was broadly evident in the case of the
Barolong: after their initial establishment as a separate *morafe* ("nation")
under Morolong, they expanded by absorbing others, and then split into
four polities in the eighteenth century. And, while these polities never
did reamalgamate, they were to come together for a period of loose
federation in the nineteenth century, when external pressures threatened
individual sovereignty.

The documented history of the Barolong ruling line begins with the
accession of Tau in c.1700–1760,[3] some fourteen generations after Morolong. Tau's chiefdom was located in an area stretching south from the
Molopo River along the present South Africa–Botswana border (see
map, below; Legassick 1969:115; Stow 1905:490; Molema 1966:4). Vari-
ously recorded as "great warrior" (Molema 1966:4) and bloody despot
(Stow 1905:490), Tau provides an example of the widespread processes

Southern Africa from the Perspective of Tswana History

of incorporative state-building among the peoples of southern Africa in
the eighteenth century.[4] His imperial exploits expanded Barolong
suzerainty from just south of the Molopo to the northern boundaries of
Batlhaping territory at Taung. Tau was killed in a battle that checked his
expansion, and his people retreated northwards under the leadership of
his half-brother, Nthufa, acting as regent for Ratlou, the eldest son of
Tau's principal wife (see fig 1). The fact that the heir to the chiefship was
younger than his junior half-brothers was a result of the rules governing
succession to the position (see chap. 3). These rules were ambiguous in
defining seniority, and hence eligibility for office, and give rise to dis-

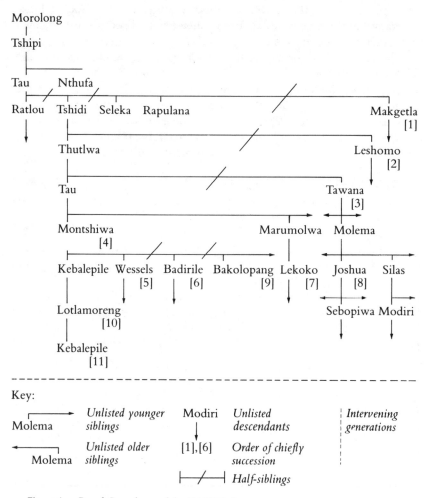

Figure 1   Royal Genealogy of the Tshidi-Rolong

putes that were an important motif of precolonial Tswana political processes. Indeed, this feature of the indigenous system, itself rooted in the very fabric of the sociocultural order, had direct consequences when the Tshidi were confronted by the initial agents of the outside world; specifically, the potentially competitive relationship between two royal half-brothers had an effect on the manner of engagement with the Methodist mission, and the enduring configuration of political and material relations that resulted.

After Ratlou acceded to office, and succumbed to smallpox, a protracted succession dispute followed among his polygynous houses, two of his sons seceding permanently (Breutz 1955–56:102). Seitshiro, the heir supported by the majority, assumed the chiefship and ruled with the assistance of his father's father's four brothers, the headmen of the constituent sections of the capital. During Seitshiro's reign, these four sections—under Tshidi, Seleka, Rapulana, and Makgetla—appear to have acquired de facto autonomy within the wider body politic, and, on his death, the final fracture occurred (Matthews 1945:13; Stow 1905:492–93; Wookey 1951:44). Following a brief period of unity, the Seleka and Rapulana sections each asserted their independence and settled elsewhere; the subjects of Tshidi and Makgetla remained together at Dithakong (eight miles west of present Mafeking), the descendants of Makgetla serving as influential collaterals of the ruling Tshidi dynasty. This was to be the last subdivision of any magnitude in precolonial Barolong history; for the rest of the nineteenth century these autonomous chiefdoms were to be drawn into the process which was to establish them at the periphery of the expanding colonial center to the south. It is largely on the basis of evidence pertaining to the period between 1800 and 1830, between the emergence of the Tshidi as an independent polity and their first conjuncture with agents of colonialism, that my account of the indigenous system will be constructed.

Defikane
Dislocation at the Periphery

When Tshidi died, another succession dispute occurred, this time escalating into what indigenous historians have referred to as a "civil war" (Matthews 1945:13). While the eventual heir, Tawana, was still in exile in 1815, his son, Montshiwa, who was to preside over the most significant phase of formal colonial engagement, was born.[5] Tawana assumed office in c. 1815 (Molema 1966:10), moving the capital to Pitsane, near the Molopo River. His reign was marked by increasing assault on the politico-economic viability of the chiefdom. The first and most immediate of these pressures resulted from the expansive state-building of the Zulu and the related military exploits of the seceding Ndebele and Kololo, a process that brought about the disruption (known in Setswana as *de-fikane*) of most of the agrarian peoples of central southern Africa. A subsequent set of forces was set in motion by the advance of colonial imperialism. In Tshidi experience, however, the effects of the latter were to become inextricably entangled in the former.

The initial impact of *defikane* on the Barolong chiefdoms occurred in 1823 at the hands of the Tlokwa, a displaced Sotho group, who preyed intermittently upon the southern Tswana and other settled agriculturalists (Lye 1969). In response to the threat, the Tshidi retired to the less accessible reaches of the Molopo region (Matthews 1945:13), while the Seleka fled southwards, to be encountered by two Methodist missionaries, Broadbent and Hodgeson. These men, who were searching for a sedentary Tswana community in which to build a station, were distressed at the sight of the fugitives (Broadbent 1865:28ff.). In fact, the circumstances of this encounter had important consequences for the missionary conception of Barolong social organization and moral status, and hence for the model of civilization envisaged for their future. The Seleka managed to create a settlement some miles away at Matlwassi in the present-day Transvaal, reestablishing cultivation and laying out a town which reproduced the preexisting forms of the Barolong sociospatial order (Matthews 1945:14). Here, on land granted by the chief, the earliest Methodist mission to the Tswana was situated (Broadbent 1865:61).

Despite their flight, the Tshidi had also subsequently been attacked and dispossessed by the Tlokwa, and their regular modes of organization and production remained severely dislocated when another missionary, Robert Moffat, visited them the following year (Moffat 1842:289). Moffat, stationed at the London Missionary Society post among the Batlhaping to the south, was summoned by Chief Tawana in the face of another onslaught (1842:414). He found that the Tshidi had been joined by the Seleka, who had left their settlement at Matlwassi in fear that they too would suffer repeated attacks. Moffat's intervention, with mounted riflemen, on the side of the Barolong, made a dramatic impression on the latter; not only did it sharpen their consciousness of their predicament, but it also had a direct impact on their understanding of available resources in the contemporary field of power relations.

For the next two years, the Tshidi attempted to maintain an agrarian base on the Molopo, but they lacked the military strength to defend their holdings against the plundering attackers and fled from place to place with their livestock in search of refuge. Travelers found them sheltering in the Molopo riverbed or in temporary grass huts on the Kalahari fringes, surviving by drinking milk and by hunting (Molema 1966:16; Matthews 1945:17).

The Establishment of the Missions

In the meantime, the Seleka had begun to migrate southwards out of the main arena of attack. In 1826 they eventually settled at Plaatberg, on the Vaal River, establishing an agricultural base and a town laid out "according to their respective wards" (Molema n.d.[a]:26). The Methodist mission was rebuilt at the new site, and both a school and a printing press were set up. Moffat's earlier Setswana biblical translations were reproduced here; these were the first written documents encountered by the Barolong, and soon became standard Protestant texts in the Tswana mission field (Broadbent 1865:185). They were to provide the basis for the introduction of literacy, the central vehicle of the general "civilizing" project of Methodist evangelism, and the source of a significant new order of power relations in the Tshidi world.

[handwritten margin notes: literacy / civilizing]

Plaatberg proved to be a safe refuge and, in 1832, the Seleka were joined there by the Tshidi and Ratlou chiefdoms (Molema n.d.[a]:33). The population expanded from some 8,000 to 30,000, however, putting extreme pressure on available resources. Records of the period reveal the central role of the missionaries in negotiating with external parties on behalf of the Barolong to obtain a new territory under conditions of increasing scarcity. Thus it was Archbell and Edwards who appealed in their name to the powerful Southern Sotho ruler, Moshweshwe; working through the latter's own resident evangelist (Broadbent 1865:180; Molema n.d.[a]:35),[6] they secured a sizable tract for the refugee chiefdoms. Such networks of exchange, mediated through the missions, were crucial in restructuring local communities in central southern Africa in the years between *defikane* and the formal extension of colonial control. In many situations, in fact, the transfer of rights in land from indigenous authorities to European agents dates back to this point. Although at this stage it was still unwitting, these missionaries served to harness the destabilizations of *defikane* to the eventual interests of colonial advance. Yet, as we shall see, the relationship between the missionaries and the various chiefs remained one of reciprocal determination.[7]

The evangelists presided over the orderly removal of the Barolong to their new domain on what was now mission land, an enterprise to which they applied the predictable imagery of a latter-day Exodus (Edwards 1883:59). But details of the creation of the community show that the indigenous leadership continued to exert its authority in established ways. On arrival at the designated spot on the hill of Thaba 'Nchu, some 250 miles southeast of the present Tshidi capital at Mafeking, the Barolong rulers took control over the allocation of land, proceeding according to long-standing principles (Molema 1966:27). Ritual experts were

called upon to draw a protective circle around the area of habitation, the
chiefs planting ritually treated pegs along its circumference (Molema
n.d.[a]:39f.). Moreover, the distribution of land reproduced the sociospatial logic of the preexisting Tswana scheme. Thus each of the three
rulers founded an integral settlement on a distinct mound; the Seleka to
the south, the Tshidi to the north, and the Ratlou to the northwest. But
there was one departure from older patterns: the mission itself was situated on the common center ground between these groupings (Broadbent
1865:189). As I show in the next chapter, the physical epicenter of a
Tswana community was also always its political and organizational
focus; hitherto it had been the place of the chiefly residence. Yet this
departure accurately depicted the articulating role that had already been
assumed by the missionaries. Not only had they come to mediate among
the parties to a somewhat uneasy confederation; but, being the van-
guards of colonial expansion, they were also the initial point of conjuncture between the Barolong and the hostile world beyond. The fact
that none of the chiefs built on the east of the town, the position of senior
rank (Willoughby 1909:233), expressed the unresolved status ambiguity
which was later to contribute to the destabilization of the Thaba 'Nchu
federation (Matthews 1945:16). For, while the Seleka had clearly been the
"owners" of Plaatberg, of which Thaba 'Nchu was seen as an extension,
the Ratlou and the Tshidi were both their genealogical superiors. Within
the distinct chiefly domains, however, existing differentiations of rank
were carefully replicated by means of spatial contrasts. Each settlement
centered on the ruler's meeting-place (kgotla), with the wards of subordinate headmen placed concentrically around it to reflect gradations of seniority (Molema n.d.[a]:40). Thus the hierarchical order of the body
politic was simultaneously the lived map of the everyday world. In sum,
despite radical social upheaval, the social organization reproduced at
Thaba 'Nchu was identical, in all essential respects, with the pre-defikane
arrangements described by early visitors to the southern Tswana peoples
(Campbell 1815:178; Burchell 1953, vol. 2:25ff.). Yet the focal site assumed by the mission, at this point a transient arrangement, anticipated
subsequent transformations.

   For a time, Thaba 'Nchu did seem to be the Jerusalem of the missionaries: they reported a slow but steady increase in the number of enrolled
scholars and converts (Broadbent 1865:181, 186), of whom they de-
manded that Western-style garments be worn, and polygyny and "traditional superstition" be set aside. They had also brought ploughs, and
demonstrated new agricultural techniques that were later to effect important changes in relations of production. Indeed, the mission projected a
systematic order of practice and ideology which, by virtue of its opposition to indigenous forms, began to engender a novel sense of collective

self-consciousness among the Barolong. Thus a notion of *setswana*, "Tswana tradition," was objectified in contrast to *sekgoa*, the cultural repertoire of the white man (Burchell 1953, vol. 2:312), and to *lehoko* ("the word") and *tumelo* ("faith"). At this point, while the senior sons of the Tshidi chief were being socialized as befitted the embodiments of tradition, their junior half-brother, Molema, became the first royal convert to Christianity, an act with significant consequences. It appears to have been motivated, at least in part, by the political implications of being a junior member of the ruling line (Molema 1966:27, 35): for, while he had little prospect of acceding to office, or of exercizing power as a royal agnate, as royal convert, Molema was to become an undisputed leader in an entirely new domain.

The Advance of the Boers

Two years after the settlement of Thaba 'Nchu, the Rapulana, the fourth and most junior Barolong chiefdom, joined the community, which was soon to become a nodal point on the path of white settler expansion into the interior. Anticipating, in 1837, the threat posed by this expansion—it was to be the cutting edge of the future subjugation of the Tswana— Broadbent (1865:182) noted: "There entered into diverse points of the same region . . . another class of persons, whose object was not the good of the aborigines, but who, on the contrary, became the reason for fresh wars and showed themselves inimical to Missionaries and their operations." The Boer Voortrekkers had left the Cape Colony in 1836, largely in protest against the liberal policy of the British regarding the emancipation of slaves and the civil status of such peoples as the Hottentots and the "Kaffirs," the southeastern Nguni peoples living along the eastern Cape frontier (Agar-Hamilton 1928:10ff.). They, too, sought their "promised land" in the heartland of southern Africa (Voigt 1899, vol.1:1), envisaging an agrarian Calvinist polity based on a mode of production extravagant both in land and labor.

In 1836, a large Voortrekker party passed through Thaba 'Nchu, and was treated with generosity by the Barolong and the missionaries (Shaw 1860:564; Theal 1926:294; Schoon 1972:7). To the north, however, the party was attacked by the Ndebele under Mzilikatzi and lost all its stock. Their wagons stranded, the Boers sent to the evangelists at Thaba 'Nchu, who organized their rescue with the aid of the Seleka chief (Molema n.d.[a]:48; Agar-Hamilton 1937:15; Voigt 1899, vol. 1:301–2). Successive Voortrekker groups now arrived at the town, and Boer and Barolong found common cause in the removal of the Ndebele from their dominant position in the hinterland of central southern Africa. For, with the exception of the Seleka, for whom Thaba 'Nchu had become a permanent base, the Barolong regarded themselves as temporary exiles from their domain along the Molopo River (Molema n.d.[a]:61). But they seriously misinterpreted the intentions of their Boer allies at this point, apparently being led to believe that if Mzilikatzi were put to flight by a combined effort, they themselves would be free to resume occupation of their former territory (Matthews 1945:17).

In January 1837, a force composed of Boers and Barolong, with assistance from neighboring Griqua and Korana peoples, routed the Ndebele some 325 miles to the northwest; a second attack precipitated the final withdrawal of the latter to their present-day habitat in Zimbabwe (Voigt 1899, vol. 1:319; Molema n.d.[a]:50ff.). This was followed by two movements (soon to be in conflict) into the interior: the Tshidi, Ratlou, and Rapulana set out in c.1841 to reestablish themselves along the Molopo (Molema 1966:30). And the Boers also moved ahead, having proclaimed, by right of conquest, their ownership of the territory formerly controlled by the Ndebele. The demarcation of this territory was to be expanded, in subsequent years, to include most the land that was regarded by the southern Tswana as their own (Agar-Hamilton 1928:51ff.; 1937:16).

The Tshidi, the Mission, and the Boers
Opposition and Alliance

The Tshidi had returned to the Molopo region by 1848, when Tawana was succeeded by his son, Montshiwa. The new chief immediately dispatched Molema, his Christian half-brother, to the Wesleyan District Missionary Society to request a resident evangelist; in January 1850, Reverend Ludorf arrived at the Tshidi capital of Lotlhakane (Molema 1966:35). This action reflected a growing consciousness among Tshidi of the state of the emerging sociopolitical field; it also revealed the direction of their efforts to protect their sovereignty in the face of implacable colonial advance. Missionaries were the most accessible source of communicative skills and of such material goods as guns; their mediation was almost indispensable to the political viability of indigenous leaders. For these leaders were immersed in an ever more complex web of external relations, in which the need for arms was increasingly being replaced by the need for literacy (Molema 1966:35). Montshiwa had seen something of the strategic benefits of a missionary presence while at Thaba 'Nchu, where the evangelists had exercised palpable influence over communication and exchange relations with the outside world. Now, in the attempt to cope with a universe of shifting power configurations, he organized his alliances in a manner which expressed the increasingly explicit opposition between Boer and missionary in the external arena, and between "converts" and "traditionalists" within.[8] The link between the two spheres was his Christian half-brother, who provided him with legitimate access to the mission network, and also the means with which to contain the growing threat to the chiefship posed by its embryonic Methodist congregation.

At this point, then, the Tshidi engagement with the mission became integral to their determined effort to retain control over the general circumstances of their own history. Initially, they attempted to incorporate the mission on indigenous terms, seeking to appropriate its resources to their own interests and to minimize its challenge to internal authority. A Tshidi historian, S. M. Molema, grandson of the first royal convert, described the chiefly attitude as follows (n.d.[a]:58).

> Christianity, they said, might do very well for servants and slaves, children and commoners, but even among them it was really introducing a state within a state, and was apt to lead to divided loyalty; still its benefits would in a way counterbalance those evils. But acceptance of Christianity by a chief would be tantamount to his voluntarily renouncing some of the highest political functions, his abdication of authority as king and priest at tribal ceremonies and festivals. . . . The best that a chief could do . . . was to put only one foot in the church, and keep the other outside; to listen to the missionary with one ear and tradition with the other. . . . "

Molema was Montshiwa's "foot in the church." But the coming of Christianity was merely the edge of the colonial wedge; its effects were not to prove containable by such chiefly strategy. To be sure, the mission was an essential medium of, and forerunner to, colonial articulation; it was *the* significant agent of ideological innovation, a first instance in the confrontation between the local system and the global forces of international capitalism. The coherent cultural scheme of the mission—its concepts of civilization, person, property, work, and time—was made up of categories which anticipated and laid the ground for the process of proletarianization. In time, these categories would also provide the basis for expressions of resistance.

Missionary mediation was a feature of the long reign of Chief Montshiwa from the start, for the Tshidi almost immediately became involved in disputes with their Boer neighbors over land, cattle raids, and the recruitment of labor; as they did, they appealed constantly to their resident evangelist to intervene on their behalf. Reverend Ludorf's initial letters to the mission society from the Tshidi capital show an awareness that he was wanted for "selfish political ends."[9] But the fallacy of trying to distinguish mission interests from political agency was evident in his self-searching correspondence. Thus, in 1852, he interceded with a party of Boers who had settled on the natural water sources near the Molopo that were utilized by Tshidi in times of drought. By his own account, he was compelled to do so, for otherwise "our mission, if not lost, at least might suffer greatly."[10] Indeed, mission interest and

political agency were to become even less distinguishable as the scramble
for dominion over central southern Africa grew more intense. Ludorf's
attempt to secure Tshidi use of the springs had been successful; but, some
months later, the new Boer Republic concluded an agreement with the
British at the Sand River Convention (1852) whereby the former was
granted absolute independence "beyond the Vaal River." Thereafter, the
Boers made a serious effort to subjugate the Barolong peoples on their
western boundary, seeking to exact both taxes and labor (Molema
1966:39). When Montshiwa resisted, they threatened to overrun his capital, claiming that it was the missionaries "who [taught] the natives to be
rebellious and to resist the white man."[11] Choosing flight rather than
domination, the Tshidi withdrew to the northwest, to the fringes of the
Kalahari. This was the domain of the Ngwaketse to whom they were
linked by royal alliance (Molema 1966:51); here, at a safe distance from
the expansionist designs of the Boers, their chief was to maintain his seat
for seventeen years. Reverend Ludorf had decided not to accompany
them, for he judged the conditions unsuitable for evangelization.

The territory along the Molopo was not left unsecured for long. When
a subsequent "treaty" with the Boers ostensibly recognized this as Tshidi
land, Montshiwa established his paternal uncle and five brothers as the
headmen of six villages that mapped out its circumference (Molema
1966:53). Like all Tswana villages, these were structurally homologous
to the capital, and functioned for most purposes like independent political communities. Molema's settlement at Mafikeng ("the place of
rocks," later corrupted to the English "Mafeking"), situated on the Molopo itself, became the center for twelve families which were closely
identified with the church. Maintaining ties with the mission network—
and being situated near the Boer frontier on the main route to the
north—Molema himself became the key intermediary for the chief; in
fact, European visitors to Mafikeng found him particularly well-in-
formed of current disputes between competing interests in the region.[12]
Montshiwa thus remained at the center of the indigenous politico–ritual
system, circumscribing the main Christian nucleus and keeping it, at a
distance, under the control of an agnate whose conversion had implied
the renunciation of his own claim to the chiefship. Molema, in turn,
resisted the presence of a resident evangelist in Mafikeng (Holub 1881,
vol.1:280; Mackenzie 1883:33). Now political and religious leader of the
town, he acquired personal authority over a nascent literate elite, later to
emerge as an alternative constituency of real power in the chiefdom.

Indeed, the opposition between the "traditional" royals and the literate elite was to underlie the most important overt political conflict in the
Tshidi chiefdom during the earlier half of the twentieth century. In 1862,
the first signs of this cleavage surfaced in the capital itself, where a small

group of "people of the word" began to protest compulsory participation in collective ritual (Molema 1966:53; Mackenzie 1871:228ff.); specifically, they sought to withdraw from rainmaking and initiation ceremonies, which were crucial to the ideological underpinning of centralized
authority. In their attempts to counter such resistance, Tshidi royals insisted that communal well-being was dependent upon the involvement
of the total population (Holub 1881, vol. 1:296). Of course, the Christian
antipathy to these rites was framed with reference to a quite different
cultural logic: prescriptive participation in public ritual performance represented the acme of heathen coercion upon the freedom of the individual
believer (see Broadbent 1865:182, 187). It was from this standpoint of
moral and economic individualism—the "freedom" so central to the
Protestant conception of civilization—that the mission opposed the political and ritual authority of the chiefs in general. On these grounds they
were also to condemn Tshidi land-tenure arrangements and relations of
production (Dachs 1972:652). As this suggests, the very foundations of
the indigenous political economy were ultimately to be incompatible
with Christian advance—and this despite the fact that, in the immediate
precolonial period, it was mission agency that provided African societies
with the support they required to protect their autonomy and structural
integrity.

The adherents attracted to the mission at this stage were, by and large,
marginal to established configurations of power and authority in the
community: they were drawn from among commoners, the young, and
women of all ranks (Mackenzie 1871:230; Holub 1881, vol. 1:296). It is
hardly surprising that the Christian advocacy of ritual and moral equality
should have appealed to those who suffered inequality in the indigenous
context. There is, in fact, some evidence that, at the time, women as a
category were conscious of the political benefits of the Christian creed.[13]
Yet, as I shall suggest, the rise of Protestantism here is not reducible to a
social cost-benefit analysis. What is at issue, rather, is the more basic
question of the historical relationship of ideology, practice, and systemic
context. To wit, the appeal of Christianity—its truth value for certain
Tshidi—is the very problem of my analysis, not its solution (cf. Kahn
1978). To resolve this problem, to understand the role of Protestantism
among the Tshidi as a system of signs and practices, it will be necessary
to move from the realm of events to that of structure and transformation.

At Moshanang, Montshiwa sought a compromise with the Christian
faction represented by Molema. He offered to allow them to worship as
they pleased in exchange for participation in collective rites (Mackenzie
1871:231). The Christians refused, however, by invoking a dichotomy
between "church" and "state": they proclaimed their loyalty to the
chiefship in all but ritual practice (Mackenzie 1871:229ff.). The evidence

suggests that, for all his efforts, Montshiwa was unable to stifle the
growth of this religious dualism and, toward the end of his reign, declared
full religious freedom in the chiefdom. The nature of this entire confrontation evokes the central theme of my analysis; namely, that the determination of practice, under conditions of historical transformation, lies in the
particular conjuncture of internal forms and external forces. The mode of
evangelism undertaken among such centralized peoples as the Tshidi was
heavily influenced by the control over mission operations exercized by the
royal establishment (Comaroff 1974, 1981; Schapera 1958). Missionaries
required chiefly permission to enter and were usually obliged to work
within the orbit of the political center. Moreover, in the years prior to
overrule (and much longer in some cases), Tswana rulers tended to permit
only one denomination access to their domains (Schapera 1958). This
contrasted with the situation among the more scattered Nguni, especially
those of the southeast, where competing denominations established more
or less independent stations outside population clusters and beyond the
jurisdiction of local authorities. Here adherents, referred to as those "spat
out" by the indigenous polity (Guy 1979:19), lived on mission land, where
their lives were configured by the culture of the church (Hutchinson
1957). In consequence, as among the Xhosa, a thoroughgoing division
arose between the "school" (Christian) and the "red" (traditional ritualist)
communities (Mayer 1961:30). In the Tswana context, church adherents
continued to reside in their own villages, under indigenous authorities,
and remained embedded in local relations of production. Despite emerging political cleavages, converts pursued their lives within the broad cultural framework shared by the rest of the collectivity; and most Tswana
developed some familiarity with Christian forms and made practical use
of the agricultural innovations introduced by the evangelists. Again, this
was to have an impact on the response of the Tshidi to the dislocations
wrought by twentieth-century proletarianization.

Among such southern Tswana groups as the Tlhaping, where the
proximity to the colonial center and to markets in produce and labor
affected local communities more radically at the time, the missions did
attempt to surround themselves with converts. But the chiefs resisted the
movement of their subjects out of the realm of their control (Kinsman
n.d.[a]:11). In fact, the style of evangelism which developed among the
Tswana brought the Christian challenge *within* the bounds of the indigenous polity itself: not only did it introduce an ideological contrast which
was to give new voice to existing internal cleavages, it also became the
basis of the renegotiation of power relations surrounding the chiefship.

However, internal dispute was soon to be overshadowed by a renewal
of strife between the Tshidi and the Boers on the borders of the Molopo
region. The services of Reverend Ludorf were again secured, and he

guided Montshiwa in a long correspondence with the British colonial administration, seeking the urgent extension of some form of protection over the Tswana peoples (Agar-Hamilton 1937:54; Molema 1966:65f.). Simultaneously, the chief threatened the Boers with British annexation in order to ward them off (Holub 1881, vol. 2:15). As Dachs (1972:658) points out, there was a shift from informal to formal missionary imperialism during this period—although, ultimately, annexation was to occur only when politico-economic considerations elsewhere on the subcontinent forced the hand of the colonial government. Yet it is important to note that, for missionaries such as Mackenzie and Ludorf, political imperialism was inextricably bound up with that of the kingdom of God. Mackenzie, for example, spoke of

> breaking the communistic relations of the members of a tribe among one another, letting in the fresh, stimulating breath of healthy, individualistic competition; and slowly, but surely and in the general tribal interest, to supercede the power and influence of the chiefs by an evidently helpful Queen's Government." (Dachs 1972:652)

This view, which neatly expresses the order of values common to the Protestant and capitalist ideologies at work, suggests that only a colonial protectorate, paternalistically conceived, could realize the mission ideal of Christian self-determination for the Tswana. This was nothing other than a liberal model of indirect rule over a community of peasants producing for the "free market." At the same time, however, the missionaries were to oppose the inclusion of the Tswana in the developing industrial state of South Africa, and their transformation from a "free" peasantry into a reservation-based proletariat. Indeed, this division of interest underlines the complexity of the motives and consequences of the participation of the evangelists in the colonial process.

The Rise of Industrial Capitalism in Southern Africa

The discovery of diamonds, in 1867, in the disputed zone between the Boers and the southern Tswana chiefdoms greatly exacerbated existing discord and drew larger colonial interests into the arena. Competing claims were laid to the territory, the British government making a telling intervention at this point. Having maintained careful distance from the conflicts in the region, they now urged the Boers to respect the rights of "the native tribes in friendly alliance with Her Majesty's Government" (Molema 1966:57). The matter was eventually brought to arbitration under the British governor of the colony of Natal in 1871. Both Montshiwa and Molema appeared at the hearings, their case being conducted "with great skill and devotion" by Ludorf (Matthews 1945:19). In the event, the rich diamond fields around Kimberley were granted to a Griqua leader who had given prior indication that he would cede his jurisdiction to the crown (Wilson and Thompson 1971:332); but the Barolong and Batlhaping were awarded most of their claim to the territories to the north, including land regarded by the Boers as falling inside the western boundary of the Transvaal. An elated Ludorf then drafted a constitution for the "United Barolong, Batlhaping and Bangwaketse Nation," establishing a consulate, appointing himself "commissioner and agent" to the chiefs, and requesting the "protecting hand" of Her Majesty to shield these "orphans" from their oppressive white neighbors (Molema 1966:67).

The Boer Republic repudiated the award and disputes continued to rage on the Transvaal border, Montshiwa pressing all the while for formal British protection. On the south bank of the Vaal, the diamond fields were rapidly becoming the focus of major industrial capital, determining the course of future social relations in the interior of the subcontinent. Here, already well-developed corporate interests were forging the core of the modern South African economy, and creating a demand for wage labor and agricultural produce to which the adjacent Tswana peoples had begun to respond. The latter had been rendered susceptible—if not adequately so for industrial needs—by the long-term effects of *defikane*, and by the ideological cast of the missions (Schapera 1947; Kinsman n.d.[b]; Marks n.d.). The pull of the labor market was felt even at Moshaneng; Holub, who visited the town in 1873, noted that many of the inhabitants worked for "lengthened periods at the diamond fields" (1881, vol. 1:294, 330.)[14] Among the Tswana closer to Kimberley, there was a rapid growth in production for the market (Kinsman n.d.[b]; Shillington 1981; Holub 1881, vol. 1:242), a growth facilitated by such mission innovations as the plow and irrigation techniques. Among the Tlhaping, for example, there is evidence of widespread sale of crops, and also of the emergence of aristocratic fiefdoms (Kinsman n.d.[b]). Although the geographical location of the Tshidi was less conducive to such transformations, they too began to cultivate for the market, both in Mafikeng (Holub 1881, vol. 1:279; 2:13) and at Moshaneng (Holub 1881, vol. 1:299). As we shall see, this process occasioned important shifts in relations of production. Holub, who also visited Mafikeng in 1873, remarked upon the prosperity of its "thriving population" but went on to state that, while the burden of agricultural work still fell on women, the introduction of the plow had brought men into this sector as well (1881, vol. 1:339). Indeed, as field crops became an object of exchange outside of the domestic sphere, men began to monopolize the disposition of the plow (Kinsman n.d.[b]). Moreover, the combination of growing pressure on arable, natural disaster, and rapid proletarianization was, by the end of the century, to consolidate the control of land in the hands of the elite, reducing large sections of the population to clientage.[15]

Formal Articulation

In 1876, Montshiwa returned from Moshaneng with 10,000 people and established himself at Sehuba, just south of the Molopo. The conflict between the Tshidi and the Boer settlers in the western Transvaal persisted, however, with the settlers managing to fan existing territorial animosities between the Barolong polities themselves (Matthews 1945:20). Several armed skirmishes followed and, in one such battle, Montshiwa was driven back to Molema's town of Mafikeng, which has since remained the Tshidi capital. Although Molema died shortly after, he had lately shown signs that he might mount a challenge to the chief's position, backed by his Christian allies (Holub 1881, vol. 2:12). This was to be the first of several disputes in which the educated descendants of Molema, and their followers among the intelligentsia, were to contest the rights to office of Montshiwa's line (J. L. Comaroff 1973:310). The fact that the capital was now situated on Protestant soil was reflected in the ruler's declaration of religious freedom, and his assertion that, while indigenous specialists would still supervise collective rites, Christian prayers would also be said at all public gatherings (Molema 1966:204). With this, the status of Methodism as "state church" was formally established, expressing the growing incorporation of the Tshidi into a colonial cultural discourse in which Protestantism was central. Compulsory initiation at adolescence was also terminated before Montshiwa's death in 1896 (J. L. Comaroff 1973:320).

While the chief himself remained illiterate and never joined the church, he continued, through his missionary aides, to bombard the British administration with requests for protection (Molema 1966:80).[16] But colonial attention at the time was tied up elsewhere; specifically, where economic incentives were more compelling. In the Transvaal, the discovery of gold had prompted the British to attempt an annexation, but this sparked an unexpectedly forceful rebellion on the part of the Boers (Agar-Hamilton 1928:129ff., 161). The inadequate imperial forces were soon overwhelmed and, in 1881, the Pretoria Convention redrew the boundaries of the settler republic, placing the western margin somewhat short of Tshidi territory and the "road to the north" through Mafikeng (Wilson and Thompson 1971:272). Meanwhile, a considerable shift of population had taken place from Kimberley to the new mining and industrial centers in the gold fields (Holub 1881, vol. 1:423).

But dispute soon returned to the border region, and missionary initiative in the area was intensified. Mackenzie, agent of the London Missionary Society among the Tlhaping and long-standing promoter of annexation of the Tswana territories by the crown, organized a campaign in Britain, addressing public meetings and lobbying politicians and the press (Dachs 1975:149ff.). He tuned his appeal both to imperial self-interest and to liberal humanitarianism, aiming to thwart designs on the Tswana territories by the Boers and by South African and international corporations. But it was not until 1885 that the Protectorate of British Bechuanaland was actually established over the southern Tswana domain, between the northern edge of the Cape Colony and the Molopo plain, its borders bisecting the Tshidi chiefdom.

During this period there was also disagreement over the status of the southern Tswana peoples within the colonial empire: whether they should remain protected subjects of the crown, to be guided toward "civilization" by the liberal missions; or whether, as capitalist interests dictated, they should become the inhabitants of reserves at the rural margins of the emerging South African state, a reservoir of labor for its growing industrial centers.[17] In the end, capitalist interests held sway, and determined policy in both the short and the long term. By 1895, British Bechuanaland was transferred to the Cape Colony, itself to be incorporated into the autonomous Union of South Africa in 1910. The Tswana peoples north of the Molopo plain, however, remained under British jurisdiction in what was now the Bechuanaland Protectorate, and so became subject to a somewhat different colonial history from that of their southern neighbors. For both groups, though, the predominant feature of their predicament was their location on the periphery of the subcontinental political economy.

By the late nineteenth century, the Tshidi leadership had come to hold a binary view of the colonial arena, opposing British protection to Boer oppression. But their subsequent experience occasioned some reformulation of this simple contrast. As Molema (1966:136) was to remark some seventy years later: "Montshiwa was happy to lose his independence to the British Government but was bitterly averse to losing it to the Government of the South African Republic. It was like a choice between drowning in clean water and dirty water. The end result is the same, namely death." This evaluation was based on the experience of half a century of subsequent southern African history, during which the Tshidi polity became an integral part of the neocolonial state, and the overlap between the interests of liberal imperialism, colonial capitalism, and Afrikaner nationalism became more and more apparent.

Wage Labor and Rural Underdevelopment

In 1896, following upon their inclusion into the Cape Colony and eleven years after they had first become subject to taxation, the Tshidi, like others in the region, were struck by the rinderpest cattle pandemic (Molema 1966:196; van Onselen 1972). This, together with a prolonged drought and increasing Boer competition in the sale of produce, forced many of the population into the labor market. At the time, this market was both local and external: the demand for mine labor was greater than the supply; and, during 1896–97, the construction of the Mafeking-Bulawayo railway provided relatively well-paid employment nearby (Parsons 1977:126), even drawing non-Tswana from as far afield as Natal. But the agricultural collapse was not total. The lack of draft cattle froze merchant lines for a while but created an inflated market for other draft animals, of which the more affluent Tshidi took advantage (Molema 1966:197).

With the establishment of the British protectorate, a white settlement (Mafeking) had been founded less than a mile from the Tshidi capital—against Montshiwa's unavailing protest (J. L. Comaroff 1973:316). The new town was the seat of the colonial administration of the region and a junction on the transport route between the Cape Colony, the diamond fields, the Transvaal and Rhodesia; it soon developed some strategic significance, to be enhanced by its improbable siege, during the Anglo-Boer War, in 1899–1900 (Grinnell-Milne 1957). While serving as an international symbol of imperial resistance, the incident also had a direct impact on the Tshidi, who were besieged along with their white neighbors, and rendered them material and paramilitary support (Matthews 1945:24; J. L. Comaroff [ed.] 1973). This reinforced their existing image of the British as allies against the Boers; but the siege also brought an assertive administration within the orbit of Tshidi experience for the first time. From then on, in the wake of the formation of the South African state, the realities of overrule were to be felt more immediately.

Oral and written records from the Boer War period suggest that the Tshidi had indeed made a limited agricultural recovery; and, while they had begun to enter the labor market in growing numbers, their low wages as migrant contract workers—wages insufficient to support them and their families—ensured that they would remain rooted in agrarian production. The latter, of course, continued to suffer great ecological fluctuations (Breutz 1955–56:45). But Plaatje does give evidence of the ability to produce agricultural surpluses, albeit modest ones, in Mafikeng in 1899–1900 (J. L. Comaroff [ed.] 1973:60).

On the other side of the border in present-day Botswana, a block of land lying between the Bangwaketse and Tshidi chiefdoms had been awarded to the latter by a Land Commission established by the British administration. Known as the "Barolong Farms," it had been surveyed and divided into forty units to be leased to individual members of the chiefdom, under a general title held by the chief. Before his death in 1896, Montshiwa distributed these holdings among his agnates, allies,

and clients (J. L. Comaroff 1973:318–319); being subject to a distinct set
of tenurial arrangements and local historical conditions, the holdings sustained higher levels of production than did arable in the Mafeking district, although the surpluses remained rather low. There was to be a
significant takeoff into mechanized commercial agriculture on the Farms
just prior to and after the declaration of Botswana's independence in
1966, a process involving fundamental social transformation. (The history of this region is the subject of a study by J. L. Comaroff [forthcoming]
and provides a companion piece to this volume.)

For the majority of Tshidi living within South Africa, however, the
recovery of agricultural and pastoral production was never more than
partial. Moreover, the completion of the railway gradually removed all
but a very limited local demand for their grain, cattle, and labor. The
white settlement of Mafeking did become the capital of the Bechuanaland Protectorate, even though it lay beyond its borders, but this
provided employment and markets which increasingly benefited white
bureaucrats and farmers at the expense of the Tshidi. Indeed, prevailing
social and ecological factors were to render the attainment even of subsistence yields ever more difficult for many of them. There had already
been progressive soil erosion in the Mafeking district, due to the aban-
donment of indigenous techniques of shallow ploughing and fallowing,
and to the inability, since overrule, to move on the land in response to
uncertain rainfall. The effects of erosion were further aggravated by a
narrowing of the range of crops planted with an eye to the market, and
by the need to counteract crop failure by protracted periods of migrant
labor. Thus, while agrarian production rose and fell during the first decades of this century (Breutz 1955–56:45–47), reasonably consistent surpluses were yielded only on the holdings of the emerging elite—the
royals, literate salariat, and petty traders—whose broad economic base
and investment in risk-reducing farming techniques enabled them to escape the cycle of progressive impoverishment.

From the turn of the century, literacy was to play an important role in
the process of socioeconomic differentiation within the community. Incorporation into the South African state had bureaucratized significant
aspects of local power-relations; for example, the office of "tribal secretary" now formally mediated all communication between the chiefdom
and the national administration. The leadership of the church had been
Africanized, as had the faculty of schools, and white government agencies in Mafeking required some black clerical assistance. At the same
time, the chiefship, despite being granted a fair degree of autonomy in
internal government, was being progressively eroded, as its real power
became diminished by the incorporation of its constituency into the encompassing political economy. Between 1900 and 1919, there were a

series of short-lived reigns, the incumbents succumbing to drink or to the temptation of appropriating the resources of office for private ends (J. L. Comaroff 1973:322ff.). The weakened royal line now faced intensified challenge from its collaterals, the descendants of Molema, who were to assert the need for educated leadership in the modern context.

Joshua, son of the first convert, inherited his father's mantle as leader of the "people of the word," and founded the first Tswana newspaper in Mafeking in 1900. His daughter married Sol Plaatje, court interpreter and diarist of the siege; the latter was of Seleka origin, and he and S. M. Molema (Joshua's brother's son) became the first published authors and historians among the Barolong (Plaatje n.d.[b] and 1957; Molema 1920, n.d.[a], 1966). Joshua's own son was to become tribal secretary, and he himself was designated regent in 1915 when the Department of Native Affairs intervened in a protracted succession dispute among the Tshidi royals.[18] But this imposed appointment, indicative of more assertive overrule, was resisted by the ruling faction, and also by the rank and file. And in 1919, the accession of Lotlamoreng, the grandson of Montshiwa, for what was to be a thirty-five year reign, effectively separated the Molema line from the office. The new chief formally opened his domain to denominations other than the Methodist—in fact, several small sects of American fundamentalist origin had already taken root. But the original church was to remain the forum of the educated elite and of a vision of the South African future based on missionary liberalism (Molema n.d.[b]). In the name of this elite, the Molemas were to mount several strong, if unsuccessful, campaigns against Lotlamoreng during his incumbency (J. L. Comaroff 1973:394ff.).

Such local tensions became part of wider conflicts in the wake of the consolidation of the neocolonial state. In 1913, the national government passed the Natives' Land Act No. 27, which limited African holdings to "scheduled native areas," largely the existing reserves, and initiated the complex legislative basis for the future apartheid system. While not directly affecting Tshidi rural territories, which had been defined as a reserve before the turn of the century, this act made utterly insecure the position of all blacks living on white farms or in the urban areas (Plaatje n.d.[b]:17). The Tshidi understood the implications of the act as opening the door to legalized dispossession, and several public meetings of protest were held in Mafeking. Both Plaatje (n.d.[b]) and S. M. Molema (1920) were to publish critical essays on this legislation, the latter describing it as "the most cruel bill ever put before parliament . . . calculated to reduce . . . Bantu and colored people to the verge of slavery" (1920:248).[19] In anticipation of this legislation, the historically significant South African Native National Congress (later the African National Congress) was formed, with Plaatje as its corresponding secretary (J. L.

Comaroff [ed.] 1973:16). But the majority of the Tshidi intelligentsia, while supportive of the struggle for African rights at the national level, remained rooted in local political processes. Thus Molema concerned himself for the rest of his writing career with Barolong history, thereby ensuring that the perspective of the liberal Methodist elite was firmly stamped on the documentary record.

The Land Act signalled the end of the early phase of colonial articulation and also put paid to the Tshidi sense that imperial protection would shield them from Boer subjugation, an impression they fostered even after the British administration ended with the establishment of the Union. A national leadership, now comprising English-speaking and Afrikaner colonials, began to tighten its control over the mobility of the African labor force and to restrict its growing politicization.

The Age of Apartheid

The Tshidi protested the effects of growing government coercion, coming into dispute with representatives of the Department of Native Affairs over matters of taxation and the control of internal political processes (J. L. Comaroff 1973:373, 391). The intelligentsia were to continue their steady support for the liberal, nonracial ideology of African nationalism; but a marked skepticism about the prospects for democracy and equality was to develop when, after World War II, the Afrikaner Nationalist Party came to power. For the Tshidi, this signalled a resurgence of their historic Boer adversary, about whose motivation they harbored few illusions.[20]

The new regime was quickly to execute its policy of segregation and domination. In 1951, the Bantu Authorities Act No. 68 abolished the already limited representation for blacks in parliament, and replaced it with "local government" comprising "tribal" chiefs and "traditional councils" (Vosloo et al. 1974:58). This was followed by the Promotion of Bantu Self-Government Act No. 46 of 1959, which provided for the "separate political development" of eight African "national" units—the future independent "states" of a putative South African federation. These units, for the most part former reserves, were to be the "homelands" from which workers would migrate as "foreign nationals" to the white farms and cities. The Tshidi were thus subsumed into an overarching Tswana polity, composed of some thirteen discontinuous and farflung parcels of land in the northern Cape Province and western Transvaal. The self-government act also provided for regional and territorial authorities, equipped with civil services, field administrators, and executive councils, two of whose members had to be chiefs. Prior to 1969, these authorities were "representative" and "advisory" to the central government (Vosloo et al. 1974:60); thereafter, further machinery (such as a legislative assembly) was established for evolution toward "self-government." In 1977, Bophutatswana ("the united Tswana people") was granted "independence", with Mafeking as its capital.

Through passive resistance, the Tshidi protested the implementation of these legislative acts, asserting in both public and private that the sinking of their identity in a generic Tswana nationality had no basis in either history or current political realities—other than those of an oppressive policy of divisive "tribalism." A modern township was built alongside the old capital to house the influx of personnel for the new administration; christened the "Government Compound" by black residents of Mafeking, it epitomized the coercive enclosure they felt at the hands of the regime. By the late 1960s, the Tswana Territorial Authority, formally named *Pusotswaraganelo* (the "government of unity"), had become known locally as *Pusokgaoganya* (the "government of dissent"). The threatening proximity of this new authority served to unify the elite in opposition; neither the chief (then Kebalepile, son of Lotlamoreng) nor the intelligentsia would cooperate with it, except in the most perfunctory manner. In fact, they had openly supported the one explicitly anti-government candidate who had put himself forward for ministerial office in the homeland—and who, not surprisingly, was unsuccessful. Those who eventually assumed the relatively well-paid positions in the puppet administration were at first unceremoniously referred to in the Tshidi capital as "sell-outs" (J. L. Comaroff 1974:44f.). However, the national government, determined to establish a stabilizing local middle-class, continued to hold out financial incentives to would-be entrepreneurs; by the mid-1970s, a small number of the Tshidi petite bourgeoisie had availed themselves of such opportunities, causing great controversy in the community.

By the latter half of the twentieth century, the chiefship had been denuded of any real power or authority over the lives of its subjects, but meaningful political alternatives had also been systematically suppressed. In such circumstances, one might expect the Tshidi to have been reluctantly acquiescent, increasingly determined by a set of historical forces that they could no longer act upon with any effect. This expectation would appear to be confirmed, at least on the surface, by conditions obtaining in Mafeking in the late 1960s: not only was the aggressive liberalism, in the past associated with the intelligentsia, absent; there was also a noticeable presence of what might conventionally be termed escapist, "utopian" movements such as ecstatic healing cults. I shall argue that such an impression would be false, however, for the Tshidi response has been far more complex. Indeed, the forms of social practice that have emerged are neither the product of global determination alone nor of indigenous cultural structures; rather, that practice is the outcome of a dynamic interaction of the two in the continuing quest for creative action upon the world. And, in order to understand contemporary Tshidi culture in these terms, it is necessary to examine the evolution of their symbolic order in relation to their changing position within the South African social system. It is to this changing position that I turn in concluding the chronicle of events.

The cumulative engagement of the Tshidi with the machinery of the modern South African state has resulted in the progressive underdevelopment of their rural base and an ever increasing dependency upon the sale of their labor power. Local records reflect a steady rise in migration. Matthews' unpublished field survey of the Mafeking district in 1938–39 (n.d.[a]), the first detailed account of production in the area, states that fully one-third of the population was away earning wages at the time.[21] He noted that, while occasioned by real need, this had had drastic effects on local agriculture, especially through the absence of workers at critical ploughing times. His census revealed a state of "dire poverty" in the reserve, the average family not raising enough food for its own subsistence, and being dependent on staples purchased with cash remittances from migrants. He also observed that, among the poor, sharing equalized meager resources among kin.[22]

In the mid-1950s, the next period for which there is detailed information, Breutz records that the output in the Mafeking district was "poor"; that, in the preceding years of successive droughts, between 30 and 70 percent of stock had been lost, and that "the majority of the people scarcely grow enough maize and kaffircorn (sorghum) for their own consumption" (1955–56:53; see also 47–51).

Domestic economic histories collected in Mafeking and its district in 1970 indicate that the drought of 1969–70 matched that of the early 1950s in its impact on the Tshidi stock population. In 1970, only 26.2 percent of the households in a sample population owned cattle, and 41.8 percent sheep and/or goats. This suggests a real decrease from the late 1930s, Matthews' census revealing that the "average family" owned animals, albeit "not more than 2.5 head of cattle, 1.5 sheep and 2.5 goats" (p.11). In 1970, the third successive season of drought, only 45 percent had attempted to plow at all: of them, some 22 percent realized subsistence-level yields and 12 percent produced surpluses, the latter category consisting largely of those with mechanized means.

These domestic histories also indicate that migrant labor—either agricultural or industrial—had long been an indispensable part of the male life-cycle for all but the petite bourgeoisie, the educated salariat, and traders, who together comprised approximately 5 percent of the population in 1970. Women had also been drawn increasingly into the labor market; by 1970, 56 percent had been employed away from home for extended periods, while 84 percent of men over the age of twenty-five had been contract workers for at least one spell of more than nine months. The pattern of female migration was different, however; women's work was more intermittent and they were primarily hired as seasonal hands on white farms or as domestic servants in the adjacent white town of Mafeking. As the value of arable production fell, and the incidence of wage labor increased, women resumed charge of the agricultural domain, except in the case of highly capitalized operations (Matthews n.d.[a]:2). By 1946, for example, census figures record that 55 percent of "farms" in the district were registered in the names of females (Breutz 1955–56:40a).[23] South African law prevents "dependants" from accompanying "labor units" (i.e. migrants) to the industrial centers; wives and children thus had either to remain on the land in the rural area or to enter the labor market in their own right.

Because neither agriculture nor migrant work was independently capable of supporting most domestic units, families were compelled to fashion strategies for subsistence which combined both sources of income. Thus the sale of labor served as an inescapable counter to underproduction in the Mafeking district; but, since wages alone were insufficient to assure the survival of households of workers, agriculture and pastoral enterprise were always required to supplement them—and to succor migrants themselves between contracts or in advanced age or disability. In this cycle of underdevelopment, then, rural poverty has ensured that the peripheral communities remain a potential reservoir of labor; quite simply, they are trapped in a predicament in which they can reproduce themselves neither through the cultivation of increasingly scarce and infertile land nor by means of wages deliberately maintained below the level of domestic subsistence. In sum, the structure of the labor market, and the political economy of which it is part, has both undermined and perpetuated the rural productive base. As I noted earlier, such simultaneous processes of reproduction and transformation, although not unique to the contact between formerly independent systems, are particularly visible in situations of conjuncture. In the Tshidi case, however, the history of articulation is not merely a matter of "contact"; its central thrust, rather, lies in the progressive incorporation of a local chiefdom into an asymmetrical social system of global scale. But, I reiterate, in order to analyze the particular form of these processes, and to explain how their historical trajectory has been mediated by a specific order of symbol and ideology, it becomes necessary to turn from event to structure.

3

From Event to Structure
The Precolonial Sociocultural Order

Let us now consider these historical events as the practical embodiments of a more deep-seated structural order. A significant feature of the period both during and after the *defikane* was the manner in which the Barolong peoples struggled to reproduce their sociocultural forms. In response to repeated evictions from their territorial domains and to the destabilization of their productive base, the chiefdoms recreated their preexisting sociospatial arrangements and political order, even when this required reunification into a single confederation. In fact, a degree of mobility was inherent in the Tswana system itself, dictated by the relationship between their centralized political economy and their dryland ecology, a relationship I shall explore in more detail below. This mobility often confused early European observers, who tended to associate large residential concentrations and complex land-utilization patterns with an evolved stage of fixed settlement.[1] Yet, as one nineteenth-century writer noted (Mackenzie 1871:370), the prevailing social and spatial forms were eminently portable: "when a tribe, driven by its enemies, or moved by its own enterprise, advanced to a new country, the whole structure of the social life was gradually redeveloped there, and domestic, agricultural and pastoral and hunting pursuits were carried on as before . . . the new settlement being as much as possible a counter-part of the old."

The precolonial structural forms to be described here continued to be reproduced as long as the indigenous leadership exercised control over the primary means of production and over those centralized institutions that underpinned the division of labor. Of course, the gradual penetration of colonial markets, the process of proletarianization, and the technical and ideological innovations brought by the mission were to cause irreversible changes in the Tswana sociocultural order. Yet, despite fundamental reorganization of the mode of production, nonmonetarized agriculture was to persist in complex and shifting relationship to peasant production and wage labor. Indeed, the transforming relationship of the commoditized and noncommoditized sectors represents the pivotal tension of modern Tshidi history; I shall return to discuss its implications for everyday practice in the closing chapters.

The Tshidi sociocultural order resembled that of the other precolonial Tswana peoples in most important respects. In the present chapter, I shall spell out the logic of this generic order, and of the forms of social action with which it existed in dialectical relationship; together they engaged with the local material context, giving rise to a set of characteristic arrangements on the ground, and setting the terms for the initial confrontation with colonialism. This account is situated in c.1800–1830, between the emergence of the Tshidi as an independent polity and *defikane*—that is, before systematic contact with the mission or other external agencies—although there is growing archaeological evidence that variants of the social, spatial, and productive structures described here had long existed among the Sotho-Tswana (Inskeep 1979:138–40; Maggs 1976; Molema 1966).[2]

Sociocultural Order

The historical sources that deal in any detail with the precolonial Tswana seem to be at odds with each other on many important issues. Thus, for instance, while all portray them as living in large, centralized concentrations, several report the existence of numerous small, unattached settlements and groups of wandering households (Burchell 1953, vol. 2:386). There is also considerable variation in accounts of internal socioeconomic arrangements: some stress the importance of agnatic rank as the central principle of organization (e.g. Burchell 1953, vol. 2:376); others emphasize the primacy of territoriality and the administrative hierarchy (Campbell 1815:187); similarly, some describe the system of government as being based on consultation and consensus (Barrow 1806:399); while others speak of autocratic domination (Lichtenstein 1930, vol. 2:414). This apparent confusion is compounded by the modern scholarly literature, which gives evidence, as Kuper (1975:71f.) has noted, of the difficulty of characterizing indigenous Tswana structures. Are they to be typified as administrative orders or agnatic lineage systems (ibid.)? And how are we to account for the fact that, while the everyday world is explicitly rule-governed, with an elaborate oral lore about principles of rank and of politico-jural procedures (Comaroff and Roberts 1981), social practice is so evidently competitive, its very rationale being that all statuses are open to negotiation (ibid.)? Then there is the problem that, although agnation provides the prevailing idiom of sociopolitical relations, being strongly contrasted with matrilaterality, descent groups themselves are not corporate units; rather, the effective kinship grouping is the *losika*, a bilateral stock. In other words, notwithstanding that Tswana culture orders the world in terms of clear-cut categories and oppositions, rules and relationships, ongoing social action seems to generate interpersonal ties that are ambiguous and multistranded, being neither one thing nor the other.

How, then, are we to make sense of these conundrums? Comaroff and Roberts (1981) have shown the value of distinguishing between structure and practice in the analysis of Tswana systems. This requires that we make a thoroughgoing separation between the underlying, *constitutive* dimension of the social order (its "structure") and the manifest forms of organization, experience, and action that are its historical *realizations* (1981:68–69). Sociocultural structure and the "lived-in" world of practice, however, are mutually constitutive: the former, because of the contradictory implications of its component principles and categories, is capable of giving rise to a range of possible outcomes on the ground; the world of practice, because of *its* inherent conflicts and constantly shifting material circumstances, is capable not only of reproducing the structural order but of changing it, either through cumulative shifts or by means of consciously motivated action. Thus, seeming contradictions in the observable features of Tswana systems at particular points in time might be seen as "transformations" (in the linguistic sense) of a unitary sociocultural structure. Our task, then, is to ascertain whether such a structure is to be found; one that, without unduly reducing the complexity of observable social systems, might yet account for their realized forms, and their variations in time and space.

In the account of social structure that follows, I have relied on Comaroff and Roberts' analysis (as well as J. L. Comaroff [1982]) in a more formal than substantive sense. The precolonial societies that are my concern in the first section of this study were different, in important respects, from the modern systems that Comaroff and Roberts discuss. Also, I am more explicitly concerned with examining how the social and politico-economic domains of the Tswana system actually came to constitute experience in both the short and the long term; in particular, how they were mediated by a system of signs which imprinted its logic upon action in the everyday world.

In the precolonial Tswana system, the administrative hierarchy comprised a nesting order of homologous units, at the base of which was the polygynous household made up of distinct uterine houses. A number of adjacent households, whose heads were agnatically related, formed the local agnatic segment, ostensibly headed by the genealogically senior male. Two or more such segments formed the core of the ward, which tended to contain additional households linked by matrilateral or affinal ties, or by coresidence and/or clientship. The ward (*kgotla*) was the most significant unit of administration in the Tswana system (Schapera 1935; Campbell 1815:187; Burchell 1953, vol. 2:348, 441) and represented in microcosm the principles and categories of that system at its most inclusive. While rarely an agnatic unit in its de facto composition, its headmanship devolved within the dominant agnatic core, putatively in terms of strict seniority, although the rules of rank were sufficiently ambiguous to make access to office a matter of political achievement (J. L. Comaroff 1978). Wards were later grouped into sections—also termed *makgotla* and organized about an agnatic core—which together composed the chiefdom (*morafe*, "nation"), the form of the latter replicating that of all the lower-order units in the segmentary structure (Schapera 1940; Burchell 1953, vol. 2:290; Spohr 1973:78). The chiefship itself devolved within the ruling agnatic segment, and its incumbent, along with collateral kin and royal affines, controlled both the section headmanships and the leadership of age-regiments (*mephato*), groupings which cut across bonds of kinship and territoriality and performed public works and military functions (Solomon 1855:43; Kirby 1939, vol. 1:271–72).

Agnatic clusters within the ward and section were the most extensive order of kinship grouping in the body politic, but they were not, as I have noted, property-holding descent groups or segmentary lineages. In fact, agnatic linkages above the level of the domestic unit served almost entirely to establish the relative distance of men from office, and groups never actually congregated for collective purposes (Comaroff and Roberts 1981:35). But the principles of agnatic rank provided the calculus of power relations and the legitimation for inequality. Thus the asymmetrical ties of clientship that gave actual form to hierarchy were contrived in terms of the reciprocal relation of senior to junior agnate; kinship, as Burchell (1953, vol. 2:384) long ago noted, furnished the "natural" model of political subordination. The Tswana themselves envisaged their system as a progressively more inclusive order of residential and administrative groupings within which the realpolitik of status and influence was negotiated in the language of agnatic seniority (Comaroff and Roberts 1981:26). And, at each level of the system, from the household up, access to position was predicated on the ability to establish genealogical rank, or influence with those who had it, for through these channels flowed control over land, labor, and patronage in all its aspects.

But this ascending order of rank and administrative groupings was subsumed within a descending order of centrist governance from the chiefly apex. Although itself validated in genealogical terms, the chiefship was founded on mechanisms of extraction and redistribution whose rationale rested in part on controlling political action pursued in the name of agnation. The relations of inequality that extended outward from the office formed a sharply stratified hierarchy, through which royals and their immediate clients secured access to three tiers of retainers: Tswana commoners, a subordinate category of captives and impoverished citizens in the towns (*batlhanka*), and an underclass of subject peoples (*balala*) living in the surrounding bush. The overall hierarchy, then, was the outcome both of the elaboration of agnatic principles of rank and of the centripetal mechanisms of the state. But, as the early ethnographic evidence suggests, these centripetal forces coexisted with other structural elements that fostered disaggregation. What appeared, in certain historical circumstances, to be a complementary inequality between chiefship and populace, in others became a conflict between the interests of center and periphery and posed the threat of dispersion. In order to examine the logic underlying these manifest features, I shall first consider the sociocultural system as an ascending order, beginning with the house as "irreducible atom" of structure. For it is in the constitution of this unit that we confront, in elemental form, both the principles of social organization and their symbolic representation.

The House as Elemental Unit of Structure

Tswana rules of rank which, as I have noted, governed the devolution of all status, office, and property from the level of the household to that of the chiefship, were ordered by the principle of primogeniture. Seniority was reckoned according to the relative age of sons within a man's house or ranked houses (Barrow 1806:398; Burchell 1953, vol. 2:376). Lineal transmission took precedence in this scheme, and a series of secondary rules and arrangements, including leviratic and ghost marriage, ensured the continuity of the agnatic line. Polygynous houses were ordered according to the relative priority of unions, but this did not necessarily coincide with the chronological sequence of the latter (Comaroff and Comaroff 1981). In fact, the principal wife might be designated at any point in a man's adult career, and in practice the rank of his houses was mutable (ibid.). This mutability opened the issue of status—and, with it, access to office—to competitive negotiation; at least, among those in the upper reaches of the social order, to which polygynous unions were confined (Mackenzie 1883:226; Campbell n.d.:66; Spohr 1973:76–77).

The prevailing rules of rank thus implied that status relations *between* polygynous houses were a matter of debate, while seniority *within* them was fixed; not surprisingly, ties between half-siblings were perceived as the very embodiment of rivalry and the prime avenues of sorcery

(Schapera 1970; Comaroff and Roberts 1981:49). In contrast, full siblings were expected to be supportive to one another, although brothers, especially in monogamous households, tended eventually to come into conflict over the patriarchal estate. The individuating identity of the house, its point of shared uniqueness in a wider agnatic constellation, lay in its specific matrilateral linkages. Children took their status from their mother and were the allies of the offspring of her natal house. Indeed, not only were these linkages strongly associated with cooperation, but the support of matrilaterals was generally an important resource in the political arena, where antagonism and dominance were asserted in the contrasting idiom of agnation.

The house was the major unit of landholding and production, and of the transaction of reproductive rights. Within it, paradigmatic categories and principles of relationship were established: those of sex, age, and generation, of complementarity and domination, and of centrality and peripherality. Moreover, its constitution underlay a cyclical process of development and fragmentation, for the unit both reproduced itself and gave rise to groupings of higher order. Thus the maturation of the sibling group produced a new set of agnatically linked households as brothers founded their own domestic groups and competed over the property and status of their father once he had died (Comaroff and Roberts 1981:34). These units, in turn, formed the core of a new segment, although hostilities might result in some households moving to the wards of matrilateral kin or affines. In like manner, agnatic clusters at the core of wards and sections would proliferate and subdivide—a process that also occured at the level of the chiefdom itself, which was equally susceptible, in the course of conflict over status and office, to fission along lines of agnatic cleavage.

If the principles of agnatic status gave form to the process of social aggregation, these principles took their meaning from their contrast with matrilaterality. At the level of the house, the uterine sibling group contained, in microcosm, the opposition between agnatic seniority and matrilateral complementarity; for the exchange of women and the ranking of men ensured not merely the eventual fragmentation of the natal unit but also the generation of two quite different orders of relations in its wake. Hence, while the devolution of the common household property tended to splinter the unity of its male offspring, the noncompetitive bond between brother and sister remained strong and gave rise to unequivocally solidary ties. Ideally, sibling pairs of the opposite sex were "cattle-linked," the sister's bridewealth being used for the brother's union (Comaroff and Roberts 1981:48). Such linkage meant that even full brothers were distinguished in terms of female ties, for it continued into the next generation in a privileged avuncular relationship between a particular mother's brother and his sister's children. As fraternal rivals entered the political arena, they counted on the supportive alliance of these matrilateral kin. In this manner, the social and moral universe was sharply divided, a distinction signified in bodily terms: agnates were typically held to "eat" (*ja*) each other, matrilaterals to provide nurture (*jesa*). Moreover, when agnates fed each other, it was with the substances of sorcery (*sejeso*). The contrast was indeed fundamental, and was reproduced at every level of the sociocultural system.[3] For example, a man found guilty of a serious crime in the chief's court could find sanctuary in the backyard of the house of the ruler's mother, who was also "mother of the nation" (Comaroff and Roberts 1981:258).

The contrast between agnation and matrilaterality also structured domestic relations of production and reproduction. Within the household, usufruct rights in land were vested in women, whose individual houses were the units of agricultural production (Campbell n.d.:64; 1815:201; Spohr 1973:77). This unit and its radiating matrilateral links was the locus of physical reproduction and nurture, culturally marked as a female preserve (see Campbell 1815:184). As such, it was spatially and symbolically distinguished from the male sphere; that of the negotiation of relations between domestic groups, and of the management of the affairs of higher-order groupings that cut across matrilateral ties. Indeed, the relationship between the principles of agnation and matrilaterality corresponded to that between male and female, a relationship both of complementary symmetry *and* asymmetry (cf. Turner n.d.[b]:5, who suggests that this dual quality is a property of symbolic polarities in general). Thus men and women possessed complementary bodily attributes and joined in the conjugal act of procreation, as well as in the provision of the regular diet which consisted of both male (pastoral) and female (agricultural) products. In addition, through their participation in the political process at the center, men secured the fields that women cultivated at the agricultural periphery, the first activity being agnatically coded, the latter one matrilaterally ordered.

Yet such symmetry, at the domestic level, between male and female principles coexisted with a marked asymmetry in their respective relationship to the total social order. For the male domain of agnatic kinship was part of the more inclusive, extra-domestic aggregations which encompassed the household and subsumed it into the ranked body politic; this was underlined by the fact the the term *kgotla* denoted alike "agnates" and all formal sociopolitical arenas. Agnation here transected matrilaterality, rendering it politically residual; indeed, the latter served as the backstage support network for public practice. As we shall see, prevailing spatial arrangements and ritual processes also stressed the circumscription of the marginal sphere of female productivity by the centralized domain of male politico-economic exchange. For control over the means of production and reproduction—land, labor, cattle, and reproductive rights—was vested in men, and was transacted in the idiom of rank and status that situated the household in the wider social field. Agnatic authority also regulated the permanent removal of the offspring from the house, male kin not only supervising the marriage of daughters but ritually "taking the sons from their mothers" at the time of initiation. In contrast, matrilateral ties, although they were the bonds of productive and political cooperation, transferred none of the values of wealth and status. Even in the realm of the dead, kin ties through women were eclipsed, the ancestors all speaking in a collective agnatic voice.

What we have, then, is the elaboration of an opposition between two domains of relationship and value which stemmed from the reproduction of the domestic unit itself. These contrasting domains were at once complementary and asymmetrical in their structural significance: the one, matrilaterality, provided for lateral, unranked linkages between domestic units; the other, agnation, for the ranked encompassment of those units into a higher-order collectivity. Where the first pertained to an individuated social field of personalized and cooperative relations, a domain symbolically articulated through females, the latter configured an aggregated social field, whose substance was wrought by male political practice. Thus far, the Tswana system, at least as I have described it, seems to have been similar to those systems more conventionally organized on principles of unilineal descent; for the latter also feature contrasting orders of relationship traced through men and women, respectively, orders which are at once complementary and asymmetrical in their structural role (Fortes 1953). What distinguished the Tswana system was, in fact, the *lack* of corporate descent groups, and the *presence* of a fluid social universe without clearly bounded aggregations or social categories, in which most close kin ties were multistranded. But how did this lack of categorical clarity arise, and how did it relate to the dichotomized social field I have outlined? Further, what, in the absence of segmentary lineages, gave form to Tswana social arrangements? To answer these questions we must move beyond the house itself to the linkages that tied it into the wider system; and this requires that the marriage system be introduced.

Marriage, Hierarchy, and Individuation

As has frequently been observed, the Tswana present something of an anomaly in the general African ethnography, for they both maintain an agnatic descent ideology and encourage all forms of cousin union (Radcliffe-Brown 1950:69; Kuper 1975). Tswana stated the following order of marriage preference: MBD—FBD—FZD—MZD, and Schapera (1950:157f.; 1963), whose data come from a later period, notes that commoners in fact conformed to this preferential order, while royals (who were more likely to marry close kin of *all* categories) selected FBD most frequently. As has been argued elsewhere (Comaroff and Comaroff 1981), the combination of an agnatic ideology and a high proportion of endogamous marriage gives rise to a particular social outcome: while descent-group exogamy produces bounded units, unambiguous categories of agnates and affines, and stable relations of opposition and alliance, agnatic marriage confounds such clear-cut arrangements. For it makes affines out of kin and overlays agnation with matrilaterality (figure 2); hence ties existing between the parties to such unions are in fact multiple bonds. And, instead of their offspring being incorporated into an objective order of enduring and bounded groupings, they were located within a kindred of overlapping linkages.

It follows that, among the Tswana, the range of kin with whom marriage was prohibited was both narrow and ego-focused: it comprised an individual's natal house, that of his parents, his children, and his siblings' children.[4] Beyond these limits, social relations were classified according to the opposed categories of agnation and matrilaterality, there being also a residual category of ties outside the field of close kinship, regarded merely as neutral (Comaroff and Roberts 1981:53). Affinity itself was seen to create bonds that were both egalitarian and cooperative.

In sum, there existed, on the one hand, a categorical order that organized the social field into unambiguous and contrasting domains, and, on the other, a pattern of endogamous marriage that gave rise to multi-stranded and contradictory kin ties. Moreover, as J. L. Comaroff (1982:152) notes, there was no Tswana term for "multiply linked relative." By implication, then, multiple links required reduction to "one thing or another," a process that appears to have occurred as the practical outcome of transactions, largely over property and rank, between the individuals and units in question (ibid.). Here again we have to return to the nature of agnatic politics, for this was the major idiom in which relations between houses were conducted.

I have pointed out how the rules of rank rendered status and office susceptible to negotiation. In the competition for resources and values—such as control over land and labor—which were transacted through the administrative hierarchy in the idiom of agnation, rivals sought to "eat or be eaten." Now a crucial dimension of such political dynamics was that they occurred within a universe which was fluid, and was governed by an ethos of active self-contrivance. As has been noted by other observers of similar social systems (Barth 1973; Bourdieu 1977; Comaroff and Comaroff 1981), the combination of agnatic ideology and agnatic endogamy not only confounds classic analytical assumptions based on

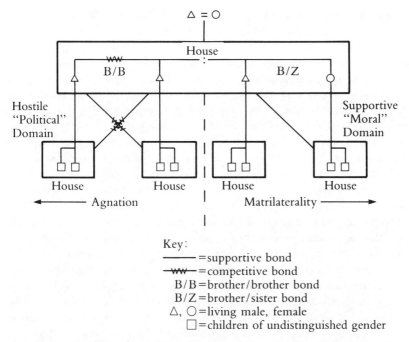

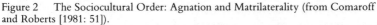

Figure 2   The Sociocultural Order: Agnation and Matrilaterality (from Comaroff and Roberts [1981: 51]).

unilineal, exogamous orders, it also gives rise to a characteristic cultural stress on individualism, and on the construction of transient alliances. In the Tswana case, the absence of stable "in-group"/"out-group" relations, and the presence of individuating maternal ties, ensured that the calculus of power lay in the seemingly infinite potential for negotiating the spheres of influence around formal, agnatically defined offices. In the process, marriage, as the most explicit mode of creating linkages, was surrounded with great strategic significance. However, for any union to have political utility, the bonds between the potential parties had first to be clarified, even though such definition might·be subject to subsequent revision (Comaroff and Comaroff 1981). Alliance with each of the three major categories of social others—agnates, matrilaterals, or distant kin— had distinct pragmatic implications; but the primary value, as Schapera (1957) and others have noted, was that of converting agnatic rivalry into supportive alliance. Such practice, of course, reproduced both endogamy and the ambiguity of the social field, which all of the actors now had to configure anew.

Thus high rates of FBD marriage became both the cause and the effect of a strong emphasis upon individual self-contrivance. But a further implication was that, in distinguishing the component houses within the agnatic field, it also provided the potential basis for disaggregation. This potential was not realized, of course, while household heads participated vigorously in centralized politico-economic institutions, but it remained an ever-present possibility, with important historical consequences. In contrast, MBD unions, when repeated over time, yielded the more familiar pattern of discrete categories of "wife-givers" and "wife-takers" and the hardening of bounded descent groups. In fact, a proportion of Tswana marriages were always of this type, in some cases leading to enduring alliances between segmentary groupings (J. L. Comaroff 1982:154). Where it occurred, this latter tendency contributed to the consolidation of larger agnatic units and also of political hierarchy. Both potentialities, the centripetal and the centrifugal, were inscribed in the precolonial system; in fact, both were realized at different moments in the life of the precolonial polities. Hence, as J. L. Comaroff (1982:155) states, the Tshidi chiefdom has at times appeared as a strongly centralized community with well-articulated descent groups; at others, it has manifested little effective aggregation above the level of the household. Disaggregation, however, was not the product of marriage patterns alone; for the opposed centripetal and centrifugal tendencies realized by them were tied in with a structural tension, in the political economy, between the chiefly center and the domestic periphery. For, just as the logic of centralized control involved the perpetuation of a tightly integrated order of inequality, and hence a ranked hierarchy of sociopolitical units, agnatic competition threatened the basis of chiefly incumbency, stressed the rivalry between households over rank and property, and exacerbated the ambiguity of social relations. Significantly, moreover, MBD marriage was a vehicle of the former, FBD marriage, a symptom of the latter. The more radical transformations of the Tshidi sociocultural order such as occurred in the past when centrifugal forces gained ascendency (J. L. Comaroff 1982), or when colonialism took hold, led to the progressive disintegration of agnatic politics and the extradomestic aggregations that supported it. Then the social field came increasingly to take the form of a network of matrilateral ties between otherwise individuated households.

In sum, the constitution of the Tshidi system—the opposed cultural categories inscribed in the house, their symbolic representation in agnation and matrilaterality, and the pattern of close-kin marriage—gave rise at once to an unambiguous classification of the social and moral universe, and to an ambiguous network of actual social linkages. The resolution of this disjuncture lay at the level of practice, in a mode of acting upon the world so as to bring it into conformity with dominant cultural values.

the household within the political economy was actually conceived of in terms of the "natural" progression of kin groups into the nation (*morafe*); and chiefly extraction was couched in the terms of agnatic seniority, a relationship idealized as one of paternal responsibility as well as authoritative license. The chief, after all, was the "father of the people."

This implies, of course, that "social" and "material" relations, whatever analytic distinction may be made between them in theory, were in fact embedded in the same practical reality. Thus the household, socially individuated within the agnatic field, was materially individuated as the basic unit of production; and its internal relations were inseparable from those upon which the division of labor was predicated. Likewise, competitive political action had economic corollaries, since the "eating" of agnatic rivals reduced them to clients or junior partners in the productive process. And yet, while they were mutually constitutive dimensions of the Tswana system, the social and material aspects of everyday practice were potentially contradictory in important respects; when elaborated into the centralized structures of the state, in fact, they gave characteristic shape to higher-order political processes.

Prior to colonial penetration, the Tswana political economy was based on both agriculture and pastoralism, augmented by hunting and gathering. Early nineteenth-century records show the southern chiefdoms to have also been partially dependent upon trade with other local communities to the north and west, a regional network which yielded finished metal tools, iron ore, and lead haematite (*sebilo*), a cosmetic powder of ritual importance (Burchell 1953, vol. 2:340; Campbell 1822, vol. 2:194). The leitmotif of this political economy, however, lay in the relationship between its dryland ecology and the politics of centralization. As I have noted, centrist domination acted upon the uncertainties of marginal rainfall, the chiefs seeking to monopolize risk-reducing resources. This applied both in the pastoral sector, where they enjoyed the best pasturage and the manpower to render large herds mobile (Burchell 1953, vol. 2:248), and in agriculture, where they regulated the seasonal cycle and exacted tributary contributions to the working of royal fields (Solomon 1855:47). The ecological necessity of plowing immediately after the spring rains called for flexible access to labor, and it was precisely here that officeholders sought to dominate their subjects by regulating *their* access to the means of production—and thereby their control over the reproduction of those means. Before the introduction of the plow, the conflict between the interests of center and periphery, while ever-present, especially for men lacking influence and client labor, was mitigated by the fact that the responsibility for agriculture was in the hands of the women, who oscillated between their duties on the chiefly holdings and work on their own (Schapera 1938:64). But the plow was to bring cat-tle—and, with them, men—into arable production, thus drawing the latter away from the court and encouraging the endemic tendency to-ward centrifugal movement.

Not unexpectedly, the ability to hold followers at the center was a crucial indigenous gauge of chiefly efficiency (J. L. Comaroff 1982:157f.; Ashton 1937). Tswana ritual and lore associated concentrated settlement and elaborate politico-jural organization with "civilization" (*rutegile*, from *go ruta*, "to teach," a state of fully socialized being [Brown 1931:265, 372]); notwithstanding this ideological hegemony, the coun-tervailing tendency, that of seeking self-realization beyond the orbit of political constraint, was a persistent feature of Tswana history. Thus states arose and fell, expanded and contracted, and regimes were con-stantly confronted with the possibility of their dominions dissolving into acephalous communities of autonomous households. In practice, given their resource base, chiefs were by and large able to limit such coun-terhegemonic processes. But, as long as the precolonial sociocultural sys-tem remained in place, so did the structural basis for the conflict itself.

Agriculture
The Female Domain of Domestic Production

Agriculture yielded the bulk of everyday subsistence requirements, while pastoralism provided for the ritual diet and for extradomestic exchange. But these were not merely distinct and complementary spheres of pro-duction and distribution: female cultivation (and, to a lesser extent, gathering) actually subsidized male extradomestic activity on a day-to-day basis, establishing a material base on which rested the exchange of cattle in the creation of lateral and vertical social ties, the activities of trading and warfare, and other forms of transaction.

Tswana fields (*masimo*), as noted before, were situated in zones beyond the residential margins of the settlement. Within these zones, usufruct rights were distributed through the ward headman, the plots of fellow ward members adjoining each other. Neither permanent homesteads nor cattleposts (*meraka*) could be established in such agricultural zones, the former being limited to the town (*motse*) itself, and the latter to the fringe of the uncultivated bush (*naga*; see figure 3). Some scholars have argued that this arrangement facilitated both the access of large sedentary popu-lations to rural holdings and the optimal exploitation of limited tracts of arable land (see Schapera 1943:128); according to this view, the practice of consolidated mixed farming by scattered productive units would have been more wasteful of scarce resources. Whatever their merits, however, such ecological arguments beg a series of questions which are sociocultural in nature. Apart from all else, there were many possible modes of relating to the existing material environment, of which the chosen one was not without severe limitations in respect, first, of hoe and, later, of plow cultivation (see Schapera 1943:130); both suffered, as centralized domicile made it impossible to time arable operations to maximum effect. Yet, despite this, the precolonial spatial arrangements persisted among most Tswana peoples well into the twentieth century—even in the face of radical alterations in the mode of production—a fact which is simply inexplicable in terms of utilitarian strategy. On the contrary, the logic of land-utilization patterns is to be found in the constitution of the contemporary Tswana system as a whole; in the social and semantic forms of the state, and in a prevailing ideology which associated "civilization" with a very particular spatial order. Notwithstanding the practical tension between center and periphery endemic to this system, politico-economic and residential centralization was hegemonic in precolonial Tswana culture: not only was it realized by the exercise of tangible power, but it was symbolically constructed in public rit' al and was embedded in the taken-for-granted forms of everyday li.. Thus, far from being the product of a utilitarian equation, patterns of resource exploitation—indeed, the mode of production as a whole—were inscribed in a dialectical relationship between sociocultural order and material circumstance.

It would seem that, under hoe cultivation, fields were seldom larger than two or three acres, and that polygynous families might have several, the only constraint being the availability of labor (Schapera 1938:201; Burchell 1953, vol. 2:362). Each uterine house held at least one, and wealthier households also maintained a common plot, often worked by clients. And, while there were clear technological and ecological limitations on land exploitation, it appears that, under optimal conditions, quite considerable cultivation took place.[6] Soil types in the nineteenth-century habitat were mixed. A range of such types were identified indigenously, only a few of which were recognized as suitable to cultivation: *mokata*, red loam, the favorite choice; *selôkô*, a heavy black clay; *motlhaba*, sandy loam; and *mósawa*, red sandy loam (Schapera 1943:129). These were unevenly distributed, most frequently being found on alluvial plains and in valleys, and their presence was an important factor in the relocation of settled communities (Schapera 1943:129). Moreover, since soils were recognized as having variable capacities to withstand drought, there was a high value placed both on certain sorts of fields and on access to holdings in different locations so as to combat the uncertainties of rainfall (Kinsman n.d.[b]:8). Thus, while there was no "shortage" of land, the best acreages were monopolized by the powerful (Schapera

1938:63). None of the soils were cultivable before the spring rains, and, prior to the introduction of the plow and of draft animals, surface water was not a major consideration in the politics of agricultural production.

As I have stressed, cultivation was a female enterprise.[7] Women held fields in their own right as daughters or wives and undertook the vast bulk of agricultural labor, receiving only minimal assistance from men (Solomon 1855:62; Campbell 1815:201; n.d.:64). Such larger-scale cooperation as was required seems to have been recruited on the basis of matrilateral ties (J. L. Comaroff 1982:156), and observers describe large parties of women who undertook in concert such tasks as breaking the ground or harvesting.[8] A mixture of drought-resistant crops was grown: sorghum (mabêlê) was the most important, and from it the staple foods of porridge and beer were derived. Millet (lebêlêbêlê), sweetcorn (mpše), beans (dinawa) and cucumbers (marotse, makatane) were also planted (Schapera 1943:117; Solomon 1855:45; Campbell n.d.:73; Burchell 1953, vol. 2:371). Nineteenth-century mission records reveal cycles in which years of good harvests were succeeded by average seasons or by complete agricultural failure (Kinsman n.d.[b]:8, 12; Moffat 1842:327); given a technology restricted to the hoe and the hatchet, and highly variable rainfall, surpluses that could offset such disasters were difficult to achieve, a fact which underlined the dependence upon diversified sources of subsistence. Women, in fact, were perpetually engaged in a complementary cycle of cultivation and gathering; while the former was possible, its pursuits structured their enterprise, and the collection of veldkos filled any spare time (Kinsman n.d.[a]:5; Borcherds 1861:128). When the rains failed or stored reserves ran low, gathering would dominate female activity and might be organized on a cooperative basis.[9]

This alternation, in the female sphere, between cultivating domesticated resources and culling the wild was mirrored in the male sphere, where pastoralism existed in complementarity with hunting. But the mode of relating to the "natural" (i.e. nonsocial) world differentiated men from women, this being reflected both in productive practice and in the role of the products themselves within the political economy at large. Women, corn, and veldkos stood in relation to men, stock, and game as did an unstable mediation of the wild to a forceful and stable domination of the exigencies of existence. Thus cattle were the very embodiments of reliability and cultural control over productive processes. They were mobile in the face of drought and disaster—a crucial factor, as the event history has shown—and were self-reproducing, if not without labor input. Grain, in contrast, was inescapably vulnerable to the climate, and frequent crop failures regularly threatened to wipe out seed altogether. Cows could be counted on to yield milk as a finished product; the agricultural counterpart, corn beer, had to be transformed by women in a delicate operation that was subject to disruption, especially by their own polluting heat. Stock also supplied dung, *boloko* (from *boloka*, "to preserve" or "save"), which was an important substance in the fabrication of domesticated surfaces in huts and courtyards; grain had to be arduously threshed, its residue serving as cattle fodder, thereby to be permanently transformed.

In fact, the entire arable cycle was metaphorically linked to that of procreation, both being associated with instability and the threat of miscarriage. For example, just as the commencement of planting, made possible by the first rains, had to be initiated by formal decree (the chief "giving out the seed time"), so the onset of the female reproductive career, while enabled by first menstruation, had to be socially initiated by ritual means. The word *tlhaka* denoted both "seed" or "grain" and "fetus," and *tlhakanèla dikobô* ("to plant," "fuse under the blanket") implied sexual intercourse as well as the work of sowing the land (Brown 1931:313, 423). Similarly, the term for "reap" (*go sega*) was also used for the "cutting" of the umbilicus in childbirth. As this suggests, there was an association between the earth and the female body, the construct of dark, moist, and secreted generation being common to both, and reappearing in the symbolism of modern rites of rebirth.[10] The identification of the uncertain process of gestation with crop maturation was further underlined by the fact that the failure of the latter was usually explained in terms of the malevolent burying in the field of an aborted fetus, the epitome of disrupted reproduction; this act, referred to as *sebeela*, was seen to "spoil" the ground and prevent rain (Schapera 1971[a]:107). Indeed, productive enterprise as a whole appears to have exemplified the meaningful contrast between controlled (male) as against uncontrolled (female) sexuality. The distinction was also given wider resonance by means of the lexicon of the natural and the social. Thus, when, in the wake of agricultural disaster, women gathered veldkos in the bush using only a digging stick and skin bag, their labor was described as *gola*. Since this was also the word for "natural growth," it suggested that, when cultivation had to be abandoned, females resorted to the appropriation of the wild, an essentially presocial enterprise. The male hunt (*letsholô*), on the other hand, was a highly orchestrated affair, often performed by age-regiments, and involving the use of carefully tooled weapons. It was regarded as the acme of cultivated skill and cultural control, and was generally undertaken to acquire the means for collective ritual and trade rather than to supplement subsistence shortfalls. The product of the hunt, and meat in general, was highly valued, whereas grain, though staple, was seen as mundane (Schapera 1953:22). Cultivated crops and female veldkos were distinguished, also, from "medicine" (*setlhare*; literally "tree"), the only object of gathering expeditions in the bush undertaken by men.

The structure of women's productive activities, then, was given by the demands of the agricultural cycle and mediated by chiefly control. The first rains fell between August and November, whereupon the officeholder had his subjects plant the tributary fields attached to his position (*masotla*) and afterwards disperse to their own holdings (Schapera 1943:184). He literally "gave out the seedtime" or the "time for beginning to sow" (*go ntsha letsema*). As we shall see, time in indigenous Tswana culture was not an abstract entity, a resource existing apart from activity and events; rather, it was the duration inherent in social practice as it acted upon the passage of the seasons. Without such practice to actualize it, there *was* no time. The chief's ability to make and dispense the seedtime was a function of his innate capacity to bring, by ritual means, the annual rains that were the essential prerequisite of arable success (Schapera 1971[a]:17); and, in bestowing it on his people, he not only accomplished a vital duty of his office but set in motion the entire social calendar. Rites calling forth the rains were preceded by the performance of *go bapola lefatshe*, the "punctuation" or "pegging out" of the domesticated area by royal doctors (Schapera 1971[a]:74). In terms of Tswana ideology at least, it was the ritual power of the chief—enhanced by his royal ancestors and his doctors—that generated fertility, and the time and space for its collective realization. Self-evidently, this was another realm in which the precolonial cosmology provided for the institutions of centralized control.

The role of the chief in the regulation of production also permitted him to extract his surpluses under optimal conditions. Able to "seize time" in an ecology where it was of the utmost significance, he harnessed the seasonal cycle, ensuring his access to public labor when it was most beneficial and protecting his superior powers of accumulation. Indeed, each stage of the agricultural process had first to be initiated on the royal tributary fields. Planting was followed by weeding and, once the crops had set, by bird scaring (Schapera 1953:22). During this entire period, the women resided at the fields, working with the assistance of daughters and female matrikin and, for those from the wealthier households, with client labor (Kinsman n.d.[a]:13). The female schedule and productive practices struck Western observers as particularly arduous (Solomon 1855:44).

Once the crop had begun to ripen, the most elaborate ritual of the entire agricultural cycle was performed: *go loma thôtse*, the "tasting of the gourd." This served to tie the maturation of the crops to the recreation of the social community, the rite being indigenously viewed as one of purification, renewal, and revitalization (Willoughby 1928:226ff.). Female producers brought their firstfruits to the chief's court, where they were to be ceremonially eaten, and a pulp of their leaves rubbed onto the body. The procedure, one of the few performed in order of seniority by the various Tswana groups, began in the chiefly household and proceeded, strictly by rank, through the entire polity down to its youngest member (Schapera 1943:187; 1971[a]:67; Willoughby 1928:229; Holub 1881, vol. 1:329). On the night of the initial tasting, each man was to sleep with his principal wife, and all the ashes in the settlement were dumped in the bush and the fires kindled anew. Members of the community who were absent from this performance had to be ritually reinstated into kin group and collectivity on their return, since they were highly polluting to its pristine form. Thus, not only was the yield of female labor symbolically assimilated into the body politic via its center; women also provided the very substance which set in motion the recreation of that body in terms of an hierarchical order that was imprinted on the anatomy of each of its citizens in turn. Such ritual renewal of the social fabric in its idealized form powerfully legitimized existing structures of domination and inequality. For the rites were a "time of reckoning," a moment at which the seeming contradiction between fixed rules of rank and shifting incumbency was resolved in an elaborate cultural statement about the nature of the system in place. Thus a fluctuating and ambiguous everyday reality was ritually objectivized in an ostensibly stable order, poised on the brink of the new annual cycle. Moreover, the rites marked the shift from the uncertain duration of the agricultural season to the more predictable social calendar, the transition from a period in delicate symbiosis with the wild to one in which the rhythm of activity was dictated again by centralized communal concerns. Now the harvest could be collected, food stores replenished, and public attention turned again to the social enterprises of collective ritual and trade, these being forbidden while the crop was still in the field and vulnerable to failure (Burchell 1953, vol. 2:381; Willoughby 1909:229).

Pastoralism
The Male Domain of Social Reproduction

The association between women and agriculture, an inherently risky enterprise which betokened a fragile hold over the wild, was consistent with the image of females as beings lacking the innate closure necessary to permit them to act masterfully upon the world (Comaroff 1983). Not only were they open to defilement from outside, their bodies were also the site of procreative processes which generated heat, a force that constantly threatened to spill over and infuse other persons and things with its disruptive qualities. Women were particularly dangerous to the more stable transformative activities of men, who, in contrast, were "cool." They were thus debarred from physical contact with cattle, and were thought to imperil the accomplishment of rituals of initiation, rain-making, and ancestral veneration, as well as of politico-jural deliberations at the chiefly court (Schapera 1938:28; Willoughby 1909:234). Effective action in the fully social domain required a state of coolness (*tshididi*); conventional salutations and benedictions at the royal meeting-place were *"Pula!"* ("Let it rain!") and *"A go nne tshididi!"* ("Let it be cool!"; Brown 1926:156; Solomon 1855:47; Schapera 1971[a]:15). The term *go hodisa* ("to cool") also meant "to heal" (Willoughby 1928:363), a socially acquired male skill which tempered the contagious heat of illness. Here, too, the semantics of everyday practice conveyed the social and material fact of female marginality.

In contrast to agriculture, pastoralism was an activity far more controlled; indeed, in the Tswana cultural order, animal husbandry represented the very embodiment of steadfast domestication. Livestock provided security in the face of crop failure and, while meat was usually reserved for ritual occasions, milk was regarded as an essential component of the everyday diet. But the value of stock stretched far beyond considerations of dietary utility—and even beyond that of counteracting ecological hazard. If the products of cultivation and gathering served to fuel physical subsistence, permitting adult men to transcend an insecure dependence on natural process, it was cattle that served as the medium for realizing their identities as social beings. Their herds enabled them to produce and reproduce enduring bonds within and between communities, and between the human and the superhuman realms; to construct marital alliances and exchange reproductive rights and labor; and to forge relations of inequality and clientship, the stuff of politico-economic domination. In addition, cattle had not only the capacity to embody value but also the wherewithal to permit its transformation: in the context of exchange, sacrifice, and ritual commensality they could construct or disentangle human relations; in initiation rites their slaughter was part of the dynamic process that made boys into men (Willoughby 1928:187, 196, 330). In short, they were the pliable symbolic vehicles through which the Tshidi formed and reformed their world of social and spiritual connections. Whereas agricultural produce appears not to have been regularly transacted outside the domestic context (except among close matrilateral kin), skins and hides, the culturally tooled fabrications of the pastoral domain, were major items of trade with non-Tswana, and were hence the source of metal ore and smelted goods (Campbell n.d.:24f.; Burchell 1953, vol. 2:293). Tswana summarized the generative power of cattle by referring to them as *Modimo o nkwe metse*, "God with a wet nose." Thus, while field crops had inherent use-value as the means of subsistence, cattle were primarily—if not solely—a medium of exchange with the capacity to objectify and transform identities and social relation-ships.

Southern Tswana herds comprised cattle, goats, and somewhat fewer sheep (Burchell 1953, vol. 2:224). Both precolonial and modern observ-ers have had difficulty in assessing the size of individual holdings, as cattle were, and are, widely dispersed under various forms of patronage (Schapera 1953:23); and any admission of wealth in animals was thought to excite plunder and ritual attack. Moreover, postcolonial history has shown that the stock population may wax and wane quite considerably over time, demonstrating long-term cycles of depletion by disease and drought, followed by spontaneous recovery. Nonetheless, the documen-tary record does suggest the presence of large herds in the nineteenth century, and it also gives evidence of visible inequalities in their distribu-tion (Burchell 1953, vol. 2:248). Most early visitors were struck by the prestige and significance attached by the Tswana to cattle ownership, and by the fact that it seemed to provide a ready index of differences in wealth and power (Solomon 1855:45; Burchell 1953, vol. 2:248). For the ordinary townsman, animals were acquired through inheritance, cli-entship, or bridewealth. Political office, on the other hand, entailed the right to levy certain fines in stock (Burchell 1953, vol. 2:248) and the chief monopolized the most profitable of all sources of supply, booty collected by the age-regiments on raiding expeditions against neighbor-ing communities (Kirby 1939, vol. 1:408; Burchell 1953, vol. 2:377). The accumulation of a large herd was an essential feature of the exercise of power, for it offered the opportunity to initiate ties of alliance and pat-ronage. But sizable accumulation was more or less confined to those with access either to royal status or office. Burchell (1953, vol. 2:248) noted that: "from the possession of property, the distribution of men into richer or poorer classes has followed as a natural consequence. Those who have riches, have also, it seems, power; and the word *kosi* . . . has a double acceptation, denoting either *a chief* or *a rich man*" (emphasis in original). He also remarked that controls built into the system effectively prevented the "poor" from transcending their economic status (p.383). The practice of *mahisa*, long-term cattle loans, served to extend the pat-ronage of the wealthy to their less favored kin and retainers (*batlhanka*) in exchange for political support and some labor. Such loans were small, merely expanding the modest herds of those who were capable of inde-pendent subsistence (Schapera 1938:246ff.).[11] Relations of servitude, in contrast, provided for the survival needs of an underclass (also termed *batlhanka*, or *balala*, those "laid low")[12] which had limited access to the means of production and was external to the politico-jural process (Bur-chell 1953, vol. 2:248). This underclass comprised former captives in war, families or small vassal communities of Bushmen and Kgalagadi, and impoverished townsmen, most of whom were forced to live outside the settlement, either at the cattleposts of their masters or in hunting camps in the bush (Mackenzie 1871:368; Spohr 1973:76). Residents at cattle-posts sent milk to the town once or twice a week (Burchell 1953, vol. 2:368); and the hunters, equipped with tools by their overlords and subsisting on a portion of their kill, brought in honey, skins, and furs (Burchell 1953, vol. 2:383; Kinsman n.d.[a]:14). Such labor, together with the input of pre-adolescent boys (Solomon 1855:44), provided the bulk of the pastoral work force, generating the surpluses that made possible the town-based existence of adult male citizens. This, in turn, was both practically and symbolically focused upon the court, the simultaneous site of political deliberation, leather work, and tool-making, activities viewed as the epitome of refined social accomplishment by the Tswana (Campbell 1815:187; Solomon 1855:42f.). Bushmen and Kgalagadi, because they resided in the bush, were regarded as "wild," innately incapable of leading a domestic life; as a result, they were effectively prevented from acquiring stock (Holub 1881, vol. 1:347; Burchell 1953, vol. 2:248). Mackenzie (1871:368) notes: "It is the mark of a freeman to have a residence in the town, while vassals are doomed always to live in the open country. . . . Bushmen indeed are not allowed to enter the precincts of the town during the day." In this manner the cultural status of the *balala* as asocial creatures of the night was perpetuated by Tswana socioeconomic arrangements.

Townsmen retained a proportion of their cows in the settlement to provide for immediate domestic requirements, but most stock was lodged at the cattleposts. The latter were assigned on a ward basis, the animals being left in the care of herders attached to individual households (Schapera 1943:218; Burchell 1953, vol. 2:368). Among southern Tswana, it seems that only the chief's herd was permitted to graze outside the allotted ranching areas and to move freely so as to maximize range (Mackenzie 1871:368). The officeholder also received considerable tribute in stock and game: the breast of any animal killed, and all ivory and jackal skins, which later became prized by white traders, had by prescription to be presented to him.

Pastoralism was complemented by hunting in the male productive domain, although, as I have suggested, Tswana contrasted the latter with gathering as secure domination to uncertain symbiosis. Furthermore, while all women, including royals (Campbell 1815:201), did identical work on the same terms, male enterprises were more diverse, this being both cause and effect of the hierarchical structure of the polity. Thus a clear distinction was maintained between the socialized activities of townsmen and the foraging of serfs in the bush; townsmen returning from activities in the wild, for instance, would be subject to ritual purification (*motlhapiso*; "washing"). From this perspective, the position of women was structurally paradoxical: as practical mediators of rank nature within the domesticated world, they both created the material basis for society and yet threatened, in the process, to destroy it. But, whereas serfs had no politico-jural rights or independent means, females did, even if as the wards of males. And, as I have noted, a pragmatic and ideological symmetry did exist between the sexes in certain basic aspects of household production. Women were also not completely without political resources: in theory at least, they could withhold their sexuality and labor from husbands who did not comply with normatively defined responsibilities; and they could, if mistreated, return to their natal homes. Nonetheless, as a category, they were patently marginal to the resources and modes of practice most highly valued within the overall political economy. Along with bush dwellers, the young, and men of junior rank, they were enmeshed in a structure of differentiation and inequality that tended to be reproduced by the very forms of everyday activity.

In order to complete this discussion of political economy, it is necessary to examine further two considerations—the indigenous conception of work and the symbolic role of cattle—since these will be of particular importance to the analysis of Tshidi cultural transformation.

The vernacular term *go dira* means to "make," "do," or "cause to happen" and was used to describe a wide range of actions upon the world, from material production to the performance of ritual or sorcery. Like time, work was not an abstract quality or a potential commodity. Rather, it was the fabrication process inherent in the Tswana perception of being: the construction of self and other and the forging of social relations in the pursuit of culturally defined values. As we have seen, "work" was of a fundamentally different order for males than it was for females, as indeed it was for the chief or for the ritual doctor, both of whom had unusual transformative powers. Women, in their uncertain mediation of nature, were associated with production and reproduction in the domestic sphere. Their innate bodily qualities required confinement and denied them the male ability to extend themselves and their personal influence in physical and social space, as well as in time. Women also had limited capacities of movement, and of inducing movement in others. By contrast, men could exchange women and clients, creating social ties through the transaction of cattle and words (*mahoko*), whose formal management was their preserve;[13] this permitted them to manipulate others and, conversely, to be manipulated by others. To be sure, the pursuit of self-contrivance and the quest for dominance—"eating" and "being eaten"—were not only two sides of the same coin; they were the quintessential expression of male "work," the form of practice that "made" the relations on which the politico-social order rested.

An important feature of this embeddedness of "work/action" in its social context was the fact that producer, process, and product were not nicely separable at any stage of their unfolding relationship. Hence the grain and beer that a woman produced were infused with her personal qualities such that to consume them was to take in something of her substance, an act which carried the connotation of sexual intimacy or close kinship. Likewise, cattle bore the identity of their owners (if not their herders) and represented them in sacrifice or in exchange. To re-capitulate Mauss's classic insight, the bonds created by the giving of stock were actually embodied in the animals themselves; over a series of transactions they acquired the quality of condensed social histories.

We are thus led to the role of cattle as signifiers. This is a perennial theme in the African anthropological literature, which has long por-trayed these animals as the symbolic extension of the human persona, linking man and spirit and providing metaphors of social relations (Evans-Pritchard 1956; Lienhardt 1961). What I wish to suggest is that they are all this and something more, for the received wisdom ignores the ideological properties of cattle; how it is that, in their key symboliz-ing capacity, they come to objectivize and naturalize an overarching order of social arrangements. Among the Tswana—and, I believe, among most so-called "cattle complex" peoples—they appear simul-taneously to personify individuated identities, values, and ties, and to act as generalized icons of the social structure qua structure. As double sig-nifiers, speaking both to the particular and the general, they infuse the former with the latter, and imbue the experience of distinct events with the ineffability of the wider social system in which they occur. Conse-quently, they underpin the hegemony of a specific world view, one that locates the basis of social inequalities outside of society itself. In this respect, cattle would appear to exhibit features associated by Marx (1967, vol. 1) with the fetishism of commodities; that is, the capacity of the commodity, and especially money, to naturalize and obfuscate the very structure of exploitative relations that it itself makes possible. And, in-deed, cattle have been equated with money, commodities, and capital in the African context, if not exactly in the ideological sense intended here.

As multileveled signifiers among the Tswana, cattle were both metonyms and metaphors of social relations. In their metonymic aspect, they indexed the perceptible inequities of wealth and status which they were to naturalize again at another level. As metaphors, their role was twofold: first, they provided what I have termed a pliable symbolic me-dium, sufficiently like human beings but contrasting enough among themselves to objectify a range of personal identities, common values, and states of relationship. In this sense, as Lienhardt (1961:23) has re-ported of the Dinka, people were "put together" like cattle and could, by the same token, be rearranged through the appropriate symbolic manip-ulation of their bovine alters. Yet, second, along with this capacity to embody particular identities, values, and social configurations, these animals shared an iconic quality that was species specific: they were also all the living products of a stratified order of social relations. Thus they could be owned only by male citizens, and it was their identity that they bore. They also had to be maintained in segregation from mature women, to whom they had a natural antipathy. Further, as fully domesticated creatures, they were not fit possessions for beings themselves not adequately socialized: women, children, Bushmen, and subject peoples of the wild. Indeed, as a focus of everyday social practice, the beast was a powerful ideological agent, pointing to the appositeness of the dictum that, in the process of dominating nature, humans find the terms for dominating each other.

Does this mean, then, that cattle were "like money" in this and other respects? The recent debate over "cattle as capital" in Africa (Schneider 1979; Sperling and Hart n.d.) does not really confront the symbolic and ideological dimension of the problem, but it does suggest that cattle might usefully be viewed as similar to money in some ways and dissimilar in others. In their account of the issue, Sperling and Hart stress the dissimilarities: they regard the analogy as a mere imprecise metaphor, based on an ambiguous use of the key concepts. If the essence of capital is "wealth used to make more wealth," and the essence of money that it serves as a fixed means of equivalence in exchange, then African cattle cannot rigorously be held to be either. Cattle do increase naturally, but they also require considerable labor input (p.330); and, while their withdrawal from some forms of everyday consumption might suggest that they serve as stores of value, they are also consumables and are used in a variety of ways, from the provision of milk, through deployment in sacrifice, to insurance against failure in other productive enterprises. These authors note also (p.331) that beasts are not easily reducible to a money form, for their value is unstandardized in terms of sex, age, and condition. However, it is precisely here where the neglect of the signifying dimension both of cattle *and* money becomes problematic. For the former are unlike the latter, at least by this definition, in a more global sense: they carry a multiple symbolic load that can never be reduced to the single-stranded calculus of utility. Above all else, as human alter egos they have a personifying function which is the inverse of money as a depersonalized "thing." Yet money, too, might be viewed in a more complex light, as both a "thing in itself" and as a meaningful sign. And in this sense, I would argue, the ideological role of cattle as naturalizers of social relations might be seen as similar to money in its "fetishized" aspect. Thus the comparison of cattle and capital need not be a literal, all-or-none equation. Perhaps Mauss's description (1966:71–2) of Trobriand *vaygu'a* valuables is the most apposite:

> [they] are at once wealth, and tokens of wealth, means of exchange and payment, and things to be given away or destroyed. In addition they are pledges, linked to the persons who use them and who in turn are bound by them. Since, however, at other times they serve as tokens of money, there is interest in giving them away, for if they are transformed into services and merchandise that yields money then one is better off in the end.

Tswana cattle were indeed social phenomena of this kind, with the addition of being themselves directly consumable. Simultaneously personalizing and naturalizing, and serving for use and exchange in a manner both material and ideological, they embodied "all the strands of which the social fabric is composed" (Mauss 1966:1). In the unraveling of that fabric under colonialism, the transformed significance of "work" and the symbolic manipulation of productive relations in the absence of cattle were, predictably, to become major themes of response and resistance. But that is an issue to be taken up in later chapters.

Rank, Hierarchy, and the Process of Centralization

It remains, finally, to consider the dynamics of politico-economic centralization in terms of the interplay of the political, productive, and semantic forces distinguished above. I have suggested that the centripetal tendency in the Tswana system, realized through the participation of men in the political process, coexisted with structural features which individuated domestic units and fostered the disaggregation of the social field. I noted also that this tension—written into the logic of Tswana culture in the opposition between agnation and matrilaterality, male and female, and center and periphery—entered into the constitution of the state itself. The latter was constructed through the agnatic encompassment of households into a segmentary hierarchy; but, as system in place, it also came into conflict with the thoroughgoing implications of agnatic competition. In other words, while agnatic principles might have consolidated the segmentary structure of the chiefdom, they also created the basis for actors to challenge existing distributions of power. As the event history has shown, this process occurred right up to the level of the highest office, posing an ever-present threat to royal incumbents, who in turn sought to limit rivalries by surrounding themselves with (nonagnatic) clients and supporters. What is more, the very mechanisms of chiefly domination carried within them the seeds of their own undoing, particularly in the prevailing ecological context. For, apart from the classic paradox faced by most rulers, the crucial balance between coercion and consensus, Tswana chiefs trod a thin line between consolidating their position through monopolistic accumulation and jeopardizing altogether the viability of domestic production. Incompetent rule and agricultural failure, especially if exacerbated by drought, could crystallize latent rebellion and give rise to a campaign to remove the officeholder. But it could also set in motion more radical centrifugal processes: individuated households might withdraw to the domestic periphery in large numbers, their heads withholding participation in centralized political processes, or might even disperse beyond the reach of chiefly control. The prevalence of secessions was demonstrated in Chapter 2, and is reflected in the early observers' accounts of the existence of numerous small, unattached groupings within the wider Tswana field (Burchell 1953, vol. 2:386); scattering was evident also in the diverse ethnic composition of the Tswana polities (Schapera 1952), the products of a continuous process of shifting allegiance on the part of households and larger segments.[14] These were the key motivating forces that ensured that the precolonial system both reproduced *and* transformed itself in time and space.

The fulcrum of the process of centralization was, of course, the chiefship itself. We have seen that the office rested on institutionalized mechanisms capable of accumulating a fund of material and symbolic resources; on the control of land, labor, booty, and trade, and rights to various forms of tribute; and on the regulation of the agricultural cycle. The spatiotemporal dimension of productive and ritual processes spiralled inwards, establishing the chiefship as the "still point" of a turning wheel. "All roads lead to the chief," says the Tswana maxim, and the incumbent came to embody the polity itself, being addressed as the personification of the nation, *Morolong* ("Rolong person"). As we shall see, too, initiation rites located him at the hub of a set of age-regiments that radiated in space and stretched through time. His personal creative powers were underwritten by the collectivity of royal dead and the greatest of living doctors, who enabled him to bring rainfall and fertility, and to shape men and events with unusual oratorical forcefulness.

Despite this cultural apparatus, and the supremacy of the apical office, the incumbent himself was seldom safe from the threat of rivalry and challenge. This was symbolically inscribed in the fact that, as metonym of the collectivity, the chief was centrally implicated in serious disruptions of its constitution. The most consequential of these was drought, never far from the politics of the chiefship (Schapera 1971[a]:17ff.), for failure of the rains suggested that the ruler himself lacked essential power and/or benevolence. Indeed, the accoutrements of office merely defined an arena and a stock of material and symbolic wealth which enabled its holders to engage in efforts to bolster their authority. Power was enhanced through the construction of alliances, the conversion of agnatic rivals into affines, and the accumulation of support through redistribution, largely in the form of cattle loans. Retainers were installed in headmanships, and loyal affines and matrilaterals were well represented among the inner circle of advisers (J. L. Comaroff 1982). These men, in turn, established further patron–client ties, creating a network of political relations that often cut across agnatic rank.

Nineteenth-century accounts of chiefly power and government show some disagreement, however. Burchell (1953, vol. 2:376) states:

> This power . . . is moderated and, to a certain degree, regulated by the opinions of the inferior chieftains or principal men of property in the community, who are very frequently called together by the Chief for advice; but I was given to understand, by the natives, that even when exerted without control, it is still obeyed without dispute. Thus should a sudden emergency require a warlike expedition to take the field, the Chief commands the inhabitants to arm; and immediately every man . . . is ready to depart. . . .

Barrow (1806:399) and Mackenzie (1871:371) also stressed the requirement that the ruler take into account the "sentiments of the people" in decision-making, and noted the role of oratorical persuasion in ensuring compliance at court. Lichtenstein, in contrast, described the chief's power as "nearly uncircumscribed," no one having the right to oppose it (Lichtenstein 1930, vol. 2:414). More recent ethnographies have emphasized the ideal of government by consultation and consent, and the reliance of the incumbent upon the executive compliance of advisers and headmen (Schapera 1938:84ff.). Such accounts also point to the need to distinguish between the office and its holder (Schapera 1938:84; J. L. Comaroff 1975, 1978), for the legitimacy of the latter might vary considerably, being dependent on the fluctuating exigencies of power relations and conflicting forces surrounding the chiefship itself. In the indigenous perception, the ruler's ability to exercise control was held, tautologically, to be determined by his ability to prove himself effective, and forceful men could exercise what amounted to dictatorship (Schapera 1938:84). In general, however, the chief was seldom beyond the possibility of being separated, as mundane being, from the superhuman powers associated with the office.

The Tshidi event history bears witness to such fluctuations in chiefly legitimacy; specifically, to the varying capacity to regulate the mobility of the populace and maximize surplus extraction. It also reflects an increasingly explicit set of structural tensions between agnatic rank and political hierarchy, centripetal and centrifugal forces, and centralized control and domestic autonomy. Moreover, this case underlines the role of the indigenous sociocultural order in configuring the initial engagement with the agents of colonialism; hence, for example, the significance of chiefly intervention in mission activity and settler encroachment. But, more than anything else, it shows how a reciprocally determining relationship developed between these sets of historical actors and the systems they represented, such that Protestant Christianity, for instance, played into the structural tensions of the Tshidi world, exacerbating and objectifying formerly implicit oppositions. Prior to this engagement, and the more thoroughgoing transformation it heralded, the indigenous system appears to have been constituted in such a manner as to contain its internal contradictions within the minimal bounds necessary to support a centralized polity; at least, it did so for a considerable period. Crucial to these processes, to the mediation of structural contradiction in the practical context, were the ideological forces that resided both in everyday activity and in magico-ritual forms. It is to these forces that we now turn our attention.

4

The Mediation of Structure and Practice
Precolonial Cosmology and Ritual

The account of the precolonial order presented in the last chapter emphasized the mutually determining relationship between structure and
practice, a relationship mediated by the symbolic scheme that resided
both in the forms of everyday activity and in the imaginative conceptions
of ritual and cosmology. In this chapter, I shall examine this process of
symbolic mediation in more detail, exploring how it shaped social practice to prevailing structural principles, and rendered tangible the values
implied by those principles. My concern, in particular, is with mythic
and ritual constructions, for these play most directly upon the signifying
capacity of symbols, using them as the means through which to grasp,
condense, and act upon qualities otherwise diffused in the social and material world (cf. Munn 1974:580). As I have noted, the relationship between two ritual complexes lies at the heart of this study; the first,
adolescent initiation, is analyzed here. In form, each ritual corpus was a
comprehensive objectification of the Tshidi system at a specific historical
moment. In the attempt to understand the relationship between the two,
however, we do more than confront a microcosm of Tshidi history; we
observe that the more global process of structural transformation is the
product, here as elsewhere, of the reciprocal interplay of material and
symbolic forces, and that historical practice, notwithstanding the canons
of a more positivist social science, must be sought also at the level of
ritual action.

Let us return, then, to the precolonial system. I have indicated that the
symbolic schemes implicit in the various domains of this indigenous
world had converging ideological implications; that, in a series of contrasting social spheres and cultural genres, Tswana symbols defined pre-

dispositions for action in respect of an often ambiguous and competitive social field. As communicative media, they asserted the priority of a hierarchical order of relationships, and an accompanying repertoire of values. Thus the different loci of practical activity gave rise to more or less partial symbolic maps, which were subsumed into an overarching scheme by such core symbols as cattle and such comprehensive rituals as the tasting of the firstfruits. It will be recalled, for instance, that the firstfruits rites, and the holistic sociospatial scheme they presupposed, symbolically encompassed the household in the collectivity. In the process, the conflicting interplay of gender symmetry and asymmetry, which characterized domestic practice, was overlaid by a definitively asymmetrical mode; one which affirmed maleness and agnatic rank as the dominant principles of organization in the community as a whole. This, in turn, realized a higher-order relationship of complementarity and potential tension between agnatic rank and chiefly dominance, between household production and centrist control, and between individuation and aggregation. Again at this level, the ritual established the undisputed prominence of one set of principles over the other, creating an authoritative model of the society as a whole, in which a ruler of unrivaled supremacy converted domestic "raw material" into a vital communal renewal. It was thus that the component domains of the Tswana symbolic system were articulated, serving to impress upon consciousness a scheme that shaped perception and practice.

I do not wish to suggest, however, that the consciousness which mediates between a sociocultural order and everyday practice is merely the product of mindless determination. For the human imagination is independently reflective, and exists in a dialectical relationship with the very material and semantic forms which give it life. As Gramsci noted, hegemony is not "given"; it has to be sustained and reproduced (Hall 1977). Of course, reflective awareness is also never wholly free from structural constraint; for there is a reciprocal relationship between consciousness and context. Dominant ideological schemes may be perpetuated which stand in tension with the mundane experience of most members of a social system; and successive reformulations may leave obscure fundamental conflicts of meaning and power, permitting their practical reproduction. At other historical moments, critical awareness might lay bare something of the structural basis of discord and engender transformations of the logic of the system and its ideological mediations.

I shall deal with the dynamics of sociocultural transformation among the Tshidi in due course; at this point, my concern is the role of the various orders of symbolic mediation in shaping perception and habitual practice, and hence in reproducing the precolonial system itself. Only when this role has been established may we proceed to examine change as a process simultaneously symbolic and material. I thus return to pick up the threads of my preliminary account of Tswana spatiotemporal categories and transformative processes, for these expressed the basic principles of the more inclusive cosmology and associated conceptions of social action. Indeed, this cosmology was the coded context in which action was performed; and action, both individual and collective, was classified in terms of its potential to affect the world. Ritual was the mode of practice most forceful in its transformative capacity, especially when performed, on behalf of the community as a whole, by those who were its living embodiments.

Cosmology
Gender, Space, and Time

The order of social and productive arrangements examined in the last chapter implied a classification of persons, actions, time, and space; a cosmology that shaped and was shaped by everyday practice. While it was given tangible form in certain mythico-ritual texts, this conceptual scheme remained implicit, for the most part, in the signs and structures of everyday life; to describe it, and its precolonial form, as "belief" or rationalized metaphysics, would be to reify it unwarrantably. As we shall see, the Tshidi term for Christian (*modumedi;* "one who professes belief") suggests that the explicitness of mission "faith" was a novelty. Thus my account of the precolonial Tswana cosmos is predicated largely upon an analysis of implicit meaning.[1]

It will be recalled that the Tswana concentric model of increasingly domesticated space implied a basic distinction between the social and the wild. The latter lacked closure or stable classification; it was the realm of spirits, plants, and animals of unruly potential, and provided the vital ingredients for transforming the status quo through healing and sorcery. Within the bounds of the community, chiefly court and homestead stood in asymmetrical opposition: the person of the chief and the body of the woman (each associated with a hearth and an ideally perpetual fire) formed the foci for two different orientations in inhabited space. This established an opposed order of relative contrasts between "core" (*kaha ntle*) and "periphery" (*ha gare*), fundamental spatial coordinates in the circular metaphor of Tswana civilization. Although these orientations are symmetrical when viewed spatially, they were subsumed in a vertical hierarchy of power relations whose comprehensive perspective rendered the domestic map both partial and marginal. The holistic order turned on the center point of the chiefship itself, in relation to which the domestic domain mediated the wild. Women provided for the physical subsistence of the community; but men controlled the media that permitted the conversion of this material into more enduring social values. Thus cattle, verbal skill, and ritual efficacy enabled the objectification, transaction, and enhancement of productive and reproductive capacity, the building of lasting bonds that constituted the polity itself. This ability to effect stable transformations and control lasting value, epitomized in the image of cattle, was central to the Tswana notion of the "social." It was also part of the male quality of endurance in time, captured in the terms of agnatic genealogy, in ancestorhood, and in history as a chronology of memorable public events. In contrast, women were associated with unstable and repetitive transformations, with seasonal production, feeding, birth, and death; all of which implied natural transformation and a less than fully social existence. The initiation rituals which I examine below recreate this contrast, enabling men to reproduce fully social beings and collective institutions by recapitulating childbirth, but substituting symbols of male permanence for those of female transience. Moreover, the ritual management of death played on the same theme; the female dead lost their identity, being subsumed into an agnatically ordered ancestor cult, which, through the mediation of cattle sacrifice, kept dead men central to the affairs of the living.

These classifications of gender, space, and time were inscribed in mnemonic form in the human body (Bourdieu 1977:87). As I have noted, the limited capacity of women to act on the world was associated with their lack of physical closure, with their natural condition as receptacles for polluting heat. Unless confined or neutralized through rites of "washing" and "cooling," females laid down "hot tracks" (*metlhala*) on the public pathways, threatening the health of others and the fall of the rain. Transactions across female bodily thresholds, and especially sexual intercourse, were ideally confined to the house. "Thirst" (*kgakgabala*; "to be parched," used of persons or landscape) connoted the destructive desiccation caused by a diffusion of polluting heat, which could disrupt the sustaining cycle of give-and-take between the body and its context, and between the community and its spiritual and material ground. "Thirst" was thus a dislocation in subject-object relations, and a primary form of disorder with physical, social, and moral implications. As we shall see, it has served as an apt metaphor for the Tshidi experience of their modern predicament, its logic shaping their ritualized efforts to act upon that predicament itself.

In contrast, the male body was inherently contained, and transactions between men presupposed a state of physical closure and control, rather than an unmediated flow of personal substance. In the world of public affairs, men tried to "eat" one another, or artfully to penetrate and possess each other's bodies and beings by means of sorcery. These processes

implied deliberate, strategic action, akin to the male role in sexual intercourse; indeed, the act of "consuming" rivals entailed their symbolic
reduction to female status. But the body metaphor that epitomized masculine activity was that of culturally mediated consumption through the
mouth, which contrasted with uncontrolled transaction of substance
through the female orifices of procreation. Forceful attempts to subjugate rivals was also referred to as *patikêgo*, literally being "forced into a
narrow space," or "pressed down," implying the constriction of the
bodily scope of another through pressure on external margins (Comaroff
1983). Such "oppression" was to take on expanded significance as the
Tshidi became part of a colonial and neocolonial world.

Human and Superhuman Capacity

The Tswana cosmos was animated by a series of beings which acted on
and were acted upon by both material elements and living persons. These
spirit forces formed a continuum, ranging from the royal dead buried in
the chiefly cattle byre to the residual supreme being, *modimo*, located in
the "far distance." As part and parcel of the total symbolic order, the
superhuman realm reproduced the logic of that order and, especially, its
division between the domesticated and the wild.

The ancestors were the domesticated dead of the settlement, a projection into the spiritual realm of the hegemonic model of social relations
among the living.[2] Death converted the spiritual component of the
human being (*moya;* literally, "breath") into *-dimo*, penetrating superhuman power (from the verbal stem *-dima*, "to penetrate," or "pervade
with power"; Brown 1926:10f.; Smith 1950:17). As death occurred, this
component separated from the body, rising like smoke to form a distil-
late which remained threateningly unstable if not harnessed through ritual (Willoughby 1928:10). Ancestors (*badimo*) had only a collective
identity, there being no singular term of address or reference.[3] Individual
spirits could also not be singled out in rites of veneration (Willoughby
1928:330), which suggests that death represented a final resolution of the
tension in the Tswana system between individuation and aggregation. In
death, then, subjective identity was eclipsed by a collective state of being,
for the *badimo* always acted in concert (Willoughby 1928:330). Predictably, given the Tshidi kinship universe, cults were largely domestic in
focus, and ancestors were thought of as comprising immediate agnatic
forebears and dead mothers (Willoughby 1928:194). The "living dead"
(Mbiti 1969) of the homestead were those who had helped propagate it
and who continued to function in it as active participants, the source both
of power and of punishment.

If the ancestor cult subsumed the individual in the collectivity, it also
subsumed the domestic group into the totality. Ancestors had the power

of unmediated intervention in the lives of their descendants, acting in "moral" defense of the established order (Schapera 1953:59ff.); in fact, this power began to concentrate in life in the bodies of senior agnates, who could curse (go hutsa) junior kin if they flouted gerontocratic authority and the principles it embodied (Schapera 1938:181; Willoughby 1928:194). More generally, the ancestors formed part of the sphere in which men, through the medium of cattle, reproduced the social order in its established form. Ancestral power, which Tshidi took to be a real force in the economy of everyday means, was tapped through sacrifice, performed only by senior agnates or household heads on behalf of their dependents. As Schapera (1953:60) has noted, estrangement from these men meant estrangement from the most potent source of effectiveness in everyday life. Further, while veneration occurred at the grave sites of both men and women, the Tswana cult (unlike those usually associated with corporate, unilineal descent groups [Macknight 1967]) provided no acknowledgment of matrilateral ties; the female dead also spoke in agnatic idiom. Thus the domestic symmetry between agnation and matrilaterality was again overlaid, this time at the spiritual level, by the preeminence of the former alone. The ancestral cult also extended to the level of the state. Important collective rituals (rainmaking, firstfruits, initiation) focused on the royal burial place in the cattle byre abutting the central court, where the chief propitiated his dead kin on behalf of the entire body politic (Schapera 1953:60). The predominance of former incumbents in the superhuman realm was unambiguous; access to their spiritual force was an important dimension of authority and of the symbolic power of the apical office.

The cult of the ancestors naturalized the ideological bases of agnatic rank and royal control by projecting the dead as intrinsic features of an ineffable cosmic order. Thus the ancestors represented socially channelled spirituality, standing in contrast to those undomesticated beings (medimo) who were left unburied in the wild. Such persons—bush dwellers and those who died "unnatural" deaths through violence in or outside the settlement—never became part of the ancestral collectivity. They were not tied by moral or ritual links to the social world, and responded to the living with random capriciousness (Willoughby 1932:110ff.). Ultimately, beyond the expanse of bush known or imagined, outside space and time itself, was modimo, the supreme being. Modimo was said to have been located "above where the clouds float and the lightning flashes" and "in the west where the sun sets and whence the streams flow" (Willoughby 1928:67). There appears to have been no explicit connection between this being and the creation of the Tswana universe. In fact, modimo did not participate in the flow of everyday events and was inaccessible through ritual, featuring as a residual referent on the margins of experience and cultural control (Broadbent 1865:82; Burchell 1953, vol. 2:388).

Ritual Practice
Go thaya and go alafa

It was within this order that the ritual cycle took form. For the pre-colonial Tswana, ritual was conceived as a particularly forceful mode of acting upon the phenomenal world, part of the inclusive category of "work." *Tirelo,* a "work," denoted a concerted accomplishment and, especially, a ritual performance. The latter implied the notion of skilled human fabrication, which concentrated qualities and powers otherwise adulterated in mundane situations. Such concentration occurred through the controlled and stylized manipulation of words, gestures, and substances with intrinsic symbolizing capacity; once freed from their normal spatiotemporal constraints, these qualities circulated between participants at "a new symbolic level of social integration" (Munn 1974:580). While certain *materia medica* were widely known, unusual ritual potency was the product both of acquired knowledge and innate creative ability (Schapera 1953:62). The *ngaka* or ritual expert combined these capacities, having superior powers to transform the lived-in world; it was he who repaired the fragile margins of cultural order, mediating categorical divisions between the social and the wild, and the living and the dead, and restoring the disrupted integrity of the personal and social body.

Ritual action was classified in terms of its explicit intent. Hence there was a basic distinction between *bongaka,* the beneficent work of the doctor, and *boloi,* sorcery. *Bongaka* comprised two modes of practice: *go alafa,* to "heal" or "reconstitute," and *go thaya,* to "strengthen," "affirm," or reproduce. Rites of *go alafa* were occasioned by a dislocation of the orderly constitution of persons and collectivities; they corresponded to the "movable" or "piacular" rituals of other African societies. Occurring both at the level of domestic group and of the chiefship as a whole, *go alafa* entailed the attempt to comprehend and reverse affliction. Divination (*go laola*) and treatment (*go hodisa*) played upon conventional symbolic media, the former to concretize an image of the malaise, the latter to transform it. Affliction, attributed to sorcerers, vengeful ancestors, or careless polluters, was associated with breaches of the normative order; its negation, therefore, involved a cogent restatement of this order in its hegemonic form (Comaroff 1981).

Go thaya, on the other hand, affirmed or renewed the orderly structure of the social world itself; it was the equivalent of what have sometimes been called "fixed" or "commemorative" rites. Such rites marked the founding of habitable space, *go thaya motse,* the redrawing of homestead and settlement boundaries, *go bapola lefatse,* and the normative redefinition of the person at moments of passage. But, just as rites of healing, which focused upon distinctive predicaments, simultaneously addressed the reproduction of the system at large, so rites of communal renewal involved the reconstruction of their individual participants. All Tswana rituals were situational applications of the same underlying logical scheme.

Rituals of *go thaya* also punctuated the agricultural cycle, ordering the calendar and marking movement between center and periphery. Such rites occurred at both the domestic and collective levels, the most elaborate of all being those which sought the articulation of the two in a cyclical renewal of the fabric of the body social itself. It is to these rites of adolescent initiation that I now turn, to demonstrate the nature of Tswana iconic process under heightened magnification. I also lay the basis here for my subsequent examination of the role of symbolic mediation in Tshidi social history.

Initiation Ritual and Social Reproduction

Precolonial initiation rites articulated personal growth and transience with mechanisms of social reproduction and continuity, reforming subjective identity and, in the process, encompassing the domestic domain in the agnatically ordered collectivity. They also subordinated male political competition to the supreme legitimacy of chiefly hierarchy, imposing on the experience of participants a persuasive, hegemonic model of the world. The ritual sequence for men effected a transition to a *social* state of being, which betokened a fully adult role within the community. Women, however, were incapable of such complete transformation and, hence, of truly social adulthood. The overall cycle of initiation rites for both sexes dramatized these differences; it grounded the complex contrasts and combinatory principles of the social universe in the distinct, "natural" capacities of maturing men and women.

Two separate but coordinated ritual sequences were performed, *bogwêra* for boys and *bojale* for girls, neither vernacular term appearing to have any connotations beyond the ritual context itself.[4] Willoughby (1909:229) provides a myth of origin associated with the rites:

> In the old, old days . . . there was a woman who had initiated her husband into the *bogwêra,* and the husband told other men that he had been initiated by his wife. All these men gathered together and discussed the matter, saying, "What shall we do, seeing that we are not initiated? Let us ask for initiation; let the woman initiate us." And they agreed. Then they said to the man: "We ask for initiation; we beg that your wife will initiate us, and that when she has initiated us we may kill her, so that the initiation may be ours." And the man agreed. And the men gathered together and were initiated, and when they were initiated they killed the woman in the midst

of their regiment. And thus women were no longer acquainted with the initiation; it came to belong to the men, whereas it used to belong to the women. But the women arose and began again to prepare their regiments, gathering the girls together and initiating them, but not in the knowledge of the men; and from that day to this there is no one who knows what these women do.

This statement links the very origins of community to the special power to initiate; that is, to give simultaneous birth to social beings and social formations. But the power to initiate, to create fully socialized men, was achieved by the appropriation, on the part of these men, of the innate transformative capacity of women. The generative potency of the latter, then, their ability to socialize others, provided the source of institutionalized male community; but, in female hands, this transformation remained incomplete. While a wife inducted her husband into a state of domestic complementarity, her actions did not give rise to the construction of a mature *social* universe. It was this that concerted male strategy was to accomplish—to seize with planned foresight the knowledge of making the social, and to apply to it collective ends through the formation of self-reproducing higher order units of male solidarity (age-regiments). In the process, the social world was itself definitively severed from its individuated domestic origins. The woman who had the power of incomplete transformation was killed, underlining the transience of everything but the enduring bonds between men. In her death, the paradoxical rootedness of all social reproduction in the innate creativity of women was ostensibly reconciled. Henceforth man was a fully social being only in the public context that was established by communally controlled ritual practice, a context that transcended the domestic nexus of sexual complementarity. Women, moreover, were cut off from the means of attaining the proto-social status they once controlled. But female creativity was not so easily to be denied. Within their marginal domain, women rose again to develop new modes of transforming nature. And, to men, the secret of their essential, dynamic force remains both inscrutable and threatening.

This mythical statement, then, addresses the relationship of gender, social form, and cultural value. It conveys, in embryo, an ideology of productive and power relations, stressing the location of the domestic unit in the incorporative structure of the state. The initiation rites themselves elaborate and detail the same basic mythological theme. But they do more than merely restate its logic in dramatic form: through the manipulation of signs and actions they engrave its message on the bodies of a group of adolescent men and women, rendering the myth both a self-fulfilling prophecy and a mystifying ideology.

"Chopping"
The Preliminary Stage

Initiation was held at roughly four-year intervals, when a son or close agnate of the chief was able to fill the role of regimental leader. The cycle could only commence once the firstfruits ceremony had marked the ascendancy of "social" time and had revitalized communal structures (Willoughby 1909:229; Language 1943:113, 117), this usually being in February or March. The rites were state-wide, and drew together all youths of appropriate age (immediately prior to or at the start of puberty). Before initiation, sexual intercourse was forbidden; the developing reproductive powers of the uninitiated had not yet been formally socialized, and cohabitation on their part was bestial, having "the same connecting effect as when dogs indulge in it" (Brown 1921:421). Every member of the community underwent *bogwêra* or *bojale,* for an uniniti- *bogwera* ated adult was a contradiction in terms and would have been excluded from any collective action (Campbell 1822, vol. 2:172). Initiation was perceived as crucial to the reproduction of a vital and enduring social order, and the authority to set the process in motion resided with the ruler alone. Indeed, the salience of the chief's control of these rites of social reproduction is underlined by the continuing, if sporadic, attempt by various modern Tswana groups to persuade their officeholders that the performance of the rites might occasion collective revitalization. Language (1943) relates that, after a fifteen-year hiatus, senior Tlhaping advisors urged the chief to hold *bogwêra,* so that the rapid disintegration of their community might be held in check.

The rites began when the chief summoned a *letsholô,* an assembly held for all male regiments prior to a collective hunt in the bush (Willoughby 1909:229; Schapera 1938:82). The *letsholô* served to mobilize these regiments for concerted physical action, executed on behalf of the entire body social. From here armed men went forth to fight wars or quell disturbances; and from here they scattered like hunters to seek those of their kin who were ready for the most forceful of all processes of domestication—*bogwêra.* It was the elaborate male rites which gave form to the whole initiation set. They were organized into two main sequences, the "white" and the "black" *bogwêra,* of which the first (*bogwêra yo o shweu*) effected the major transformation in the novices, while the second (*bogwêra yo o ntsho*) involved the subsequent impression on them of collective norms. The white cycle started with a phase called *go rema,* "to chop," which lasted nearly a month and focused on the severance of prospective initiates from their natal domestic contexts (Willoughby 1909:230). The candidates from each ward were gathered together as a group, spending their days in the wild under the guidance of senior agnates and other adult men of the unit. The father of every youth chopped down a *moshu* (*acacia litakunensis*), a green-leaved thorn tree with long thin pods which twist and twine into large knotted balls (Burchell 1953, vol. 2:320). The boys were required to remove the inner bark (*lodi*) of the smaller bran-ches and chew it well, producing long, fibrous threads (*dithodi;* Willoughby 1909:230). The threads were then taken by members of the regiment that had been formed during the past initiation cycle (referred to as *badisa,* herders) and woven into kilts (Willoughby 1909:230). These garments were to be worn during the central phase of the initiation rites and looked uncommonly like the conventional dress of young girls— short skirts of leather strings (see plate 2). The chewing and weaving, accompanied by intermittent dance and song, were the main activities of this phase. By night, the novices returned to their natal homes, each ward group remaining distinct from the others in the bush.

The preliminary stage of the rite was dominated by the image of the *moshu* tree, which was severed from the wild and transformed, through a series of increasingly specialized operations, into an artifact with inherent ritual power. During this stage, the conversion of natural substance into social product would not be completed; but sacred elements were con-structed whose manipulation would contribute to the crucial chain of transformations to ensue in the liminal period. Yet it was not only that the active symbolic ingredients for the subsequent rites were assembled at this point: the preparations also laid out the metaphoric structure, the paradigm for the entire sequence to follow. The tree was taken from the bush, and was dismembered and processed: it ceased to exist in its former context, being refined and transposed into a new order of meaningful elements. Through the act of chewing, itself a decomposition of form, raw material was generated for the manufacture of a manifestly social product. Thus the herders wove kilts from these fibers, creating the clothing of young girls and prefiguring the liminal phase, in which the newly circumcised would relive an androgynous childhood. Bark (*lodi; also meaning "cord"*) was made into thread (*thodi*) and then into fabric. *Lodi* is the root of the word *moeledi,* human umbilicus, from which the social fabric itself may be said to have been fashioned. This is an icon of social rebirth which invoked female procreative capacity; but physical birth was eclipsed by images of male transformative processes, implying a more stable domination of nature than that achieved by female creativi-ty. Thus chewing, for instance, symbolizes definitive male appropriation (the role of the "tooth" in this regard recurring throughout the rites); and the making of cultural artifacts and herding of cattle were themselves prototypical acts of male domestication. Here, then, is a composite meta-phor through which the social is made to give birth to the social, without

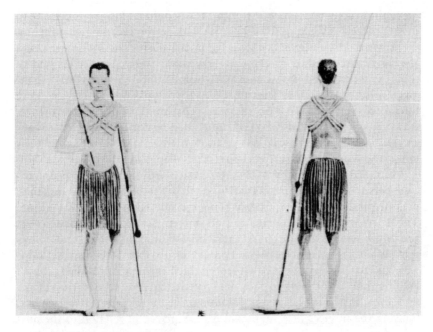

Plate 2   Male initiation dress.

recourse to less stable female processes of gestation, physical birth, and nurture. The symbolic association of the male mouth and female reproductive organs was also underlined, and would be elaborated upon in the stages to come.

As for the *moshu* tree, like all trees of the wild, it captured in concentrated form the diffuse dynamic power of the bush. As I have stated, the Setswana term for trees (*ditlhare*) is also the word for "medicine," for substances which bring activating natural force to bear upon human beings and their social projects. The use of *ditlhare* was central to the symbolic ministrations of the *ngaka,* who was always male. The *moshu* tree appears to have had little practical or metaphorical significance outside the initiation rites. But perhaps a clue to its particular appropriateness among other like species of sinewy acacia trees lies in the modern Tshidi observation that its wiry, tangled pods were like human hair (*moriri*).

"Circumcision"
The Liminal Phase

The initial severance enacted in the rites of separation was followed by a more definitive removal of the novices from their natal homes. On the evening when the moon of *Mophitlho* (March) was seen, all boys to be initiated proceeded in ward groups to the chief's court, where they spent the night in song and dance. After this they could no longer "go home to their mothers" (Willoughby 1909:230) and, in the morning, the men of the town escorted them to the lodge in the bush. The lodge itself was always situated near a river or natural water source, and consisted of roughly constructed wood and grass huts (Willoughby 1909:231; Language 1943:114), each of which had a low doorway so that novices were forced to enter and leave on all fours. The building of these structures was subject to a strict division of labor, men performing the woodwork and women thatching the roofs. Immediately after completing their work, the women were dispatched to the village, and the lodge was ritually founded (Willoughby 1909:234). Henceforth no woman or uninitiated person was even permitted to catch sight of the enclosure, their presence anywhere in the vicinity being considered dangerously defiling. The activities which occurred within it were a strictly guarded secret, and any breach was thought to cause misfortune, individual and collective. While distinct from the settlement in obvious respects, the lodge was held to "resemble the town from which the neophytes [had] come" (Willoughby 1909:230). In fact, its spatial structure echoed that of the settlement in one crucial respect: within its encompassing fence each hut, housing the novices of a single ward, was placed in relation to the next according to the rank of the respective units (Willoughby 1909:231; Language 1943:114). Concentric arcs of huts faced a central meeting-place where the boys of the royal lineage were housed.

Participants in this liminal world were referred to in a nomenclature specific to the *bogwêra*. The chief was the fixed point of reference for the entire cycle; he remained at the center of the settlement, and was referred to as *setlhaba molao* ("summit of the law"), a phrase with an interesting web of connotations. *Setlhaba* was a "flat place at the top of a hill" or a "flat roof"; apart from implying a summit at right angles to the path of ascent—an apt image for the relation to the chiefship to agnation—it derived from the verb *go tlhaba*, "to sacrifice" or "pierce," suggesting a site of reckoning or sacrifice. The senior chiefly advisors who supervised the rites were termed *dinare* (buffaloes) and *manong* (vultures). Significantly, those introduced earlier as "herders" were known during this phase as *bakganye*, from the verb *go kgayayêga*, to rage or trumpet as an elephant in anger (Willoughby 1909:232). These attendants now became the executors of the severe discipline crucial to the transformative power of *bogwêra*. Indeed, the activities which took place at this stage were replete with images of fierce creatures of the wild. Thus the sharpened pegs or thorns with which the novices were prodded were called *ditshoshwane* (ants), *dinotshe* (bees), and *mentsane* (mosquitoes). In fact, the numerous songs associated with this phase drew upon the general cultural propensity of the Tswana to signify social relations in animal allegory (cf. Alverson 1978:206). Such songs opposed animals wild and domesticated, an opposition mediated by the various totemic species that signified distinct Tswana chiefdoms.

During the liminal stage of the rites, it was critical that initiates be kept away from the heat generated by adult sexuality, and men having contact with the lodge had to refrain from intercourse for this period (Willoughby 1909:233; Brown 1921:423). Sexual pollution was contagious, and a man's physical and social identity were entailed in that of his fellows. While all the food for the camp was prepared in the town by the boys' mothers and sisters, these women, too, had to refrain from cohabitation for the duration of the liminal rites. They carried their pots to an assigned place in the bush where they were collected by the herders, who, in their capacity as *bakganye* ("wild trumpeters"), drove the bearers back to town with considerable ferocity (Willoughby 1909:235).

Circumcision was the ritual act that triggered the transformative process of the *bogwêra* cycle, which, as a whole, might be referred to as *go rupa* ("to be circumcised"). It occurred on the day of arrival at the lodge, and was performed by a man of experience and skill, for whom no specific term existed (Willoughby 1909:233). The boys, moreover, were blindfolded during the operation and were not allowed to know the identity of the one who cut them. They assumed a supine position and were expected to respond to the ordeal without emotion or protest, although most screamed with pain and bled profusely (Brown 1921:422). The foreskin, termed *molomo* ("mouth"), was discarded in the bush after the operation. Considerable attention was paid to the order of precedence in which the boys were cut. All the Tswana polities contained members originating in other chiefdoms, and relative rank between, as well as within them, was observed. Among those of the home community, the senior royal novice and future regimental leader was operated on first, and strict status order was followed thereafter (Willoughby 1909:233).

From the time of circumcision until they left the lodge, the youths remained naked and slept on the bare ground. The only exception to this was the ritualized dressing in *moshu* kilts, performed for the first time on the day following the operation. Thereafter, the kilts were donned daily to the accompaniment of song and dance, and the novices' chests were smeared with a mixture of white clay (*oolitic hematite*) and fat. They assumed the impassive demeanor that was to characterize their bearing throughout the liminal and postliminal phases: as novices, they could only hear and repeat (*buabua*), not speak or react assertively (*bua*). The recurrent text of the *moshu* dance ran as follows (Willoughby 1909:234):

A bo itlhamêla!	Take warning!
Boshweu yoa rara	The whiteness of the father
Borona molomo	Is unbecoming on the mouth.

The novices had also to bathe in the river each day at sunrise and sunset. For the first week after the operation, they ate only sorghum porridge and did so in a ritually prescribed manner. Unable to dip their fingers in the food in the normal way, the boys of each ward ate from a common bowl; kneeling on the ground with his left hand above his head, a boy scraped up the porridge with the side of his right hand, and passed it to his mouth. After the first week, meat was consumed in quantity, for the men of the settlement engaged in the uncommon practice of regular slaughter in order to foster a concentrated process of growth in the novices (Language 1943:118).

The most tangible symbol of the postcircumcision rites was the bark switch (*thupa*). The switch orchestrated the *moshu*-clad figures in their recitation, and set the tempo for their collective physical activities. Unlike those switches used in such mundane contexts as herding (where the *mosêlêbêlê* tree—*Rhus viminale*—was preferred), this one was made from the *moretlhwa* (*Grewia flava*), a bush whose profuse brown fruit remains a Tswana delicacy (Willoughby 1909:236; Brown 1931:215). My own observation of the more public sequences of the *bogwêra* cycle, those associated with the postliminal stage, revealed the switch to be *the* palpable symbol of emerging manhood: it was brandished by the herders in minding their charges, moved up and down suggestively in dances, and used to swipe lustily at any women or uninitiated men who happened upon the proceedings. In the lodge, the novices were beaten each morning in the place of assembly, and any irregularity in the daily repetition of songs and praise-poems called forth similar correction. The boys were also thrashed while being made to repeat a series of formulaic transgressions typical of boyhood—largely concerned with careless ("selfish") neglect of domestic duty (Willoughby 1909:236). As the Tswana proverb puts it: *bogwêra go utlwa bo ditèwa*; "*Bogwêra* is understood/heard through thrashing" (cf. Willoughby 1909:236). Indeed, the whistling switch beat the rhythm of the transformative rites onto the bodies of the initiates themselves.

The days in the circumcision lodge were deployed in continuous and carefully structured activity. Much time was spent on rote instruction through the medium of song and dance. *Dipina tsa molao* ("songs of the law") provided the semantic frame: at the level of explicit reference, they dealt with the normative basis of the social order and with the principles that underpinned authority. They also catalogued the chronological order of age-regiments present and past, stressing their durability in the face of what, for the novices, must have seemed a tangible personal frailty. But their rich metaphors also spoke to a meta-theme—the potential challenge posed to established order by the vigor of youth. Their rhetoric evoked a continual four-way interplay between images of the social and the sexual, and of challenge and domination. Willoughby (1909: 238ff.) provides several texts of such songs, some of which were all but identical to those recorded in 1970:

[a] *Mogae! Rramotho! Rramotho!*   At home! One's father! One's Father!

Rramotho ga a rogwe   One's father is never cursed.
Oa re a rogwe   Should one curse
Go cwa a boifhshê   He will be afraid,
Go boifhshê ino   Afraid of the tooth,
Ino letêlêlê   Even the long tooth
Le yañ nchotlwane   Which eats tripe
Le bokutukutu   And chitterlings,
Nama tsa bogolo   The meat of old men.

[b] *Segodi se marulaneñ*   The hawk of the roof ["in the *marula* trees"]

Se itsa maeba go sêla.   Forbids the doves to feed.
Bonnaka lo so bolaêê   Kill it, you younger brethren;
Lo se chware le so bolaêê   Catch it and kill it;
So leta tshimo ea Morena   It scares the birds from the chief's garden.[5]

In contrast, *pina ya letswae,* "the song of salt," formed part of a stylized and highly codified performance; this occurred every morning and evening at the central meeting-place, and involved the participation of much of the male population of the town (Brown 1921:424). The rites entailed the use of material objects which were all transformations of the core symbol of the switch (*thupa*). The meeting-place was marked out in a square: to the west were several rows of poles (*mekgoro*), behind which were the novices, each holding a bundle of thin twigs (*dithupana,* the plural, diminutive of *thupa*) bound together with a sinew from the neck of an ox (*losika*). Boys from commoner families had bundles of twenty-four; those of royal status, of twelve. Each bundle was referred to as *polo ea podi,* "goat penis." Facing the poles on the eastern side of the ritual space stood the herders and other "clean" officiants of the lodge and, behind them at some distance, any widowers present. To the left of the novices stood their fathers and the men of their regiment with switches in hand; while to the right, completing the square, were initiated men who were sexually unclean. The latter were screened from the ritual enclosure by a thick brush fence (see figure 5).

The ritual was marked by the incantation of the "song of salt," punctuated by the novices beating on the poles with their *dithupana* (Brown 1921:425). The beating had to be continuous; should a boy falter, his father would reprimand him with the switch. The song was chanted, line by line, by the herders and repeated by the novices. Its form and content addressed the experiences of sexual arousal; sequentially ordered so as to suggest mounting excitation, its metaphors spoke of waxing potency (Brown 1921:425:

Shupañ kgwedi ka nakana	Point to the moon with the little horn (the penis).
Lecwai le yele bosimane	Salt has eaten boyhood.
Lecwai le tla bina kae?	Where shall the salt dance?
Setlhako sa me se la malekana	My shoe has been torn to pieces.
Ke rile ke le mosimane	When I was a boy
ke dihela tlou	I served in the elephant (*penis erectus*).
Tlou ea gola ea mpheta	The elephant grew and passed me.
Nna lecwai ga ka ye motho	I, salt, don't eat the person.
Ke tlosa letlosho	I take away the foreskin. ["that which is to be removed"]
A di lele diphorogotlho!	Let the *dithupana* cry!
Re letile maheho (basadi)	We are waiting for women.

The missionary sources stress that these songs were "saturated" with "indecent suggestion"; that the "whole atmosphere in which the initiate lived was lascivious," and that he was encouraged to view "all womankind [as the] hunting ground" (Brown 1921:426). Yet these observers also noted perplexedly that "like castration . . . *bogwêra* claims to keep in bounds the sexual passions."

The novices remained at the lodge for the moons of *Mophitlho* and *Moranang* (March and April); at the appearance of the next moon the chief signaled that formal closure of the liminal rites should commence.

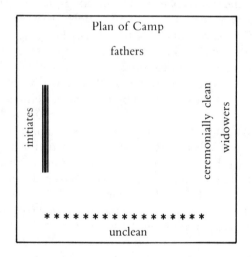

Figure 5   Male Initiation Rites: The "Song of Salt" (from J. Tom Brown [1921:425]).

Interpretation of the Rituals of the Liminal Stage

At their most inclusive, the rites performed in the bush may be seen—in the classic terms of van Gennep—as the marginal phase of a *rite de passage*. The novices were placed in a liminal capsule outside of social space and time, between domestic childhood and social manhood. This stage was the epicenter of the entire transformative cycle, and it served to reconstruct the person in terms of the dominant meanings and interests of the social collectivity. In the process, fundamental bodily experiences of separation, pain, fear, and death were invested with vivid new associations, and paradoxes of the lived-in world invoked and redressed.

The bush was a domain of dynamic vitality, unconstrained by the categories and relations of the social world. The novices, likewise, were in a ritual space where boundaries were fluid and shifting. It was upon this dynamic formlessness that ritual practice was to impose the order of a determining process. Preexisting form, here the initiate's childhood identity, was to be reduced to its natural substrate and shaped anew (cf. Turner 1967). With the assistance of male attendants, the youths were to be reborn into a more refined existence, one which replaced subsocial boyhood with a persona shaped by membership in a practical and moral collectivity. The transformative stage of the ritual effected its object through the positioning of elements—their juxtaposition, contrast, and transposition—in a multilayered poetic structure.[6] Its order, as I have suggested, derived from the sequential logic of the transformation of the *moshu* tree in the preliminary stage. This composite image was both a temporal model for the overall metamorphosis and a guide to the distinct subphases that made up its totality. For the liminal stage contained a series of segments, together producing a cumulative transformation, but each in its own right playing upon a set of paradoxes to be ritually resolved before the next phase could proceed.

Let us examine the structure of the rites layer by layer, so that its sequential logic may emerge. The bush lodge was the context which framed the liminal stage, and its internal organization and spatial location displayed telling conundrums. Situated in the wild, beyond the confines of sociocultural containment, the lodge related to the settlement as unstable flux to ordered predictability; yet it nevertheless replicated the structure of the town in important respects. Thus, while its constituent huts were made of grass and branches—untransformed natural materials used by bush dwellers, not townsmen—the division of labor which effected their construction expressed conventional relations of production. Men chopped branches and built durable frames; women gathered grass and secured perishable thatched roofs, an activity expressly associated by Tswana with unstable transformation. Females were excluded from the lodge and its surrounds as soon as the work was done and before it was ritually founded. Their innate physical heat was held to be particularly threatening to novices in their liminal condition; and, indeed, the rites in the bush explicitly excluded them. Here the paradox posed by the essential yet dangerous continuity of the social and the wild was "resolved" by the careful separation of women from crucial social transactions. Yet, as it did in the settlement, female creativity—the provision of cooked food—subsidized male activity. Thus the latter still rested pragmatically upon the mediating role of women, despite their elaborate exclusion from the process of ritual generation, a situation which recapitulated but did not remove the conundrum of the origin myth of *bogwêra* itself. In fact, the female creative principle had a subtle presence throughout the rites in the core metaphor of physical reproduction. The juxtaposition of continuity and discontinuity between rank nature and the social was further evident in the spatial organization of the lodge. Despite the remoteness of the site and the simplicity of its construction, it recapitulated the spatial contrasts of rank and royal privilege obtaining in the town. Its structure was an architectural expression of ordered inequality in the heart of the unordered bush.

It would seem that it is the very contrasts built into the semantic structure of the rites which gave rise to their transformative power; specifically, the tension between the categories appears to have motivated a process whereby one set was actually transformed into the other as a function of their sequential position in the ritual (Silverstein n.d.:9). The contrast between dynamic formlessness and static hierarchy recurred at different levels throughout the liminal phase; indeed, the categories were so arranged that the power of the wild was harnessed to defined social ends, and the natural sexual energy of the novices overlaid by normative constraint.

It was circumcision that actually set in motion the pivotal metamorphosis. Indigenously perceived as emblematic of the whole *bogwêra* cycle, it initiated the dynamic movement of the ritual by literally cutting off its subjects from their former, physically indexed existence. The severance, a message of bodily violation, blood, and suffering, was carved on the organ bearing the major symbolic load of emerging adult identity. But, while it distinguished the present from the past by invoking separation, pain, and death, the operation also introduced the terms of an alternative theme—that of rebirth. Yet, while this classic paradox of rites of transition was boldly announced by the circumcision itself, it had already been anticipated in the central image of the preliminary stage, the felling and processing of the *moshu* tree. The same logical entailment of death and rebirth was suggested there by the metaphor of sacrifice, which, while not explicitly marked, was clearly implied by the blood-letting enacted on the supine victims. Sacrifice was the quintessential act of male generation, and the term of reference used for the chief during the rites pointed to his role as sacrifier. The act itself was implicitly acknowledged by Tswana to be a confluence of life and death; the word for sacrifice (*go tlhaba*) also meant to "germinate" or "rise." For the immolation of the victim epitomized the transformative power of the entire ritual complex, its capacity to create a "higher-order ground" in which the fixed categories and relations of the everyday world might be reclassified (cf. Turner 1977). The same confluence of life in death was to be confronted, of course, in the logic of Christianity; in the practice of full immersion, in the rituals of reconstruction and resistance which are examined in Chapter 6. In initiation, while the novices were detached from their former domestic and presexual identities, they were simultaneously reborn to an existence at a new level of vitality. But their metamorphosis into full adulthood would be achieved by way of a transformative sequence that would first evoke and then domesticate the natural process of maturation.

The operation itself was performed by an unidentified expert on the blindfolded and supine boys, who were physically restrained while they bled profusely. This operation condensed two images, sacrificial victim and neonate, the latter to eclipse the former in the subsequent development of the cycle. As total event, the ritual might be seen to reproduce the structure of sacrifice: the core roles of sacrifier, sacrificer, and victim were filled, respectively, by the chief, his anonymous circumciser, and the novices. The bodies of the latter, like those of sacrificial victims, became the media for the symbolic reordering of social categories, both specific and general in reference. Thus in the painful destruction of an old identity, and the emergence of a new one, the bodies of the youths served as icons for the renewal of the community at large. But the theme of childbirth was also clearly visible in the circumcision, and it was to provide the dominant image to be carried forward into the stages to come. Thus the initiate lay on the ground like a newborn baby—Tswana women gave birth on the floor of their houses—and was cut with a sharpened spear, as was the umbilical cord (Schapera 1971[b]:209). Like the infant, he was born "blind," a state which denoted inertness and the inability to make distinctions in the world; for sight was associated with informed, purposive action, and the verb *go bona* ("to see") also meant "to achieve." Despite normative injunction, the novice cried like a baby while being cut. And the foreskin, like the placenta, was disposed of beyond the margins of human habitation.[7]

Birth was a subsocial process, occurring in domestic seclusion and ending with the ritualized reincorporation of mother and child into the wider community. Like death, it was associated with the floor of the

house, with planes below the normal level of social interaction. Birth
established a personally individuating link between mother and child,
itself the origin of matrilateral relations. By contrast, circumcision was a
social process; while it also occurred in seclusion and ended with reincorporation into the social world, it was done on the floor of the public
meeting-place (albeit that of the bush lodge) and was organized in terms
of agnatic rank. As this suggests, it established a generalized link between
the novice and the adult male community, which superseded all individuating kin ties and subjected them to centralized control. Thus it was
that the expert who "gave birth" to the novices as men was anonymous
to them—without face, title, or agnatic identity, a mere representative of
the capacity and authority limited to the preeminently powerful (cf. La
Fontaine 1977). He was the agent of the collectivity and of its metonymic
figure, the chief, who was ultimately responsible for the forces that begot
the state of manhood.

Linguistic evidence also underscores the notion that circumcision proclaimed the birth of sexually distinct identity out of childish androgyny.
The main song of the ritual segment that followed the operation would
declare that "the whiteness of the father is unbecoming on the mouth," a
reference to the incompatibility of the foreskin with adult sexuality. For
"mouth" blurred the clear dichotomy of gender; it described both the
foreskin and, colloquially, the vagina ("the mouth without teeth";
Schapera 1971[b]:166). And "whiteness" connoted semen, which, on the
foreskin rather than the female orifice, seems to have been an image of
retentive self-negation, the failure to participate in creative heterosexual
exchange. The metaphoric connection between "mouth" and male
adulthood had a further dimension, however, for social potency entailed
a man's acquisition of a mouth of a higher order: the verbal ability to
represent and transact values and relations in the world. Whereas the
woman's communicative capacity was eclipsed by her consignment to
mute physical reproduction, that of adult men was the vehicle of knowledge and control.[8] And the male mouth, unlike the female, had "teeth";
it had the power of both physical and social domination, the power to
consume the interests of others.

Of course, birth into social being was not an entry into a homoge-
neous male community. The polity was stratified by agnatic rank and
politico-economic inequality, and the attainment of manhood required
that personal identity be articulated with a structure of asymmetrical relations. But rank was also subject to ambiguity and individualistic management. The careful order according to which circumcision was
performed left engraved on the body an ideal and unambiguous model of
seniority. Thus the ritual conveyed the paradoxical message that, while
all were equal under the knife, some were "naturally" more equal than

others. At the core of the act was a tension between two meanings: (a) that men, through the traumatic birth of adulthood, shared a common identity and potential; and (b) that the male social world was organized in terms of agnatic status. The latter was the construction to be reinforced most cogently in the sequence of images to follow: for the hold of the ruling elite, as undisputed seniors, became ever more evident in the rites, the young royal leader being distinguished from his undifferentiated age-mates. Thus circumcision played off images of death and procreation, natural and social birth, matrilaterality and agnation, and equality and hierarchy. In each case, again, the presentation of these elements was asymmetrical, the first term of each pair being dominated by the second in the unfolding logic of the ritual cycle itself.

Once circumcised, the novices were metaphorical infants in the domain of the social. The ritual was structured so that signifiers of social and physical development ran parallel, the former impressing their significance on the latter. The remainder of the liminal stage represented a condensed passage from birth through childhood and an accelerated growth into social maturity. Thus the newly circumcised boys were naked by day and slept at night on the bare floor of their huts—both signs of a condition minimally refined by human socialization. For the first week after the operation, moreover, they ate only porridge, the diet of babies (Schapera 1971[b]:215). Nor was this food taken in the usual manner; the initiates had to kneel over the common ward bowl, like dogs, their incapacitated lapping resembling that of those who had yet to learn the basic human accomplishments of physical independence. Another reference to the state of infancy was afforded by the doorways to the novices' huts, which were so low that they were compelled to enter and leave on all fours, an activity characteristic both of animals and the very young. After a week, however, the boys were able to feed themselves normally and to eat meat, which diet suggested that they were being ritually "nurtured" by the men of the settlement.

Metaphors of subhumanity thus came to be juxtaposed with others representing a more highly socialized state of being. Indeed, the asymmetry between the two states again motivated the transformation from one to the other. If circumcision was the first subphase of the liminal stage, spelling out the ideological themes of the whole sequence, the next was introduced by the rites of the *moshu* kilts. Commencing the day after the operation, these rites were concerned with realizing the developmental process it had initiated, and centered on the material objects of earlier manufacture. The kilts were now placed on the novices in a manner which signaled the onset of androgynous childhood, and focused on the body as the site of continuing transition. As I have noted, the kilts resembled the regular clothing of young girls, but they also embodied the power of the wild inherent in the fibers of the *moshu* tree. At this point in the ritual its metaphoric elements were structured so as to induce acceler- ated growth. Novices, while dressing, sang of the father's "whiteness" which was "unbecoming on the mouth"—i.e. of the emergence of sexu- al identity—a song which stood in contrast with the androgynous state proclaimed by the kilts. The transformation effected in this subphase was further enabled by smearing the youths' chests with white clay. The color white signified activating force, the potency of semen, salt, and lightning. The whitened bodies above the skirts served as a pathway between childhood and the maturity foretold by the songs, urging the participants forward in a concentrated spurt of growth. But the sym- bolism of the *moshu* kilt must also be seen in linear relation to the prior state of infancy imposed by circumcision; for the organization of imag- ery permitted a dynamic relationship to develop *between* the two, so that infancy was overlaid by childish androgyny (evoked by such practices as the resumption of normal modes of eating). In addition, the repeated "washing" of the boys marked the renewal of a social identity residing on the "social skin" (Turner n.d.[a]), laying yet another image on the crowded surface of the body. Such ritual washing expressed the role of water as solvent, an issue I shall take up again in relation to modern Tshidi rites of personal reconstruction.

The poetic structure of the liminal rites was also multilayered, playing upon the imagination of its participants as would a contrapuntal sym- phonic score. After "wounds had begun to heal," yet another sequence of symbolic action was introduced, the recitation of "songs of the law," punctuated by the discipline of the switch. During this segment, explicit reference was made to the normative organization of the social world and to the subsumption of careless, childish identity into an order of institu- tionalized roles. The law (*molao*) was the corpus of oral prescriptions which gave shape to politico-jural action, a world in which symbols of male identity were simultaneously instruments of control. But these au- thoritative images also signified, albeit in unmarked form, another kind of dominance—that of "might and right," of the rule of strength with- out the mediation of law, rank, and privilege. This apparent paradox recalled again the tension between male equivalence and asymmetry; and, again, the ritual process effected a transformation whereby the marked signifiers, in this instance those of the hegemonic order of the polity, overlaid the unmarked ones, the implicit recognition of the *real- politik* of competitive equality. In so doing, the ritual achieved at the ideological level what the assertion of political dominance did at the social.

The "songs of the law" catalogued a normative repertoire of catego- ries and principles, grounding filial piety and chiefly authority alike in the transcendent power that controlled the formation and activities of age-regiments; and the fact that the creation of these groupings marked historical time, from the origin of the state into perpetuity, gave that power an eternal quality. The synchronized gestures of the dance and stylized repetition of the songs also underscored the sinking of individual subjectivity in collective conformity. But the unmarked meanings that inhered in the same multivocal metaphors spoke of waxing sexual power, of the physical potency of the young, ever challenging to gerontocratic right. Thus the first song addressed the father's fear of the son's curse, itself an inversion of the norm according to which agnatic elders alone enjoyed the capacity to afflict their kin with words; it spoke, too, of their apprehension of the "long tooth" (old age; lack of physical incisiveness), which condemned them to eat "tripe" and "chitterlings" (flaccid intestines), the meat of old men. I have noted the link between eating and political domination in Tswana cultural usage, and sexual consumption is to be added to this fan of associations. Here and elsewhere the tooth was seen as an agent of virile male appropriation. The second song, that of the hawk and the doves, further elaborated the theme. The image of the powerless birds in the chief's garden evoked the notion of the illegitimate feeding in the preserve of authority; birds in Tswana agriculture were prototypical pests and bird-scaring was a time-consuming female chore. The opposition of hawk and dove upheld the contrast between an elite that monopolized command and an impotent rank and file. The hawk sits "in a *morula* tree," a place both lofty and fecund, whose fruit, *thola,* was a prized food; the term also was used to refer to the first physical movements of the neonate. The hawk, in other words, commandeered sexual and reproductive rights in the community, and the song urged resistance to such domination of sexual access, defending the rights of the powerless to "eat in the chief's field."

The theme of the politico-economic control over sexual and reproductive rights, itself an aspect of the equality-hierarchy tension, was to recur in the postliminal stage of the *bogwêra*. Here, too, the appearance of this unmarked motif alongside marked references to the social order in place served to impose images of normative right upon those of youthful insurrection. Not inconsiderable in this process was the role of the switch, an overt agent of domination and an implicit symbol of sexual vigor. The switch ensured that the immediate experience of the novitiates would remain in the hands of the representatives of authority. It also expressed another dimension of the normative values attached to adult sexuality: the wood used in its manufacture was *moretlwa,* a bush which yields clusters of profuse and tasty fruit. For, properly channeled male sexuality would, in time, produce households, and hence assure the continuity of the social domain. The switch thus stood for the predominant model of male reproductive power; its impact on boys left no ambiguity as to the ascendance of the marked meanings in the ritual sequence. The beating, moreover, gave palpable reality to the passage from selfish childhood—*vide* the formulaic repetition of past wrongdoing—to adult responsibility. In a manner reminiscent of Needham's association of percussion with transition (1967), the thrashing punctuated and actualized the transformative process. Significantly, too, the staff, both as symbol of male aggression and as ritual baton, turns out to be equally important in modern Tshidi rites which seek to recapture control over an estranged world.

The final level of the multilayered structure of the liminal stage was the segment centered on the "song of salt." This addressed the arousal of adult sexual potency in the novices and their articulation, as new men, with the community of the sexually mature. Anticipating reincorporation into the community, its performance necessitated the participation of most adult males of the settlement. Again, its meaning is to be found both in the internal transformative logic of the segment itself and in its role in the more inclusive ritual sequence. The rites associated with the "song of salt" were the most elaborate of all in the liminal stage and made use of objects that were themselves transformations of key elements in prior phases—the tree and the switch, which here signified male sexuality in its various forms. But, unlike the foregoing rites, which acted upon the novices as patients, this set sought to evoke their assertiveness. It called upon them to take up the cudgels, albeit diminutive ones, and beat an entry into the adult male community.

The entire congregation was sexually categorized at this stage, using the ritual space to mark out the salient classes. Thus the novices faced east, the source of waxing power, with an obstacle between them and the herders, who were about to assume full rights of adult sexuality; behind the latter, stood those now past the phase of procreative potency and activity. This axis, which recapitulated the processual chronology of the male career, was "cold"; it included those not actively engaged in sexual consummation. Crosscutting it was the "hot" axis, composing the two poles of legitimate and illegitimate sexuality. It was the intersection of these two axes, however, that gave dynamic impetus to the ritual: the herders solicited the novices across the barrier ahead; the "fathers," to the one side, drove them forward with raised switches; and their alter egos, those polluted by illicit sexuality, served as tangible foils (see figure 5, p. 94).

The barrier that separated the novices from the mature men was made of poles (*mekgoro;* "markers of the gateway" or "entrance"), the latter being both enlargements of the phallic switch and the threshold to a new social and sexual status. The boys were to beat on the poles as on a maidenhead, striking rhythmically with a bundle of diminutive switches, secured with a sinew taken from the neck of an ox. The word for sinew was *losika,* which also implied an "artery," a "generation," or a "unit of kin," reflecting the role of cattle in establishing enduring social bonds. The bundles would thus seem to have signified a generation or aggregate of individual men, united by a tie which was the product of the social refinement of nature and entering the adult male arena with a common identity. The fact that the royals held smaller bundles was perhaps a recognition of their elite status among the regimental rank and file. These bundles were referred to as goat penes, *polo* (penis) being a term of abuse, and the goat being associated, at least by modern Tshidi, with unrestrained lechery. Thus the assault of the bundles upon the barrier was an epic of defloration, an entry into the world of sexual experience between the twin poles of legitimate and illegitimate practice. In making this assault, the novices were supervised by their fathers as representatives of normative sexuality.

The performance of the song was also structured in such a way as to induce transformation. Not only did the herders coax their changes forward through a series of formulaic statements and responses, but the linear form of the song itself evoked a mounting urgency and worked up to a climax, both in semantic content, with the image of the child overtaken by sexual desire, and in poetic form, with a progressively decreasing gap between marked and unmarked meanings; the metaphors ("little horn"::childlike penis; "elephant"::erect penis) giving way to circumlocution ("that which is to be removed") and finally to explicit declaration ("we are waiting for the women"). In the symbolic context of the song, the salt was the agent of transformation, eating the foreskin and boyhood like a corosive acid. Salt, moreover, was associated with whiteness, a color signifying concentrated, activating power. One exemplar was the penetrating force of forked lightning, and regiments going into battle painted white jagged lines on the body to resemble it (Willoughby 1909:242); similarly, white animals were sacrificed at times of serious collective crisis or when estranged kin were to be joined together again in close harmony (Willoughby 1928:196, 351). These were all processes of movement, dynamic transformation, and fusion. In contrast, black signified depressed activity, severance, and coolness; it was the color of beasts offered in rain rites in order to "cool" a community overheated by promiscuity, lightning, or general disorder (cf. Willoughby 1928:351; Schapera 1971 [b]: 109, 113). The use of black to neutralize white is seen also in the follow-up "black" *bogwêra,* when, during a brief ceremony, the burgeoning vitality of the initiates was "blackened" to impress upon them the full weight of the collective social order (Brown 1921:420; Willoughby 1928:298). Red, on the other hand, signified the natural cre-

ative potential, the fertile ground of humankind, especially female heat as
concentrated in menstrual blood. Thus Tswana notions of conception
held that it was the mixing and coagulation in the womb of blood (red),
or creative heat, and semen (white), or activating force, which formed
the composite "seed" from which the fetus developed (Schapera
1971[b]:194). And red would be the color of the novices' bodies when
they left the lodge, filled with sexual potential but not yet ready for adult
consummation. Indeed, the triad of red, black, and white featured centrally in the subsequent "black" *bogwêra* and has continuing salience in
modern Tshidi ritual as we shall see.

Salt, then, was linked to whiteness, movement, and fusion. Just as
semen energized inherent female fertility, so salt, in cooking, brought
out characteristic flavor and permitted the full transformation of raw
matter into "food" (see Hugh-Jones 1979:195 for a comparable case).
This association of salt with such complete metamorphoses, and hence
with the fully "social," was seen in Tswana mortuary rites: those persons
for whom bereavement had severed the normal pattern of interaction
were placed in subsocial seclusion, being spatially confined, withdrawing
from sexual activity, eating with the left hand,[9] and taking saltless food.
The activating force of this valued social commodity was subject to purposive use on the part of those who had access to it: women utilized it in
cooking, as did men in the preparation of skins; but, above all, it was the
object of external trade relations monopolized by the royal elite (Campbell 1822, vol. 2:204). In the liminal rites themselves, the role of salt was
to motivate the novice's final passage to the state of sexual potency,
while harnessing its challenge to the established order by hedging it
about with normative constraint. The song itself dramatized the stages of
male sexuality in their distinctness and interdependence, stressing that
social maturation was a relational process and that individual identity
was a function of a position in a total gestalt. The boys were urged by
their fathers to take their place in an ordered community of men who,
while ranked, were yet sexually and morally interrelated, each alike serving as a potential channel for the contagious pollution that perpetually
threatened the social world.

This theme returns us to the central paradox of the myth of the origin
of *bogwêra,* that of the contradictory rootedness of the social world in an
unstable mediation of the wild. For, while male sexuality might be socialized, men remained tied to each other through women; through a
relationship, both complementary and contradictory, like that between
the collective and the domestic domain within the community at large.
Indeed, the *bogwêra* rites played upon the metaphors of sexuality in order
to impose a particular social form upon that universal human paradox:
the continuity and discontinuity between mankind and nature.

"Spring Plumage after Moulting"
The Rites of Reaggregation

Once the chief had given the signal to disband the lodge, rites commenced which simultaneously terminated the liminal stage and introduced that of reaggregation. The first performance to address this shift was termed *thalalagae*, "the visit home" (from *go ralala*, to "visit" or "pass through").[10] The rite began in mid-morning: initiated men of the town gathered at the lodge, and any women and children on the path between it and the settlement were driven back by officiants (Language 1943:118). The novices were assembled outside, wearing skin shoes and *moshu* kilts, and carrying the characteristic markers of the reaggregation sequence, a metal-topped spear (*lerumo*), a stout stick (*thobane*), and a wooden club (*molamu*). Accompanied by men carrying switches, they moved homeward in tight formation (Language 1943:119). All sang in unison and, as they drew near, the boys were encircled so as to be invisible to observers. The phalanx came to a halt a little distance from the town borders, where the female population had gathered, eager for a sight of the initiates. The older men now moved to the front of the column, forming a dense barrier between their charges and the women, and between the bush and the settlement. At this point, the novices took to their heels and returned to the deserted lodge. In *bogwêra* rites observed in this century, one of the senior men, who had acted as leader of the lodge, accompanied the novices on horseback, waving a white flag.[11]

That night, after dark, a second and related rite was performed, that of *ditime* ("grass torches," i.e., those rapidly extinguished; from *go tima*, "to be extinguished"). The novices proceeded a distance from the lodge in the direction of the settlement, each carrying a torch of fiber made from the now obsolescent *moshu* kilts. At an appointed spot they formed a long row, facing the population of the town, which had assembled at its outskirts to witness the scene (Language 1943:119). When the torches were ignited, women rushed forward with shouts and ululations, attempting to drive the novices into the settlement. But the latter, bearing their rapidly extinguishing torches, made for the bush lodge for one last time.

The following morning, the initiates bathed in the river, and smeared their bodies with a compound of red clay and fat (Schapera 1971[b]:231). Their hair was roughly shaved so as to leave only a circle on the crown— a practice known as *go beola setlopo*, to shave around the "pointed head of the hornless ox." The remaining hair was dressed with *sebilo*, a cosmetic of lead powder and ox fat used only by adults, which gave it the flat and iridescent appearance of a metal cap (Burchell 1953, vol. 2:342). Finally, they would don new skin cloaks (*dikobo*, standard adult male dress) pre-

pared by their fathers from the skin of an ox sacrificed on their behalf.[12]
Toward evening, the lodge was finally razed, its former occupants setting off for the town, once more encircled by adult men bearing switches
(Willoughby 1909:242). This time the phalanx proceeded directly to the
chief's court, while the women of the town lined its route, ululating and
lurching forward in mock attempts to thrust the guardians aside and reveal the initiates to the public gaze. But the men wielded their switches in
stylized ferocity, as if to herd the women like cattle. The young men
were deposited in the chiefly cattle byre, whose entrance was barricaded.
The entire adult population then passed the night dancing and singing on
the outskirts of the court.

Such dance and song had a characteristic form, being associated with
occasions of social reconstruction such as the reaggregation stage of *bogwêra* and *bojale,* the bringing in of the harvest, and the making of rain.
The core formation of dancers was a circle of men, which moved either
in clockwise or anticlockwise direction and kept up a rhythmic shuffling,
punctuated by leaps in the air with switches held erect. The women
sometimes composed a loose circle about the men, dancing in the opposite direction, with body movements more continuous and flowing
(Spohr 1973:82). But they provided the rhythm for the whole performance, clapping their hands, singing, and stamping their rattle-clad feet.
They might also stand on the sidelines, or rush forward, playfully but-
ting the slowly rotating circle of men (Burchell 1953, vol. 2:292ff.).
While the early sources say nothing of the songs themselves, those recorded among the Tshidi in 1970 indicate a clear theme:

He! Dumela moeng!	Oh! Greetings stranger/guest!
He! Dumedisa moeng!	Oh! Stranger, you are being greeted!
He! Moeng, dulafatshe moeng!	Oh! Stranger, sit down!
He! Dula fa moeng!	Oh! Sit here, stranger!
O re bokete tsa kwa otswang, moeng!	Tell us where you come from, stranger!
He! Dumedisa moeng!	Oh! Stranger, you are being greeted!

The novices were now termed *dialogane,* "those who lie on skin sleeping
mats," and were indeed to sleep on mats in the court for the following
week. Early in the morning following their arrival, their heads were
shaved again, this time very neatly, and their faces were smeared with a
decoction of pumpkin seed and pith, giving them a red-brown glow.
Skins were then laid on the floor of the royal enclosure, where the whole
population had gathered, this being the only occasion on which women
were allowed in *en masse* (Language 1943:120). The *dialogane* were led

from the cattle byre, wearing their cloaks and carrying their weapons, and being screened from view by their herders. Once they were arranged on the skins in ranked ward groups, the herders drew back, revealing them to the general population for the first time. The sight called forth a crescendo of ululations, to which the *dialogane* responded impassively, with downcast eyes and expressionless faces (Willoughby 1909:242). They were then formally greeted by the chief and given their regimental name, the latter leaving little doubt as to the normative role of the regiments (*ma Tlotlakgosi,* "honor of the chief"; *maGodu,* "the [cattle] raiders" [Schapera 1938:316]). Thereafter, praise-poetry was recited which extolled the virtues of the ruler and his predecessors, and recounted the mythical history of the chiefdom and its totemic relationship to other Tswana polities. Finally, the newcomers were welcomed by their kin of both sexes, who placed gifts of personal adornment (bracelets, beads) in their laps. The young men then spent the night in the royal enclosure.

The following day, the *dialogane* took up their newly acquired weapons and hunted or herded cattle in the bush (Willoughby 1909:242). Towards evening, those who had presided at the lodge went to meet them, and painted their faces with white lines which framed their eyes—one line down the center forehead and the ridge of the nose, the other crossing it on the forehead and extending down past the eyes on to the cheeks (Willoughby 1909:242). Thus adorned, they returned to the court before sunset and lay on their mats, covered by skin blankets. The adult male and female population now gathered around them for the rite of *thoyane.* This comprised a lengthy session of song and dance, during which the women attempted to expose the "sleepers" by pulling off their coverings. The herders, in turn, were to prevent their charges from being seen, and the *dialogane* were to make no visible response; most particularly, their teeth were not to be seen by the taunting women (Willoughby 1909:243). This rite formed the point of articulation between the *bogwêra* and *bojale* cycles, for the parallel female rites, while far less elaborate, gave rise to a complementary age-regiment bearing the same name as the male. The *bojale* commenced after the *bogwêra* and ended before it, and it was these young women, newly inducted into mature sexuality and nubility, who now taunted the *dialogane* most energetically.

For this week, during which the *dialogane* would hunt in the bush by day and sleep in the court at night, they were to communicate only with other men and to remain phlegmatic in the face of female provocation. The women sang songs from a repertoire termed *dipina tsa maitisho a dialogane a motlhapudi*—"the songs of the evening leisure of the clean ones on the sleeping mats"—performed as dialogues between them and any males present, besides the *dialogane*:

One girl
He! He! Naledi!
Mosipidi! Mokotlamêdi!

Oh! Oh! Star
Traveller! Thou who sinkest below
the western horizon!

Men, all
Ka re, Tsela ga u e bonê, he!
Mosipidi! Mokotlamêdi

I say, Oh! do you not see the road?
Traveller! Thou who sinkest below
the western horizon!

One girl
Bao boo tsêla ka ba gago
Mosipidi! Mokotlamêdi!

Those who travel are thine,
Thou traveller! Thou who sinkest
below the western horizon!

Men, all
Ka re nna ka re molala a tladi
Ga u o bonè, he!
Mosipidi! Mokotlamêdi!

I say, this I say, the milky way
Don't you see it, oh!
Thou traveller! Thou who
disappearest below the western
horizon!

One girl
A ga utulwê ñwana a lailwê, he!

Oh, dost thou not hear the child
who is instructed!

Mosipidi!
Mokotlamêdi!

Thou traveller!
Thou who disappearest below the
western horizon!

Willoughby 1909:244

After the week of *maitisho a dialogane a motlhapudi*, the initiates returned to their homes. They were now termed *botshotlwana*, "those who
have put out spring plumage after moulting" (Willoughby 1909:244).
Their bearing was proud and confident, and they were entitled to participate in the courts of headman and chief. But, until they had acted as
herders to the next group of novices, they were expected to remain celi-
bate. Together with the uninitiated, they drank the beestings of cows
who had newly calved. If this were done by the sexually active, it would
have caused the calf to sicken and die, and the cow to miscarry in the
future (Willoughby 1909:244).

After about one year, the *bogwêra yo o setsho* (black *bogwêra*) was performed (Schapera 1971[b]:231). Information about this rite is limited, but
it seems that the young men were reassembled at the chief's court and
smeared with a mixture of charcoal and fat. They were then made to
clamber through a circuitous tunnel or maze in the royal cattle byre, at the
center of which was a pointed, decorated pole. The pole was "painted
black, white and red in horizontal bands of a hand-breadth and crowned
with ostrich feathers and the tails of wild animals" (Willoughby 1928:299;
Brown 1921:420). "Songs of the law" were repeated and the switch re-
introduced. After the rite, the group was sent on its first collective assign-
ment as a regiment (Schapera 1971[b]:231). It then remained for the

initiates to gain their sexual freedom through participation as herders in the subsequent *bogwêra*.

Interpretation of the Stage of Reaggregation

As I have suggested, the sequence of liminal rites proceeded from an act of deconstruction of the novices through their gradual reformation. In the process, the poetic structure of the rite built a cumulative image of social being, shaping the person in terms of an increasingly inclusive order of categories and relations which transcended individual subjectivism and subsocial existence. But the impetus which triggered the shift from the liminal to the postliminal phase came from outside of the ritual structure itself, from the epicenter of the polity. The chief, to whom ultimate control of the whole process was attributed, set in motion the rites enabling the integration of his now transformed subjects.

The rites of *thalalagae* in fact highlighted the semantic structure of the whole ritual process by providing a negative instance: an abortive effort to return the novices to the social world on terms which ensured that the attempt could not be consummated. The young men, still carrying the "dirt" of their gestation in the bush—they were unwashed, unshaven, and unsmeared, and wore the kilts of androgynous childhood—sought entry into the community in the heat of the day, the categorical confusion being further underlined by the juxtaposition of symbols of uncompleted growth (the androgynous kilts) with those of manhood (the weapons of war and control). While still creatures of the bush, they now wore shoes, a sign of socialization. Such flouting of the logic of the ritual process was fated to miscarry, and therein lay its significance. Despite the fact that the attempted reentry of the initiates anticipated features of their subsequently successful arrival, it contradicted the very essence of a sequential, nonreversible development. When confronted by the full force of active female sexuality, the novices could not stage a commanding return to the social world; shielded from disaster by their male seniors, they fled back to the bush like frightened animals.

The *thalalagae* thus made a statement about the process of orderly articulation through which the novices, as new men, were to assume a position of stable dominance within the community. The ritual construction of male sexual potency had now to be translated into practical social control: these new men had to confront and domesticate the threat of female sexuality and all that it implied. They had to be able to penetrate the heterosexual world confidently to its center. To do this, they were dependent upon the mature capacity of their seniors, upon an established hierarchy of male social authority, a dependency which contradicted and subverted the challenging vitality of their rising manhood (cf. La Fontaine 1977, who stresses that the efficacy of initiation rites is self-validating, for it impresses upon the novices the power of secret knowledge controlled by the elders).[13]

The following rite of *ditime* set in motion a cycle of reincorporation more in keeping with the developmental logic of the liminal stage. Here the *moshu* kilts, the agents of transformation which had linked the pre-liminal and liminal phases, were destroyed, signaling the irreversibility of physical and social maturation. Once again, the young men confronted the assembled population of the town. But maturation, even in the encapsulated world of ritual time, is a process. The novices, as new men, were not yet equipped to take up the challenge of female sexuality; the women, demonstrably ready, attempted to drive them into the town on their own terms. After the kilts had been consumed, however, the initiates could wash off any residue of their rebirth, and prepare for an effective reentry. They smeared themselves with red clay, a mark of social and sexual potential, if not yet of consummation. The clay was mixed with cattle fat, an important emulsifier in ritual cosmetics. This, and the oxhide they wore, underlined the role of cattle in the realization of male identity and politico-social domination. The novices now dressed as adults, carrying the instruments of masculine aggression—a war club, a spear, and a herding stick. Their hair was shaved roughly; that is, in a manner not yet fully refined, but indicative, in the shaping of a small residue on the crown, of a harnessing of natural energy. Human hair, in its protrusion from the body in space, its quality of both life and lifelessness, and its capacity for styling, is well suited to signify the extension of the persona in the social world; it lends itself to constriction through socialization (Turner n.d.[a]; Vlahos 1979). The shaving of the initiate's head to resemble a hornless ox expressed the cultural harnessing of waxing physical power. But the use of *sebilo* to anoint the crown also prefigured a regular adult status; for this substance was a token of normal maturity. It had a cumulative effect upon the hair, overlaying natural contours with the artificial luster of a socially derived aesthetic (see Burchell 1953, vol. 2:348).[14] Its use was suspended only at points when natural forces intruded into everyday social life: after childbirth or bereavement.

Before the youths left the bush, the lodge was fired: this time there would be no return. Now, buttressed by their elders, they made for town, moving in a tight formation whose shape resembled a large phallus. This solidary formation, protecting its still vulnerable offspring from a hostile environment, suggested that the phalanx was a male metaphor of consummation, and that, in the stage of reaggregation, images of gestation and growth were to give way to those of sexual conquest. The phalanx moved ahead determinedly, penetrating to the heart of the settlement and depositing its charges in the chiefly cattle byre. The initiates had now regained the social world, but still as creatures of the night; they had yet to confront the body politic in the light of day.

Meanwhile, the adult population sang and danced, welcoming the novices as "strangers" from a place unknown. The verb *go bina* connoted "to sing," "to dance," and "to venerate," implying the act of honoring by means of the aesthetic of harmonious collective performance. This activity articulated individuals and categories in a unified body of sound and movement; it was a supremely social activity, a dramatization of community in its highest moral aspect. Indeed, the form of the Tswana dance may be read as a metaphor of the construction of the social world itself, and the related roles of males and females within it spoke of their idealized positions in the system. Thus the movement of the men was more formalized than that of the women, commanding the inner circle and dictating the direction of the whole scheme. Men did not touch, and took care to synchronize their steps so as not to tread on each other. But they broke their circular motion from time to time by leaping in the air with sticks upright, suggesting a vertical, or phallic, movement which contrasted with the lateral, rolling motion of the women (cf. Gell 1975:234, whose similar New Guinea material suggests the operation of very widespread bodily metaphors in such dance forms; see also Comaroff 1983). This difference implied not only the complementarity of male-female sexuality but the distinction between agnatic rank and matrilaterality. While men periodically broke the ring to eject themselves assertively upward, women participated on the margins, their circle only intermittently and loosely integrated and their directionality being taken, by contrast, from that of the men. Much of the time they stood on the sidelines, but it was they who provided the continuing rhythm for the entire formation. In a manner isomorphic with their role as mediators of natural processes, a role which set the basic tempo of the alternating ritual and social calendar, they furnished the temporal framework for the dance, although themselves often not obtrusive participants in it. The map of the dance floor also replicated the spatial order of the social world, its organization of center and periphery, and its opposed yet complementary relations between male and female.

The initiates were now referred to collectively as *dialogane*, "those who lie on the sleeping mats." These mats connoted adult sexuality; to "share a sleeping mat" was to engage in intercourse. However, the sleeping mats of the new men were not in the usual domestic context but in the chief's court, for the political center took precedence over individuated relations with women, a fact whose recognition was integral to the emerging social identity of the youths.

Before their debut, the *dialogane* underwent a process of bodily refinement. Their heads were deftly reshaved with close-cutting implements, and the crude preparation of red clay and fat was replaced by a carefully rendered vegetable substance. The young men were arranged on mats in strictly ranked formation and revealed to the public as newborn social beings. While presented with personalized gifts, they made no acknowledgment of them, their impassive reaction to the excitement of the women being a demonstration of their disciplined self-control, their subjection to cultural form. As new regimental members, they shared a unitary identity, exemplified in their uniform dress and demeanor. But this identity was firmly overlaid by hierarchy, both within and between age-grades, and in relation to the chiefship.

The day after their public debut, the initiates were sent to the bush, their characteristic male activities being articulated directly with the royal court. While there, their faces were painted by the men who had supervised their earlier transformation, their eyes framed by white lines which accentuated the point of sight which, it will be recalled, embodied the quality of personal assertiveness and determination. In the ritual battle that was to follow, such determination had to win out over feminine challenge and self-indulgence. The boys were not to "show their teeth"; that is, to give sign of sexual arousal or response. During this ensuing battle (*thoyane*), the initiates were defended by their herders who, being more thoroughly socialized, were about to engage in their own first sexual encounters. Here the less socially constrained sexuality of the young women was contrasted with that of the men who, despite provocation, could contain their physical potency. The association between the teeth and male appropriation had already been made at several points in the ritual sequence. By keeping their teeth hidden, the young men conserved a sexuality itself not yet ready to withstand the threatening attractions of its female prey. At this juncture a concluding statement is made about the paradox of female generative power (expressed in the acts of provocation) and male social domination (dramatized in the show of collective masculine resistance and control).

The contest between female sexual urgency and male restraint was expressed at various levels during the week of ritual at the court. The initiates consolidated their esprit de corps by pursuing masculine exploits, such as communal hunting in the bush. But they remained the "clean" ones on their sleeping mats; during the time of nocturnal domestic intimacy, they stayed huddled as a regiment in the public center. It was their elders, secure in their senior status, who engaged the nubile girls in a nightly dialogue, in songs whose metaphors talked both of sexual arousal and of the physical incompetence of the new men. The give-and-take between the older males and young females, and the countering of images of youthful sexual inadequacy with those of experience underlined a generational asymmetry in Tswana marriage practice; an asymmetry which linked younger women to older men. The idioms of the duets opposed maturity to ineptitude by juxtaposing verticality (star; milky way) with laterality (western horizon; road). As elsewhere in the *bogwêra* ritual—for example, the counterpoint of "horns" and "tusks" against "tripe" and "chitterlings"—these directional contrasts had phallic significance. But the distinction between linearity and laterality was not merely one between penes erect and flaccid; it also evoked the more general division, noted in the dance, between linear masculine and lateral feminine principles. Thus the traveler who sinks below the western horizon was the star that failed to remain in the heaven above—that was lateral rather than vertical—and hence drew scorn from the young women. The men replied by laying the blame on the traveler himself; he did not "know the road," the correct route to consummation. The women, in turn, suggested that this traveler failed to hear the child who had been instructed; failed, that is, to respond to those made sexually adept through initiation. In culmination, the men advocated as a contrast with the lone sinking star the stars of the milky way (literally, "the path of lightning"), a profusion high in the heaven, which formed a pathway of white activating power.

The image of the young men as *botshotlwane*—"those who have put out spring feathers after moulting"—expresses the sense of beings clothed in a new, externally marked identity; one acquired after having been reduced to nakedness. But, despite their fine plumage, they remained in a condition of protracted marginality, jurally adult while sexually restricted. Indeed, they were to remain "clean" for some time yet, as their dietary connection with the beestings connotes. Their female coevals, however, could be taken as wives by the older men of the community any time after their initiation. In a situation where the elite controlled access to both storable wealth and the reproductive rights that such wealth indexed, they were in a position to practice polygyny—itself an important feature in the negotiation of political alliance. This pattern ensured that the marriage age of all women remained low, whereas that of commoner men was kept high (cf. Campbell 1822, vol. 1:66f.). Thus the ritual proscriptions which distinguished male and female initiates linked innate gender differences to the politico-economic realities of the social world.

As I have already suggested, the black *bogwêra* entailed a further "cooling" of the potency generated by the "white" cycle. The central activity of these rites required that the initiates clamber through a circuitous maze in the chiefly cattle byre; that their youthful vitality undergo additional channelization, being constrained by socially constructed artifice. The decorated pole at the nucleus of the ritual again introduced an icon of verticality, here bearing the weight of the depiction of the whole cosmic order. This pole evinced several themes simultaneously: it suggested a *pinegare,* the central load-bearing stave of the conical dwelling hut, which connoted both founding support and genealogical continuity (Comaroff 1974:96). In the black *bogwêra,* it stood with its foot in the chief's cattle byre, the burial ground of the royal ancestors, the most potent of superhuman beings; but at its head were the feathers and tails of wild beasts. Its middle combined in equal measure the three basic colors of the Tswana cultural order—the red of natural potential, the black of social constraint, and the white of dynamic activation. The pole was hence a condensed symbol of the perceptible universe, the cosmic context containing within it the social domain. Both the pole and the color triad that encircled it were to recur in the transformed symbolic practice of the modern Tshidi, practice likewise directed towards social reconstruction, if in sociopolitical circumstances which had radically redefined the accession to adulthood.

Bojale
Female Initiation

Not only was female initiation considerably less elaborate than *bogwêra,* but the contrast between the two held the key to the full ideological significance of the whole ritual complex. For just as the male rites projected man as skilled social being, the creator of a domain which transcended the female periphery, *bojale* complemented this with an image of woman as incompletely socialized, capable of producing value but not of transforming it into enduring social form.

The *bojale* took place on the margins of the town, in a homestead which was derelict or belonged to the "poor" (Kirby 1939, vol. 1:400).[15] It was held during April and May, being timed to coincide with the concluding stages of *bogwêra* (Schapera 1971[b]:233). Smith's observations suggest that one royal daughter might have taken precedence in the rites but that this would have been the only distinction of rank made in the female cycle (Kirby 1939, vol. 1:400). Girls participated after the onset of menstruation (Brown 1921:421) for, after the month-long process, they were formally nubile. No elaborate rites of separation occurred, as the status of the participants was not to be drastically transformed. Their maturation appears to have been perceived as a largely "natural" one, attendant upon their physical development; the adult female estate of wife and mother remained rooted, ultimately, in the mediation of extrasocial process.

Immediately after seclusion, an operation was performed on each girl. The inside of her right thigh was cut and the glowing end of an ignited stick was twisted in the wound, a procedure to which she was required to respond with fortitude. After this was done, a second rite, the core of the *raffirming social roles* [margin note]

social construction of nubility, was performed: every initiate was examined to ensure that she was a virgin and had not been opened to intercourse in a manner unmediated by social regulation. Her hymen was then pierced by means of a tuber (Kinsman n.d.[b]:15; Jennings 1933:18). This done, sexual instruction commenced, punctuated by severe flogging carried out by older women or widows (Kinsman n.d.[b]:16; Kirby 1939, vol. 1:400). Once their thigh wounds had healed, the girls spent much of the day in the bush, being educated in what Schapera refers to as "matters concerning womanhood" (1971[b]:232–34); namely, domestic skills, agricultural practice, and sexual technique. Moffat noted that they were "initiated into all the duties of wives, in which it merits notice that passive obedience was especially inculcated" (1842:250). Indeed, the ritual stress on subordination was both predominant and unambiguous. Within the marginal homesteads, the novices assumed the role of "servants of the lowest caste" (Methodist Mission Society correspondence of Kay, quoted by Kinsman n.d.[b]:16). They performed such menial domestic duties as gathering wood and fetching water, work done by *balala* in wealthy homesteads or young girls among the rank and file.

During the entire month, no men might approach the novices; the latter carried hooked sticks or mimosa thorn branches, ostensibly to resist any advances (Schapera 1971[b]:233). Yet several of the ritual performances were semipublic in nature, involving masking, the singing of sexually provocative songs, and the apparent expression of hostility toward males for their inadequate participation in domestic labor (Kinsman n.d.[b]:16). A further public rite, observed by Campbell, involved the whole female population of the town, which assembled in a circle around the novices and was then encompassed, *in toto,* by a skin thong. As a solid mass, they danced, sang, and filled the air of the settlement with great noise (1815:188). Campbell also describes a rite in which the novices danced around an image of a "horned serpent" in the sand, being observed by some 600 to 700 women (1815:195).

After the midpoint of the period of seclusion, the girls were made to don "vests" made of damp corn stalks, which were worn until the end of the ritual, by which time they had become dry and uncomfortably chafing (Kinsman n.d.[b]:16; see plate 3). During this period, their bodies were smeared with a mixture of white clay and fat. Toward the end of the liminal phase a rite was performed that again called for a show of passive endurance. The novices were made to hold a bar of hot iron without letting it drop, to show, in Moffat's words, "that their hands [were] hard and strong for labor" (1842:250). They would then wash in a river, or a similar natural water source in the bush, and put on the dress of adult women—a leather skirt and a skin bodice covering the breasts. Their heads were shaved around the crown (though not as radically as

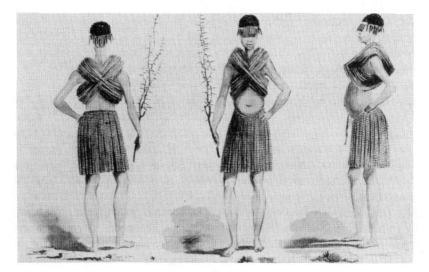

Plate 3   Female initiation dress.

those of their male counterparts) and the remaining growth was an-
nointed with *sebilo* (Moffat 1842:250). The initiates were then taken to
the royal court, where they were given their regimental name and declared ready for marriage (Schapera 1971[b]:233).

The *bojale* clearly paralleled the *bogwêra* to some degree: it addressed
the social construction of adulthood and the collective appropriation of
natural procreative powers; it effected a transformation on its subjects;
and it was centered on a liminal phase set off in time and space from the
everyday world, during which those undergoing metamorphosis were
attended by those sexually inactive. On the other hand, the female rites
took place at the margins of, rather than outside, the community. Wom-
en's adult state did not oppose nature but mediated it; and the ritual expressed this continuity by moving back and forth between the social
periphery and the bush. Moreover, female fertility developed as an unde-
niably natural process with the onset of menstruation; unlike male potency, it was not itself constructed by initiation as much as channeled by it.
Thus the emphasis within *bojale* was upon the "opening" of the young
women to sexual access, preparing them for marriage and all that it entailed. And, as their bodies were made receptive, their consciousness was
shaped through concentrated and symbolically marked instruction. The
"taming" of female sexuality, with its stress on docile endurance, differs
markedly from the inducements to aggressive conquest provided in such
male performances as the song of salt. This was most apparent in the

closing act of the sequence—the woman taking the hot metal bar into her bare hands. Here woman clearly had to prove herself passively recipient of adult male potency (metal being a product of male exchange and fabrication). Yet, while this might have been the culminating statement of the cycle, it stood in tension with a second order of meanings contained within the logic of *bojale* itself, meanings already encountered in the origin myth above.

The *bojale* began with an ordeal of pain and blood which, while less extreme than that of *bogwêra*, ushered in a culturally induced alteration in physical and social identity. The cut and the burning stick were in some senses the complement of circumcision; for, rather than liberating unambiguous sexual assertiveness, they imprinted on the bodies of the young women their opening to potent intrusion and generative process, a kindling of the fire. This was reinforced by the ritual act of defloration, which prepared the way for intercourse within the socialized confines of established norms. Here the confrontation with the "horned serpent" was also relevant; while there was frequent identification of snake and phallus in Tswana metaphoric usage, this rite focused on a culturally contrived snake drawn in the sand—i.e., a conventional image of natural potency. The emphasis, as in the ritual as a whole, was on a socially refracted order of human sexuality.

Yet the ritual might be seen to carry another, discordant, message: the burning stick and the tuber were symbolic constructions of male sex organs made from female substances (firewood and veldkos)—the analogues of the male appropriation of female generative symbols in *bogwêra*. Women here took the sexual initiative, in this context at least regulating their own generative capacity. There were also other elements in the performance that expressed female resistance to established gender relations: provocative song and dance, intrusive noise and explicit accusation. Indeed, the origin myth itself associates the secret rites with the uncontrollable, sui generis character of female creativity. Still, women appear to have taken control of their own emerging fertility only to have to deliver it, when socially encompassed, into male hands. In the ritual, despite the tension between female assertiveness and subservience, the former was systematically overlaid by the latter; again, a transfer of meanings seems to have occurred within the *bojale* itself, such that it concluded with the image of woman as passive recipient of male dominance, both sexual and politico-economic. Thus females approached the public spaces with curved and blunted sticks, weapons which had been neutralized, or branches whose sting remained "natural" and unhoned; and they wore constricting vests made of corn husks, rather than dynamic *moshu* kilts, prefiguring the yoke of agricultural production. Moreover, although they engaged in playful physicality, even critical social comment, the overall structure of the rite appears in the end to have depressed such exuberance in its participants. But the enthusiastic response of Tshidi women to the Methodist mission was to suggest that the church tapped a suppressed, but continuing undercurrent of female discontent in the precolonial system. For in *bojale,* the movement from natural fertility to social nubility, underlined by the use of white clay on the novices' bodies, was a passage to unambiguous social marginality. While the male rites played on the endemic paradox between equality and hierarchy, their female counterpart, by binding all women young and old into a single body or *losika,* stressed their unitary peripheral status within the cosmology and political economy.

The fact that women were less completely transformed by *bojale* than were men by *bogwêra* was captured in the practice of shaving less of their hair on reincorporation into the community. Females remained "open" to the ebb and flow of natural processes, subject to disaster, decay, and death. Their activities were tied to the transience of the individual lifespan, a transience which could be overcome only by the fully social intervention of man; for the latter alone had the capacity to fabricate an enduring social order. And it was this order that was celebrated in the regular re-creation of age-regiments in the *bogwêra* ritual.

Ritual, Action, and History

Let me return to the issue raised at the start of this chapter, namely, the role of symbolic mediation in the relationship of structure and practice. I have suggested that the principles underlying the sociocultural system of the Tswana impressed themselves, through the intervention of a complex symbolic order, upon the flow of everyday life. But this system, as constituted in the precolonial period, gave rise to specific contradictions in the manner in which value was defined and action potentiated. It was these contradictions that were dramatized most elaborately in the collective ritual that has been my major concern here. In my analysis of these rites, I have attempted to show how they addressed and redressed systemic conflicts, their poetic forms imposing a dominant set of meanings upon the experience of paradox.

The initiation cycle provided a particular model for the articulation of the individual and the collectivity, the periphery and the center, the male and the female domains, projecting an authoritative map of social and symbolic relations that overlay, but did not totally eclipse underlying structural tensions; the latter were reproduced as part of the overall system, their implications continuing to threaten its constitution. Hence it was necessary to repeat the hegemonic charter in this and in other genres.

hegemony

For hegemony, as Williams (1977:108ff.) has noted, is itself a process that always engenders opposition and resistance. Also, symbolic mechanisms of the sort examined here, while clearly part of the apparatus of power, are not coterminous with material forces. Yet they mediate such forces in human experience, and are essential to their reproduction and transformation. To paraphrase Sahlins (1981:52), symbolic mechanisms are not condemned to serve as mere "superstructural foam on the wave of history"; as we shall see, their manipulation was of particular importance in the practical response of peoples coercively marginalized from the material basis of power—the predicament of the Tshidi and others in modern South Africa.

I have noted that, in the Tswana conception, ritual was a mode of activity particularly forceful in constructing and transforming the features of the tangible environment. In the nineteenth-century system, communal rites played a major role in reproducing established structures of inequality and in managing the tensions they embodied. But ritual is never merely univocal and conservative, papering over the cracks in the cause of hegemonic social forces. As the example above suggests, it is always the product of a more or less conflicted social reality; a process within which an attempt is made to impress a dominant message upon a set of paradoxical or discordant representations. Indeed, the power of ritual may come to be used, under certain conditions, to objectify conflict in the everyday world, and to attempt to transcend it. This became particularly evident among the Tshidi when engagement with the colonial system began to alter the precolonial order in radical ways, to engender a discrepancy between dominant ideological forms and practical experience, and to crystalize tensions formerly implicit in the lived-in universe. Also, as historical exigency introduced new contradictions and new orders of symbolic mediation, "traditional" ritual was to serve increasingly as a symbol of a lost world of order and control.

In such situations as colonialization, novel symbolic orders come into being through a process of reorganization; a *bricolage* which not only alters existing relations between signs but also integrates them with others bearing forms and forces of external origin. Complexes of signs are thus disengaged from their former contexts and take on transformed meanings in their new associations, a process constantly repeated in relation to modified material circumstances. We shall see, in the Tshidi case, how such syncretism—observable in productive technique, built form, dress, cosmic maps, and so on—created a dynamic force-field in terms of which the people themselves acted upon the circumstances of articulation. The innovation sprang from a disjuncture between received categories and changing everyday experience. The attempt to regain control

over the practical world most frequently entailed implicit symbolic reformulation, but it also took the form of concerted action through syncretic ritual. In order to understand the mediation of symbols in the
process of structural transformation, I now turn to the engagement of the
Tshidi system with the South African political economy.

Marxism

Part

2

5

Culture, Consciousness, and Structural Transformation

In the last two chapters I have constructed a model of the social system of the Tshidi, c.1800–1830. Before considering the process through which this system became articulated with the forces of European colonialism, it is necessary to draw out a number of summary conclusions about its form—and, especially, about prevailing modes of consciousness—at the point of first sustained contact with the agents of the industrial West. By this time, the dislocating effects of *defikane* had prompted the Tshidi to leave their base on the Molopo River and to reaggregate temporarily with the other Barolong peoples. Yet, despite this visible upheaval, the structure underlying the lived-in world was itself left intact. As Chapter 2 indicated, characteristic relations of power and production, and the sociospatial order at large, were reproduced by each of the chiefdoms once access to adequate land had been obtained. The fact that control over this land had been secured by the Methodist mission did not have an immediate impact on the Barolong communities, although it did prefigure the process of subjugation to follow. But, at this juncture, the indigenous polities were relatively unconstrained by the presence of the evangelists, and, when circumstances permitted, all but one of them set out to reestablish their independence.

Nonetheless, the migration to Thaba 'Nchu had made the Tshidi aware of the nature and implications of the Christian presence, and had exposed them to the wider cultural order that underlay its project. For the Protestant mission bore the symbolic forms, the ideological commitments, and the imperial intent of nineteenth-century Europe. True, there were significant features that were specific to the English evangelical vision and to Methodism itself, for they were products of a particular social history; and there were differences, as we have seen, between the ideologies of missionary paternalism, of Boer nationalism, and of colonial capitalism. But, despite distinctions of express motivation, these agencies had converging effects, stemming both from their common European origins and their ultimate unity of interest in the thoroughgoing binary logic of a racially ordered South Africa. Thus, in the mutually transforming relationship between the Tshidi and the Methodist mission, we observe the first stages of the articulation between a local society and the global forces of the European political economy.

The conjuncture between these two systems and the subsequent changes it engendered were shaped by the structure inherent in each; but the actual encounter occurred in the practical engagement of participants from each side. And, while the historical processes that ensued cannot be understood merely as the product of the purposive interaction of those involved, it was through such culturally mediated practice that transformations were realized on the ground.

The Forms of Tshidi Consciousness

In my account of the precolonial system, I stressed how spatial organization, built form, and everyday practice were the silent bearers of a symbolic scheme, a scheme which impressed itself upon human consciousness as the process of socialization inserted the person in the world. I noted, too, that this process was centered upon the body, the medium through which the meanings and values of any social system become internalized as categories of individual experience and identity. Because this is a universal phenomenon, the signs and functions of the organism act as a "memory," a condensed model of the collective order (Bourdieu 1977:94); by the same token, significant changes in that order must entail a reconstruction of the mnemonic scheme inscribed in physical form, a point which will prove important later on. Moreover, while the logic of these symbolic processes is universal, they take on culturally specific contours. The precolonial Tswana system was founded upon the relationship between agnatic descent and endogamy as principles of social reproduction, between agnation and matrilaterality as bases for constructing social relations, between agnatic rank and politico-economic hierarchy as modes of aggregation, and between centralization and household agriculture as forms of ecological exploitation. As Chapter 3 indicated, this configuration of principles generated a series of contradictions, the practical resolution of which gave concrete shape to the community at any moment in time. But pragmatic action did not occur in an ideological vacuum: powerful symbolic mechanisms underpinned contemporary sociopolitical arrangements, and infused perceptions of the possibilities of practice. In this everyday world, cattle were comprehensive icons of the existing alignment of social relations. As both utilitarian objects and media of exchange, they condensed several levels of signification: they provided an index of individual status within a structure of inequality; they served as a metaphor of stable transformation and social durability; they presented a natural image of the division of labor. And, as a symbol of the male productive capacity and social estate, these animals stood in contrast to grain, which embodied the more transient transformative potential of women. Such mundane icons of social relations were complemented by more elaborate ritual statements. Thus both rites concerned with the disruption of the lived-in world (healing and ancestral sacrifice) and those of renewal (firstfruits and initiation) addressed conflicts and paradoxes in experience, striving to invest them with a model of hegemonic social order.

This cultural scheme had several corollaries for Tswana modes of consciousness. First, what we might term "worldview," a holistic vision of the cosmos, or "ideology," an order of values supportive of a given set of social arrangements, were almost entirely implicit in Tswana thought and action. Models of space-time, the phenomenal world, and the community were borne by material forms and activities explicitly directed toward practical ends—the human body, agricultural production, and the built form of the settlement. Of course, the poetic structures of ritual did carry a more complex and elaborate semantic load than did the inconspicuous signs of the everyday context. But such rites as healing, firstfruits, or initiation were not merely expressive vehicles either; for the Tswana, they were pragmatic acts which effected the transformation of the world; from an analytic perspective, they constructed, rather than merely reflected, meaning. Thus no simple distinction between instrumental and symbolic practice makes sense here, or indeed anywhere; instrumental action is always simultaneously semantic, and vice versa.

However, what does appear to be distinctive about precolonial Tswana culture—and others which lack a complex division of labor, monetized exchange, and literacy—is the absence of an awareness of the process of objectification itself. With the exception of the unevenly systematized repertoire of norms that governed rank, succession, and legal procedure (*mekgwa le melao*), and the even less explicit body of ritual technique of the specialist (*bongaka*), there was no indigenous notion of formal knowledge, of "myth," "tradition," "history," or "belief." Established cultural forms were conveyed largely through participation in everyday practice, and involved a mode of communication which, as Bourdieu (1977:120) has pointed out, seldom attains the level of open discourse. Indeed, such implicitness is a feature of ideology everywhere, notwithstanding the tendency of a positivist social science to treat human thought (especially in the modern West) as if it were merely the stuff of unidimensional concepts, not polysemic signs. The symbols that lie in the shadow of the explicit always provide powerful hidden persuasion, deriving their force from a fan of connotations that are neither consciously perceived nor evaluated, in our "rationalist" culture or any other. There is also a tendency to minimize the role of self-conscious, critical discourse in non-Western contexts; as the Tshidi case shows, such peoples both experienced and sought to reconcile conflicts generated by the social system that encompassed them.

Despite these universal features, however, there would seem to be important distinctions between modes of consciousness in societies like that of the Tswana and those where generalized media have been developed for the express purpose of systematic abstraction (through writing, enumeration, and theories of knowledge) and "rational" exchange (by means of money and models of exchange). In these latter contexts, there is an awareness of the *process* of representation through signifiers of specialized and universal relevance, and hence an overt concern with the accuracy of depicting the world ("realism"), with the transparency of symbols (see note 5 below), and with the logical coherence of their arrangement in "texts" (cf. Horton 1967, although this ideology is actualized in only a partial sense). Such self-consciousness about knowledge, its absolute "truth," and its systematicity was to develop unevenly among the Tshidi as a result of the encounter with Christianity, colonialism, and the money economy. As we shall see, identification with the symbols of these global forms and a concern with the coherence of "belief" and practice in the face of cultural syncretism was to mark an important line of differentiation within the community.

A second and closely related feature of Tswana consciousness has been implicit in much of the discussion above, especially that of cattle and grain, time and work. This is the quality I have already identified by recourse to Mauss's notion of the "total social phenomenon" that carries within it the multiple threads of the entire social fabric (1966:1). In the precolonial system, relationships were "multiplex," and mundane signs carried a symbolic freight that condensed plural frames of reference. Thus, for instance, cattle were at once objects of consumption and exchange and, while they appeared to function like money in certain respects, storing and enhancing wealth and mediating transactions, they lacked its ostensibly depersonalized quality. The circulation of animals permitted the human persona to extend beyond the spatiotemporal confines of physical being; similarly, grain and beer contained something of the substance of the producer, so that to consume it was to imbibe her self. Among modern Tshidi, clay beer pots are usually made by groups of female matrikin, and the firing of the pots is regarded as a delicate operation that may be threatened by social discord or polluting heat. Completed pots retain individual identity, being typed by the circumstances of their manufacture, the hand that shapes them, and the degree of accord among producers. Taussig (1980:36) has noted that, in such contexts, "Products appear to be animated or life-endowed precisely because they seem to embody the social milieu from which they come"; in such systems, both "work" and "time" remain immanent features of the social process itself.

According to this conceptual scheme, human subjects and material objects are not definitively set apart: the moral, spiritual, and physical components of the perceptible world exist in an integrated and mutually transforming relationship. For precolonial Tswana, the social universe imposed a fragile order upon the dynamic flux of the wild and was constantly threatened with dissolution into rank confusion. The "wild" itself was not constrained by social classification; here cultural categories had limited purchase, and unstable transformative processes prevailed. The interface between it and the domesticated world, moreover, was fluid: the wild was constantly being tamed for social ends, but social constructions constantly stood in danger of losing definition and reverting to an uncontained state. As Radin has remarked of this relationship in "primitive" contexts: "Nature cannot resist man, and man cannot resist nature" (1957:373; see also Taussig 1980:37). Thus occurrences such as drought, which signaled a breakdown of human control over natural process, required the ritual redrawing of blurred boundaries between domesticated space and the bush.

The maintenance of order was a function of both normative prescription and ritual reinforcement. Hence any breach of the agnatic code threatened to disrupt the divide between the living and the dead, matter and spirit. Aroused ancestors could take possession of the bodies of offenders, eclipsing their human qualities and their identities; or they might withdraw their spiritual support, rendering those concerned vulnerable to malignant intrusion. Indeed, socialization entailed the construction of bounded selfhood on the part of members of the community, for only a stable and contained persona could engage in give-and-take with its immediate context. Mature identity was constructed through the rites of initiation, and its physical margins were regularly renewed thereafter by symbolic practice, both mundane and elaborate. Affliction, in turn, flowed from a disruption of ordered subject-object relations; this was typically referred to in Setswana as an involuntary contraction of bodily space (*patikêga*), or as a process of being "overshadowed" (*khurumeditse*, to be "snuffed out" like a flame; Comaroff 1980:643), i.e., the erasure of subjective being by an obliterating world. Ritual treatment involved the iconic manipulation of the bodies of sacrificial victims or those of the sufferers themselves, in the attempt to reestablish the bounded integrity of the person and his/her separation from intrusive elements of the material and spiritual environment.

The definition of identity in the precolonial Tswana context, then, stressed self-construction and individualistic management. But such self-determination is not to be understood in terms of a unidimensional political pragmatism: the subject was enmeshed in a web of forces that promised to invade his bodily domain and placed moral limits upon the scope of his activity. In this scheme, personhood was not confined in space and time to a corporeal cocoon: it permeated the world through its material and spiritual extensions. An individual's name, his personal effects, and his footprints in the sand bore his influence, and could be used by sorcerers wishing to attack him. Malevolent thoughts toward others might cause them tangible harm, and the Setswana proverb has it that "the greatest sorcery is that of the heart" (*boloi jo bogolo ke jwa pelo*).[1] Indeed, the heart (*pelo*) was the physical and experiential center of being. Lacking a concept akin to that of "mind," Tswana regarded the heart as the epicenter of feeling (*utlwa,* which also meant "hear," "understand," and "sense" in a physical manner). It registered impressions that impinged on the person from outside and radiated influence beyond the self. As in many cultures, personal disposition here was imaged in the physical state of the heart: *peloethata* ("strong-hearted" or "brave"); *peloetelele* ("long-hearted" or "patient"). A sudden thought or recollection was understood to be the impact on one's sensory center of the mobile dimensions of persons and forces in the external world.

This cultural order would seem to contrast sharply with a Western epistemology in which persons appear as self-contained, determining individuals, acting out of rational utility upon a compliant world; one in which, as a Tshidi commentator put it, "the air is empty of forces and powers." Here products become unhinged from the circumstances of their production, and "time" and "work" are discrete commodities exchangeable against like "things" in a pervasive market. In this context, too, the embeddedness of persons and objects in the social field appears to be overlaid by a cosmology that proclaims the natural discontinuity of the social, the material, and the moral. And yet, the culture of industrial capitalism is not as definitively opposed to that of peoples such as the Tshidi as our own dualist notion of "self" and "other" might suggest. In comparing cattle and money, I noted that for us, the latter is itself a sign, expressing a fundamental continuity of the social and material beneath a more explicitly reifying ideology. For just as money, the archetypal depersonalized medium, may be invested with a life of its own, so, as Mauss (1966:64) remarks: "things sold have their personality even nowadays." To be sure, in our own society, identity is securely personified in things, and self-construction is pursued through the consumption of goods which, as either hidden or more obvious "status symbols," are imbued with social meaning, shaping us and the "needs" we deem "natural" (Baudrillard 1981). Marx captures this anthropomorphic process in his account of the twofold effect of capitalism upon the fetishism of the commodity: first, as product, the commodity is torn loose from the social relations that constructed it; then it is reinvested with seemingly autonomous life (1967, vol. 1:71ff.). Indeed, this process of alienation and personalization seems endemic to our culture, for the reification inherent in our mode of production stands in tension with the ever-present experience of social, material, and moral continuities (cf. Mauss 1966:64ff.). We are caught on a treadmill, forever materializing the social and socializing the material; for peoples relatively new to wage labor and the commodity economy, this presents itself as a paradox which is often addressed through ritual means. Among the Tshidi, for instance, the response to proletarianization was to involve an elaborate, ritualized attempt to reintegrate, once and for all, things and persons objectified in capitalist production.

The Tshidi were to encounter the depersonalizing effects of such productive processes when they became directly integrated into the labor market. But, before this, as I have repeatedly pointed out, they were to find the cultural images of industrial capitalism prefigured in the ideology and organization of the mission. It is to this that I now turn my attention.

The Cultural Logic of Mission Methodism

The Methodist mission to the Barolong grew out of the British Protestant tradition; specifically, out of the Nonconformist sects of the late eighteenth century. While a range of European denominations—Congregationalist, Moravian, Baptist, and Lutheran—were at work in the South African field at the time,[2] the Wesleyans were the most numerous and the most influential. Their church came to be the dominant context of conversion until the early twentieth century, especially in the burgeoning industrial centers; not only did its ideological forms mediate the process of proletarianization, but they also gave coherence to the black national culture emerging at that period. At the same time, however, Methodism provided the liberal terms of middle-class African reaction to the colonial society whose image the missions had borne; it furnished the blueprint for the growing Independent church movement, and afforded both a practical model and an educated leadership for the African National Congress in its early years. This mission, in fact, was not merely the bearer of British Protestant culture and the intellectual traditions, both religious and secular, of its broader European context; it was also a particular variant of this culture that had been fashioned in relation to the predicament of the newly industrialized "Christian poor" of northern England and had evolved a theology and institutional structure that was to prove relevant to those caught up in the rise of a black working class in South Africa.

Methodism had been a product of the industrial revolution in Britain, the last great revival, as Weber (1958:117) noted, of the European Puritan tradition. This tradition, stemming from the Calvinist rather than the Lutheran confession of early Protestantism, was associated with the doctrine of predestination, ascetic labor, and antiemotionalism. But, in Methodism, this strain was to be brought into somewhat uneasy articulation with Lutheran values—the equality of all legitimate worldly "callings" and a stress on the emotive outpouring of God's love through man's execution of his neighborly duty (Tawney 1926:96ff.). While early Protestantism had been a "church civilization"—one in which a unitary spiritual creed governed both church and society—modern Protestantism, of which Methodism was a development, recognized a dichotomy between church and state, and replaced the absolute authority of the Bible with a humanistic, subjective spiritualism based upon inner conviction (Troeltsch 1912:43ff). Early Protestantism had substituted for the Catholic priestly hierarchy and sacramental ritual the certainty of Scripture and decisive acts of faith; but in the Calvinist tradition, the notion of "good works" was overlaid by a theology according to which only a small proportion of mankind had been "elected" for salvation. Such doctrine conferred upon the elect the confidence that they were "lords of the world" (Troeltsch 1912:63), "self-confident saints" empowered by God to construct society according to their will (Weber 1958:112). Indeed, it was this theology, routed through the Dutch Reformed Church, that gave form to Boer and Afrikaner national consciousness in South Africa, while the culture of the mission and the first generation of black converts stemmed largely from subsequent transformations of the European Puritan tradition.

From the earliest period, Protestantism had stressed that the world had been provided by God as the context in which man was to labor in His name. *Lex naturae* (the law of nature) set the terms in which the dutiful were to prove the transcendent glory of *Lex Dei* (the law of God). Life was a "vale of suffering and tears" in which man, through struggle and service, was to show either that he was indeed one of the elect (in the Calvinist tradition) or that he could attain salvation by his own efforts (in the more "democratic" sects). Even where belief in "election" remained strong, the utilitarian individualism inherent in all Protestantism urged the person toward self-construction through rational and punctual duty

(Tawney 1926:234). In contrast to the medieval Christian, who, as Weber (1958:116) put it, lived "ethically from hand to mouth," the Protestant's career was cumulative and long-range, unmitigated by atonement and absolution; it centered on the individual as self-determining agent of planned activity and moral accounting. Man's reason was to control his state of nature through effective "system" or "method"; and it is hardly surprising that this model of a utilitarian moral economy found expression in the imagery of bookkeeping and commerce (cf. Weber 1958:124) and in the notion of the great ledger in the sky. Implicit in this scheme is a cosmology, a classification of personhood, agency, and space-time, which rested on a set of thoroughgoing oppositions between body and mind, flesh and spirit, emotion and reason, and lifetime and eternity. As symbolic system, Protestantism mediated a protracted transformation of European social and productive relations. In its early form, it gave coherence to the worldview of mercantile capitalism as this emerged in a feudal Europe; but it was subsequently to shape and be shaped by the rise, in those same contexts, of industrialism and wage labor.

[margin handwriting: Protestant gave legit. to mercantp capt'm]

In this dialectical process, Protestantism was also involved in the development of the European nation-state, for the Reformation spawned a series of national churches which were, in turn, to offer a powerful spiritual legitimation to such newly centralized administrations as those of Prussia, Geneva, and England. (They were also, where Catholic hegemony prevailed, to afford tangible examples of radical resistance.) The Christian commonwealth now became the parallel of the secular, urging upon the latter a "civilizing" ideal based upon the ethos of material and moral meliorism. What is more, the patriarchal concern with spiritual welfare within the nation-state was to converge with the interests of expanding mercantile colonialism, giving rise to an ideology of global moral imperialism. If the law of nature provided raw material for "God's gardeners" to shape the world in his image, then their toil would seem even more glorious where unmitigated wildness still reigned, untempered by a knowledge of the Word.

Within this wider Protestant context, Methodism had its specific genesis in the radical reconstitution of productive relations set in motion by industrialization in England. Originally a revival within the established church, it aimed to: "awaken the masses, which, under the influence of an 'enlightened' church and the pressure of industrial capitalism, had become indifferent, dull and coarse" (Troeltsch 1949, vol. 2:721). The Methodist revival was directed at the workers and the middle classes of the northern industrial river valleys, ignoring in the main the rural agriculturalists and the aristocratic and professional sectors (Warner 1930:165). At great open-air meetings, its leadership projected a rousing message of salvation from original sin, hellfire, and damnation; a salvation attainable through a direct and consciously experienced passage from condemnation to joy and peaceful duty. The Wesleyan creed represented an attempt to reconcile intense religious fervor with sober Calvinist discipline; it brought a sense of self-worth to the depersonalized, and charted a methodical and closely supervised route to moral improvement. In fact, its innovative genius seems to have lain in its organizational form, which consisted of local democratic societies under strong lay leadership, which operated in terms of a system of highly ordered, if mutually exercised controls (Troeltsch 1949, vol. 2:722). The church provided a framework that impressed the reality of spiritual conversion onto the practical details of the everyday world; its ramifying structure of districts, united under the supreme General Conference, situated the individual member within a coherent social and moral community, giving discernible shape to a social world in flux.

In its symbolic forms and rhetorical imagery, Methodism addressed those caught up in the expansion of capitalist production. The emotive individualism of revival spoke to the still novel experiences of urbanization, wage labor, and monetarization. Once aroused, enthusiastic identification was channeled toward the values of discipline, of self-realization through work, and of peaceful acceptance: the values most desired by management in its employees. In this, the Wesleyan message revealed its essentially double-sided ideological role: from its inception, it addressed the conflict generated by the industrial labor market, especially as this impinged upon its lowest participants; yet it reconciled these conflicts in such a manner as to reinforce the overall system that produced them. This fundamental contradiction was to alienate subsequent generations of the politically aggressive British working class (Hobsbawm 1957; and Thompson 1963); in South Africa, too, it was eventually rejected by large numbers of the black proletariat, who sought a more radical solution to their social predicament.

In its mediation of the experience of industrialization, Methodism played more directly than any of the sects before it upon the symbols of the market and the workplace. Natural law, in Wesley's elaboration of the creed, became the law of free enterprise; spiritual democracy entailed the right of each individual to pursue redemption through providentially bequeathed activity, whose constraint in terms of collective social considerations was of no great moral concern to the church (Warner 1930:152). Money featured prominently in this scheme, being the universal denominator that made possible the incorporation of the person into the free market of the spirit. It represented all the core values of the system, permitting them to circulate and accrue to those who engaged in earnest moral endeavor. Wesley (quoted by Warner 1930:155) noted:

"Although God has committed to our charge that precious talent which contains all the rest—money—it is definitely to be desired only if we are wise and faithful stewards of it." Money, here, was no less than a divine icon of a moral economy created in the image of the market. But it was a symbol which served also to sanctify the social roots of production and the forces that controlled them. Wesleyan teaching naturalized the essential relations of industrial capitalism by encompassing them in a supernaturally inspired cosmos. As Warner (1930:146–47) states:

> The habitual assumption of the [Methodist] revival was that the labor relationship was an ethical one in which one group had a definite function to perform as workers, and a second group had another function to perform as masters. Neither function was a determinant of one's status as a man. . . . If they are Methodists, it was affirmed, they must be continuously industrious, respectful and reliable. They must perform their work as a divine calling.

system of complacency

Drawing from the Lutheran stress upon the equality of all legitimate human vocations, Methodist teaching turned inequality into a sacred instrument of moral correction: God had decreed that "a diversity of ranks [should] subsist to the end of the world" (Warner 1930:125).

diversity of ranks

Central to the ideology of the free market of the spirit was a particular conception of labor. Marx made the distinction between labor as a social process, carried on by an organized plurality, and work, the exertions of individuals or groups expending energy to produce energy (Marx, as quoted by Wolf 1982:74). The former becomes conceivable only when money permits previously distinct kinds of activity to be equatable and interchangeable in a discernible system. As the seminal analyses of Weber and Tawney have shown, the Protestant ethic served to objectify this emergent form, elevating labor, in the collective consciousness, to the price of life eternal; it was a commodity to be deployed wisely in the pursuit of grace. Along with "time" and "money," labor was a "talent" provided by Providence in order that man might transcend a state of nature.

For the Protestant, in other words, work had become an end in itself (Weber 1958:63), the alienating effects of wage labor being the just cost of salvation. As Thompson (1963:365ff.) has noted, Methodism was an extension of this ethic in a specific set of historical circumstances: its ideology of sober self-discipline, routinized application, and uncomplaining acceptance shaped the worker especially well to the needs of the expanding British economy. But the forms of consciousness to which it gave rise were not a product of nature; they required cultural codification and effective symbolic mediation if they were to be internalized as axioms of existence (Weber 1958:62). Before this occurred, and until the Protestant work ethic had become hegemonic in European societies, in-

dustry was severely hampered by an inability to recruit the kind of employees most suited to its needs, since it was compelled to draw on a
population for whom "work" had not yet become equatable with such
absolute currencies as money and spiritual capital. A similar problem
dogged the subsequent advance of capitalism into the Third World,
where indigenous conceptions of action and self-construction were typically incompatible with the logic of the commodity economy. As the
event history indicated, the mission preceded capitalist penetration into
South Africa, bearing its image and values. But the masters of industry
and the state were to find the local population reluctant proletarians, despite physical and ideological coercion and the continuing effort to regulate the quantity and quality of requisite labor. Indeed, local black
resistance, both explicit and implicit, has consistently contested the
nature and conditions of work as defined for blacks by the neocolonial
order.

    The Protestant church played a significant part in establishing the
hegemony of a worldview compatible with industrial capitalism in both
Europe and the colonized Third World. Methodism, in Britain and its
colonies alike, was to prove well-equipped to carry the culture of the
bourgeoisie to the emerging proletariat, at least under the conditions of
economic expansion. In order to understand its apparent ability to unify
these two classes as integral components of an unequal social state, we
must return to the ideological role of Methodism alluded to above. More
successfully than any creed before it, Wesleyanism addressed crucial contradictions in the development of industrial capitalism in Britain. It did
so by recognizing working-class displacement, yet harnessing it to the
perpetuation of the overall system. For example, Wesley himself spoke
quite explicitly to labor relations, advocating that management set "fair
prices" and "just wages"; but he simultaneously decried workers' efforts
to disrupt the divinely established market in the interests of their own
betterment (Warner 1930:150). This juxtaposition expressed the conflict
within Methodism between spiritual democracy and temporal authority,
emotionalism and repression, and proletarian and bourgeois interests.
Thus, on the one hand, it depended upon the power generated by physically experienced religious conversion (Thompson 1963:365); yet, on
the other, it stressed that the active repression of bodily arousal was the
path to grace. As Foucault (1980[b]) has pointed out, such contradictory
excitation and denial has characterized modern Western treatment of the
body more generally, revealing how physical being becomes subjected to
social control. In Methodism, passionate excitement coexisted with a
condemnation of lechery, drunkenness, and hedonism, and contrasted
strongly with the rational forms of Anglican orthodoxy. Thompson
(1963:368ff.) has observed that the enthusiasm of revivalist ritual was of

great appeal in the depleted emotional landscape of the working class; but it alternated, both in the lives of its members and the ethos of the church in the nineteenth century, with periods of sober repression.

The persistence of enthusiasm and emotive forms of expression in church practice seemed to deny the dualisms of a bourgeois worldview and reflected the continuing inseparability of emotion and reason, matter and spirit, and body and mind in the cosmology of those not completely assimilated to the Protestant ethos. In fact, the vitality of nondualistic consciousness among populations peripheral to the establishment in the nineteenth century is well documented, both in the context of everyday life and in religious ideology (Thomas 1971:666), and I shall argue for its continuing salience in the modern world. Indeed, I return to one such creed, explicitly counterhegemonic, in the following chapter; for it was to supersede Methodism in its ability to provide modern Tshidi with a viable Weltaanschaung that countered the reifications inherent in mission ideology.

But, just as the ethos of sober rationalism came to control emotional effervescence within the nineteenth-century Methodist church, so the interests of spiritual democracy were accommodated to the prevailing civil order. Wesleyan doctrine appears to have done this by playing up the dichotomy of church and state; in its name, a strict separation was maintained between the free individualism of the spirit and the hierarchy of the temporal world. The ultimate realization of the former was not to be gained by contesting the latter, but by suffering it, and practical political activity was strongly discouraged. As I have noted, this accommodation was to prove increasingly inadequate for those among the working class who developed a critical awareness of their social predicament; more specifically, however, the unresolved contradictions of contemporary Methodism had a direct consequence for the history of such peoples as the Tshidi. As Hobsbawm (1957) has suggested, the Wesleyan mission enterprise in the early nineteenth century served to channel sociopolitical energies in a strongly conservative manner and was supportive of existing secular structures. Drawn from the strongholds of the church in the northern weaving districts, the emissaries who first made contact with the Barolong were sent abroad in the industrial boom years between 1820 and 1824 (see Hobsbawm 1957:124). Mission ideology of the time was relatively unselfconsciouss; whereas, by the end of the century, the mission boards in London and Boston were to formulate policy statements about the relationship between "parent" and "native" churches (Sundkler 1961:31), the earlier evangelical efforts rested on a set of more rudimentary assumptions. Of central importance was the tenet of universal grace: any man capable of recognizing his sinfulness was open to salvation through the blood of Christ. But the mission to the natives, the reclamation of a world "lost to the Church for centuries" (Whiteside 1906:30), also had less altruistic motivation. As Thompson (1963:365) has recorded, Wesley stressed "faith" above "good works" in the attainment of grace, and the most effective demonstration of faith was "the attempt to reproduce the convulsions of conversion." Thus the first evangelists to work among the Tswana peoples expressed their joy at the challenge the natives presented:

> the hitherto unknown and unpenetrated domains of paganism are unfolding before us; regions where Satan has his seat and riots in cruelty and bloodshed. . . . However imperfect and mixed the motive of the heathen may be, they welcome [the missionaries] to commence their labors. In this we again see the preparing and directive hand of God (Broadbent 1865:176).

We saw earlier how the circumstances of initial contact with the Barolong reinforced the mission expectation of "riotous" paganism. But this is a statement of righteous imperial charter; a legitimation to engage, in this moral wilderness, in the sort of social reformation expressly forbidden by Methodism in its own context. As long as Satan reigned, comprehensive social intervention in the cause of "civilization" was the divine duty of the enlightened.[3]

The ideology contained in the writings of these missionaries is predicated upon a set of oppositions which gave form to the evangelical charter that justified spiritual colonialism. Thus Satan contrasted with Providence as did "darkness" to "light," "riot" to "order," "wilderness" to "civilization," and "death" to "life." In summarizing the progress of the early mission to the Barolong, Broadbent (1865:179) states:

> the people [display] all the essential elements of a Christian community; in an infant state, I allow, but a spiritual church against which the gates of hell shall not prevail, raised up among a people who not long ago sat in darkness, and the shadow of death, and in a land of war and bloodshed, where they knew not the way of peace.

He continues (p. 204): "In fact, the incipient civilization begun is on the spread, as seen in improved habits, decent and comfortable dwellings, gardens and cultivated lands, so that the wilderness literally become [sic] a fruitful field . . ." Where Satan prevailed, the law of nature had been corrupted, and civilization—discernible in the social vision of the European bourgeoisie—had first to be established before human beings could set good apart from evil and work for their own salvation. The uncivilized were as unruly children in the moral world, in need of paternalistic discipline: "[the natives] must in many respects, for their own good, be treated like children. To benefit them, there was a time to give, and there was a time to withhold, a time kindly to say Yes, and a time firmly to say No" (Edwards 1883:63). The dark heathen, like the sinner in the civilized world, had first to be furnished with the "talents" necessary for industrious self-construction, to learn that uncomplaining service in this world brought life eternal in the next. He had, in other words, to realize himself as the subject of relations of production and exchange in the capitalist marketplace—to find his image in the universalist symbolic media that permitted his integration into a global economy of matter and spirit.

The Conjuncture of Tshidi and Methodist Forms

The Methodist missionaries made first contact with the Barolong in terms of those universal gestures of social intent, prestation and exchange. Like other Europeans in the native heartland, they presented small gifts to the "chiefs," tokens to "gain their regard, and so open the way to further intercourse" (Broadbent 1865:108). By then, regular exchange relations had been established between itinerant white traders and peoples of the interior, such transactions being governed by an explicit hierarchy of values, in which guns and ammunition occupied prime place (Burchell 1953, vol. 2:267, 288). Already by the time of *defikane,* the southern Tswana had developed a keen awareness of the utility of firearms, and those skilled in their use—as were the missionaries—had become scarce resources.[4] In fact, experience soon reinforced the view that the presence of evangelists was an effective deterrent against marauding attack (Broadbent 1865:128–29). For their part, the Methodists were eager to demonstrate goodwill, and signaled their readiness to provide material goods and practical assistance. Not surprisingly, the Barolong classed them with the other white visitors they had known; as motivated primarily by material considerations.

Well before the arrival of the missionaries, the term *lekgoa* (pl., *makgoa*) had come to be applied by the southern Tswana to white men (Burchell 1953, vol. 2:312). Nouns of this class (sing. prefix, *le;* pl., *ma*) characteristically denote animals, plants, and natural features of the world, as well as persons of demeaned, subsocial status (*legodu:* "thief"; *lerolo:* "simpleton"; *lesetlha:* a Griqua). *Kgoa,* moreover, is a tick or a bush louse most commonly found on the hindquarters of domestic animals (Brown 1931:125). Burchell records the fuller term *makgoa ma shweu,* which refers to a "white bush louse," this possibly being evocative of the fact that white men were usually first seen approaching on horseback (i.e., fastened to the body of the animal), a mode of locomotion foreign to indigenous peoples.

Like all other white visitors, the evangelists were *makgoa,* strange and extrasocial beings associated with the distant colony to the south, from which travelers and their material trappings were known to come. This alien status was reinforced once it became understood that they were the "emissaries of God" (*modimo*); all the mission agencies among the Sotho-Tswana used the term for the indigenous supreme being to denote the Protestant deity. But the Tswana construct conveyed the sense of an otiose power residing on the margins of the apprehended universe, a remote spiritual force far removed from the paternalistic God of the church. Nonetheless, the concept of *modimo* was to provide these missionaries with an apparent point of contact between their own cultural scheme and that of the natives; it seemed proof of the divinity inherent in all humankind (Broadbent 1865:81; Moffat 1842:180). But the real conceptual discrepancy was, and remained, wider than the Methodists ever really perceived; for the overlap was in fact a serendipitous convergence of signs, whose superficial similarity belied the fact that they derived their meanings from their respective positions in two very different symbolic systems. Broadbent's attempts to explain the Protestant deity to the chief of the Seleka Barolong illustrate the breadth of this epistemological gap. The chief asked, "Where is God? How big is he? Does he have hair?" The missionary commented (1865:177) despairingly: "I have never felt more forcibly the difficulty of conveying spiritual ideas to the heathen, arising from their carnal view of spiritual things." Indeed, the nondualistic cosmology of the native was taken as proof of his inability to transcend base confinement in the flesh.

If the obstacles to spiritual conversion appeared formidable at first, the parallel effort to disseminate the practical trappings of "civilization" was to yield more tangible results. Although the Methodist notion of labor was shaped by the circumstances of industrial production, its underlying commitment to rational self-construction was held to be universally applicable. But its pragmatic imagery required translation for the African context. Indeed, agrarian metaphors came to pervade the evangelists' vision of a Christianized Africa: it was a "wilderness" to be turned into a "fruitful field." In England itself, the Wesleyan doctrine was not strongly represented in the countryside (Hobsbawm 1957), the emergent urban industrial sector being its real stronghold; but the now anachronistic rural peasantry provided an appropriate model for preindustrial societies elsewhere. Noncoincidentally, several of the first generation of missionaries were themselves from rural backgrounds (Edwards 1883:2), the children of farmers being regarded as particularly well-equipped to labor among peoples living off the land. In fact, the Protestant initiative among the Tswana was founded on a notion of civilization that came to celebrate peasant production in biblical clothing:

> In order to complete the work of elevating the people, we must teach them
> the arts of civilized life, if we exhort them to lay aside the sword for the

ploughshare and the spear for the pruning hook, we must prepare them to use the one with the same dexterity which they exhibit in wielding the other. If they are no longer to start upon marauding expedition, if they are not to depend upon the precarious results of the chase, then we must teach them to till their own land, sow and reap their own crops, build their own barns, as well tend their flocks (Mackenzie 4/19/1858 [in Dachs 1975:72]).

It was in the sphere of agrarian production that the missionaries to the Barolong were to make their most influential innovation. No sooner had the first station been established among the Seleka than the missionaries set to work as living embodiments of the Protestant doctrine of useful toil. They began to lay out fields and to address the most palpable limitation upon local farming—the uncertainty of rainfall—by digging simple wells for domestic and agricultural use (Broadbent 1865:96). Highlighted by the fact that the previous year had been one of drought, the ability to draw water from beneath the ground impressed the Barolong; it was taken as a sign of unusual power, and the activity soon found many willing helpers. But the wells sparked off one of the first conflicts between the evangelists and the chiefship. The Seleka officeholder, Sefunelo, resented the new influence wielded by the outsiders over so symbolically charged a resource (Broadbent 1865:102). After all, the capacity to make rain was a highly valued component of indigenous authority; as the physical and spiritual embodiment of the nation, an effective ruler controlled its fertility, which was epitomized, when the social world was in an auspicious state of balance, by timely showers. It will be recalled too that the issue of rainmaking was a significant aspect of the competitive politics surrounding the chiefship.

The missionaries were soon to be made aware of the political implications of the control over water. For them, too, rainmaking took on symbolic significance, and became an index not merely of ritual power but also of religious authority. For the value accorded to rainmaking rites by the chiefship served as a prime instance of "superstition" or, worse, of "vile imposture" (Broadbent 1865:102). That this should be the case is hardly surprising: these rites conflated categories set apart in Western thought—instrumental from symbolic action, the "political" from the "religious"—and were taken as clear evidence of the mental chaos of the savage (Broadbent 1865:178). The decline of the rites thus became a crucial marker of mission success. Reports from the Barolong field regularly noted with pride that the "public interest" in rainmaking was decreasing (Broadbent 1865:102, 182)—notwithstanding the fact that historical sources suggest that the rites remained closely tied to the chiefship and persisted, albeit unevenly, as long as the office retained substantive spiritual and temporal power (Schapera 1971[a]:24). Their eventual demise, in other words, was a function of the more general effect upon Tshidi culture of articulation with a colonial system. However, the incident concerning the wells was an early sign of a developing awareness on the part of both parties that there was a more thoroughgoing conflict between the mission project and the indigenous sociocultural order.

Cultural Transformation
Space, Time, and Literacy

I return below to the effect of the mission on Tshidi productive practice, because it was to induce profound transformations. But first it is necessary to examine the early conjuncture of symbolic forms. As we have seen, the circumstances of initial confrontation confirmed missionary expectations of the state of Satanic savagery. The records make it clear that the historically specific upheavals in central South Africa, attendant upon the rise of the Zulu state, were perceived as the characteristic "anarchy and misery" of peoples living in spiritual darkness (Broadbent 1865:203). Theirs was a condition of moral chaos:

> *They had no marriage,* nor any proper domestic order, nor acknowledged any moral obligation to the duties arising out of that relation. Females were exchanged for others, bartered for cattle, given as presents, and often discarded by the mere caprice of the men. . . . The absence of the proper domestic affections, and unnatural treatment of children . . . has been in part stated. . . . Yet the Divine institution has been introduced (Broadbent 1865:204; emphasis in original).

In terms of the categories of mission culture—the nuclear family as the basis of a private family estate, marriage as a sacralized union between consenting individuals—the Barolong lived in a sociomoral vacuum. The nuclear unit, the "atom of structure" in industrial capitalist society, was sanctified as the "holy family" of the Christian cosmos; moral duty enjoined its reproduction through rationalized, complementary productivity of husband and wife. Such forms found no counterpart in either the polygynous or the monogamous Tswana household; there, marriage was a multistranded alliance between domestic *groups* and the essential unit of production was the uterine house, which was linked to others in a cooperative matrilateral network. The house was also part of a compound household, itself incorporated in an agnatic segment. Under these conditions, relations of production, property-holding, and parenting were not easily identifiable in terms of reified Western categories. Indeed, close kin ties among the Tswana were frequently ambiguous, and individual identity and normative expectation existed in a complex relation with each other. Given the discrepancy between the two cultural systems and the binary logic of the mission view, it is to be expected that Barolong social arrangements would be adjudged "unnatural" and "chaotic."

To the Protestant evangelists, then, the need to make the natives conform to a European bourgeois model of "natural" order appeared as the essential prerequisite of conversion. They began the attempt at reform with the more tangible breaches of that moral order—polygyny and bridewealth (Broadbent 1865:85). But their ethnocentric model implied a holistic sociocultural scheme and they were soon to realize the impossibility of a piecemeal reconstruction of institutions that were securely embedded in a total system. Nonetheless, would-be converts had, in their probationary period, to commit themselves to monogamy and minimal literacy; only after a period of sustained instruction were they examined as candidates for baptism.

Of course, the challenge that the missionaries posed was not limited to explicit efforts to persuade the Tswana of their theological cause. In addition to their early demonstration of productive techniques, they applied themselves diligently to acquiring Setswana; and, with the assistance of Moffat's biblical translations, they soon began systematic instruction in literacy. But, most generally, the very organization of the church itself conveyed an implicit symbolic scheme and an ideological message. The structure of the mission faithfully reproduced the system devised by Wesley himself; the local "societies" were constituted as voluntary associations, subsumed under district- and national-level administration. Members were issued with "tickets," whose renewal on a quarterly basis was subject to an assessment of moral standing; close supervision of spiritual commitment had been the essence of the "method" of the parent church (Broadbent 1865:179). These arrangements coexisted with a routine of everyday practice which reproduced the order of space-time relations identified with Methodism at large, and with the more general Protestant tradition. The mission church set the potential Christian on the path to redemption, objectifying his career as the focus of long-term planning and the rational accumulation of value. Time, in this vision, was a unitized resource to be seized and "put to work"; for man's duty, as Thompson (1967:95) notes in the words of Watts, was to "improve each shining hour." As this suggests, the timetables and calendar of the church served to differentiate and classify what, in the Tshidi cosmos, was a continuous flow of events and a cycle of seasons. To the religious schedule of the Sunday service, weekly classes, quarterly communion, and annual feasts, they soon added the secular routine of the British schoolroom. Tickets, registers, and ledgers plotted the progress of each participant. The printing press produced vernacular religious tracts, introducing the written word, the list, the two-dimensional page, and the sequence of the text (Goody 1977:103ff.). The prayer book tabulated the fixed order of the divine service, and the hymnal a repertoire of songs of praise. Moreover, the content conveyed by the biblical passages contained an explicit notion of cumulative moral development and also of linear history, both personal and collective.

As Thompson (1967) has argued, the impersonal clock is the fundamental instrument for internalizing the organization of work essential to industrial capitalist production. If labor is to be reducible to a compensation independent of the value it generates, then time becomes its irreducible measure; for time itself is then equatable with money, and provides the yardstick "fair wage." During the process of proletarianization, the impartial clock prizes labor free from its embeddedness in undifferentiated social practice, setting apart "work" from "leisure," and masking the unrequited surplus value transferred from the wage earner to his employer. The Tshidi were to experience its regimen once they entered the industrial sector; and they were to be judged, like neophyte proletarians elsewhere, as inherently undisciplined and incapable of punctuality (Weber 1958:63, 67; Thompson 1967). As we shall see, their response to this experience included the ritualized attempt to reformulate the temporal logic of the workplace. But their first introduction to the commoditization of time came in the schedules and routines of the mission.

The temporal order of the church also implied a set of spatial coordinates. Just as the schedules of worship and instruction were printed out on the two-dimensional page, so the institutional timetables of religious and secular activities were legible in the architecture of the mission in the Tswana landscape. The early stations were set apart on their own plots of land, a measured distance from what one evangelist described as "a heap of Bechuana huts jostled together without any apparent order" (Cameron, in Broadbent 1865:189). As the event history showed, however, the location of the mission became increasingly central within the settlement; and it did so in proportion to its growing role within the expanding Barolong universe. Within the mission's confines, the distribution and design of buildings expressed the division between the sacred and the secular, the public and the private. Distinct units for schooling, printing, and agricultural activity (Broadbent 1865:189) reflected the differentiated domains of the civilizing project, each deemed appropriate to a particular segment of the face of the clock (cf. Moffat 1842:339).

Mission buildings were all four-sided boxes into which other boxlike shapes could be fit with rational efficiency. The contrast between these square freestanding forms and the concentric structures of Tswana domestic architecture was to become a symbolic focus in the confrontation between the two cultural systems, typifying, in the Tshidi imagination, the distinction between sekgoa (the way of the white man) and setswana (Tswana tradition). I have dealt in some detail with the significance of the circle and the arc in the precolonial context. For the modern Tshidi, the act of encirclement still implies encompassed cultural control; the stereotyped government townships comprising square houses on rectangular plots convey to them a sense of calculated regimentation and exposure. Indeed, as the mission had done in its time, the South African regime was to attempt to "rationalize" African community structures by imposing upon them the geometric grid of civilization. Goody (1977:148ff.) has suggested that alphabetic literacy has encouraged such conceptual formalizations as the list, the table, and the matrix. Certainly, the four-sided figure is the key shape in the spatiovisual construction of the West, from the nave of the medieval church, the page of the book, the market square, to the enclosed field, the shop floor, and the modular blocks of modern urban built form. The nineteenth-century evangelists placed pressure on their converts to construct "civilized" and neat houses—square structures on fenced sites, the visible icons of propertied individualism. For the "undifferentiated heaps" of Tswana homesteads connoted the irrational shapes of "primitive communism."

The fact that much of the mission culture was communicated in written form had an important impact on indigenous consciousness, just as literacy was to have a transformative effect upon the Tshidi social system at large. The Bible was the embodiment of divine truth in the Protestant tradition, and the spiritual liberalism of Methodism required that each convert should have independent access to it. Thus the evangelists devoted considerable energy to the translation and printing of texts in Setswana and Dutch and, by 1830, were teaching some two hundred scholars on a regular basis (Broadbent 1865:175). Although systematic instruction was interrupted at several points during the nineteenth century, the spread of literacy was sustained, accentuating emergent patterns of social differentiation and the rise of a salariat within the community. For, as Goody and others have stressed, writing is not merely a utilitarian medium of communication; it is a mode of practice which implies specific relations of production and particular conceptual formalizations (1977:46). In South Africa, the colonial process was mediated by bureaucratic forms, making local peoples dependent upon those who had the necessary skills; the printed word was to assume great symbolic importance for illiterate Tshidi workers, who later sought to regain command over an estranged world through the iconic manipulation of letters and newsprint.

Perhaps the most palpable effect of literacy is that it transforms the consciousness of those who acquire it, setting it off, in unprecedented ways, from the worldview of their illiterate fellows. As I have pointed out, both literacy and monetization generate an awareness of the process of abstraction and a concern with knowledge and value as explicit systems beyond the immediate contexts that generate them. That such an awareness developed, over time, among Tshidi is indicated by their increasing elaboration of a series of objective constructs, such as *tumelo*— "faith," literally "collective consensus" (from *dumela*, "to agree")—to describe coherent bodies of knowledge. The effects of commoditization

were also patent: a visitor to Mafeking in 1873 remarked of its inhabitants that they had "learnt the value of English money" (Holub 1881,
vol. 1:121). Moreover, as shown by the writings of S. M. Molema in the
next generation, there developed among the literate a reflective concern
with the process of cultural evolution itself. He states:

> Superstitition and witchcraft were, perhaps, the two greatest curses among
> the Bantu, and so universal and deep-rooted were they that their death has
> been necessarily slow and hard, so that to this very day many, even those
> who pretend to enlightenment and Christianity, do not cast a shadow of
> doubt on the reality of witchcraft . . . (1920:170).

A notion of metaphoric form has also emerged for some: a Tshidi Methodist minister with whom I discussed the matter of church ritual in 1969
remarked to me, in English, that the majority of orthodox Tswana Protestants "understood the Eucharist in magical rather than symbolic
terms."

Such evidence would suggest that, among the educated elite, cultural
articulation has generated a reflective concern with the objectivity and
systematicity of their own emergent symbolic scheme. For, as Goody
(1980:131) notes, literacy "takes language out of immediate referential
context," appearing to drive a wedge between the "word" and the
"world." In the same way as money and time permit the detachment of
value and productivity from their total context, so written words—impersonal, functionally specific, and seemingly transparent—permit the
reification of speech and knowledge.[5] Like money, too, written words
circulate at a new level of abstraction; they are not embedded in the holistic social fabric. Indeed, literacy and commoditization reinforce each
other under conditions of colonial conjuncture, constituting an order of
seemingly rationalized signals which replace the polysemic signs of the
indigenous cosmos.

Nevertheless, it is important not to overestimate the reifying effects of
literacy and monetization upon the Tshidi; their influence has been great,
but they have not induced an evolutionary passage from "magical" to
"rational" thinking, or a "shift from signs to concepts" (Goody
1977:150). I have already noted the fallacy of assuming that Western consciousness is itself depersonalized in any simple sense, or that the role
within it of polysemic signs is rationally delimited; neither can we assume that its cultural forms are the inevitable terminus of all peoples
incorporated by the world system, unless we are to deny to such peoples
any powers of sociocultural determination. As I argue here, Tshidi transformations must be understood as the outcome of a reciprocally determining interaction of local and global forces whose logic must first be
comprehended in its own terms. Thus, while the literate elite may be

understood from within the modern Tshidi system as symbolically identified with *sekgoa,* the orientation of its members is the product of a specific articulation of local and colonial forms. This is exemplified in the substance of the construct of "faith," *tumelo,* which objectifies for the Tshidi the defining feature of Protestantism but overlays its sense of subjective commitment with one of collectively derived consensus, such as characterized precolonial sociopolitical relations.

In contrast to the elite, the less educated rank and file have opted for a more radical solution to the conflicting implications of the colonial and postcolonial worlds, although it is a solution that necessarily addresses the same discourse and deploys the same signs—if only to seek to revalue them. In order to analyze these cultural transformations over the longer term, and to account for their various refractions among the Tshidi, it is necessary to return to the politico-economic context of the colonial process itself.

Technological Innovation and Structural Change

The introduction, by the mission, of the plow, simple irrigation devices, and high-yielding crops precipitated the most significant transformations within the precolonial system and fostered articulation with the colonial political economy. These technological innovations occurred in a broader context, however. During the nineteenth century, Tshidi participation in regional trade networks expanded significantly and became more exclusively channeled through merchants based in the Cape Colony. This trade was increasingly monopolized by the chiefs, who attempted to extend the scope of centralized institutions and extractive mechanisms. Thus control over such products of the wild as ivory and skins was carefully husbanded by officeholders; these products were exchanged for guns with which to equip yet more client hunters (Burchell 1953, vol. 2:285; Parsons 1977:118). Lower-order headmen were bypassed in the process, and mission mediators served to reinforce this by insisting that all commerce should pass through the chiefs, not through their "vassals" (Mackenzie 1887, vol. 1:263). The political effects of regional trade—its intensification of inequalities—were to be both magnified and modified with the commoditization of agriculture and the growth of the market. For despite the importation of an agrarian technology designed for commercial farming, monetized distributive mechanisms did not yet exist; their penetration, in due course, was to make peasants of the southern Tswana.

The plow was an essential element, at once practical and ideological, in the Methodist model of peasant production, and was adopted quite widely among the southern Tswana peoples between the 1830s and 1950s (Kinsman n.d.[b]:1). Its first systematic use among the Tshidi was in

Mafikeng after 1857, where the settled and relatively properous Christian
population employed rudimentary irrigation methods and grew "European cereals" such as maize (Holub 1881, vol. 1:278, 339). As elsewhere
in southern Africa (Ranger 1978:109), such technological innovations
had a thoroughgoing impact upon the mode of production. The plow
made possible more effective (short-term) exploitation of rainfall and
soils and, along with irrigation and higher-quality seed, provided significantly greater surpluses on larger acreages (cf. Parsons 1977:123); it also
required the use of animals for draft and this, in turn, led to the intersection of the formerly discrete agricultural and pastoral sectors. For
Tswana sociocultural arrangements precluded the management of cattle
by women and, therefore, disqualified them from plow cultivation; in
the upshot, the latter, at least in its dominant technical aspect, became a
male pursuit. Indeed, not only did men participate in this previously
female domain, they also assumed direct control over it (Holub 1881,
vol. 1:339; Kinsman n.d.[b]:1). As this suggests, the logic of pastoralism
came to be imposed on arable production, the greater inequalities of the
first overriding the more egalitarian character of the second. Of course,
only men with access to a team of draft animals could plow at all, and the
value of cattle clientship took on new significance. Women, for their
part, were relegated to the devalued tasks of tending and reaping
(Kinsman n.d.[b]:2; Crisp 1896) and appear to have lost their influence
over the disposition of the agricultural product, which became disengaged from its embeddedness in matrilateral ties of domestic nurture. In
fact, when produce markets arose, it became necessary for some Tswana
chiefs to control the proportion of grain sold to forestall domestic hunger
(Schapera 1943:203).

Given the organization of productive relations, and the entailment of
the sexual division of labor in articulating the political center and the
domestic periphery, these shifts were of considerable structural moment.
The increased value of agriculture drew men from their former pursuits,
thereby narrowing the general economic base at the expense of hunting,
regional trade, and manufacture (Ranger 1978:116). It thus exacerbated
the deep-seated systemic tension between the centralized interests of the
chiefship and the centrifugal pull of household production.

These transformations were more fully realized, however, with the
interaction between the Tshidi and the expanding colonial economy. The
development of the diamond fields, as well as the market for foodstuffs
among the Boers in the Transvaal (Holub 1881, vol. 2:22), set up a steady
demand for southern Tswana produce. The enlarged surpluses of Tshidi
agriculture were soon directed to these markets, via the mediating offices
of merchants (Holub 1881, vol. 1:242; vol. 2:7; Kinsman n.d.[b]:1); thus
Holub observed, in 1873, that increasing numbers of Barolong were par-

ticipating in monetized transactions (1881, vol. 2:13), involving a range of everyday Western commodities. Among the Tlhaping to the south, Moffat had arranged for a resident colonial merchant to supply textiles, so that the people might satisfy the mission insistence upon modesty in attire (1842:605). Among Christian Tshidi, likewise, Protestant dress codes ensured a flourishing trade in fabrics from the northern English strongholds whence the evangelists themselves had come. The further extension of British interests into what were to become the Rhodesias, brought heavy traffic to the "road to the north," providing a greatly expanded produce market for the Tswana people living along it (Molema 1966:173; Parsons 1977:123). By this time, the Tshidi had begun to favor cash crops ahead of food, and grew increasing quantities of maize and wheat (Holub 1881, vol. 1:121; Mackenzie 1879, as quoted by Kinsman n.d.[b]:2). These crops required more intensive cultivation, but permitted a second planting each year. Christian observers noted that the prohibition in Mafikeng of the sale of liquor, motivated by Methodist notions of sobriety, greatly enhanced the relative productivity of the Tshidi in relation to other southern Tswana (Holub 1881, vol. 1:278).

It is to be stressed, however, that the construction of a peasantry in this context is inadequately perceived as a mere "response" to the extension of international capital through the colonial system. As Ranger (1978:110) has noted, the data indicate that surpluses of varying magnitude had long been generated in the precolonial southern African polities in reaction both to internal and external modes of extraction. These surpluses, in other words, may have been enlarged and redirected by exogenous mercantile interests, but they were not created by them in the first place. Moreover, regular production for the market by some Tshidi was soon entailed in the proletarianization of others, for both sectors were encompassed in the conjuncture of the indigenous and colonial systems. Thus, at the local level, changing relations of production led to a process of "enfeudalization," and to the movement of relatively disadvantaged sectors of the population into the expanding labor market; but, at the more global level, the effects of progressive underdevelopment, which prevented the migrant labor force from reproducing itself by wages alone, kept workers dependent upon the produce of the land (cf. Foster-Carter 1978).

Let us examine the process more closely from the local perspective. Technological and ideological innovation was spearheaded by the Christian community in Mafikeng; but, once this settlement had become the Tshidi capital, and the worst frontier disputes had abated, relations of production among the entire population were restructured. Of most general significance, in this respect, was the involvement of men in agriculture. However, such changes in the division of labor were mediated by established internal politico-economic forms. For not all men were equally able to avail themselves of the plow and the market, and the control executed by royals and their clients over the cattle economy and the allocation of land took on new significance in light of growing scarcity: settler encroachment had depleted southern Tswana holdings, especially near surface water (Ludorf M.M.S. Box XVII, Lotlakane 3/1/1852; Motito 10/16/1852), and expanding production was putting new pressure on arable resources (Holub 1881, vol. 2:22). Mackenzie, both a missionary and a mediator for the imperial government, noted in 1878 that everywhere in the region there had arisen "a farming class, men who had led out the water of some fountain, and who annually raised a few muids of wheat as well as the usual kaffir-corn and mealies [maize]. . . . many of the farmers have been possessors of considerable property" (In Dachs 1975:110). Mackenzie also notes the "inveterate desire" of ambitious men to "collect power over weaker people than themselves and make them vassals." And Kinsman (n.d.[b]:1) points to evidence from the period shortly after the opening of the diamond fields, suggesting that "roughly two-thirds" of the formerly independent townsmen had become "clients" on fiefdoms under "aristocratic" control, which produced for the market. This evidence points to radical change in indigenous tenurial arrangements, and growing inequalities in access to the means of production. Prior to the colonial era, clientship among the Tswana had been restricted to the sphere of pastoralism and hunting; all adult men had usufruct rights in land, and no form of ground rent existed. Now scarcity of good arable and the inability of some to plow at all in their own right ushered in a variety of formerly nonexistent feudal arrangements.

These transformations, however, had a contradictory impact on the Tshidi political economy. On the one hand, as male agricultural participation increased, the politico-ritual mechanisms which reproduced the values of allegiance to the center were being undermined; thus, even before the establishment of the British protectorate over the southern Tswana there was a general weakening of chiefly control and a scattering of formerly concentrated populations (Holub 1881, vol. 1:250; Dachs 1972). On the other hand, the evidence also indicates a simultaneous extension of royal dominance in productive relations, as ruling cadres privatized the benefits of office and extended their own arable holdings at the expense of others (Kinsman n.d.[b]:22, n. 1). The chiefs retained such privileges as the right to exact tributary labor and to control seasonal activities, practices which later became the focus of an explicit confrontation between the interests of center and periphery (cf. J. L. Comaroff 1982:155f.). At this time, too, an increasing number of southern Tswana were moving into the labor market, both that of the diamond fields

(Mackenzie 1871:521; Holub 1881, vol. 1:294) and of the Boer farms in the Transvaal.[6]

Much of the source material concerning the southern Tswana peoples during this time is based upon observation of the Batlhaping.[7] Detailed accounts of relations of production among the Tshidi do not really exist prior to annexation, when tribal and government records suggest that very similar processes of transformation had been occurring in Mafikeng. For all the chiefdoms of the region, however, the documentary record establishes that incorporation into the colonial state coincided with both a cattle pandemic and a protracted drought; this, together with heightened Boer competition in the produce market, induced extensive proletarianization, thereby putting paid to a self-contained Tshidi peasantry. Henceforth, the vast majority of the population was to be dependent upon wage labor, for economic recovery was to remain limited under conditions of progressive erosion and centrally engineered underdevelopment. Neither wage labor nor subsistence farming was capable, on its own, of supporting the rural domestic units; indeed, the articulation of the two underlies both the structural basis of the modern community and its cultural response to the labor market.

Before examining this response, I shall conclude the analysis of articulation by returning from the level of structural transformation to that of cultural mediation, to the role of consciousness and agency in the historical processes that preceded overrule.

Consciousness and Agency

The actors in the colonial encounter made its history in a manner that was constrained not only by their relative structural positions but also by their respective cultural orders. The interaction of discrete formations that follows an initial conjuncture dramatizes discrepancies and conflicts between them; it also provides contrasts that make participants aware of formal aspects of their own world previously below the level of consciousness. Thus, in the Tshidi case, confrontation with the mission engendered recognition both of *setswana* as a system and of the tensions inherent in the indigenous political economy. A similar process of objectification occurred for the evangelists, since work in the southern African field crystallized the discontinuities within Methodism between spiritual activism and political quiescence. Moreover, the role they had come to assume in the field of precolonial relations also made them cognizant of, and gave impetus to, the stakes of the church in the politics of imperialism.

In such colonial encounters, however, the interaction between formerly distinct systems is not merely one of contrast but of contradiction;

the confrontation occurs within a global order of relations, in which the respective parties wield unequal powers of control and determination. Thus the Protestant mission, armed with a universalist moral charter, entered South Africa with European technical resources and the ultimate political backing of the British Empire. Its objectives, like that of the embracing colonial venture itself, stood in direct opposition to the struggle for self-determination and viable independence on the part of indigenous preindustrial peoples. Articulation, therefore, involved domination and resistance, the imposition of hegemony and the evolution of protest. But it was a lengthy and complex process. As the event history showed, the initial attempt by the Methodists to project the ideology of the church was unsuccessful. On the other hand, their technical innovations were compelling from the start, and presented an implicit threat to the indigenous sociocultural system, which was quickly perceived by its rulers. More sustained coresidence with the mission between 1822 and 1851 induced certain individuals to identify with the symbolic and practical resources it offered. The church flowed into the cracks of the existing structure: the earliest converts—junior royals, poor men, and women in general—were those who, in one way or another, were marginal in terms of indigenous social categories and authority relations. For them, Christianity promised a novel source of influence and control; the mission was a tangible embodiment of force—guns, water, the plow, the written word, and the underlying power that animated them—which professed its availability to all who would "believe." It also offered a positive social identity: within it, structural marginality was redefined as membership in the society of the saved. Hence a new set of categories came to give voice to implicit conflicts in the existing Tshidi world, this being especially evident in the emergent opposition between "tradition" and "true believers," a contrast that objectified antagonisms surrounding the access to political office. The conversion of the chief's junior brother, Molema, crystallized this opposition as one between conservative ascription, personified by the chief and his allies, and a liberal individualist ideal of achievement, represented by the converts. The Christian royals and their supporters were henceforth to challenge the "traditionalist" ruling line on the grounds that education and proven ability were the rational basis for chiefly selection. This was countered by the accusation that the educated elite sided with *sekgoa* against *setswana*.

The presence of the mission was also to give expression to tensions in the indigenous relationship between the chiefship and the populace. In the British context, as noted above, the contradiction within Methodism between authoritarianism and democracy was resolved, in part, by the dichotomization of church and state. But this same Methodist order had rather different implications in relation to precolonial African systems, where the entailment of the "religious" and the "political" permitted no simple division and where the evangelical pursuit of personal salvation ran counter to the undifferentiated forms of the collectivity. At the outset, the missionaries to the Tshidi had no choice but to work through extant politico-economic structures; thus their first efforts were directed against "uncivilized domestic arrangements." Later, at the collective level, they focused their challenge on communal rites which, to them, were a graphic instance of nefarious political coercion, exercised by the chiefship on the moral freedom of the individual. But their opposition to rainmaking, initiation, and firstfruit ceremonies brought them into direct confrontation with officeholders over the issue of spiritual power. Public ritual performances became the arena of contest, symbolically as significant to the evangelists as to the rulers themselves. In fact, collective dance and song were especially offensive to the Christians. Broadbent (1865:187) noted: "I feel happy also in saying, that the Bechuana customs and ceremonies are considerably on the wane. The native dance is, in some instances, kept up; but I frequently go at the time of the dance, oppose it, and preach to those who are willing to hear." If collective rites in general offended the Protestant sense of the religious, seeming to celebrate mindless superstition in the place of individual contemplation, then dancing was particularly distasteful. In its obvious "salacious" Tswana form, it conflated body and spirit, and proclaimed an ascendancy of the flesh that was inimical to the Puritan temperament. Activity of this sort was also a dramatization of the vitality of the system it represented; early visitors to Tswana communities were struck by the energy, duration, and obvious ritual salience of these performances (Burchell 1953, vol. 2:291; Campbell 1822, vol. 1:84). It will be recalled that the Tswana term for dance (*go bina*) also implies to "venerate," and *dipina* (songs, dances) had the power to motivate social and symbolic transformations. For the missionaries, not unexpectedly, they epitomized Satanic animation; it was the withdrawal from such communal activities that marked the first popular opposition to the chiefship by Tshidi converts. Of course, the rites were at the heart of chiefly power, so that the refusal to take part in them in the name of "religious freedom" was perceived as a direct affront to central authority. The ruler countered this with a response that likewise challenged the logic of his Christian opponents: participation in public ritual was to be the price of religious freedom itself.

As the process of articulation proceeded, the fundamentally contradictory implications of the two systems took more explicit form in the consciousness of the participants. The Protestant faction coalesced, welding the various bases of individual marginality—junior rank, poverty, and gender—into a unitary identity, at least for a while. At the same time as relations between the church and the chiefs were becoming more overtly

concerned with power, missionary mediation between the local polity
and the imperial government moved into an explicitly political phase;
where earlier evangelists had protested the utilitarian intent of African
rulers who had attempted to use them as brokers, they now espoused
their role in eliciting British protection as a moral duty. This was entirely
consistent with their contemporary goals and interests, namely, the formation of a stable social order within which "civilized" self-realization
for Christian converts would be possible. Mackenzie's statement of the
need to break "the communistic relations" among "tribesmen" so as to
permit the growth of "healthy, individualistic competition" expressed
this vision with clarity. As he himself put it:

> We must teach them to till their own land, sow and reap their own crops,
> build their own barns as well as tend their own flocks. Nor is the mission-
> ary in Africa content even when all this is accomplished. He longs to see
> the African united as friends, interwoven with the general brotherhood of
> the race. He desires to behold the African ship weighted with the produce
> of African soil and the results of African industry, mingling on the great
> ocean with ships of other lands, and returning home laden with the varied
> treasures of commerce. (In Dachs 1975:72)

The imperial pursuits of the missionaries were dictated by the logic
inherent in their project from the start—even if their recognition of the
appropriateness of colonization per se to their goals evolved only in their
interaction with indigenous peoples and other would-be colonists in
South Africa. This does not, of course, imply that they were mere "colonial agents" (Asad 1973), a view which does not discriminate between
intended and unintended outcomes or distinguish subtle motives from
structural effects. Conversely, apologetics on behalf of the humanitarian
motives of the mission fail to bring such values into any historical relation with their practical implications (Wilson 1976). Dachs, who has attempted to trace the development of "missionary imperialism" among
the Tswana, concludes that it was engendered by the experience of "the
resilience of Tswana resistance," the product of the "secular" role that
the chiefs "chose to allocate" to the evangelists (1976:657ff.). But this
answer also simplifies the problem, since it does not place the encounter
in its total historical context. Thus the position allotted to the missionary
by local rulers was the product of the "structure of the conjuncture"
itself (Sahlins 1981:33), a conjuncture which could not but define them in
terms that they perceived to be "utilitarian" and "secular." This encounter occurred within the wider precolonial field, which, in its impact upon
local sociocultural systems, created the structural niche filled by the missionaries. And, while the chiefs clearly did attempt to limit the internal
threat of Christianity, their dependence upon its agents in the field of
external relations kept the latter at the heart of the polity, where their

general cultural impact—not neatly separable, in any case, into the "religious" and the "secular"—continued to be felt. The issue of Tswana resistance is also more subtle; as the Tshidi case shows, communities varied in their response along indigenous fault lines. While the majority initially resisted the mission along with the chief, a minority resisted the chief along with the mission. Although these local rulers were indeed opposed to formal conversion, the increasingly global threat of subjugation caused them to embrace the evangelists as political allies to a greater extent than they might otherwise have wished or deemed prudent.

Similarly, while the model of civilization inherent in Protestant evangelization was the product of its own social history, the vision of the missionaries was mediated in complex ways by their field experience and by South African political conditions. For example, it was only once they had been successful in making converts that the limitations of Christian self-realization *within* the centralized structures of Tswana chiefdoms became clear (Moffat 1842:242ff.; Broadbent 1865:203; Dachs 1975:14); and this occasioned a shift in objectives, pointing, as it did, to the appropriateness of formal colonization. In any case, by that stage it was not so much a matter of whether there would be overrule but of which imperial power would assume control; it was here that the model of the Christian peasantry held by the Protestant mission was to encourage its activists to oppose the annexation of the Tswana to the Boer Republic or the Cape Colony. For the cynically unambiguous proletarian fate envisaged for rural communities within the South African state appeared to preclude the evangelists' paternalistic ideal of a "free" African Christian peasantry, "protected" on its *own* reservation land (Molema 1966:157). In fact, the divergence between the Methodists, the Boers, and the Cape colonial government over the destiny of these communities underlines the poverty of teleological reasoning in analyzing the rise of the South African state. For, while the implications of mission endeavor, Boer nationalism, and colonial concerns were to overlap, their convergence, far from being the product of a conspiracy of interests, was the practical outcome of a set of initially distinct, competitive, and often contradictory orientations.

Articulation and the Analysis of Transformation

This account of Tshidi history as dialectical process makes central use of the concept of "articulation." As several commentators have noted, the construct has two denotations in English, "to join together" and "to give expression to" (Foster-Carter 1978; Post 1978; and J. L. Comaroff 1982). It thus permits us to view the joining of distinct systems, themselves dynamic orders of practice and meaning, into a unitary formation, the novel product of particular historical circumstances. The most con-

sistent use of this construct in the modern literature has been in the context of the so-called "modes of production" debate (Foster-Carter 1978),
where it denotes the interplay of local and global formations characterized in terms of their distinctive relations and forces of production
(Rey 1973; Meillassoux 1972). Within this debate, there is also a position
which regards the very notion of articulation as chimerical. In this view,
global history is a function of the extension and total penetration of the
world capitalist system, a penetration that denies determination to forces
outside of itself, therefore rendering the idea of interaction between formations logically impossible (see Frank 1967; Wallerstein 1974).

I am unable here to enter into a critical assessment of these analytical
positions.[8] At the most general level, any approach which characterizes
sociocultural formations and political economies in terms of the exclusive priority of "modes of production" would seem to oversimplify
an inevitably complex, multidimensional reality. Forces and relations of
production are disengaged, in such an approach, from their embeddedness in wider orders of material, ideological, and moral relations; conse-
quently, the dynamic interplay of these relations, my analytical concern
here, is reduced to a mechanical determinism. Instead, I use the concept
of articulation to imply the multilevel process of engagement which follows the conjuncture of sociocultural systems. My usage thus attempts
to preserve both the subtle interpenetration of levels characteristic of all
social systems, and the reciprocal quality of the interaction of such systems with each other—whether this be between local formations or between local and global orders.

In fact, there is nothing inherent in the concept of articulation which
dictates a priori what is being joined or how—it merely conveys the
sense that it is indeed the *joining* of systems, rather than the mere encompassment of one by another that is at issue. The concept therefore lends
itself to several possible theories of history. Its most consistent use to
date, while still inadequate for my purposes, has yielded two useful in-
sights. The first is that, in the process of conjuncture, formerly distinct
formations become subsumed in an indissoluble unity (Foster-Carter
1978:50); we might add that articulation, proceeding from an initial point
of contact, establishes relations between orders of relations and, in so
doing, generates the emerging social structure. The second insight is
that, in the interaction of global and peripheral systems, the conjuncture
is one between unequal orders, and between systems in contradiction
(Meillassoux 1972; Bettelheim 1972). Following this, a grounding construct is required within which these processes may be located—perhaps
a notion of a "world system," which subsumes both exchange and production, polity as well as economy, and symbolic as well as material

forms. But the relationship of such a global system to local formations has to be viewed as a historical problem; it is a relationship which, while inherently contradictory and unequal, is not universally determining.

As I have argued, the articulation between the Tshidi world and the colonial order was profoundly unequal; it was a vertical relationship structured by centralized domination and extraction. But the conjuncture was mutually transforming, and the encompassing formation that emerged was the product of the interplay of both systems. Of course, the conscious intentions brought into this encounter by the Tshidi and the mission, respectively, originated and remained embedded in very different orders of meaning; yet there was a contingent, if limited, overlap between the two and a converging notion of strategic practice that surfaced under conditions of historical disruption—enough, that is, to set the process in motion. As this process unfolded, the evangelists, initially forced to operate within the parameters of the Tshidi system, developed an emergent order of values, rooted in a model of an idealized African Christian peasantry under British protection. This, in turn, motivated the development of formal missionary imperialism. But their technical and ideological innovations had already initiated significant sociocultural transformations among the Tshidi, on whose experience the signs and practices of Christianity were imprinted, whether or not they were "converted." These signs and practices were soon to resonate with those of colonial politico-economic institutions—their dualistic categories, their constructs of time and agency, and their projection of the world as an order of material relations.

Yet the process of articulation involved neither a mechanical supersession of the institutions of the industrial world nor the obliteration of indigenous forms; and it cannot be represented as a neat transition from precapitalist to capitalist modes. Rather, it operated within the logic of existing peripheral structures to transform them, reordering relations between their component elements and undermining prevailing arrangements. In so doing, it also reproduced and elaborated certain internal relations, changing their role within the social system itself. In this way, novel formations which were neither "traditional" nor "capitalist"—the southern Tswana royal fiefdoms, for instance, and the ritual movements to be examined below—developed within the colonial arena, yet persisted within an embracing universe increasingly dominated by the logic of capitalist forces. This touches upon a more general issue in the confrontation between global and peripheral systems: from the empirical record, the extension of ubiquitous capitalist structures itself appears to be a complex and contradictory process. As Foster-Carter (1978:51) puts it: "capitalism neither evolves mechanically from what preceded it, nor does it necessarily dissolve it. Indeed, so far from banishing pre–capitalist forms, it not only coexists with them but buttresses them, and even on occasion devilishly conjures them up *ex nihilo*." The comprehension of such processes raises problems for a social science that, whatever its ideological persuasion, is still steeped in a binary conception of economy and society; a binarism that opposes "West" to "non–West," and tacitly asserts a neo–evolutionary trajectory for the history of the Third World. Among the southern Tswana, precolonial arrangements were transformed into peasant fiefdoms which, with waning markets for food and growing demands for labor, gave way to the classic forms of underdevelopment, wherein subsistence production and wage labor became indissolubly conjoined under the neocolonial state. Such uneven change involves the interplay both of systemic contradictions and of conflicts of experience and value. It entails the simultaneous reproduction and transformation of precolonial forms, giving rise to novel structures which challenge the dualist categories of conventional social science. It is the challenge posed by the rise of such sociocultural forms in the modern Tshidi world that is the subject of the remainder of this study.

6

Alienation and the Kingdom of Zion

Let me pause in this account to step back and frame my initial confrontation with the modern Tshidi world. I first visited their capital at Mafeking in 1969. The mudbrick settlement, established in the latter half of the nineteenth century, still sprawled between the rocky outcrops along the seldom flowing Molopo River. The royal court and "tribal office," which administered what remained under the control of local government, were situated at the old political centrum; but the town stretched for several miles to the east, south, and west. Now known by all as the "stad,"[1] it comprised a motley array of red-brown dwellings set in walled yards. Some buildings were rectangular with tin roofs but most were of "traditional" circular design, standing in carefully finished surrounds and thatched with grass. Apart from the recently settled fringes of the town, individual homesteads were grouped in semicircular concentrations; despite the scattered dwellings on the outskirts and the several dirt roads that traversed the stad, the wards retained an air of enclosed seclusion. The overall settlement pattern still took the form of concentric arcs, which reproduced the contrasts between *ha gare* (core) and *kaha ntlè* (periphery). The stad exhibited certain obvious signs of its colonial and neocolonial history—the large and somewhat delapidated Methodist church near its center, the offices of the Bantu Commissioner overseeing the main access route to the white town, the ubiquitous police vans with uniformed white occupants, and the clothes, bicycles, and plastic shopping bags of the market economy. Yet the predominant shapes, colors, and rhythms of the town accorded with nineteenth-century descriptions of Tswana settlement. In the latter half of the twentieth century, the capital still lacked any plumbing or electrical power, and the passage of a car on its roads still excited attention.

Half a mile from the northwest fringe of the stad, and set apart from it and the white town by a curve in the railway line, was Montshiwa Township. As I have noted, this had been built to house the population serving the "government" of Bophutatswana; it will be recalled that the Tshidi chiefdom now fell within the more inclusive "homeland" from whence its population migrated to the industrial centers as "foreign nationals." By the late 1960s the headquarters of the Tswana Territorial Authority consisted of a small staff of white officials of the Department of Bantu Affairs,[2] and the six Tswana "ministers" of the embryonic administration. The latter had been equipped with chauffeur-driven cars and new houses, erected in Montshiwa Township in the style of the suburban, white, lower middle class. The accoutrements of ministerial office served to project the government ideal of stable black bourgeois leadership, just as the forms of the township spoke to the rationalized and bureaucratically serviceable existence envisaged for the rank and file. The new settlement housed an ethnically mixed population, some of whom had long been in the area, others of whom had recently migrated in search of work. There were also a number of Tshidi residents who for various reasons had been unable to build homes in the stad.[3] Montshiwa Township harked back to the "locations" built for black workers in colonial times on the ground plan of an unfocused grid. It embodied the physical structures of proletarianization, its two-roomed, rented houses being designed at most for a small nuclear-family unit. No stock might be held in its yards, which were also too small for cultivation. Houses stood in relentless monotony on rectangular plots, on well-lit and eminently policeable thoroughfares. The vast majority of the population of the township relied on wage labor, either as local workers or as dependents. The Tshidi, as I have stressed, were generally opposed to the homeland administration and the system it represented, and they resented the concrete embodiments of its values that had been erected on their familiar landscape. There is a historical irony to the fact that this regimented settlement, which Tshidi call the "Government Compound," is named after their own last independent chief—and this did not escape wry comment. As one informant remarked: "Those in the Township are naked and live with strangers; they sit in yards that everyone's eyes can pierce, without the shelter of a homestead wall."

The Tshidi Social System, c. 1970

In 1969–70, the population of the Mafeking district was some 45,000, of whom approximately 19,500 lived in the stad and the remainder in twenty-five small hamlets scattered throughout a hinterland of some 153,650 morgen (1 morgen = 2.116 acres; see Comaroff 1974:33). A further 1,000 Tshidi lived in Montshiwa Township, constituting one-fourth of its population. I have stressed that as part of the black rural periphery in modern South Africa, the community has been subject to progressive impoverishment, the result of the mutually reinforcing relationship between soil erosion and a dependency on an exploitative migrant-labor system; moreover, only a small proportion of Tshidi—a petite bourgeoisie of local traders and clerical workers and, recently, a minuscule middle class—has been able to escape the cycle of wage labor and failing agricultural production. To recapitulate: Breutz had stated in 1956 that "the majority of the people scarcely grow enough maize and kaffir-corn (sorghum) for their own consumption" (1955–56:53). By 1969–70, after a period of severe drought, I estimated that no more than 45 percent of the households in the Mafeking district had been able to plow at all, and of this proportion less than half realized yields sufficient for their basic requirements. Household surveys suggest, further, that only 26 percent of Tshidi units owned or had usufruct rights in cattle, and 42 percent held some small stock.

In such economic circumstances, where rural poverty becomes both cause and effect of labor migration, a lifetime of contract work had become the norm for adult males. Local employment was limited: in 1969, white Mafeking had a population of some 6,000, selling goods and services to the surrounding black communities and neighboring white farmers; government attempts to induce "border industries" to take advantage of rural African labor *in situ* had been unsuccessful. As a result, most ablebodied men had little choice but to seek work in the mines or in the industrial complexes around Johannesburg. Seasonal employment on the white farms in the Western Transvaal provided support for women and was the source of food for the destitute in the local population. Entire families were transported to the fields, to be paid in bags of maize. In 1970, a sample survey in the village of Mareetsane, southeast of Mafeking, revealed that 35 percent of the residents had "gone to work for the Boers" for the reaping season. These maize farms are the heartland of Afrikaner rural culture, and the Tshidi regarded working on them as a distasteful strategy of last resort. But conditions in the mines and industrial centers tended to be equally exploitative and discouraged longer-term identification with the values of the workplace. Indeed, while the urban areas might have offered a vibrant black culture that brought popular Western forms into relationship with African experience, the Tshidi regarded their sojourn there as uniformly exploitative and degrading. Their attitude was well summarized by an old man who sat in his delapidated yard, the product of a lifetime of migrant labor, and remarked: "Here I struggle, but I see the result of my work [*tiro*] and I call no one '*baas*'" (Comaroff 1974:36).[4] Such consciousness must be borne in mind as we examine the response of Tshidi to their modern circumstances.

Certain limited commercial opportunities were exploited by members of the community in Mafeking: in 1970, thirty-nine registered traders, mainly small general dealers, operated in the chiefdom. But such ventures faced considerable competition from the national chain stores, whose outlets in white Mafeking catered specifically for the local black population. Competition came also from the several new and well-capitalized businesses in Montshiwa Township, whose Tswana proprietors had been the beneficiaries of a government interested in developing a small, "stabilized" rural middle class. Of the Tshidi stores in the stad, however, none was found to exceed a monthly taking of R25.[5] There were numerous other local enterprises in the struggling "informal" economy: liquor brewing, hairdressing, bicycle repair, a few owner-driven taxis. Women, who in any case formed the bulk of the resident population, were active in this sphere. In the late 1960s, monetized exchange remained a source of tension in the Tshidi community. A large sample was questioned in Mafeking about the sale of goods and services to close kin, and 95 percent responded that it was both "bad" and "widespread." Also singled out for criticism were the ground rents and share-plowing arrangements imposed on the rank and file by the small elite of successful farmers, whose consolidated holdings dated back to the immediate precolonial period. As we shall see, such tensions over exchange relations have emerged as a visible theme in modern Tshidi ritual; indeed, monetized transactions came to replace agnatic rivalry in local perception as the key focus for sorcery accusations and general social conflict.

It should be noted that the consolidation of the neocolonial economy at this time ensured the progressive socioeconomic polarization of its total population. As underdevelopment and overall dependency increased at the rural periphery, so did the gulf between the proletarianized majority and the few with independent access to the means of production; only the latter were in a position to take advantage of the limited material prospects provided by the establishment of the "homeland" system. Despite initial ideological opposition, some of them eventually began to seize these opportunities, and, by 1974, the one Tshidi minister in the Tswana Territorial Authority and the few local recipients of government loans had become the subject of much debate. But, if the consolidation of a bourgeoisie proper within the community was limited, so was upward mobility from the ranks of the worker-peasants. Stark poverty militated against any real accumulation by members of this class; indigenous patron-client links had all but disappeared, and the government had engineered the demise of the mission schools, former avenues to higher education and advancement. In this sense, the internal dynamics of stratification in the modern Tshidi community no longer constitute a "system" but a fraction of the overall process of class formation in the neocolonial state.

Of course, these conditions also imply complex sociocultural transformations. What were the effects, for instance, of the dramatic decline in the cattle population, given the centrality of these animals as signifiers of value in the precolonial system? While stock became reducible to cash, and were bought and sold under certain circumstances, they remained significantly opposed to money in the Tshidi conception. Indeed, cattle still served as repositories of wealth and the preferred mode of investment among the elite and came, for the majority, to signify a lost world of politico-economic independence—the seemingly unobtainable symbols of freedom from the need to earn wages (cf. J. L. Comaroff 1973:54). This seldom-realized goal tantalized most migrants; the values of control and self-realization that beasts have always had for the Tswana took on new significance in contrast to the alienating experience of the industrial workplace.

One of the few circumstances in which Tshidi still transacted stock in the modern context was marriage; domestic histories gathered in 1970 suggested that over half of the unions formally contracted over the previous twenty-five years involved bridewealth. This would seem to underline the cultural importance of cattle in the construction of enduring social ties. Yet it must also be noted that local records show a general decline in the rate of marriage in the community over the same period, especially among those dependent on migrant labor. Thus, as the stock population diminished, so did the social transactions they mediated—at least, that is how it appeared in Tshidi perception. Among the rank and file there was a rise in transient unions, quite widely referred to in South Africa as *"vat en sit"* or *"donkie trou"* (Afrikaans for "sit and squat" and "donkey marriage"), which evoke the unceremonious coupling of animals. The general social disruption spawned by underdevelopment, and by migration under South African conditions, led to a rising proportion of children born out of wedlock, and also of female-headed domestic groups.

This rise in the proportion of female-headed households was accompanied by the declining salience of agnation in the constitution of the social field. The eclipse of the precolonial state apparatus removed the values formerly transacted in the idiom of agnatic politics; the small elite in the rural area defined their interests largely in terms of individuated productive enterprise and did not participate in what remained of the activities of the chiefly court. As might be expected, given the structure of the procolonial system, this entailed the ascendance of matrilaterality as a principle of social organization, for the female-headed grouping was a transformation of the indigenous "atom" of structure, the uterine house. The latter, located in its web of supportive lateral ties, emerged as the dominant unit of interaction and cooperation for the large sector of the community that serves as a reserve army of labor. In fact, the domestic domain itself became the periphery of the distant urban centers, tied to them by an order of relations, rules, and bureaucratic procedures that bypassed almost entirely the apex of the indigenous system, its public sphere having been swept away by external forces both pervasive and unsusceptible to local control. As this suggests, the significance of the house was altered by a radically transformed relationship between "inside" and "outside" in Tshidi cosmology. Indeed, the residual family with its female head bore testimony to the centripetal processes that drew adult males not to the local chiefly center but into a national vortex. For labor migration was a form of forced mobility in time and space, one that wrenched people from their local worlds in a process coercively channeled from the white nuclei of power. The passage of blacks between town and countryside was to become the subject of increasingly close physical and bureaucratic control, a major arena for the graphic demonstration of state authority. The infamous laws of "influx control" cynically regulated the oscillation of African labor to and from the cities, making permits and passes a condition of movement and providing the most frequent cause of arrest and detention. Everyday activities became determined by the curfew, the official stamp, and the day-long wait in line; in the black perception, the world of work was that of a forced march down an obstacle-ridden corridor, under the constant surveillance of uniformed police and bureaucrats. The usurpation of the freedom of movement and the setting up of barriers and boundaries seemingly as capricious as they were insurmountable was a basic fact of Tshidi reality. All this occurred within the overarching logic of the apartheid system, whose very terms implied forcible separation, the creation of barricaded "group areas" and of legal restraints. Thus the homeland policy had seized black rural space, redefining historic maps by lumping and splitting populations at will, and by injecting novel realities into the familiar landscape of native South Africa.

It was this regimentation of space, time, and passage that Tshidi rites of resistance sought to redefine. Earlier I examined how collective ritual practice in the precolonial context served to articulate center and periphery, to subject the spatiotemporal forms of the domestic domain to the logic of the collectivity; below we shall see how, in altered historical circumstances, Tshidi attempted to reverse this process, to disengage their local world from the exogenous structures that encompassed it, and to reconstitute a bounded community centered upon the elemental relations framed by the house. Thus modern Tshidi rituals of reconstruction came to address paradoxes in the experience of the wider neocolonial arena, seeking to overlay its alienating forms with the procreative metaphors of the domestic unit, with its basic images of shape and process and its rules of productive relations.

Agnation has continued to organize formal access to office and status, but, with the erosion of the chiefship and indigenous political and economic arrangements, its structural and pragmatic relevance has been greatly reduced. Thus agnatic segments, which formerly were shaped in the course of political processes, were rendered as moribund as the power relations which they expressed. Indeed, the last factional opposition of moment to mobilize along agnatic lines was the conflict between the Christian elite and the chiefly establishment, in which the former argued that educational qualification should replace rank as the criterion for access to office. More pervasively, such internal debate has been increasingly submerged, with the advent of the homeland scheme, in the politics of the Tshidi relationship to structures of global incorporation; here, agnation has had little relevance. In the argument that developed among Tshidi over whether to resist or comply with the institutions of apartheid, it was the cultural markers of class that were to play an increasing role.

Given this displacement of the realm of agnatic politics, and also the noted suppression of African nationalist movements, are we to assume that these rural communities were left in a power vacuum? Of what does modern local-level politics consist? This raises the issue of power itself; specifically, how we are to conceptualize it without either reducing it to a crude synonym for domination or extending it so broadly as to cut it free of any relationship to structural constraints (cf. Giddens 1976:110). I shall return to this matter after I have examined the role of symbol, ideology, and ritual transformation in modern Tshidi culture. At this point, it is sufficient to note that, in the late 1960s, the Tshidi appeared to lack the capacity to intervene directly in the course of events that determined their social predicament. Yet, like similar peoples elsewhere, they continued to act upon their circumstances in a manner which had historical implications both local and more global. True, much local-level politics seemed at the time to be divorced from broader social issues—it concerned the residual activities of the chiefly court, now the preserve of aging royals—and most evidently, it turned around the limited leadership opportunities offered by the Protestant churches. Such activities seemed securely in the hands of the educated elite and were carefully set off from macropolitical concerns. One Tshidi migrant used a telling English idiom to describe the situation: "The church is a 'chatterbox,' talking about everything except what really matters to black people in this country." Indeed, the radical dichotomy of church and state was central to the ideological apparatus of the South African regime, which has long determined that the church should provide the legitimate and apolitical mode of cultural expression for blacks; and Protestantism, in all its variants, was to become an important source of metaphor and organizational form for the repressed population. But its complex and changing historical role cannot merely be written off as "mystifying," or even "prehistoric" (see Hobsbawm 1959:10). For the categories and modes of practice of the church have had a significance that extends far beyond their manifest form and function: it was in this context that black South Africans first experienced and gave voice to colonial inequality; and, under transformed, if equally repressive circumstances, the church has continued to afford the terms that frame an awareness of social differentiation—if not a consciousness of "class." In fact, for some of those most dispossessed by the neocolonial system, the less orthodox forms of the Western Protestant tradition were to provide the very basis for a more radical expression of cultural resistance.

The Religious Spectrum

Notwithstanding the visible significance of "religious" movements in the culture of modern black South Africa, I was struck initially by the profusion of churches on the skyline of the Tshidi capital, and by the prominence of signs of Christian origin in their everyday life. Delicate, if now infirm, spires rose alongside hand-hewn crosses; and many buildings seemed to serve both domestic and ritual purposes. At the weekend, a cacophany of competing sounds filled the air—pulsating drums, identifiable Methodist hymns, and other Protestant forms so altered in rhythm and tempo that they were barely recognizable. Church members, predominantly female, hurried by on the pathways, clad in brightly colored uniforms; public gatherings, whatever their purpose, were opened and closed with liturgical formulas. Everyday "cultural debate" (cf. Parkin 1978:295) among the Tshidi was clearly about the operation of spiritual power in the world. Ordinary practice expressed for the most part a nondualistic engagement of spirit and matter that harked back to the precolonial semantic order, for notions of pollution and ancestral intervention existed alongside the now explicit idea of a universal deity.

While the original Methodist church still stood near the center of the stad, and continued to represent Christian orthodoxy, there had sprung up around it a clamorous throng of distinct movements that repudiated its hegemony. These, collectively known as "Zionist" or "Spirit" churches, centered on a range of inspired leaders who were conceived of as healers rather than ministers in the Protestant mold. The movements were all referred to as *dikereke*[6]—"churches"—and, while they varied somewhat in sociocultural form, most were multipurpose associations, each organized around a focal ritual place and a holistic ideological scheme. Their energy and creativity were palpable; they seemed given to continual fission and symbolic innovation. Most of the movements centered explicitly upon the ritual reconstruction of the body—on rites of healing, dietary taboos, and carefully prescribed uniforms. The latter were composite statements which proclaimed most accessibly their challenging stance: for these uniforms parodied the insignia of Western authority, reversing essential indices of Protestant orthodoxy and seeming, in the process, to announce a unique access to superhuman power. Was this quest for "Zion" to be understood as yet another instance of millenarianism among a population dispossessed by the advance of the world system? If so, how are we to account for the decidedly this-worldly social commentary contained in its already long-established modes of practice? In some respects, the plurality of uniformed movements appeared to serve a totemic function; in others, their striking and irreverent transformation of orthodox symbolic schemes was akin both to cargo cults and chiliastic movements in the colonized Third World (Worsley 1968; Bastide 1971) and to the countercultures of marginalized populations in the modern West (cf. Cohen 1980; Hebdige 1979).

Also, it seemed that inspired faith-healing, that bastard child of our own religious establishment, was here in the process of eclipsing the forms of Protestant orthodoxy—at least in their local guise. Clearly, before me was a dynamic system of signs and practices which had both configured and been configured by, the changing predicament of the Tshidi; and, at its center, was the ritualized attempt to reform the body and the location of the person in the world. But why had such ritual practices become the key symbolic domain in which these pragmatic concerns were being addressed? Why was it the church that had come to provide the signs that these and other Tshidi had appropriated in their ritual practice, their lusty song, and their ingenious uniforms? Plainly, the emergence and coexistence of a ramifying spectrum of religious associations and forms, from those of the orthodox mission church to those of the flamboyant Zionist sects, gave expression to a growing differentiation in the consciousness of Tshidi themselves; a differentiation that expressed the local experience of a wider process of stratification through which they and like peripheral peoples were being incorporated into the South African political economy. I began to see, in other words, that the "churches," here, were the indices of a more encompassing dynamic, and that by unraveling their transforming logic, I would understand a crucial dimension of Tshidi cultural history.

Person, Cosmos, and the Experience
of Proletarianization

Of course, the ritual movements which featured so prominently among
the Tshidi in the late 1960s were in no sense unusual phenomena in black
southern Africa. Indeed, throughout colonial and neocolonial Africa,
orthodox European culture had felt itself challenged by the flowering of
the so-called "sects," "cults," "syncretic movements," and "separatist
churches." The emergence of such phenomena, both from within the
mission denominations and out of spontaneous indigenous growth, has
been noted since the turn of the century; but Sundkler's classic study of
Zulu "independent churches" (first published in 1948) was to confirm
that a particular "hypertrophy" of these movements had developed in
South Africa (1961:13). Sundkler related this fact to the thoroughgoing
structures of inequality there, and highlighted an important feature
shared by the otherwise diverse array of novel religious formations: the
apparent ease with which African peoples internalized the forms of the
Western church masked an often trenchant resistance to the culture of
colonial domination (1961:19). He traced the emergence of two modes of
such resistance; for, in the symbolic and ritual contrasts between "Ethiopian" and "Zionist" sects, he observed different modes of reconciling the
social and conceptual contradictions that configured the contemporary
Zulu world. Sundkler also stressed the creative interplay between indigenous religious innovators—and the changing cultural order they represented—and the forms of mission Christianity; and in the addendum to
the second edition of the volume (1961), he pointed to the growing polarization of consciousness and socioeconomic status among the Zulu, a
polarization clearly indexed in their set of contrasting religious movements (1961:304ff.).

Much of the subsequent work on black religious movements in central
and southern Africa has failed to match Sundkler's sensitivity to their
broad structural significance and to their character as complex symbolic
systems. A host of more explicitly sociological studies has provided ample evidence of the mediating role of these movements under conditions
of rapid and uneven transformation, often viewing them as buffers in the
wake of social dislocation. Thus those movements have been described
as "places to feel at home" (Welbourn and Ogot 1966); as examples of
"incapsulating" or "totalitarian syndromes" (Mayer 1961); as the "syncretistic" foci for "modification and adaptation" (Murphree 1969), and
as "small reference groups in relation to the wider society" (West 1975).
In reaction to the limitations of such sociological analyses, there have
been efforts to understand the religious movements in idealist terms: thus

Peel's neo-Weberian ethnography of the Aladura churches of West Africa (1968) treats them as an attempt to reconcile the "this-worldly" vision of African cosmology with the "other-worldly" focus of Christianity; and Horton's "intellectualist" account concentrates on their pursuit of "explanation, prediction and control" in circumstances of change (1971). But, like the sociological focus it ostensibly opposes, this idealist perspective fails to situate these movements within more encompassing structural orders; indeed, by regarding them either as "religious associations" or "modes of explanation and control" it extends to them a literalist, ethnocentric theory of meaning which ignores their embeddedness in total social and cultural systems. Notwithstanding the clear evidence that their emergence is tied to the politico-economic processes of colonial domination (cf. Sundkler 1961; Worsley 1968) few studies have given these processes real analytical weight; and despite the classic demonstration, especially in pre-industrial African contexts, that "religious" forms are explicable only with reference to the inclusive symbolic systems in which they arise, the practices of "sectarian" movements have seldom been treated adequately as modes of cultural signification, as meaningful creations more complex and resonant than the mere literal "explanation" of things threatening or strange.[7]

In light of this critique and the problem at hand, two recent approaches to religious innovation must be singled out. The first is the work of van Binsbergen (1976) on religious innovation in modern Zambia, especially his account of the Lumpa church, in which he seeks to relate the violent confrontation between its members and government forces to the formation of class and the postcolonial state. Van Binsbergen suggests that this rising, which took place among Bemba at the time of independence in 1964, was a peasant resistance movement. It presented a challenge, in the idiom of spiritual power and agrarian regeneration, to the unseen forces that had undermined a world formerly known and controlled (1976:113). He goes on to contrast this rural movement with other forms of "super-structural" reconstruction; in particular, those that sprang up among migrant workers in response to the experience of industrial wage labor, which had rendered the forces of politico-economic control especially palpable. In this second context, the perception of alienation was expressed in different forms: initially in the conservative terms of the mission church, with its inherent dichotomy of "religion" and "politics," which encouraged acceptance and suffering rather than rebellion; then, in reaction to white domination within that church, in the dual idiom of independent Christianity and black nationalism (1976:113). Van Binsbergen notes that the peasant response was in fact more radical than the proletarian one, for its symbolic forms

rejected encompassment by the colonial-capitalist system. The proletarian movements, on the other hand, sought to negotiate the position
of blacks within existing social and ideological structures (1976:117).

This account is not without problems. For example, van Binsbergen's
rigid dichotomy between infra- and super-structure makes the analysis
unduly mechanical, and it is unclear whether his thoroughgoing distinction between processes of "peasantization" and "proletarianization" is
legitimate in the Zambian case. Nor, ultimately, does he explain why
Lumpa, if indeed a peasant movement, should have been confined to the
Bemba; a problem which may only be resolved with reference to the
dialectic, which he does not confront, between external forces and local
sociocultural structures. Still, the study is noteworthy for its attempt to
synthesize consciousness, symbolic action, and politico-economic process, and for its treatment of novel ritual movements as orders of perception and intention, themselves the outcome of particular colonial histories.
In this sense, it is directly relevant to the Tshidi case and raises issues that
require to be addressed if this case is to be adequately analyzed.

Werbner's recent account (n.d.) of "The Argument of Images" in the
iconography of Zimbabwean churches is also relevant here. It examines
the imagery of space and location in a series of religious movements,
seeking systematic variation in the consciousness they express of dislocation and marginality, and in the attempt to transform the position of the
person in the ritual universe. Werbner draws on Fernandez's insightful
notion that processes of "decentering" and the "acute sense of peripherality" which these engender may be "imaginatively negotiated in
primary images of body and household, field and forest life" (see Fernandez 1978:229ff.; these constructs are sensitively developed in the
more extended study of the Bwiti movement; 1982). By Werbner's account, three contrasting tendencies may be distinguished among the
Zimbabwean cults, each with distinct implications for the location of the
person in ritual space and for the homologous relationship of the ritual
community to the colonial state. Thus "territorialism" characterizes
movements whose spatial maps resonate with the established geographical divisions and "central place hierarchy" of that state (n.d.:27). "Re-
gionalism," in contrast, is found in those which focus on sacred sites at
odds with the geographical and religious structure of the establishment,
and which through their "disharmonic" semantic structure, redirect the
perception of participants away from regnant center-periphery relations
(n.d. 30). And "communitarianism" occurs in movements which reject
altogether the conceptual forms of the known temporal world; anti-
hierarchy prevails in their symbolic schemes, and they are motivated by
the continuing search for an ultimate sacred focus (n.d.:33).

In this short paper, Werbner does not aim to demonstrate the symbolic and conceptual contrasts between these "cults" in detail; neither does he relate the three tendencies in any systematic manner to the embracing historical structures which generate them (n.d.: 25). Yet his account does raise important issues concerning the relationship of bodies personal and social as this is realized in the ritual context, stressing the role of religious innovation in marking the complex and shifting relations among marginal groups, and between them and established sociocultural foci. Such issues are clearly salient in the Tshidi case. I shall attempt to address them by showing how ritual, through its practical and poetic structures, locates persons in space and time, a process inseparable from the wider forces of social history.

The Tshidi Case

I have suggested that in the nineteenth-century Tshidi universe systematic values and predispositions were impressed upon consciousness in large part through the symbolic management of the body in everyday practice. Ritual addressed and attempted to reconcile conflicts engendered in personal experience, conflicts which stemmed from the constitution of the embracing sociocultural order. This process was at its most elaborate in such communal rites as initiation, where symbolic manipulation of the bodies and personae of pubescent boys and girls served to reproduce established "natural" definitions of the social world in the collective consciousness. These rites structured Tshidi perceptions of the real, dramatically working through paradoxes of perception so that they harmonized with established social arrangements.

In the latter half of the twentieth century, collective ritual among the Tshidi no longer spoke in a single voice. In fact, ritual discourse seemed now to be engaged in a process of argumentation about the "real" and the "valued." Such discourse was obviously an expression of conflict, but it was also an effort to transform the world through forces inherent in the form of ritual itself. A considerable proportion of the rites focused explicitly upon the construction of the human body, upon its relation to "spirit," and upon its location in the everyday order of events in space and time.

In 1969, research in the Mafeking district revealed the existence of some fifty-six distinct religious movements (*dikereke*) and several hundred congregations. At least forty such movements were represented in the stad itself. However, by their very nature, many of these organizations were difficult to identify; for, while there were fourteen denominations of established international status, only four of which were not of orthodox Protestant affiliation, there were also at least thirty-three distinct "Zionist" movements which were small, constantly proliferating, and often embedded in the kin networks of their leaders.[8] Of all the churches distinguished in the area, nine were of a type whose formal structure resembled Protestant orthodoxy, but which were organizationally autonomous. These were African Independent churches of national scope, formed through secession from mission institutions, and retaining their essential form.

Elsewhere I have described the emergence of this spectrum of movements in some detail (Comaroff 1974:54ff.); here it is necessary only to recount the major trends. The Methodist mission church had retained undisputed tenure of the Tshidi field until the time of overrule. However, when they founded the white town of Mafeking to serve as the administrative center of British Bechuanaland, the British built both an Anglican church and a Methodist chapel. Standing within half a mile of the indigenous settlement, this town represented a different social and cultural universe, except for its direct dependence on local black labor power. But white Mafeking impinged directly upon Tshidi consciousness; for the experience of colonial rule at such close quarters was to contradict the liberal message of the moral and spiritual equality promulgated by the mission church and the European civilization it was seen to represent. Henceforth, black and white Methodists—and, soon, Anglicans and Catholics as well—were to worship in segregated churches built within walking distance of each other. At the regional and national levels, white Protestant leaders were to retain strict, paternalistic control over black congregations, and such religious authority was paradigmatic of hierarchical state structures at large.

The closing years of the nineteenth century saw growing numbers of Tshidi drawn to the polyethnic mining and industrial centers, first to Kimberley and then, increasingly, to the Witwatersrand. By this time, the established missions had begun to practice in these urban areas; despite earlier protest, they soon came to regard the advent of large-scale labor migration as a blessing to their cause.[9] The expanding industrial complexes, especially the gold fields, drew many Protestant converts, now no longer under the paternal supervision of the rural churches (Sundkler 1961:39). During the final decade of the century, secessions had begun to occur within the mission denominations in various parts of southern Africa,[10] a range of precipitating conflicts expressing fundamental contradictions within the churches themselves and their relationship to the colonial state. By far the most numerous of these secessions occurred among the Methodists, for their African church had reproduced the same tension between democracy and control that had characterized the parent movement. The "grass-roots" egalitarianism of the latter had dictated a policy of native leadership within the church, at least at its lower levels, and a relatively large number of literate lay preachers had been trained. These men now began to protest their lack of real power (Sundkler 1961:39). Here, as in the case of the Zambian proletarians (van Binsbergen 1976) the conflict was exacerbated by their exposure to throughgoing oppression in the mines (cf. Marks n.d.:8ff.). Not only was the experience of mine labor brutally at odds with indigenous precolonial concepts and values; it also violated the ideal of liberal "freedom" projected by mission ideology—particularly as this was interpreted by those not yet predisposed to such conceptual dualisms as would make emancipation a condition of the spirit alone. Thus, while the categories of the mission church had clearly anticipated the practical experience of proletarianization, its constructs of person and agency contained no preparation for the realities of alienation, for the segregation of physical, social, and spiritual being attendant upon entry into the urban labor market.

In this account I employ Marx's concept of alienation without subscribing to all the theoretical assumptions originally built into it. Marx made a radical distinction between the alienation or estrangement of the worker under capitalism—estrangement from himself, from his labor power, his product, and his fellows—and the objectification that is part of all productive activity (Marx and Engels 1970:42ff.). The former rests on two defining features: that man's product "exists outside him, independently, as something alien to him and that it becomes a power on its own confronting him" (Ollman 1971:142). Under such conditions, the worker's product is the property of another, and he cannot use it to sustain himself. Indeed, rather than augment the producer, the severed product appropriates his vitality, making it its own—and being, in this sense, the inverse of the Maussian gift (see Marx 1959:70). This severance is experienced by the worker as self-estrangement; he "feels himself outside his work" and no longer "recognizes" his product as his own (Marx 1959:72; Ollman 1971:143). Ollman notes that, for Marx, "capitalist labor does not belong to man's essential being in the sense that it leaves most of the relations that constitute the human being . . . unaffected" (1971:137).

I have argued that a thoroughgoing dichotomy between capitalist and precapitalist formations does not do justice to the real complexities of similarity and difference that obtain in historical societies. In this sense, the opposition between "use" and "exchange" value, between transparent and mystified modes of domination, or personalized and reified consciousness is not all or none. I have suggested that, in the precolonial Tswana context, cattle had value both in use and exchange, and that they both personified and naturalized relations of inequality. In that context, too, client producers neither controlled their product nor saw themselves reflected in it, but they were able to use it to keep themselves alive. Conversely, following Mauss and Baudrillard, I have noted that the depersonalization of the industrial capitalist workplace is not a totalizing, mechanical process; this is particularly obvious among those whom Weber labeled "traditionalist" (1958:59), those who still recall the experience that Tshidi Zionists refer to as "eating the work of our own hands." But Marx's concept of alienation does capture the implications, both structural and experiential, of production that is abruptly cut loose from its embeddedness in the social fabric by the mediation of money and the clock. It speaks to the effects on human practice of a drastically reduced control over the dimensions of the self invested in the labor process— and of a disrupted subjectivity provided by the consumption of goods which, if not impersonal, embody a persona that appears alien. We shall see how Tshidi rites of personal reconstruction focus on the symbolic reintegration of such alien commodities and images of being. Ultimately, what Ollman says of Marx's formulation might be applied to the Tshidi: in their consciousness, wage labor seems to fail to engage those crucial dimensions that constitute human existence; it unravels the total social fabric so as to utilize only those strands that suit its purpose. As they aptly put it: "The mine, like the grave, has use only for your body."

By chance the word for money in Setswana, *madi* (derived from the English by established vernacular principles of transposition), is the indigenous term for "blood." The condensation of meanings here is rich and, at times, explicit. As I stood lamenting price increases with an impoverished Tshidi migrant in a supermarket in white Mafeking, he took a coin from his pocket, handed it to the cashier, and said bitterly: "*Ke madi a me*" (This is my blood/money). The association of money and blood is particularly plausible in a context where work conditions are often physically threatening, as they are to the miners. Indeed, the Tshidi notion of money would seem to parallel closely Marx's formulation of the commodity that feeds off the substance of the worker (Marx 1959:70). But the term also taps a wealth of other overlapping associations, such as redness and polluting heat, slaughter and the dangerous potential of female sexuality. *Bothitho*, "heat," was a state of interrupted flow induced in the sufferer's blood by menstrual pollution or by adult sexuality that was not normatively constrained. Money, particularly when the basis of strife in local relations, was referred to as "hot," implying that its passage was intense and destructive, bearing the polluting substance of persons unknown. The indigenous conception of *madi* also suggests the life-giving motion of blood within the body (Comaroff 1981), for the state of health among the Tswana was a function of the blood's relative viscosity and ability to course freely through the whole system. "Hot blood" was a condition of dangerously unmoderated flow; indeed, the

Tshidi perception of money would seem to imply a process of circulation which, from their point of view, is unregulated and uncontrollable. The mannered incorporation and regulation of *madi,* as we shall see, is an important theme of the Zionist rites.

Just as they had done in Britain, the sociocultural categories of orthodox Protestantism legitimized the categories of commoditization and of the workplace in South Africa. For the migrant, these categories were no longer cut across by the practices and physical forms of a preindustrial rural world. Moreover, the strict dichotomy of "religion" and "politics," on which the ideological efficacy of Protestantism rested, militated against any active concern on the part of its establishment with the political aspects of African proletarianization. Thus, when the experience of neophyte migrants challenged received categories, they directed their disaffection against the church itself. While the agents of political and material domination could be neither encompassed nor cast out, the more tangible colonialism of the mission afforded an accessible target. The growing repudiation of the church was also a symbolic rejection of the system at large, a rejection based on the sedimentation of a class of black wage-laborers. And, while the rise of the Independent churches might not have signaled the development of a "working-class consciousness," it objectified a cultural scheme that was to give more explicit voice to the conflicts inherent in the shared experience of wage labor. As Marks (n.d.:21) put it, this scheme "gave strategies for surviving in a new and harsh world, if not yet for transforming it."

The foundations of the African Independent church movement in South Africa had been laid by the early years of the twentieth century. One of its most vital new offshoots was the Ethiopian church, which, as its name suggests, combined the symbolism of a biblically indexed millennium with an evolving African nationalism, itself cross-fertilized with the neatly overlapping ideology of Marcus Garvey—that blacks were the "dispossessed of Ethiopia."[11] This condensation of meanings was to give form to the black political consciousness emerging in the first quarter of the century. A further offshoot of this movement was to become affiliated with the African Methodist Episcopal Church in North America, thus widening the fan of referents in the politicized Protestant culture that addressed a black experience, in some sense structurally equivalent, on both continents. During this period, the Ethiopian and the A.M.E. churches, while under the leadership of the educated products of the Methodist mission, presented a novel ideological discourse to the growing proletariat, offering what seemed to be a reconciliation of some of the conflicts attendant upon their lot. As membership grew, the movements began to radiate outward from the urban areas and move, with returning migrants, to the rural communities.

In their organization and ideology these Independent churches rejected the political hegemony of white orthodoxy, but they did not seriously challenge its constituent sociocultural forms. In fact, they addressed the repressive situation of the peasant-proletarian in one limited dimension only: the visible domination by whites in the ostensibly "democratic" world of the church itself. Protest was framed in terms of the orthodox Protestant categories, those of spiritual democracy and the right of the individual to self-determined freedom, the categories of European liberalism we have already encountered in the worldview of the Tshidi Christian elite. The Independent churches did not, then, contest the structure of the colonial order; rather, they debated the place within it of the aspiring black Protestant elite. In this sense, they left untouched the deeper social and cultural contradictions facing the majority of the peripheralized African population. The nationalist imagery was cut across by the orthodox division of church and state; and it was ultimately syphoned off into the emerging "secular" nationalist movements that crystallized around the passing of the Natives' Land Act in 1913. But even within these movements, the influence of liberal Christian ideology remained strong; as Gerhart (1978:39ff.) notes, "nationalism" here was to mean liberal, multi-racial integrationalism and rarely black activism per se.

There was, however, a second religious movement among migrant workers during the same period; one which did address the fundamental contradictions of the peasant-proletarian predicament in a more thoroughgoing manner. This movement emerged out of what was first a limited white fundamentalist secession in South Africa, itself fertilized by a system of utopian reform developed among the urban poor in North America in the late nineteenth century (Sundkler 1976:13ff.). This "Zionism" was to construct a symbolic order in direct opposition to that of Protestant orthodoxy and the rational, dualistic worldview it presupposed. Through its key metaphor of healing, it emphasized the reintegration of matter and spirit, the practical agency of divine force, and the social relocation of the displaced; in short, it drew together everything that had been set apart in the black experience of colonialization and wage labor. Like the radical Lenshina church in Zambia, Zionism was to offer the apparent possibility of reconstructing a holistic community within which the impact of industrial capitalism could be resisted. As in the Zambian case, reconstruction proceeded through the management of ritual symbols and of practical social relations (cf. van Binsbergen 1976:117). In drawing upon the image of Zion, this movement shifted the emphasis of Protestant cultural logic; for Protestantism had rendered the Bible accessible, presenting a set of ready analogies to the consciousness of the persecuted. Indeed, Zion and Jerusalem served as predictable icons for those whose experience urged the shift of focus from transcendent salvation to a more immediate utopia. Thus in Britain the millennial siting of "Jerusalem" in "England's green and pleasant land" was to be reworked in a range of dissenting contexts before the Mormons were to mark—in their exodus in search of an American "City of Zion"—a further shift in the symbolic location of the earthly heaven (Armytage 1961:259ff.).

The Cultural Logic of the American Zion

The Christian Catholic Apostolic Church in Zion (C.C.A.C.Z.) was founded in Chicago in 1896, and was introduced to the black populations around Johannesburg and in Natal in 1904 (Sundkler 1961:48; 1976:28ff.). It is necessary to describe something of the sociocultural background of this movement, so that its conjuncture with the emerging proletarian culture in South Africa may be analyzed. The Zionist church provided indigenous workers with an order of symbols, concepts, and practical forms that promised novel resolutions to the problems of living between the impoverished worlds of rural subsistence and wage labor. In this process, the incoming movement was itself to be considerably transformed. But its initial appeal lay in the resonance of its cultural categories with the historical experience of such peripheralized peoples as the Tshidi.

The overlap between the cultural forms of the American church and the consciousness of black South Africans at the turn of the century had a sound basis. The C.C.A.C.Z. drew the bulk of its following from the impoverished urban communities of the industrial Midwest: a population itself alienated from such experiences of self-determination and rational achievement as were celebrated in nineteenth-century American Protestant ideology. Not only was there a structural equivalence between the two populations of the newly proletarianized dispossessed in South Africa and the United States, but both alike sought a language through which to protest the inappropriate image of themselves presented in the established church and in the dominant culture at large. Both cases, too, involve the expression of class conflict, not explicitly voiced or nicely articulated as class consciousness per se, but couched in the flexible symbols of Christian dissent (cf. Worsley 1968:225ff.). The C.C.A.C.Z. claimed to stand for the "restoration" of an "original and native" church, one that had become corrupted by the evil and apostasy of the orthodox Protestant denominations. As Worsley (1968:226) has noted, such irreverent, anti-authoritarian innovations are usually treated with the utmost suspicion by the religious establishment and the state. Indeed, the C.C.A.C.Z. called forth considerable attention both in its native Illinois and further afield, for it challenged hegemonic interests and the symbols in which these were enshrined. A doctoral dissertation presented to the Graduate Divinity School at the University of Chicago in 1906, for example, is devoted to a "rational" theological refutation of the movement (Harlan 1906), based upon detailed historical research and firsthand observation. It notes that in the church's early years, several formal indictments were made against its leader, John Alexander Dowie, by "Chicago authorities," prominent medical doctors, and ministers of orthodox denominations (34).

This dissertation, which includes material drawn from interviews and correspondence with church members and from contemporary reactions to the movement, provides a fascinating account of its origins and sociocultural form. Dowie was born in Scotland in 1847, and trained in Australia as a Congregational pastor. Earlier work there on behalf of the poor through the Social Reform party gave way to a conviction that he could provide more pragmatic relief with his own powers of divine healing (Harlan 1906:29). He came to North America in 1888 and moved to Chicago in 1890, where he established the headquarters of his controversial church. His crusade, firmly centered on the power of divine healing, gathered great momentum at the time of the Chicago World's Fair in 1893. Mapping the entire city into "parishes," he organized an energetic evangelical mission, founding the Christian Catholic (later Apostolic) Church in Zion in 1896, with himself as "General Overseer" (35). In 1899, he formed the Zion Land Investment Association and, largely on the basis of tithes from his followers, secured 6,500 acres on Lake Michigan, 42 miles north of Chicago, on which he founded Zion City (6). Within a year, the city boasted a population of several thousand, a bank, a brickyard, and several stores and small factories. There were also schools and a printing press, all registered under the absolute ownership of Dowie himself (9). A current observer summarized the popular cynical reaction to this conflation of the "sacred" and "secular" by remarking that "there they make a business of religion" (12). But the semantic logic of the venture was much more complex. Centered on the imposing Zion Temple, the town was to be a haven of purity from the sinful environment, signified in the Zion cosmology by "that most wicked city," Chicago. Zion was the focus of physical and spiritual reunion, of pragmatic "cleansing and healing." Here the habitual practices of everyday life were reformed and the social universe reclaimed and circumscribed by the church. *Lex Dei* was to regain control of an unruly secular world, reversing the division enshrined in the Protestant Reformation. Most crucially, these transformations were played out upon the corporeal body, whose metamorphosis symbolized the healing of a homologous social order. Church law dictated detailed physical reform, specifying conventions of diet, casual interaction, and the organization of everyday space and time.

The testimonies provided by participants in the Zion movement give reasonable evidence of its socioeconomic basis. Despite the founding of several branches abroad, its major following was drawn from the Midwestern cities of the United States (Harlan, 1906:161ff.).[12] Its leadership and a proportion of the membership appear to have been of petit bourgeois origin—clerics, self-employed artisans, and struggling small businessmen—but the majority were both poor and working-class. Several appear to have been labor migrants, and the general "lack of education" and "inability to succeed anywhere else" were noted by many middle-class observers (169, 175). Clearly, this was a population marginal to the late nineteenth-century industrial and commercial "take-off" in such cities as Chicago, and sufficiently distanced from the forms of bourgeois experience to reject the assumptions fundamental to its ideology, especially those of power and agency; a population, in other words, protesting what appeared to be the uncontrollable invasion of their everyday world by forces inscrutable and alienating.

The Zion movement was millennial in ideology: through the moral reformation of everyday life, the restoration of the "primitive" church, and the revival of apostolic mediation, the second coming would be realized (Harlan 1906:96ff.). This restoration implied a return to a shared image of "origin" residing in the reunification of man and spirit, and in a recentered social world whose valuables, like cargo, would then lend themselves to control by the faithful. First and foremost, however, God must acquire again the direct material power denied him by the orthodox churches, a power which would revitalize the church of Zion and reverse the marginality and impotence brought upon them by an evil world. Man's dualistic state, his divorce from spirit, was a fiction of modern "human philosophy and ordinary Christianity" (151). In truth, the human being was tripartite; each person was centered on the Holy Spirit, which flowed through the psyche and the soma, uniting them, and also fusing the congregation of the faithful in a single, dynamic whole (150; see figure 6). Thus reconstituted, the person became a part of "one great family" of Zion and could set about constructing a community in which industrial production, commerce, and politics could be encompassed and reformed. The runaway urban world would be reclaimed again, its alienating logic replaced by that of the "original" theocracy. Man and his material context would together be "healed and cleansed." The healing of affliction was the most pervasive metaphor of the culture of Zion. This, of course, was also the case for several other urban apocalyptic movements in North America at the time—Christian Science, and the many small groups referred to collectively by one contemporary observer as the "Mind-Cure Movement" (110).

The specific form of such a chiliastic ideology can be understood only in relation to its particular sociocultural context. Like other millenary movements, the Church of Zion was the product of radical social change and of subsequent structural contradictions which, while not perceived as class conflict by the displaced, yet formed their consciousness in a manner at odds with the hegemonic culture (Worsley 1968). But why, in the case examined here, should this rejection have been couched in a discourse about somatic symptoms, about a mode of "healing" that also required the transformation of relations of production and exchange? This question is particularly apposite in light of the appeal that such symbols were to have for black workers in South Africa.

The American Zionist movement emerged in an urban milieu structured by the growth and consolidation of industrial capital, by technological advance, and by the aggressive meliorism aptly embodied in the staging of the Chicago World's Fair. The dominant ideology of Protestant industriousness and utilitarian individualism resonated with the secular Emersonian myth of personal achievement, both ideology and myth implying a thoroughgoing division of spirit and matter, church

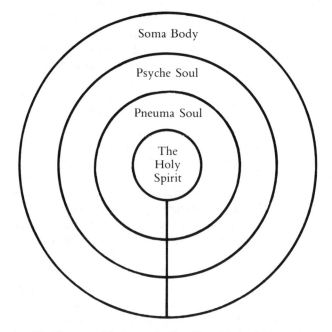

Figure 6   The Concept of the Person in Zion (from Harlan [1906:150]).

and world. But between Protestant utilitarianism and rational meliorism there was no model of collective being and no reflection of the alienation experienced by the wage laborer and struggling small businessman, de-centered in a landscape progressively dominated by industrial and com-mercial monopolies. Zionism and movements like it arose to heal this breach. In the Zionist scheme, the consciousness of marginality was framed in terms of the loss of "original" integrity; and the sense of loss entailed in alienation was described as the uncoupling of man and God, body and spirit, self and other, and church and state. Zion attempted to counter estrangement by constructing a bounded community whose so-ciocultural logic appeared integrative, contained, and controllable. Such movements are products of their context; notwithstanding their claims to originality, they draw their signs from the encompassing discourse which they seek to reform (cf. Lipset and Raab 1970 on similar processes in right-wing "extremist" movements). In the case of Dowie's Zion the paradise to be regained was not cast in some preindustrial peasant idiom, or even in the terms of early mercantile capitalism. The cultural elements were contemporary—somatic health, industrial production, business en-terprise, and the forms of state government. But these elements were used to fashion a new structure of categories, a *bricolage* which reordered their preexisting relations, and replaced the alienating logic of the market with the "original" nondualistic law of God.[13]

The particular elements that made up the Zionist scheme, then, were preeminent symbols of the world that they sought to reform. As social historians have noted, a dominant metaphor in the various cultural dis-courses of Western Europe in the nineteenth century was that of organi-zation; organization modeled on the physiological structure of the human being, who had been increasingly objectivized and reduced to a biological individual (Foucault 1975; Figlio 1976). In a dualistic world in which spirit was ever more residual and the terms of secular materialism increasingly pervasive, the contrast between physical health and disease came to edge aside less reductionist sociomoral categorizations of the human condition (Foucault 1975; Zola 1972). Health came to replace sal-vation in this scheme (Foucault 1975:198), and the reduction of human existence to biological individualism was reinforced by the growing le-gitimacy of the applied life-sciences and the rising status of biomedicine as a bourgeois profession (Starr 1982). Biomedical knowledge, especially after the emergence of the germ theory of disease, served to exacerbate the process of reduction, its increasingly influential image of the person as a decontextualized and amoral being reproducing rather than cutting across the categories of alienation (Powles 1973; Comaroff 1982[a]). It would thus seem hardly surprising that movements trying to reverse the experience of estrangement and to protest established ideologies should do so in the idiom of physical illness, and that they should resist its bio-medical coding and seek a healing power both personalized and spir-itualized. The wider culture might have come to index disease almost exclusively in biophysical symptoms, but the testimony of many of the recruits to Zion reveals a distinct ambivalence toward secular medical practice. One, for instance, speaks of the "unsanctified methods of sur-gical butchery" (Harlan 1906:167). Such testimony might well reflect inadequacies in the medical services available to the poor in North Amer-ican cities at the time. More fundamentally, however, it also expresses a rejection of the categories of the cultural scheme in which healing was purely a matter of rational technical intervention, the repair of the body physical alone. Dowie strongly opposed the secularization of healing, which he saw as undermining the power of a pragmatically conceived Holy Spirit: "The heathen[s] have sense enough to know that the book in every page teaches divine healing. . . . Your missionary boards send out your infernal lies, and your medicine chest, and your surgical knives, and tell the Heathen Christ is not the same [i.e. as the miraculous healer of biblical times]" (Harlan 1906:89). Dowie's evangelists were indeed to find black migrant workers in southern Africa very susceptible to his nondualistic concept of healing.

But the explicit stress upon bodily healing in the Zion movement was also a particular cultural manifestation of a more general symbolic pro-cess, one arising out of the universal role of the body in mediating be-tween personal experience and the social and material context. Anthropologists have long insisted that physical disorder indexes social disruption, and that healing is a simultaneously individual and collective process (Turner 1967:359ff.). Indeed the body may be manipulated, *pars pro toto,* in the attempt to reform the immediate world. Thus, the symp-toms of the Zion followers, symptoms regarded by contemporary ob-servers as "hysterical" and "hypochondriacal," may be seen as soma-tized signs of a wider social malaise. This was a cult of affliction, but the ills it addressed spoke of more than mere physical dislocation. They ex-pressed the desire to reconstitute, through the ritualized reconstruction of the body personal, the encompassing orders of power and production that it signified. Divine healing sought to reintegrate body, soul, and spirit, to cast out "disease," the intrusive influence of Satan (Harlan 1906:113). But the frequent parallel of healing and social cleansing in Dowie's rhetoric explicitly linked the personal and the social corpus. Thus the reintegrated self, referred to by Dowie as the "temple of God" (Harlan 1906:90), was focused on the inner presence of the Holy Spirit, its form a microcosm of the city of Zion—which, in turn, was centered upon the great Temple and the supreme human mediator of divine power.

Radical personal and social reconstruction were also pursued through the careful reform of the "natural" structures of everyday practice, and of the taken-for-granted organization of space and time. In his dissertation, Harlan notes:

There are a number of peculiarities of a religious nature one sees in Zion City. The ordinary greeting is "Peace to Thee" instead of "Good morning," and the usual response is "Peace to Thee be multiplied," and if the Hebrew language were being used instead of the English translation, one would imagine himself among the Israelites of old. At nine A.M. the whistle at the power house blows and for two minutes, Mohammedan fashion, everybody turns to pray in whatever place and from whatever work or occupation, until the same whistle bids them turn their thoughts to secular things again. A number of things are entirely forbidden in Zion City. Billboards at the cross streets caution one that swearing or smoking or bad language of any sort are not allowed. Zion City will tolerate no breweries, no saloons, no drug or tobacco stores, no physician's or surgeon's offices, no theaters, no gambling places, no dance halls, no secret lodge rooms, no keeping or selling of swine's flesh. During the history of the city these regulations have been rigidly enforced, in fact there has seldom been any attempt at infringement (Harlan 1906:15–16).

The new center of Zion was fixed, via the apostolic mediation of its leader, on the "original," personalized, and pragmatic power of God, whose true followers were now locked in combat with the tangible intrusions of Satan. As Harlan (1906:139) observes, the stress upon the intervention of "a personal Deity and personal Devil in mundane affairs" was out of step with the theology then "commonly heard in Christian pulpits." This graphic opposition of personalized moral forces provided a model for the seemingly inexplicable features of life in a world out of control, a model which permitted action upon that world by those who suffered it. Taussig (1980:18) has noted that, for peasants in South America whose contact with industrial-capitalism has been short-lived, the figure of the devil served to anthropomorphize their experience of subjugation. In contrast, he suggests, for those living within mature capitalist systems, the "subjugation of social relations to the economic laws of commodities" acquires "the stamp of fact" and is no longer the focus of such resistance (Taussig 1980:29).

Yet there is growing evidence from within mature industrial-capitalist systems that the thoroughgoing effectiveness of this process of naturalization, of the "stamp of fact," cannot be assumed, particularly in respect of those excluded not only from the realm of bourgeois control but also from the experience of some degree of self-determination as workers in a "free" labor market. As I have noted, citing Williams (1977), dominant cultural orders and the modes of consciousness they configure never enjoy absolute hegemony in any social system. The followers of Zion, like many subsequent "sectarians," "apocalyptics," "deviants," and "folk devils" (Cohen 1980), saw as unnatural the image of themselves projected by an industrial society whose contradictions were inadequately reconciled—at least, for them—by dominant ideologies. They experienced the cultural categories of nineteenth-century capitalism as inauthentic, and strove to reanimate a disenchanted world, to encompass the production and exchange of commodities that had been set loose by the Devil, and to resituate them in a social order based on clear anthropomorphic foundations.

The logic and legitimacy of this "primitive" order was to be found in the text of the Bible, which represented a common myth of origin to a diverse population unified only by a shared structural predicament. But it was a Bible read as an inscription of the pragmatic power of the spirit; not one understood in terms of modern Western theology, which viewed these same texts as both social history and allegory. Yet if the Bible was to be metaphor, it was by its very nature polyvalent, capable of yielding a message very different from that of Protestant orthodoxy. As Hebdige (1979:33) notes, it can quite easily be interpreted as recommending not a patient suffering but an "immediate internal 'healing of the breach' between pain and desire." The sociocultural forms of Dowie's Zion incorporated the person in a dynamic social order, in which human relations boldly recaptured and reintegrated the world of spirit and matter. But, like the cargo cults it resembled in many respects, the thrust of Zion's symbolic practice was not a mere return to a *status quo ante;* for it was motivated by pain and desire that were products of the process of alienation itself, a disjuncture between means and ends, and between subjective being and the objective world. Dowie's movement was an attempt to render the cargo of the industrial capitalist world, whose value was captured in his emphasis on manufacturing and commerce, susceptible to the control of the faithful. It was not these values themselves as much as the logic that determined their flow and distribution that Zion sought to reform. Its communal rituals proclaimed with splendid clarity the structure of this reorganization, one in which the invisible forces of political, economic, and cultural domination were objectified and brought under the control of the Kingdom of Zion.

Of course, this exercise in reconstruction was itself riddled with contradictions: the economic basis of the American Zionist movement, despite considerable ingenuity on the part of its founder, was soon in severe difficulty; for the organizational principles of theocracy and community in Zion City soon showed themselves incapable of delivering the cargo, being inhospitable to modes of production and exchange that could subsist, let alone flourish, in relation to the wider market (Harlan 1906:8ff.).

Zionists in a Strange Land

By 1904, when the first "overseer" from Zion City arrived in Johannesburg to bestow instant membership by triune immersion upon twenty-seven black South Africans, the parent organization was foundering on these very contradictions. Dowie had been replaced as leader in 1906, and the "religious and ecclesiastical side of Zion's work" had been severed from the commercial (Harlan 1906:7). The church was subsequently to split into six distinct organizations (Sundkler 1961:48). This is significant for our concerns, because the fission inherent in the structure of the original church has been a continuing feature of the movement it spawned in southern Africa. Indeed, the rate of subdivision has increased steadily over the years. While the precipitating conflicts have concerned disputes among the leaders over the exercise of authority, typically in respect of financial control, these disputes express a more deep-seated contradiction inherent in Dowie's original vision and especially evident in the South African context: that the Zionist community, founded as it was upon principles disharmonic with those of the embracing socio-economic system, could be viable within that system and could reverse the conditions which had given rise to dissent in the first place.

As Sundkler (1976:16ff.) has shown, the first evangelists of Dowie's Zion, in contrast to their orthodox counterparts, were actually solicited to the South African field. In fact, it was from the Dutch Reformed mission to the Zulu that the first Zionist church was to emerge; the Boer missionary, a renegade from staunch Calvinism, established a center for pragmatic healing in the image of "Zion." The name "Zion," in this case, appears to have come directly from a Dutch Moravian hymnal, *Zions Liedere*. Ostracized by the Dutch Reformed community, he soon sought to identify with the movement in Zion City, Illinois, which shared both the name and the pragmatic emphasis of the embryonic Zulu church (Sundkler 1976:30).

Dowie responded immediately by sending an emissary from Zion City, who was later followed by representatives of the other groups that had seceded from the parent movement. Each projected a transformation of the founding scheme, a progressive revelation, drawn from the same biblical repertoire, each held to be the true and final completion of the vision of Zion. Thus, while the original church had claimed inspired leadership, apostolic mediation, and divine insight, it had set itself firmly against "excessive emotionalism." Dowie, apparently, "was never friendly to those who are in the habit of seeing things" (Harlan 1906: 189); indeed, his strict control of enthusiastic outbursts appears, for a time, to have limited challenges to his leadership on grounds of rival spiritual election. Subsequent secessionists exercised less restraint and, by 1908, emissaries of one such group arrived in Johannesburg, proclaiming that, while Zion had taught immersion and divine healing, it had neglected the Pentecost (Sundkler 1961:48). Black Zionist converts incorporated the pentecostal theme with great readiness; it seemed to accord with indigenous notions of pragmatic spirit forces and to redress the depersonalization and powerlessness of the urban labor experience. Soon the alliance with white Afrikaner fundamentalists was left behind.

The inclusion of spirit possession and inspired leadership into the Zionist repertoire enhanced the potential for fission, since, as Weber long ago pointed out (1947:358ff.), charismatic authority militates against stable institutionalization. This mode of exercizing power, of course, stands in contrast to Western notions of routinized clerical authority; the fact that the original Zionist leaders were ascribed spiritual gifts, therefore, was itself a defiance of the established principles of power relations and consistent with the movement's overall iconoclastic stance. But the opportunity cost of such power is that it remains unstable and transient unless routinized by normative means (Weber 1947:363), and Dowie only managed to restrain it for a limited period. Zionism in southern Africa was in fact to institutionalize instability early on, an instability characterized by a process of repetitive revelation and secession that constantly gave rise to new churches while reproducing their stereotyped formal structure. In part, this pattern was the product of a double set of structural constraints: prophetic figures were unable ever to remove the fundamental contradictions that had given rise to their contesting movements, and so were only occasionally able to maintain secure followings; yet the state apparatus prevented the prospect of extending such protest beyond the ritual domain, thereby reinforcing affiliation to the movement itself, if not to a particular church. It is this that seems to account for the widely noted tendency of Zionists in South Africa to move frequently between similar groups (cf. Berglund 1967).

From the initial clutch of converts in Johannesburg a spate of proliferating Zionist groups emerged, moving outward from the epicenter to other urban areas and to rural communities. The initial conversions had drawn many migrant workers from the Methodist and Independent ranks; some, however, had never been formal members of any denomination. From the start, the Zionists were stereotyped as poor and uneducated by the literate Protestant elite. As we shall see, these churches may be regarded as a unitary class of religious movement; not only do they display a common structural form, but they also constitute an indigenous category, both from within and without, as *Basione* ("Zionist") and as *dikereke tsa moya* ("Churches of the Spirit"). Sundkler remarked on the surprising degree of uniformity that underlay the seeming diversity of these sects (1961:55), all exhibiting such key features as healing, glossolalia, purification rites, and behavioral taboos.[14] But he also noted that significant transformations had occurred "in the transfer from Lake Michigan to the streams and ponds of Zululand" (1961:49). Indeed, the thirty-three or more churches in the Mafeking district in the late 1960s, while structurally similar to those described by Sundkler and others,[15] also bore clear signs of a mutually transforming relationship with the local Tshidi system. In fact, the form and significance of the Zionist groups could only be adequately understood when placed within the wider context of this relationship and the endogenous cultural elements from which it was constructed.

Tshidi Churches and the Signs of Inequality

The records of the Tshidi Tribal Office reflect the fact that a steady stream of mission associations and Independent churches have sought to establish branches in the chiefdom since overrule. These Protestant denominations went through the formal procedure of seeking chiefly permission; bureaucratic forms were basic to their organization, and they required sites on which to build their churches; in this, they reproduced the symbolic and institutional practices of the dominant neocolonial culture. In contrast, the Zionist denominations all entered the Tshidi domain with returning migrants or lone itinerant "prophets" in search of local followings. They tended to dispense with the formalities of official permission, organizing collective rites in domestic contexts or under trees at the periphery of the stad. This, of course, is consonant with the fact that the sociocultural bases of these movements contrasted with those of established authority; they did not recognize its maps—or its categories of center and periphery, church and world, or public and private. Zionist organization was predicated upon personalized rather than bureaucratic principles, and both leaders and followers were mostly illiterate.

Around the time of formal overrule, the majority of Tshidi became nominal converts to Methodism. The mission, as we have seen, had offered a *lingua franca* for colonizer and colonized; it established the initial terms for an emerging black national culture and provided schooling for what seemed, at the time, to be a future of "Westernization" and integration. In Mafeking, the original church came to replace the chiefly court as the focus for such collective ritual as prayers for rain, and emerged as the power base for the educated elite. The Anglican and Roman Catholic denominations both subsequently established congregations in Mafeking, the new leadership prospects of the former recruiting a small following from the nonroyal elite, and the latter being associated with the ruling line itself,[16] and the poorest inhabitants of the town, for whom it provided alms and education. But the Methodist church remained the recognized "official" denomination of the Tshidi.

At the same time, a steady stream of Zionist groups were attempting to recruit followings in the district (Comaroff 1974:83).[17] The majority managed to found small congregations, some comprising only a clutch of kin, but many soon disappeared without a trace. During the second and third decades of the century, more than fifteen African Independent churches established themselves in the area, but only half of them remained viable in the late 1960s.[18] Records suggest that, in the first two decades after the accession of Chief Lotlamoreng in 1919, an increasing number of rank-and-file Methodists were joining these churches; a realignment of cultural categories was taking place, in which Independent Christianity was providing an alternative for many Tshidi who perceived themselves marginal to the status of the literate elite. After World War II, a further shift was discernible, for both the mission and the Independent denominations were increasingly losing members to the Zionists. In fact, by far the largest number of new churches established in the Mafeking district in the postwar years were of this category, and many of them underwent further subdivision on local soil. Surveys and personal histories show how the trajectory from orthodoxy to Zionism was realized in the structure of individual biographies; older Tshidi had typically been "born" in the Methodist church, moved to the Independent groups during early adulthood and labor migration, and joined the Zionists later in their careers, often when suffering personal affliction. But younger Tshidi were often recruited directly to the Zionist ranks. Within the latter, there was frequent movement between groups.

The polarization between orthodox Protestants and the Zionists had proceeded apace, marking, by 1970, yet a further realignment of categories, a distinction between "orthodoxy" (dikereke tsa molao; "churches of the law") and "Zion" (Basione; or dikereka tsa moya; "churches of the spirit") which paralleled the pattern that had developed in other black South African communities (West 1975:18). The emergence of this distinction was itself entailed in the socioeconomic polarization within the Tshidi community outlined above: the contrast between orthodoxy and Zionism which arose out of the articulation of indigenous and external cultural forms came to mediate processes of structural differentiation, themselves of more global origin; and it provided a conceptual order through which Tshidi perceived and acted upon their world. Orthodox Protestantism was now explicitly associated with the establishment, both local and national, while Zionism stood for the repudiation of hegemonies. The binary opposition between them, which has increasingly eclipsed subtle symbolic contrasts, has been brought into relation—if not strict alignment—with the cleavage which sets Tshidi peasant-proletarians off from the mainstream culture and from their bourgeois and petit bourgeois fellows. Thus the constructs and practices, the colors, spaces, and schedules of Zionism have become the generalized markers of the illiterate poor, of an entire mode of being that is counterposed with the legitimacy of orthodoxy and those who subscribe to it (see plates 4 and 5).

Yet the binary contrast between Zionism and orthodoxy, albeit a clear expression of the dynamics of class formation, reflects the mediation of local cultural categories. Thus, while it provides the signs of inequality, this religious opposition neither generates a neat alignment along class lines nor does it precipitate a class consciousness in any strict sense. There remain in the Methodist church many poor Tshidi, most of them elderly, whose reverence for its authority still outweighs the conflict it engenders; and a large number of orthodox Protestants will turn to Zionist healing in the face of personal affliction, although they might do so in secret. Also, despite their dwindling ranks, the Independent churches still hold a position in the Tshidi field which cuts across the dichotomy of establishment and counterculture. At the same time, such statistics of church membership as are obtainable do suggest a continuing process of polarization.[19] The records that were available in 1970 indicate that there were some 6,000 Tshidi in the Mafeking district formally affiliated with international Western denominations. Of these, some 4,750 were orthodox Protestants, the rest being associated with such churches as the Catholic or Seventh Day Adventist.[20] Only 3,750 Zionists were enumerated by this means, but I estimate that the figure pertains to no more than two-thirds of the local groups, and it takes no account of the "floating population" in these churches, which is far larger than the regular membership (cf. Sundkler 1961:167). The African Independent churches numbered just over 1,000 members, nearly half of whom were in the African Methodist Episcopal Church, which, while independent of orthodox Methodism, retains its North American links. A detailed analysis of membership samples suggests that while a proportion of the poor and uneducated remain in the orthodox churches, the Zionist ranks draw none of the petite bourgeoisie as formal adherents (see Comaroff 1974:164ff. for a fuller account). The few cases of mobility from Zionism to orthodoxy were associated with attempts to gain government employment or entree into a state-controlled secondary school; for Zionist affiliation was a handicap, being associated by whites, as well as by the local elite, with "primitiveness" and general "unreliability."

The fact that this religious differentiation did not generate an explicit awareness of "class" ought to be regarded in light of Wallerstein's reminder (1979:177) that mature class consciousness is rare, not only in African history but in history in general. The contrast between Zionism

Plate 4   The External Forms of Orthodoxy: The minister and the women's
Manyano of the Bantu Methodist Church of South Africa (Independent) seated in
front of their church.

and orthodoxy is appropriately understood as a relation between "status groups" in the sense specified by Wallerstein (1979:181): "status groups are the blurred collective representations of class," representations whose outlines are sharpened in the context of heightened conflict. Thus global processes of social differentiation have been perceived, from the local Tshidi perspective, as relations of inequality; relations now indexed less in terms of agnatic rank than in religious denomination, which itself encodes such features as education and wealth. Denomination, in turn, has become subsumed in a segmentary order of status-group signifiers, nesting into ethnicity (as exemplified in the Tshidi response to Tswana nationhood) and, ultimately, race. While Tshidi notions of status are informed by an awareness of economic exploitation and political oppression, they are not conceived in terms of relative access to, and control over, the means of production. Thus, while they may be seen as expressing and acting upon class conflicts, Tshidi perceptions of differentiation only partially overlap with class divisions.

The rise of Zionism marks the emergence, within a formerly unitary semantic universe, of a systematic counterculture, a modus operandi explicitly associated with those estranged from the centers of power and communication. As we shall see, its adherents have seldom directly resisted the mechanisms of politico-economic domination—a formidable prospect in such coercive contexts—but they have contested the logic of the sociocultural system of which they are a part. Drawing on a notion of power that remains embedded in ritual practice, the Zionist has attempted to encompass and transform alienating structures of control. The model of proliferating charismatic leadership and small face-to-face congregations is eminently suited to the task, but Zionism speaks a language greatly different from that of the established cultural order. Its very existence is an exercise in determined estrangement from an effacing world, a holistic stance that has been judged as decidedly "other" by members of the local establishment. As one local teacher put it: "you can see the Zionist anywhere. His dress, the way he holds his body, and the look in his eye. What he eats, whom he may marry—its all laid down. He's not the same person once he starts to follow the drum."

In contrast, the petite bourgeoisie continued to espouse Protestant lib-

Plate 5   The External Forms of Zion: The prophet leader and the people of the Morians Episcopal Apostolic Church in Zion gathered at the leader's homestead.

eralism; their worldview was reinforced by the experience of some control over the nature and conditions of work and over established modes
of communication. This consciousness also rested upon a bed of contradictions that threatened its stability: for it existed within a social context
in which racial divisions cut across unities of class, and black social mobility and political expression were severely limited. There were, in other
words, structural impediments to a comprehensive identity with the categories of neocolonial culture. Moreover, the Tshidi petite bourgeoisie
remained part of the local community, within which the ideology of
liberal individualism was being challenged. As a result, Protestant
orthodoxy was subtly transformed, and developed features and emphases which varied from the nineteenth-century mission paradigm. Indeed,
Tshidi Protestant practice expressed a continuing nondualistic logic
which enmeshed the individual in processes of sorcery and pollution, and
placed ancestral mediators between man and God. But in local terms,
such "orthodoxy" represented the self-conscious cultural scheme of the
Tshidi elite, whether or not they were active participants in the churches.
The elite "drew the line" between themselves, Zionism, and "tradition";
while the contradictions of this predicament might motivate them to engage occasionally in "traditional" practice, they perceived this as going
outside the formal bounds of their cultural system.

The dwindling of the African Independent movement has been due to
the fact that it occupies the middle ground in an increasingly polarized
community. Its reformism prevents it from offering the radical alternative presented by the Zionists, but it also lacks the emblems of established status—the material trappings, educated leadership, and rational
bureaucratic structure—favored by the liberal bourgeoisie. In the latter
half of the twentieth century, as black political consciousness in southern
Africa developed its own secular models, both liberal and radical, the
embryonic nationalism of a biblical Ethiopia lost all salience and was
quite simply eclipsed.[21]

To summarize, Tshidi tended to perceive the structural contradictions
of their predicament in terms of the opposition between an idealized and
objectivized *setswana*, "traditional Tswana ways," and *sekgoa*, "white
culture." The referents of these reciprocally defining categories, however, had shifted since their specification in the nineteenth century. For
modern Tshidi, *setswana* now connoted modes of production and social
relationship obtaining "in the time of our chiefs," before the advent of
coercive white domination; it entailed "eating the work of our hands,"
nonmonetized exchange, and the performance of ritual whose logic contrasted with that of the Protestant orthodoxy. *Sekgoa*, on the other hand,
was the world of wage labor (*bereka*) and of "Pretoria," a metonym for
the whole apparatus of state control. But white culture was also the

world of the orthodox church; among the petite bourgeoisie at least, this was associated with the "English"—both English-speaking South Africans and Britons—who contrasted with "Boers" and were the ambiguous fellow travelers with apartheid rather than its cynical architects (cf. Marks n.d.:17).

During the course of this century, two distinct modes of reconciling these contradictions have emerged in the Tshidi context: one identifies with the sociocultural forms of industrial capitalism in their benign aspect, and continues to be associated with the Protestant church; the other, represented by Zionism, seeks to subject the symbols and values of *sekgoa* to indigenously derived notions of practical control. The former has been the mode of resolution most frequently adopted by the petite bourgeoisie, the latter by the proletarianized or semi-proletarianized. The contrast between these two ritual foci, and between the ideological and practical orders they index, has increasingly come to mark the line of emerging class divisions in the Tshidi cultural debate. This symbolic divide has become increasingly salient to Tshidi social discourse, which now generally assumes a stable overlap between religious orientation and social position: the educated are "Methodists"; the illiterate, Zionists; and so on. The articulation between Tshidi sociocultural forms and the southern African political economy has been a continuous process, however, and constituent social relations are engaged in progressive transformation. Local cultural resolutions, such as the religious orientations described here, are themselves in a state of flux and are, in any case, unable to address persisting contradictions in any definitive manner. Yet Tshidi social history in this century *does* move in a perceptible direction, that of increasing dependency upon wage labor, a process that has involved both the perpetuation and the transformation of precolonial structures. It is in relation to this process that the emerging structure of modern Zionism must be seen.

7

Ritual as Historical Practice
Mediation in the Neocolonial Context

The emergent contrast, among the Tshidi, between Protestant orthodoxy and Zionism has not merely provided their most articulate collective representation of social stratification; it has also defined a context within which the transformation of their world may be acknowledged and addressed. It is this latter process which concerns me in this chapter; specifically, the manner in which, through the idiom of Zionism, the peasant-proletarian majority objectifies and reacts to its predicament. In line with my general argument, I shall suggest that modern Zionist signs and practices are the product of a dialectical interaction between indigenous social forms and elements of more general currency in the culture of colonialism. This religious movement, then, must be understood as a unique sociocultural phenomenon, a dynamic construction wrought by the universal process of symbolic mediation working itself out in a specific historical context; as such, it is simultaneously unique and yet one instance of a very general class of social movements.

The Tshidi have been purposive actors in the process of articulation despite the superior determining force exercised by the neocolonial state. I have traced the pattern of their response, noting their growing awareness of the structures of oppression and the developing resistance to the cultural forms of colonialism. I proceed, now, to examine further the logic of such contemporary resistance, for it is in these terms that the significance of Zionism must be viewed.

This, of course, presupposes a particular conception of "resistance" as a social phenomenon; in fact there has developed a lively debate over the meaning of the construct in both Western and colonial contexts (Hobsbawm 1959; Hall et al. 1976; Eco 1972; Hebdige 1979; Prins 1980; Cohen 1980). The debate turns on the definition of the prior constructs of "power," "consciousness," and "intentionality," and positions range along a predictable continuum from a crudely literal, mechanistic view of agency to an emphasis upon iconoclastic texts and "semiotic guerrilla warfare" (Eco 1972). In my conclusion, I shall return to the relationship of symbol, consciousness, and agency as they have been illuminated by this study. At this point, my concern is not to assert the viability of Tshidi resistance but to demonstrate the cogent, if implicit, logic of their opposition to neocolonialism. This logic resides in the historical and symbolic coherence of their practice; I shall suggest that, while the act of resistance has not often been expressly reflected upon, its force is compelling and its meaning, *in situ,* unambiguous. But this meaning is yielded only to a careful and systematic examination of its coded vehicles in their wider sociocultural context. Moreover, "resistance" is typically neither an all-or-nothing phenomenon nor an act in and of itself; it is frequently part and parcel of practices of subjective and collective reconstruction.

That the Tshidi response to colonialism should take a highly coded form is hardly surprising. As van Onselen (1976:239) said of the equally coercive environment of black miners in what was then Southern Rhodesia:

> The analyst who seeks for an index of worker consciousness or an outright demonstration of African resistance should not . . . look for dramatic responses. Compound police, spies, censorship and the *sjambok* [a hide whip, used to discipline black laborers in southern Africa] do not produce an environment conducive to the development of public ideologies, organizations, meetings, petitions or strikes. In tightly controlled situations, such as the compound undoubtedly was, the patterns of resistance amongst black miners should in the first instance be sought in the nooks and crannies of the day-to-day situation.

He goes on to suggest that, in such repressive contexts, resistance is a matter of practical defiance: in the mines, desertion was a rational response to conditions in which disease and death were rampant; "loafing," poor-quality production, and crime directed at employers were implicit rebellions against exploitation (1976:242). He concludes (p. 244):

> These largely silent and unorganized responses of black workers offer eloquent testimony to the existence of a consciousness of who the exploiters were. . . . For Africans to resist spontaneously and directly, they simply needed to perceive the single dimension involved in the relationship of exploiter and exploited (1976:244).

Tshidi came to realize the stark contours of oppression under similar conditions: in the segregated church, the brutal mine compound, and the degrading rituals of apartheid. Suppression of African resistance in South Africa has been an elemental feature of state policy from the beginning, but equally long-lived has been the resilient black struggle. I have noted that, while they made their contribution to the national protest movements in the earlier decades of this century, the Tshidi had, by the late 1960s, entered a period of apparent acquiescence, part of the more widespread hiatus that followed the violent Sharpeville confrontation (Gerhart 1978:212ff.). Although the flame of resistance burnt low during those years, it was to flare up at several points in the 1970s in defiance of the local imposition of the structures of homeland government. Indeed, in the years immediately prior to the "independence" of Bophutatswana, more than one building erected in the name of the new regime in Montshiwa Township was actually burnt to the ground.

In these historical circumstances, while awareness of oppression obviously runs deep, reaction may appear erratic, diffuse, and difficult to characterize. It is here that we must look beyond the conventionally explicit domains of "political action" and "consciousness"; for, when expressions of dissent are prevented from attaining the level of open discourse, a subtle but systematic breach of authoritative cultural codes might make a statement of protest which, by virtue of being rooted in a shared structural predicament and experience of dispossession, conveys an unambiguous message. In such contexts, ritual provides an appropriate medium through which the values and structures of a contradictory world may be addressed and manipulated. And it is in this capacity that the sociocultural forms of Zionism have been pressed into service.

Ritual Form and Cultural Iconoclasm

Hebdige has noted that those marginal to established hegemonies, both in modern Western and Third World contexts, frequently challenge authority in the medium of style; following Volosinov, he examines how focal signs become the objects of contest, how the battle waged at the level of the symbol expresses a more fundamental confrontation: "The struggle between different discourses, different definitions and meanings within ideology is . . . always, at the same time, a struggle within signification: a struggle for the possession of the sign which extends to the most mundane areas of everyday life" (1979:17). Hebdige's account is most successful when dealing with the often self-consciously provocative reworking of orthodox Protestant signs in Jamaican Rastafarian culture (1979:30ff.). In fact, black religious innovation in southern Africa has likewise sought to wrest the Christian "message from the messenger" (Vilakazi 1962:101); and its history has been peppered with battles over the control of master symbols, such as the "right" to baptize or dispense communion. For the guardians of European orthodoxy did not remain passive in the face of an African "heresy" that challenged their imperialist designs for the Kingdom of God. Where early black Independent Christianity was to seize key sacred signs, Zionism was to revalue them radically, and the missionaries were to reflect sorrowfully upon this satanic reversion to "nativism" (cf. Lea 1928). Repeated government commissions in the early years of the century expressed the suspicion that such black iconoclasm might be "mischievously" crossing the boundary between "religion" and "politics."[1]

In appropriating core signs from Protestant orthodoxy and the secular culture that bore it, Zionism resituated them in its own holistic landscape and, by extending them into the mundane "nooks and crannies" of everyday life, naturalized them as the captured bearers of alien power. For all the reasons considered earlier, such cultural construction tends to focus upon the body and its immediate life-world. As in the ritual of the parent movement, it was the images of physical affliction that were to present contradictions inadequately resolved by reigning institutions and ideologies; and it was the polyvalent metaphor of healing that was to provide the means for effecting personal and collective transformation. Of course, the construction of messages through the medium of symbols is the essence of all ritual; it is symbols that convert implicit social meanings into "communication currency" (Munn 1974:580). In my discussion of the precolonial initiation rites, I stressed how their poetic structure permitted the pragmatic transformation of meaning through the ordering of signifiers in the ritual text itself; by this means, paradoxes of everyday experience were presented and "resolved" in accordance with prevailing ideologies. Such symbols as the *moshu* tree were graphic instances of this process: severed from the wild, it retained the powerful substance of its natural context; once located within the text of the ritual, it existed at a new level of significance, its acquired meaning being a function of its position in a novel syntagmatic chain. Though revalued in this manner, it still carried with it preexisting meanings; a "paradigmatic" association, in other words, with the dynamic qualities of the wild, which were subsumed in the new formulation. The domestication of the *moshu,* then, was achieved by resituating it in a more highly coded symbolic context. In the same sense, all ritual constructions present novel associations, even if only to re-present, in fresh guise and new combination, the paradigmatic meanings of the wider culture. Equally, all symbolic innovations are *bricolages,* concoctions of symbols already freighted with significance by a meaningful environment (Lévi-Strauss 1966).

The reconstructions we label "subversive" or "syncretistic" operate according to this same logic, even though their motivation, be it implicit or explicit, is iconoclastic—in the literal sense of the breaking of existing images. Their intent is to deconstruct existing syntagmatic chains, to disrupt paradigmatic associations and, therefore, to undermine the very coherence of the system they contest. Yet, as we saw in the case of American Zion, purposive reconstructions invariably work with images which already bear meaning; and the latter itself comes to be built into the novel system, for signs are never transparent and innovations are always partial. As a result, subversive *bricolages* always perpetuate as they change. At a formal level, then, such processes draw upon the same principles of symbolic construction as do all cultural reproductions and transformations; they are merely rendered more dramatic and, at times, self-conscious by conditions of radical structural change, especially where it involves the confrontation of markedly asymmetrical social systems.

The widespread syncretistic movements that have accompanied capitalist penetration into the Third World are frequently also subversive *bricolages;* that is, they are motivated by an opposition to the dominant system. While they have generally lacked the degree of self-consciousness of some religious or aesthetic movements, or of the marginal youth cultures of the modern West, they are nevertheless a purposive attempt to defy the authority of the hegemonic order. Their substantive forms, of course, vary according to context-specific contradictions arising within the process of articulation (cf. Worsley 1968); but addressing the implications of proletarianization and colonial domination, iconoclastic *bricoleurs* everywhere struggle to control key signs and to construct an order of practice that might domesticate the divisive forces that have come to pervade their environment. Such exercises do more than just express revolt; they are also more than mere acts of self-representation. Rather, they are at once both expressive and pragmatic, for they aim to change the real world by inducing transformations in the world of symbol and rite. Hebdige (1979) suggests that youth stylists create *bricolages* as icons of their own structural marginality: but African Zionists construct rituals so as to reform the world in the image they have created, to reestablish a dynamic correspondence between the self and the structures that contain it. Their epistemology remains "magical" in the sense that they make no thoroughgoing distinction between symbols and their phenomenal referents. The former have the power to affect the latter, just as "spirit" and "matter" might act upon each other in the course of everyday life. To these Zionists, in other words, healing is not an explicitly expressive process; it is a pragmatic reality achieved through the manipulation of words, objects, and gestures capable of channelizing diffuse power in such as way as to alter the state of bodies physical and social.

Patently, the rituals of Zion have no direct impact on the structural predicament of black South Africans, although this does not mean that the rituals lack historical significance. Quite the opposite, their influence on the consciousness and practice of *all* South Africans is considerable, a point to which I shall return. More immediately, however, it is the very fact that these rituals must inevitably fail in the long run that accounts both for the sociocultural form of the Zionist groups and for their stereotypic reproduction. For, on the one hand, the Zionist presentation of experiential conflict and its message of estrangement and resistance loses none of its exclusive salience; yet, on the other, its ineffective resolution of these very contradictions leads directly to the high level of fission and mobility between groups, often remarked on but never satisfactorily explained (see Berglund 1967). This constant process of subdivision and movement is realized through an ideology of progressive revelation: while Zionism promises an instant millennium, indexed in the tangible restoration of depleted physical and social being, each prophet offers his/her followers a more perfect vision, a more effective route to the realization of "apocalypse now." The potential for fission and proliferation, a structural feature appropriate to South African conditions, is itself a function of the institutionalization of iconoclasm and ritual reconstruction. At the same time, though, despite the ideological stress on innovation, prophetic revelations may be understood as a string of *bricolages* that endlessly recycle a limited stock of symbols. The latter are themselves ordered in a relatively stable system, one which describes a coherent redefinition of the neocolonial world.

The Symbolic Structure of Tshidi Zion

While the Zionist church constitutes a marked and unitary category, I never encountered a Tshidi adherent—leader or follower—who was able to offer an explicit account of the history or theological charter of the movement. Several prophets (*baporafota*) stated that it had originated in America rather than in England, the home of the Methodists and, for Tshidi, of white orthodoxy in general; and two leaders of the local branch of the Zion Christian Church, the largest Zionist group in the country, stated that their "law" (*molao*) was that of John the Baptist and the prophet Immanuel. As Sundkler (1961:59) has noted, John the Baptist is a central figure in the South African Zionist cosmos, personifying the pragmatic harnessing of divine power through the baptismal waters of the River Jordan. Dowie, whose use of Scripture had been eclectic and literalist, had placed much emphasis upon baptism as the practical route to healing and salvation (Harlan 1906:165) and had referred to himself as Elijah the Restorer (Harlan 1906:4), thereby linking divine healing to an imminent millennium. Tshidi Zion has its sights fixed on a distinctly this-worldly utopia; the prophet Elijah has been eclipsed, for the ZCC church at least, by Immanuel, the name given to its now deceased founder, who had claimed to be the living instantiation of the Holy Spirit. Such prophetic identification is a common mode of rooting congregations in the soil of a biblical Zion, though the place of the emblematic figures within the wider scriptural text is seldom a matter of express concern. As Sundkler (1961:181) long ago observed, pragmatic ritual replaces expository scripture in the Zionist cultural scheme; to wit, for illiterate Tshidi, the "book" and the "word" have their prime significance as condensed ritual symbols of the power of literacy.

In fact, Zionists were most frequently described by other Tshidi as people who "baptized," "practiced healing," "observed taboos," or "followed the drum." Their system is one whose meaningful cohesion resides in the context of action, of both codified ritual practice and mundane daily routine. Zionists are what Zionists do; and their primary mnemonic is lodged not in Scripture but in the physical body and its immediate spatiotemporal location.

The association of "spirit" and "water" is widespread in South African Zionism (Sundkler 1961:205); in the Tshidi context, these constructs condense meanings that contain the essence of Zion itself. First there is the focal role of the Holy Spirit, the distinguishing feature of the whole movement, whose very name—*moya,* "breath/life," rather than *modimo,* a distant, disembodied supernatural force—underlines its physical grounding. Harking back to the pragmatic "breath of God" envisaged by Dowie (Harlan 1906:152), *moya* is also the indigenous term for the spirit force practically incorporated in human life, standing in stark contrast to the transcendent God of Protestant orthodoxy. This contrast is reinforced by the linking of spirit and water, for the latter serves as the impersonal embodiment of spirit in this scheme, the means through which it becomes accessible to manipulation. Spirit, breath, and water are all seen as essentially animating; they are substantial yet fluid, containable yet self-regulating, and they are capable of pervading space within and outside the body.[2] In this manner, the Zionist scheme reverses the process of reification, inverting the progressive segregation of matter and spirit that was central to the mission church and the industrial workplace. The materialization of spirit is not a mere return to a "traditional" cosmology, notwithstanding the fact that the concept of *moya* does incorporate the notion of concentrated ancestral power (cf. Sundkler 1961:249ff.); the Holy Spirit is also the potent universalist God of the colonizers, whose might is thus channeled and domesticated by the practices of Zion.

It will be recalled that control over water was an essential part of politico-ritual power in the precolonial system; moreover, rainmaking and wells became focal signs in the colonial encounter, the object of struggle between missionaries and chiefs. Water also had an important role in the indigenous symbolic scheme, Tswana rites of purification in healing and initiation playing upon its universal significance as solvent. Zionism, too, makes central use of the transformative capacity of water, the icon of the biblical Baptist uniting the precolonial notion of *motlhapiso* ("ritual washing") with *kolobetso* (literally, "to make wet"; or baptism in the Protestant lexicon). In the Zionist scheme, holy water serves to dissolve form and usurp space, constituting a medium within which categorical relations can be reformed and physical and social boundaries redrawn. The baptism of initiates dissolves former identities indexed in the corporeal body; and the circulation of water among the members of the church establishes a fluid unity of spirit that cuts across the social and physical discontinuities of the neocolonial world.

Indeed, the act of imbibing holy water to "quench the thirst" (*go tima lenyôra*) is a crucial element in the ritual of Zion. The churches are referred to as *didiba* ("wells"),[3] an image which conflates biblical vitalization with what was one of the most dramatic innovations brought by the Methodist mission; in this drought-ridden landscape, it signifies the damming of quickening spirit, achieved through the force of encapsulating ritual and reformed habitual practice. The damming of spirit is itself paralleled in a wealth of imagery associated with moisture. For example, *pula* ("rain") and *tsididi* ("coolness"), as elsewhere in the Tswana world, serve here as terms of auspiciousness; and the Zionist color scheme emphasizes green and blue, associated with lush plant growth and water. It was to the wells that the afflicted, the "thirsty" and "oppressed," came to drink (*nwa*), to be inspired ("entered"; *tsenwa*) by spirit. Here deflated body margins were restored and the reciprocal exchange between person and world reestablished.

The metaphors of thirst and oppression appear widely in Zionist ritual and connote existential states through images of bodily affliction, affliction which entails an imbalance in the relationship of "inside" to "outside," of individual and context. These images, again, are transformations of precolonial constructs: thirst (*kgakgabela*) implied a desiccation of bodily substance through the disruptions caused by pollution or sorcery, and oppression (*patikêgo*) suggested a forcible compression of bodily space through pressure on its margins. These concepts have in fact been subtly revalued, tuned to the novel system of meanings through which Zionism speaks to the effects on the body and person of a changed social world. As we shall see, these metaphors function in healing rites to describe specific symptoms; in so doing they link particular cases of suffering to a more global existential malaise. For they place individual experience within its structural context. "Thirst" refers both to suffering due to malign physical intrusion and to the general disruption of relations between persons and their contexts; it also images the explicit preoccupation with wresting a living from the parched soil of the rural reserve. Similarly, "oppression" conveys a bodily wasting or shriveling; it also connotes the forcible contraction of physical and social space engineered by the South African state. In fact, Tshidi colloquial usage *pitlagangwa* "oppressed"; "crushed") conveys a sense of the routine harassment of trying practical conditions.

Let us proceed to examine the sociocultural features of modern Tshidi Zionism in more detail. This account is based on the observation of a number of churches in Mafeking in 1969–70. I deal here with two in particular—one main example, and one subsidiary—each of which is a transformation of a common underlying structural order. My analysis will thus move between the specific instances and the more inclusive class of phenomena they represent. At the time of fieldwork, the Full Witness Apostolic Church in Zion and the Zion Christian Church had had established followings in the district for at least fifteen years. These two groups lay at the opposite ends of the spectrum of the Zionist movement in South Africa. Each had a central place which was its main ritual focus, and subsidiary branches, known locally as "descendants" (*dikokomana*). But, whereas the small Full Witness Church had been founded by secession and the leader's homestead was its "great house" (*ntlo ya bogolo*), the local Z.C.C. was a branch of the largest Zionist church in South Africa; centered on its founder's seat in the Northern Transvaal, it was estimated to have a following of over 200,000 (cf. West 1975:22). In analyzing these groups, I shall consider their social organization and their symbolic and ideological structures, seeking to draw out their meaning both as cultural texts and as social movements.

The Full Witness Apostolic Church in Zion
Social Organization and Habitual Practice

The organizational and ritual forms of the Full Witness Apostolic Church are typical, in most respects, of the majority of Zionist groups in Mafeking and elsewhere in southern Africa. The church was founded in 1956 by Bishop N., a semi-literate Zulu who, for many years, was a contract worker in the mines in Johannesburg. A former member there of the Full Witness of Jehovah Apostolic Church of Africa, he had had a vision instructing him to "go out and preach to the peoples living on the fringes of the desert"; this was interpreted as an injunction to found a church in Mafeking, for he was working with several Tshidi men at the time. By 1970, Bishop N., now fluent in Setswana, had about one hundred followers, forty-five of whom regularly participated in activities at the "great house" in the stad; the rest were distributed among three small groups in the Mafeking district. The entire membership, the majority of which was Tshidi, met at the "great house" twice a year—at Easter ("Passover"; cf. Soundkler 1961:215) and at the Judaically inspired New Year in September.

The "great house" contrasts with the physical forms of Western orthodoxy; it is not "traditional" either, being a 240-foot-square mudbrick structure standing on a barren rectangular plot with a wire fence. Situated on the fringes of the settlement, it is far from the center where most of the Protestant churches are located, and serves as the homestead of the prophet and his polygynous family. It has no external signs marking it off as a ritual site, save the frequent presence in the yard of women dressed in distinctive Zionist uniform—in this case, a white robe, green tunic, and white headscarf. There is also nearly always a knot of people sitting patiently in the shade of the sole tree in the yard, await- ing the leader's attention. The house is the epicenter of the church's re- ligious domain. Its inside space is divided into two cubicles, one serving as a kitchen for the bishop's family, the other being both their sleeping quarters and the place of collective ritual. In the latter, the mud floor is bare, except for one rickety table and a pile of sheep skins (the bedding of the leader's family) in a corner. A yellow satin cloak and large brass staff (*thobane*), the insignia of the prophet, hang from a nail, and a pile of Bibles rests on the ledge of the single small window. On one wall there is a large, outdated calendar sporting a photograph of a sleek American car; calendars and advertisements, which combine images of manufactured goods with signs of literacy and enumeration, are common in South Af- rican Zionist churches (Sundkler 1961:183; Berglund 1967). On a second wall is a highly colored, mass-produced picture of the "Good Shepherd" tending his sheep along the banks of what the bishop assumes to be the River Jordan.

In 1970, Bishop N. was sixty years old. He had been married and had had children prior to coming to Mafeking; but he had arrived there alone and, subsequently, in response to a visionary injunction, had married two local sisters. Such sororal polygyny is not uncommon, either among Tswana or Zulu. Since being called by the spirit (*moya*) in 1956, he has held no other employment, living frugally off the meager donations in cash and kind provided by his following, and off the less than successful cultivation undertaken by his wives in the back garden. Apart from occa- sional visits to the other branches of his church or to sufferers too ill to come to him, he is always in his yard. His life-style does not really re- quire any acknowledgment of existing temporal authorities, either the local Bantu commissioner or the Tshidi chief. Indeed, his domain is remarkably self-contained. Most of his followers live in homesteads clustered about the "great house"; they acknowledge N. as their only leader. Nearly all are female, women with young children from female-headed households. Of the forty-five members of the main congregation, only nine are men, all but three of whom are over fifty and have long careers of migrant labor behind them. Fifteen of the members are kin, mostly claiming matrilateral links, but several recognizing agnatic or multiple ties. None of the females are employed, while two of the men have irregular work in the white town. Given the protracted drought, all live primarily off the proceeds of seasonal migration into the nearby Transvaal.

Male members of the main congregation are referred to en masse as *bagogi* '"leaders") and, as a category, take ritual precedence over the women. But, apart from the bishop, only three men really exercise any leadership: the "minister" (*moruti;* literally, "teacher," the Setswana term for a cleric), the "deacon" (*modiakona*), and the "seer" (*molori;* literally the "dreamer"). The minister is chiefly responsible for practical matters in the ritual context; the deacon acts as the minister's general assistant; and the "seer" shares with the elder of the bishop's wives the role of assistant visionary, diviner, and healer. The bishop himself (*mpisopo*) is both prophetic founder and vessel of the spirit; he determines the distinctive practice of the church and channels divine power (*thata*) on behalf of his following. He is the pivot of all ritual action but takes little part in the everyday organization of the church. While charismatic leadership might be distinguished from "legal" authority in the Full Witness Church (Weber 1947:328ff.), the role of minister is less impersonal and normatively defined than the Weberian ideal-type might suggest,[4] and he is clearly subservient to the prophet. Also, the latter performs certain of the functions of the indigenous ward head, such as hearing disputes among his congregants. Outside the ritual context, members maintain the gender separation characteristic of most Tshidi social life but behave with the easy informality of kin and often cooperate in domestic and agricultural tasks as had matrilaterals in former times. They use conventional Setswana terms of address, marked only by gender—*Rra* ("father") and *Mma* ("mother"). The bishop addresses them all collectively as *ba ga etsho* (strictly "my agnates," but used widely in modern contexts to mean "my people").

Bishop N.'s appearance is remarkably like that of the biblical prophet projected in Protestant Sunday School illustrations distributed by the missions at the turn of the century. In common with many Zionists, he never cuts his hair, which stands about his face like a white mane; and he also has a long, matted gray beard. He wears flowing white robes and no shoes while at his sacred place, asserting that the Spirit has instructed him "to put off his shoes on holy ground as Moses did" (Exodus 3:5; cf.

Sundkler 1961:196–97). At his neck, waist, ankles, and wrists the bishop wears sacred cords (*dithodi*)—twisted lengths of red, white, and black yarn—enjoined by the Spirit as a protective measure. When not attending those who have come to consult him, he is usually found reposing under a tree, Bible in hand. Since coming to Mafeking he has acquired quite a reputation as a healer and many of those who seek his help are members of other denominations, or of the local petite bourgeoisie.[5]

The sociocultural forms of the church ostensibly derive from the revelations of its founder. As its origin myth suggests, the bishop, a Zulu in Mafeking, is, like Dowie before him, a "prophet in a strange land." But his church reproduces the general features of South African Zionism and, within them, specific forms of local origin—no doubt the result of the fact that the rest of the congregation, including the subsidiary visionaries, are Tshidi. The name of the church, clearly a transformation of the name of the parent body, its uniform (*diaparo;* "apparel"), and distinctive practice (*molao;* "law") have all come to the bishop in dreams in which a "hand wrote on the wall as in the Bible." (The relevant biblical passage—Daniel 5—was not cited.) Here again we see the symbolic significance of literacy to this largely illiterate population.

Like most South African religious movements, the Full Witness Church places great emphasis upon uniforms, which, in contrast to those provided by the Protestant associations, are worn almost continuously, at least by the women (cf. Sundkler 1961:213). Such uniforms are held to be infused with power, to encase the body of the wearer like a shield; indeed, in the densely populated stad, the apparel of the various denominations, and the distinctions they signify, appear to be an important dimension of personal identity. Female members of the Full Witness Church wear long white cotton skirts, which are kept scrupulously clean and pressed; emerald-green tunics with large white lace collars, reminiscent of the Victorian blouses introduced by the mission as the dress for female converts; and white headscarves. As I have noted, white, green, and to a lesser extent, yellow, are the distinguishing colors of South African Zionists (Sundkler 1961:213ff; West 1975:18; Berglund 1967); but members of the Full Witness Church, like those of several local groups, also wear cords of twisted red, white, and black yarn at the neck, waist, wrists, and ankles. Moreover, for ritual performances, the women don a more elaborate headdress of green satin, shaped like a bishop's mitre, and also wear broad yellow and green satin sashes over the right shoulder, with the letter "H" picked out on the chest in dark green (see plate 6). The bishop explained that this letter featured prominently in all his visions. He seemed unclear as to its significance—like the other signs, it is not the subject of discussion in the church—and suggested that it might stand for both the English "holy" and Afrikaans "heilig."

Plate 6   The Full Witness Church: female ritual dress. The bishop's senior wife
leads the outer dance circle.

Male congregants generally let their hair grow and wear flowing
white gowns fixed at the waist by a green sash, again reminiscent of
Victorian biblical illustration. While engaged in labor in the white town,
they wear regular, Western-style work clothes; but they put on uniforms
whenever visiting the "great house," an occurrence which marks the end
of the work day. And they never remove the red, white, and black yarn
cords. For ritual performances they wear satin cloaks of gold, dark or
light blue, with gold fringes and gold military frogging at the neck. They
also wear yellow banners bearing the letter "H" and carry ritual staffs.

As in many reformist movements, dietary prescriptions are important
signifiers of the reconstructed life of Zion. Those of the Full Witness
Church stem almost unchanged from the instructions of Dowie and,
through him, from Leviticus. Baptized members eat no pork, and no
animals that have died of natural causes or have been killed in the hunt.
They also do not smoke, drink alcohol, or (in theory) consult doctors,
either native or Western. The prophet's visionary injunctions repeat
that congregants should be persuaded to "eat the work of their own
hands"—that they should strive as a collectivity to produce for their own
consumption and desist from using money. In fact, while not engaging
in communal production, they do practice generalized reciprocity in the

exchange of foodstuffs. Moreover, as is common among Tshidi Zionists, all their purchased commodities—household utensils, food, and clothes—are brought to Bishop N. for "strengthening" (*go thaya*). He also treats the water drunk by his congregants, and uniformed Zionist women bearing water containers are an everyday sight on the Mafeking thoroughfares.

Zionist groups in South Africa, like social units elsewhere that seek closure, attempt to proscribe sexual and marital relations across their boundaries. Many prescribe endogamy, if not within their own churches, then within the ranks of the wider movement; most also stress marital fidelity. The membership of the Full Witness Church, like the local population from which it is drawn, has a high proportion of unwed mothers; sexual reform tends to be focused around the denunciation of "looseness" (*repile*), said by unsympathetic Tshidi to apply only to liaisons with non-Zionists, although endogamy remains a stated ideal (cf. Simpson 1970:197 on the comparable case of Jamaican Revivalism).

The Forms of Ritual

The restructuring of personal relations implied in Zionist habitual practice is paralleled at the more codified level of ritual. While the Full Witness Church conforms with the wider Zionist tendency to stress "Passover" and the Judaic New Year as occasions for the gathering of the whole congregation, the ritualization of these events varies little in form from that of the regular Sunday service (*tirelo*) and even the frequent unscheduled healing sessions (similarly named). Baptism at a local dam or water source marks initiation into the congregation, and also "washes" (*tlhapisa*) those polluted by birth and death. But such rites tend to be recombinations of the four genres which together constitute the logic of the Zionist ritual process: the rites of summoning the spirit (*go bitsa;* "to call"), of testimony (*go bolela;* "to tell"), of strengthening or prophylaxis (*go thaya*), and of healing (*go alafa*). As we have seen, the latter two were the major categories of precolonial Tswana ritual; the former pair stem from Protestant tradition, implying situationally motivated and individually voiced communications with divinity, what Tshidi sometimes refer to as "praying with words" (*go rapela ka mahoko*) as against "praising with the feet" (*go baka ka dinao*).

Scheduled services in the church take place on a Sunday morning; healing sessions most frequently occur at night. Starting times are variable, marked by sunrise and sunset for the two kinds of services. At sunset on a typical evening, both members and those "guests" who have come in search of healing begin to gather in the bishop's yard. Some thirty women and nearly as many children wait under the tree, and seven

or eight men sit on the dung-smeared step before the "great house." All
but the guests are dressed in ritual uniform, and a large skin drum and
two rattles made of wire and metal bottle-caps rest against the house.
The bishop's wives and several female congregants tend large cooking
pots over an open fire, for a communal meal precedes the start of the
ritual "work" (*go dira*).

When all have eaten, the bishop's senior wife signals the start of the
rites by rising to her feet and beating her staff on the ground to the
rhythm of a rousing hymn. Words and music are of Methodist origin,
but the form has been domesticated by quickening its tempo, accentuating its beat, and introducing a complex four-part harmony (cf. Sundkler
1961:196). Of the original six verses only the one referring to Zion is
sung:

Tumisang Mothusi	Praise the Redeemer
To' tletseng Siona	Come and make Zion great.
Baporofeta le dikgosi	Prophets and kings
Tsa swa di sa mmona	Died before seeing him.
	(See *Hymns of Praise*, 90, 5;
	Methodist Publishing House,
	Cape Town, n.d.)

The verse is repeated many times, and slowly the other women rise to
their feet, rouse their children, and begin to clap and sing. They form a
stamping, swaying column, moving in unison toward the house. The
men now rise, straighten their cloaks, take up their staffs, and join in
with the bass harmony. The bishop appears from behind the house, having been sitting apart from the throng. A teenage girl takes charge of the
drum and beats it energetically and the bishop's wives take up the rattles.
Inside the small cubicle that serves as the ritual space, the table has been
pulled to the center of the floor and covered with a white cloth; on it
stands a large basin of water, several tins of condensed milk, and packs of
tea. The men group themselves in a semicircle behind the table, the
bishop stands in the center, flanked by his officers. The women crowd in
front of the table, forming the second arc of a large circle. The single
small window and door are carefully covered with sacking, for, as in
most Zionist churches, rites do not begin before the sacred space has
been closed off from its encompassing context (cf. Kiernan 1976). The
bishop informed me that this "encircled" (*dikanyeditse*) the Holy Spirit.

Within the confined cubicle, dust begins to rise, and the singing,
stamping, and drumming reach a deafening volume. The rhythm is
compelling, and the few guests participate with gusto; the excitement
and urgency is palpable. Suddenly the minister raises his hand and the
singing stops in mid-verse. The men sink to their knees, facing East; for
the bishop had been enjoined in a vision always to call upon the Spirit

while facing the rising sun. The women follow suit, each commencing to recite an individual prayer, first in a whisper but rapidly raising their voices until all are shouting simultaneously. The utterances lack set formulas, and consist of a breathless recounting of practical needs, outpourings of suffering, and pleas to the Spirit to descend in strength and deliverance (cf. Sundkler 1961:185). The sound in the little room seems overpowering, the babel of clamoring tongues being the essence of mutually negating confusion. The Spirit "called" in so discordant a manner begins to descend, but uncontrolledly. Several women begin to gabble senselessly, to snort, grunt, and tremble, the conventional Zionist symptoms of having "been entered." All are now perspiring profusely under their robes. After about ten minutes, the men, who have shown few signs of possession, rise at a signal from the bishop. They turn inward again to form a circle and begin a song of complex harmonies and lilting rhythm, unmistakably indigenous in all but its words, which consist of the single phrase: "Amen, Morena, Amen" (Amen, Lord, Amen).

The Spirit has now seized several female members encircling the room, but it remains disaggregated and unfocused. The seer holds up his hand; the singing ceases and he begins to testify. In an agitated but articulate narrative, he recounts a dream which reveals the meaning of the illness of a female congregant. She has been afflicted by an evil spirit at the behest of another woman, a stranger (*moeng;* i.e. not a fellow Zionist) with whom she worked for a time in the dairy in the white town. There was trouble, and both lost their jobs. They are now unemployed and the "stranger" bears a grudge. The woman named in the testimony listens with bent head, muttering in assent. The testifier utters his statement in short rhythmical bursts, every few sentences being punctuated by the responsive formula "*Go siame Morena?*" ("Is that correct, Lord?"), to which the congregation shouts "Amen!"

Such testimony, as Sundkler (1961:192) noted among Zulu Zionists, replaces formal preaching or clerical exegesis.[6] Among Tshidi, it tends to be framed by fixed formulas of commencement and conclusion, and is structured so as to objectify and generalize a personal insight or subjective experience. The recitation comprises short phrases of mounting speed and volume, punctuated by exclamations which evoke standardized confirmations from the audience:

Kagisho, Borra le Bomma mo Sioneng!	Peace, Fathers and Mothers in Zion!
Ke a patikêga.	I am oppressed.
Pelo ya me e botlhoko.	My heart is sore.
Ngwana wa me o ya lwala.	My child is sick.
Mala a gagwe a siana jaka metse.	His stomach runs like water.
Yo mongwe ngwana o ntshigile fa ke ne ke dira Randfontein.	One (child) already died while I was working in Randfontein.[7]

Go siame, Morena! Amen!	It is correct, Lord! Amen!
Fao, ke ne ke sena mogaesho, ke sena mothusi.	There I had no kin, no help.
Fa, ke legae.	Here I am at home.
Go siame, Morena! Amen!	It is correct, Lord! Amen!
Janong ke na le yo mongwe.	Now I have another child.
Ene ke wa Mpisopo.	This one comes to the Bishop.
Go siame, Morena! Amen!	It is correct, Lord! Amen!
O nwa metse a kgalalêlô, o apara dithodi.	He drinks holy water and wears cords.
Go siame, Morena! Amen!	It is correct, Lord! Amen!
Mma, o sa lwala.	But still he is not well.
Go siame, Morena! Amen!	It is correct, Lord! Amen!
Jaka fa ke le fa le Mpisopo,	Now that I am here with the Bishop,
Ke fa le borra le bomma,	Here with my fathers and mothers,
Ke tsholohêla gore moya wo wa boshula o tla huduswa.	I hope this evil spirit will be sent away.
O ntswele motseng wa me.	Away from my homestead.
Go siame, Morena! Amen!	It is correct, Lord! Amen!

Such testimony is typical of those offered in Tshidi Zionist churches, both by visionaries and sufferers, and epitomizes the form of *rapela ka mahoko,* ritual verbalizations, stylized in form but based in particular personal experience. In this context, however, the end is not individualistic communion, but the objectification and extension of subjective perception such that it may serve as a focus for collective ritual action. Testimonies employ rhetorical formulas to crystallize a set of physical symptoms in the bodies of a few patients, patients serving as metonyms for the social group itself. Moreover, the images that convey this distress—"oppression" for instance—link personal bodily disorder to a more embracing malaise. As the two examples cited suggest, the interplay of the physical and the social, of the individual and the community, rests on an opposition between "outside" (wage labor, the city, strangers) and "inside" (home, the congregation), a tension between depletion and wholeness that is to be mediated by the rites of healing.

Congregants listen to such testimony with rapt attention, their formulaic responses reinforcing each breathless phrase. When the narrative ceases, they extend their hands to steady the speaker and draw him or her back into their midst. The distress of the few has concretized the diffuse state of disorder that characterizes all the participants, thus making tangible the object of the healing process. The crucial rites of reconstitution can now begin.

The Full Witness Church is a cult of affliction. With little exception, its members were recruited in the wake of organically indexed distress.

Indeed, their material circumstances ensure that this is a population in which malnutrition and biophysical morbidity is high.[8] As a solidary band of "wounded healers" (cf. Lewis 1971:192), Zionists extend the metaphor of personal suffering to embrace the broadest perimeters of everyday life itself. For them, the state of the body is a vital indicator of being, providing a discourse upon their location in the social, material, and spiritual world. The physical signs negotiated in Zionist ritual are sometimes ordered in terms of biomedical symptoms ("diarrhea"), but participants still seek the sociomoral logic that underlies them. While they recognize the operation of sorcery and, to a more limited extent, ancestral wrath, these etiological principles tend to be collapsed, in their cosmos, in a thoroughgoing opposition between the healing spirit and the corrupting "outside." But the attribution of cause is less significant than pragmatic intervention. In this sense, Zionist "mythology" seems to dehistoricize and depoliticize the social roots of affliction (cf. Barthes 1973:142ff.). Still, as I have suggested, Tshidi metaphors of suffering are polyvalent, and invest the experience of physical distress with global sociomoral associations; the aim of healing rites, for example, is to reverse both bodily lesions and the encompassing forces of which those lesions speak.

The bishop now signals to the minister and his assistant to remove the central table, and the congregation begins a spirited hymn to a heavy drum beat. The lyrics are the English phrase: "Holy, holy Spirit." The removal of the table (*sebesho*; the word used for "altar" in the mission church, but also the ritual hearth of the rainmaker of old) signals the shift from *go rapela* to *go bina*. Under the leadership of the prophet's wives, the women begin to clap their hands and shake the rattles, providing a rousing rhythm. The bishop takes up position in the center of the cleared space, amidst a motley array of water containers. He sways gently and beats his staff on the ground, and the men form a circle about him, dancing in clockwise direction with small shuffling steps. The pace quickens and the dancers tighten their coordination; they begin to leap up in the air, each intermittently breaking the circular formation. As the drum pounds, they brandish their staffs and thrust them aloft, the total movement recreating the structure of the dance in the precolonial initiation ritual. The tempo becomes ever more urgent, and the women, several holding infants, form an outer circle, dancing in the opposite direction. The dust rises and the sound wells up in the airless cubicle. Suddenly the minister requests that the singing stop and, to the beat of the drum, he leads the men in a closely articulated formation. They move backwards and drop to their haunches as one, then rise and march forwards in what looks like a parody of a military parade. As the song is resumed, the participants return to the twin circle movement, their pace quickening again. The energy generated by the whirling circle was explicitly associated by participants with the descent (*bohologô*) of the Spirit.

The prophet stands in the center of the rotating circle, serving as the vertical path of the descending power. He begins to show physical signs of being "filled" with Spirit: he snorts, shivers, and sweats profusely. It merely remains for him to transmit this force to the ailing bodies of his followers. He holds up his staff and one by one his congregants come and stand beneath it—first those few whose symptoms signify the communal affliction, then each of the men, and finally the women and children. Alike they draw from the fund of power that flows into this "well" of healing. The bishop presses his hand down firmly on each head, "filling" (*tlatsa*) each person with the Spirit, and repairing damaged bodily margins and the disrupted balance of inner and outer being. Those who imbibe the Spirit will become "perfect" or "sufficient in themselves" (*itekarela*), at least in the context of the rite. Where before they were parched and wasted, they now "bulge" or become replete (*totoma*). They drink the waters of Zion and "quench their thirst" (*itimola lenyora*). When all have been "healed," the bishop entreats the spirit to pervade the water and all who drink it with his reinforcing power. The water will leave the "great house" with the participants, extending the force of the ritual in time and space, and sustaining them till the next healing session.

As the rite winds down, the circle disaggregates and the dancers resume a quiet demeanor. The table is replaced and a Methodist hymn of more conventional style marks a return to the more orthodox ritual form that frames the entire healing process. The minister places an empty jam jar on the table, and the congregants dance up to it, one by one, in carefully individuated manner. With exaggerated, caricatured gestures, they exhibit the coins to the assembly and then drop them in noisily. The standard donation—referred to by the seemingly paradoxical *go koleka* ("to collect")—is one cent. The bishop now intones a conventional benediction and then he and the men leave the house, standing in a line outside so as to greet each woman with the customary three-clasp handshake. The ritual performance is at an end.

Zionism as Symbolic Mediation

Let me now consider the significance of the order of practices I have described. Writing of the cultural forms of Jamaican Rastafarianism, historically and ethnographically comparable, Hebdige (1979:37) notes:

> Not only did the Rasta fix the dreary cycle of solitary refusal and official retribution within the context of Jamaica's absent history, he broke that cycle altogether by installing the conflict elsewhere on the neglected surfaces of everyday life. By questioning the neat articulation of common

sense (in appearance, language, etc.) the Rasta was able to carry the crusade beyond the obvious arena of law and order to the level of the "obvious" itself.

Tshidi Zionism is also a crusade at the level of the "obvious." It is at once a statement of denial and an art of radical reconstruction, both effected at the level of everyday practice. But the crusade of the Zionists has also been carried out in the one arena which enjoys relatively generous license in their coercive environment—that of organized religion. By seizing the church as their preeminent communicative domain, black South Africans, like their Jamaican counterparts, have turned the structures of Western orthodoxy inside out, transforming marginality into esteem, and subordination into defiance. Like the Rastafarians and their Creole antecedents (Brathwaite 1971:64), the Zionist effects a novel resolution of the contradictions of his peripheral structural predicament. Ritual movements have here been made to assume the major burden of meaning in the culture of the colonized; as we shall see, their semantic forms frame the constructs of person, context, power, and value that order the cosmos of the impoverished majority.

Dowie's Zion was a statement of estrangement from, and resistance to, the cultural hegemony of late nineteenth-century urban America. Black proletarians in early twentieth-century South Africa recognized a resonance in these Zionist forms, which seemed to model their own relationship to the forces of colonialism. The parent movement provided terms that fetishized marginality, and the signs and practices of the Full Witness Church are, in this sense, a transformation of the original vision, the outcome of a reciprocally determining relationship with the process of Tshidi social history itself. The evolving symbolic order of this and like Zionist movements has given particular meaning to the experience of politico-economic domination. It has provided a system of knowledge and practice which seems to have a secure existence outside the terms of the neocolonial culture, permitting the marginalized to separate themselves definitively from it, to hold it at arm's length.

Organizational Form

The founding of the Full Witness Church was typical of the emergence of such movements, both among the Tshidi and elsewhere in southern Africa. Its origin myth calls upon a humble mine-worker to become a vessel of the Spirit in the wilderness, sending him out from the center of urban industrialization to the barren periphery on the "fringes of the desert" (see Brathwaite 1971:254 for a similar theme in nineteenth-century Jamaica). Voluntarily moving to this liminal domain, he sets about establishing a collectivity of those involuntarily marginalized by that same center and all it represents. He is a stranger made local, an outsider bearing an innovative vision through which the dross is revalued and the afflicted are made whole. In many Tshidi Zionist churches, the journey from Johannesburg (*Gauteng*—the "place of gold") to the rural Zion provides a message of continuing relevance—the exodus from the social and semantic forms of white control to a categorically distinct and ritually recentered Canaan. However, myth plays fast and loose with history (Barthes 1973:11): the metaphor of revelation brought by the charismatic stranger is a mystification. Bishop N.'s church is continuous in important respects with the urban house of bondage he has ostensibly forsaken. Not only is its name an obvious derivation from the parent movement; its forms are the Zionist stock in trade, and bear the tangible impact of the politico-economic context of which it remains a determined part. While ostensibly a haven beyond an alienating world, the Zionist cosmos is structurally encompassed; its texts are *bricolages* whose elements come from the cultural schemes from which it seeks to escape. By setting itself up in self-imposed exile from both "tradition" and white orthodoxy as it perceives them, the Zionist movement is placed in a position in which it has to mediate both. Thus the bishop's utopia might see itself as drawing on divine innovation; but the movement is in fact a reconstruction of existing reconstructions, a transformation of a cogent, syncretistic cultural scheme.

The structure of the Full Witness Church presents a clear instance of "central place competition" (Werbner n.d.:30). Its ritual focus contradicts the center-periphery relations of both state and indigenous cultural maps, yet combines features of each. The movement projects its own iconoclastic spatial order, carefully bounded by symbolic action, yet permeable to external forces. Accordingly, the origin myth provides a statement of the rationale that underlies the recentering of the church at the periphery, a point emphatically made by its location on the margins of the stad. In fact, its spatial logic is a function of the historical transformation of the precolonial order; in particular, with the eclipse of the agnatic domain and the centralized institutions of the chiefdom, the uterine house emerged as the elemental social unit in the rural sector, where it stands in complementary opposition to the urban core, its centrifugal force pulling against the centripetal pressures of labor market. The homestead in its modern guise constitutes the basis from which the Zionist churches tend to elaborate their sociocultural scheme—a *tertium quid* between the elemental unit of the uterine house and the collective world of the orthodox institutions and the industrial workplace (figure 7). Thus the house itself is the ritual nucleus for most Zionist congregations, and the female body with which it is associated is a central metaphoric referent in their ritual. As the account above suggests, the iconography of healing is that of spiritual insemination, of gestation and re-

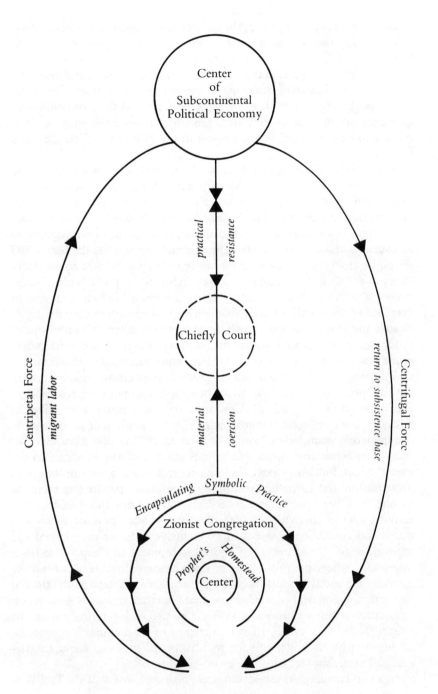

Figure 7   Center and Periphery in Zionist Practice

birth, of ritual reproduction in the cloistered seclusion of domestic space. But this locational scheme also combines formal properties of the hegemonic order in church and state. Many Zionists, for instance, cherish the ideal of movements that will spread out from a relocated center on the model of a hierarchical voluntary association, with headquarters and branches. But their template for these structures defines constituencies that defy hegemonic spatial arrangements. The significance of these maps will become particularly evident in the case of the Zion Christian Church below.

The organizational arrangements of the Full Witness Church stand between the bureaucratic forms of industrial capitalism and the integrated politico-territorial structures of the precolonial system. Its institutionalization of charismatic leadership defies both Western rationalist and indigenous Tswana constructs of authority; and the theocratic quality of its charter—the merging of the religious and the secular, the public and the domestic—contrasts with the established dichotomies of colonial ideology and Tshidi Protestant orthodoxy. Also, the explicit "cultic" identity of Zionism differs markedly from the embedded ritual forms of "tradition." In practice, the Zionist congregations vary in their degree of closure and in the extent to which they attempt to restructure relations of production and exchange within the bounds of the movement. Members of the Full Witness Church do not form a community of production, but they do engage in a considerable degree of cooperation, again working with adapted "domestic" models. The group does not own resources in its own right (as do some of the more elaborate congregations, like the Z.C.C.), but a collectivist ethos encourages the pooling of assets and the counteracting of individual risk (cf. Kiernan 1977 on the Zulu case). In this sense, while the movement cannot affect patterns of access to the means of production, it nevertheless attempts to cut across processes of privatization and to reduce commoditization. But productive relations among members also contrast very obviously with those of the precolonial system, in which nuclear or polygynous domestic units produced and consumed within a more inclusive order of matrilateral and agnatic kin ties. In a context of underdevelopment and large-scale labor migration, where the proportion of female-headed households is on the increase, the social organization of the church may be seen as an effort to reconcile the practical contradictions that constrain domestic production and reproduction (cf. Kiernan 1977). The use of kin terms within the congregation, the residential concentration of its membership, and the assumption by its leader of such regulatory functions as dispute settlement all underline its status as a proto-ward unit.

In a similar manner, the ideological and ritual forms of the Full Witness Church defy the cultural orders of "tradition" and of neo-colonialism yet recycle elements of each. Of course, the Old Testament is quite easily translated into the language of preindustrial society, its pastoral ethos, kin-based relations of production, and theocratic models of organization seeming to evoke a lost world of "traditional" African integrity. At the same time, the message of exile and redemption contained in both Testaments resonates with the position of the peasant-proletarian. The text, in fact, yields signifiers capable both of evoking and of transcending the everyday context of the modern Tshidi. And the fundamentalist interpretation of Dowie removes the Bible from the discourses of bourgeois orthodoxy, replacing it in a universe of ritual pragmatism and apocalypse. It is primarily the metaphors of the Old Testament (Zion; Moses; Exodus; prophecy; the proscriptions of Leviticus) which are incorporated into the Zionist *bricolage,* to be revalued, in turn, by being brought into relationship with the other elements of a total scheme, itself motivated by the desire to subvert the forms of neocolonial culture and society. In the hands of the southern African movement, the Bible becomes a mandate for returning tangible coherence to a world that had been rendered alien.

Let us examine in more detail how this process actually occurs. Douglas (1966:122ff.) has asserted that dietary and sexual proscriptions indicate a cultural concern with the dangers of bodily pollution and, by extension, with the threat of a disrupting intrusion into the bounded categories of the social order. Now South African Zionists, like their American forebears, do indeed display such a bodily indexed concern with sociocultural margins—and with the paradox of their independence of, yet encompassment within, a wider structural order. They proscribe certain foods and medicaments, prefer endogamy, and like to "eat the work of their own hands." But to view these practices merely as expressing danger to "community boundaries" and "group survival" (Douglas 1966:123, 124, 148) is to stress their role in perpetuating a group seen in functionalist isolation and divorced from its historical context. In the Zionist case, the prescriptions and taboos of everyday life are part of an order of meaningful actions which seek to intervene in the contradictory relationship between local peoples and the larger system that contains them. We have seen, for instance, that the uneven monetization of relations between close kin and across class divisions has been an explicit cause of conflict, and it is in this light that Zionist attempts to reverse commoditization must be seen. But these efforts do not negate existing contradictions; as individuals and as a collectivity Zionists remain dependent upon, and are determined by, more embracing politico-economic forces. This, at least, would seem to be the message of their taboos:

substances and activities regarded as defiling are proscribed not merely because they signify boundaries but also because they are emblematic of the world from which the Zionist wishes to be severed and of the means by which this may be accomplished.

Zionists have explicit notions about the generalized corruption that resides in the domain of those who eat "filth" (*makgapha*); the proscriptions of Leviticus set them off from the bodily indexed modes of production and consumption of a defiling society. Food production is a widespread metaphor for communal action on the natural world, and its consumption may image both participation in a social order and the process of constructing human substance (Comaroff 1983). As I have indicated, eating was a polyvalent indigenous metaphor for physical consumption. But the latter, while capable of enhancing the person, could also be the means of his destruction: *sejeso,* the prototypical form of sorcery, was the admission into the body of disrupting concoctions. Indeed, food was never neutral; it was loaded with social valence. For that reason, Tshidi were, and are, careful about what and with whom they eat, the body being "opened" only in what seem to be unthreatening conditions. The taboo of pork, tobacco, and alcohol expresses the desire to exclude from Zion items that have become emblems of white colonial culture and bearers of its defiling substance; indigenous South African peoples knew no pigs, and high rates of local alcoholism have made Tshidi very sensitive to the role of liquor vending in the subjugation and impoverishment of the black community (cf. van Onselen 1982:44ff.). Sundkler (1976:44ff.) has noted how abstinence from smoking among the first Zulu Zionists was perceived by Afrikaner farmers as an act of resistance against a labor system that used tobacco as a mode of payment. This is part and parcel of the general injunction to "eat the work of our hands," informed both by the desire to know the social origin of one's food and by the value placed by Tshidi upon freedom from the need to sell their labor power. Cattle were icons of this ideal of self-sufficiency, but most Zionist congregants had long ceased owning or handling them; yet their own symbolic media also spoke of the desire for economic independence.

Tshidi Zionists deal with the manifest contradictions of their separatist ideology in the same idiom of material consumption. Despite their negative injunctions, traffic with the market remains essential. They address this paradox by focusing on the very objects that embody it—purchased goods. All outside commodities are ritually processed before being used: shoes, blankets, and foodstuffs are brought to the church, stand on the table for the duration of the service, and then are sprinkled with holy water. In this manner, goods that are the work of the hands of others are purified and incorporated through a kind of baptism. As in the American

Zion, the cargo of the rejected system is not itself repudiated en masse; rather, it is reformed, and resituated within an alternative order of values. As alienated products are given a new social and spiritual identity, the experience of alienation is reversed. But Zionist proscriptions also express a rejection of *setswana,* this being reflected in the taboo on eating animals that die of natural causes, a common indigenous practice. Once again, this reveals that the process of symbolic mediation is not a simple return to the "nativism" of a precolonial Africa; it is the work of an African Zion whose syncretistic constitution is perceived by its agents as a unique and novel revelation.

The focal role of the "healer" in these symbolic processes recalls that of the precolonial *ngaka* as master of transformative ritual power, but it also evokes the image of Dowie as Elijah the Restorer. In Zion, healing was the crucial act of innovative reconstruction; as a leader of the Z.C.C. put it, "All we *do* is heal" (*re alafa hela*). In Dowie's church, the rejection of biomedicine was a rejection of secular, depersonalized professionalism, and of the sociocultural order from which it derived. South African Zionists also proscribe biomedicine, and, indeed, all Tshidi make only partial use of it alongside indigenous healing practice (Comaroff 1981). But the Zionists dismiss this more general syncretism as well, for they also eschew the *ngaka.* Bishop N. stressed that "those who practice *setswana* spoil [*senyetsa*; "pollute"] the body while pretending to heal." Here too, then, the repudiation of these doctors is a denunciation of the wider system that they, in particular, embody; for, in the Zionist code, the healer constructs the human form in his image of the world, according to a revealed vision of agency, power, and collective well-being.

Dress and Style

The clothing and presentation of the body are also crucial dimensions of the Zionist scheme, uniforms having assumed an important role in all South African churches from the start. It will be recalled that the conjuncture between the precolonial Tshidi and the mission was played out, in significant measure, in the domain of body management; the dressing of the "social skin" in mission garments marked off converts and would-be converts, signifying, along with their recruitment to "civilization," their initiation into a world system of industrial production and commoditized consumption. Indigenous dress codes had made primary distinctions between adult male and female apparel, not so much in the substance or color of materials as in the extent to which they covered the organs of reproduction; men wore hide loincloths and women wore long aprons and breast-coverings of skin (Spohr 1973:67). Whereas male attire communicated differences of status—the rich donned fine skin karosses—that of females reflected a uniform channeling of natural fertility. The mission revalued this gender contrast, introducing the characteristic Western distinction between severe male garb, expressive of self-disciplined production in the workplace, and more opulent female apparel, signaling domestic consumption (cf. Turner n.d.[a]). Zionism, in turn, seeks to reformulate this opposition, along with the order of relations and values it betokens.

The missions were soon to realize, if not really to understand, the complex significance of uniforms for African converts. The various denominations developed emblematic outfits, in particular for their women's associations; indeed, the women's association (*manyano,* a generic South African term derived from the Xhosa *ukumanyana,* "to join together") was frequently the de facto core of the congregation. Church women were known among the Tswana as *basadi ba seaparô,* "women of uniform" (cf. Pauw 1960:90), the term for "uniform" being coterminous with Western usage, denoting also military and service apparel. For the Tshidi in the late nineteenth century, the Methodist dress of red, black, and white served as a particularly appropriate icon of the new ritual establishment, its forms explicitly revaluing the basic color triad of the precolonial symbolic order and overlaying it with the overt associations of blood, sin, and redemption, respectively. The power of uniforms in Tshidi perception was both expressive and pragmatic, for the uniform instantiated the ritual practice it represented. Observers have frequently commented on the "magical" quality attributed indigenously to ritual attire among modern Batswana (cf. Pauw 1960:90), and a (Tswana) Methodist minister working in Mafeking in the late 1960s remarked: "In all the churches they think that when they put on the uniform, they take on the divine power itself—and the Zionists put it on and never take it off! Our Methodist women say that if they break church law while wearing the uniform they might be strangled by it!"

Methodist and other Protestant women put on uniforms for "sacred" occasions. Ritual dress for men in these churches is the regular Western "suit"; that is, the prestige attire of the nonproductive classes or of nonproductive occasions (cf. Turner n.d.[a]:59). In other words, Methodist garb is a transformation of the code of the modern West, setting off sacred from mundane, men from women, production from consumption, and productive from nonproductive activity. Church uniforms, here, are worn specifically for "religious" practice.

Zionism, in contrast, has developed a code which reformulates these established categories. As Sundkler has shown (1976:48), Dowie had clothed himself (if not his congregants) in flowing robes, photographs of which appear to have been seen by the first black Zionists in South Africa. This does not explain the symbolic role of the attire; why, that is, it seemed so appropriate, in both contexts, as an image of the reconstituted person. To understand Zionist dress, we have to locate it within the wider system of signifiers of which it is a part. Zionists, especially the women, are semipermanent inhabitants of the domain of the Spirit, wearing their robes at all times and places as evidence of a holistic transformation of personal identity. Of course, to the extent that the congregation is still an integral part of a wider system, such total identification with the Kingdom of Zion cannot be realized, particularly for male members, who interact with that system through the labor market. Men, in fact, wear their apparel when away from the workplace—at the "great house" or in domestic contexts. It is in the sphere of male dress that the Zionist code contrasts most dramatically with that of the modern West, supplanting somber work-clothes—the "uniform of mature capitalism *par excellence*" (Turner n.d.[a]:51)—with gleaming white skirts. These delicate and impeccably laundered robes reverse, in color and line, the functional severity of Western garb; they seem thereby to protest the values and pragmatic implications of proletarianization. Bishop N. remarked that to work in the robes would "spoil" them: "this is the uniform of the spirit," he asserted. By placing men in skirts, moreover, Zionists blur the stark Western contrast between male severity and female opulence, itself rooted in the logic of capitalist productive relations and the gender-indexed opposition between production and consumption (cf. Turner n.d.[a]). By inverting this distinction, they state again the motivation to "eat the work of our own hands," to return to a world in which producer is not severed from consumer, or use from exchange, and where direct and controllable social relations replace commoditized transactions.

More generally, the Zionist's outward appearance is crowded with signs that speak to a particular relationship between bodies personal and social. The sparkling robes and flowing hair of the men, and the Victorian tunics of the women, are conspicuously set off from the mass-produced, often threadbare clothing worn by the majority of rural Tshidi. The Zionist might also trudge on the dusty roads of the stad, or on the bustling streets of the modern town; but he is visibly of neither place. The colors and contours of his appearance make reference to images of distant times and contexts; his style communicates his "otherness," a fact which all Tshidi perceive. He personifies the distant biblical world of Victorian mission illustrations, which still line the walls of many Tshidi homes, conveying a general message both of disillusion and passionate intention—a message at once of deconstruction and recreation.

The role of color is also central to the Zionist symbolic order. West (1975:18) has recorded how, in Soweto, an explicit association is made between black and white and the "Ethiopian-type" (i.e., Independent) and Zionist churches, known respectively as "Churches of the Law" and "Churches of the Spirit."[9] Among the Tshidi a similar distinction obtains, except that black is linked to the mission denominations, in whose uniforms it predominated, and then, by extension, to the Independent churches, both groups being regarded as *kereke ya molao,* "churches of the law." In fact, both mission and Zionist uniforms combine a series of colors, but these are subsidiary signs planted, as it were, on the basic ground of black (for mission uniforms) or white (for Zionist ones). Thus the indigenous Tshidi opposition between black as normative control and white as activating power echoes the Weberian contrast between bureaucratic and charismatic authority, implying a distinction between hegemonic and countercultural orders. The black, disciplined conformity of Protestant orthodoxy coalesces with the meaning of the "black" initiation, which was concerned with the "law" and with normative constraint upon human creativity. Furthermore, "law" (*molao*) in the precolonial system conveyed the repertoire of rules that governed the exercise of established authority. The mission association of "black" with "sin" seems to have tied in with this, for, as an English priest among the Tshidi observed, their notion of sin is more one of a careless but reprovable "breaking of the law" than of a moral offense threatening to salvation.[10]

On the other hand, the white of Zion combines orthodox purity with unorthodox pragmatic spirituality, and both with the dynamism of the "white" initiation, which evoked the activating power of lightning, semen, and salt. Precolonial color associations are perpetuated among modern Tshidi: mourners continue to abstain from salt; lightning still connotes dynamic power; and menstrual blood still signifies fertility yet pollution. The revival of initiation rites on the outskirts of the chiefdom in 1970 represented an attempt to revitalize a distressed community. It was a minority effort, regarded by the Tshidi elite as "backward." But its faithful reproduction of precolonial symbolic forms spoke to the continued salience of such sign complexes as the color triad. The contrast between black and white, then, aptly captures the opposing role of the two church types in modern Tshidi life: normative orthodoxy and dynamic reconstruction. Each, in fact, makes limited use of the primary color of the other by way of contrast, and both draw from a common stock of signs, building their respective *bricolages* according to logically opposed combinatorial principles.[11]

In the construction of novel formulations, as I have noted, signs simultaneously retain their earlier significance and acquire new meanings. For Tshidi, the distinction between black and white brings a fan of preexisting referents to the emergent opposition between neocolonial orthodoxy and dynamic counterculture. The Zionists' most widely used color combination is white and green, with blue providing a frequent addition (Sundkler 1961:213ff.; West 1975:116). In Southern Bantu cultures in general, blue and green appear to be widely linked to the activating power of white—in contrast with red and black—and are the hues of rain, water, freshness, and growth (cf. Ngubane 1977:118). For Tswana, blue and green connote vegetable fecundity, distilled from the blackness of rain clouds by the force of lightning, whereas human fertility is drawn from the redness of the womb through the white potency of semen. Green (*tale*) specifically signifies origins or points of growth; *bogologolo tale,* for example, refers to "long, long ago, when all was green." Blue (*bududu*) is associated with development and maturation; *budula* (to become blue/gray) means to be "ripened" or "cooked." Blue is also the color of water (*pula,* "rain," is from the same root). Together, these colors evoke a sense of fluid process, of regeneration and animated flow, such being the active qualities imparted to the body when the colors are worn. Modern Tshidi explicitly refer to "shade" as "blue" and "cool" (*tshididi*), and Bishop N., when explaining why Zionists did not wear red, said that it was "hot" (*bothitho;* polluting "heat"), the color of blood (cf. Sundkler 1961:214); explicit reference to the blood of Christ was important in the mission message of salvation. The term for blood, *madi,* is, of course, also the term for money and Tshidi Zionists wryly talk of the Methodist church as *kereke ya madi,* the church of "blood, redness, money" (i.e. the church of the rich, those immersed in monetarized transactions). The cool flow of water in Zion, as this implies, contrasts with the hot flow of money/blood in orthodox Protestantism.

As Sahlins has noted (1977), red, yellow, and blue are all primary colors, which, together with black and white, are perceptually unique and not visually decomposable into constituent hues. They would thus seem, as a set, to be universally suited to serve classificatory functions; that is, to signify a systematically related order of meanings. Moreover, these hues comprise two opposed dyads (red–green and yellow–blue) and four dyads of compatible colors (red–yellow; red–blue; green–blue; and green–yellow) which again are widely used as signs of combination and contrast (ibid.). The Zionist scheme condenses a range of harmonious, context-derived meanings in one statement, that of white–green, which exists in primary opposition to the red–black of Protestant orthodoxy. On this basic ground, additional color-coded messages are mapped out. Thus, on the white-green base of the Zionist uniform, many groups, like the Full Witness and the Z.C.C., introduce the compatible color yellow; and the contrast is emphasized by the texture and sheen of the fabric used, satin marking off a ritual banner from the everyday cotton uniform. Similarly, blue often distinguishes office bearers from the rank and file, suggesting distinction within unity. Colored cords, to be discussed below, introduce the opposing hues of black and red, intertwining them with white in a replication of the three bands of color on the pole in the indigenous "black *bogwêra*," which connoted the ideal of cosmological balance. Red and black are limited to the cords, and seem to be a uniquely Tswana practice; Sundkler (1961:214) states that Zulu Zionists expressly forbid the use of these two colors.

But color is only one dimension of the semantic structure of Zionist dress. Indeed, the assemblage of features combined in the total style amount to a commentary on the wearers' social history, evoking elements emblematic of indigenous and colonial culture, only to revalue them in their iconoclastic juxtaposition with others. Thus the uniform itself is associated with church vestments, the military, mine labor, and domestic service; it is manufactured from industrially produced and marketed fabrics, and evokes a past of mission acculturation and politico-economic incorporation. Yet the Zionists seek to apply the associations of this mode of dress to very different ends. For the constituent parts of their uniform appropriate and transform the signs of mission culture. The tunic with lace collar, worn by women in the Full Witness Church, is a stylistic replica of the Victorian blouses introduced by the Protestant churches; the latter churches retain the original but, in the Full Witness Church, the red has been replaced by brilliant green. Instead of serviceable black, the women wear flowing white skirts, and white rather than black headscarves. Such headscarves are still widely worn by black women in South Africa and express the canons of mission modesty, which overlaid the elaborate indigenous code of hairdressing. Female members of the Full Witness Church reproduce this dimension of mission sobriety, at least in form if not in color; what is more, their headdress contrasts with the bareheadedness of males in a manner reminiscent of mission practice, in which men's heads were uncovered during worship. But here again, orthodox form is subverted, for Zionist men allow their hair and beards to grow, evoking both Victorian images of biblical prophets and the more universal connotation of unrestrained locks—that of threatening, uncontained power. Like the long-haired youth of the modern West, or male Rastafarians, the Zionist men are regarded by the establishment, both black and white, as harboring unstable, subversive power.

These examples point to the fact that it is in the sphere of male dress that the explicit rebellion has occurred against the functionally constrained style of the dominant culture. Indeed, male hair and clothing styles have been more closely regulated by the idioms of discipline and production than have those of females, reflecting the greater engagement of men in the world of industrial capitalist production (Turner n.d.[a]). Women, on the other hand, remain closely associated with the domestic sphere; even where they are employed outside, they tend to do house-work. As in the precolonial context, there is less discontinuity, in symbolic terms, between their productive activities and the rest of their social existence; also, they tend still to be less fully socialized, and comparatively undifferentiated from each other in relation to the means of production. Where male Zionist apparel seeks to reverse colonial styles, women's attire is more congruous with precolonial dress *and* with modern Tshidi garb, both inside and outside the workplace. However, within the church itself, the gender contrast in hairdressing expresses a further feature of the Zionist order; namely, that it is predominantly men who wield spiritual power on behalf of a more passive female congregation. While Zionism protests the marginalization of the black peasant-proletarian, its symbolic practices continue to proclaim inequalities of gender. For women were marginal to the organized exercise of authority in the precolonial system and they remain so, both in the neocolonial world and in the Kingdom of Zion.

Zionist uniforms also include elements donned for ritual performances only, these playing with heightened emphasis upon the emblems of power inscribed in the colonial encounter. During services men in the Full Witness Church wear satin cloaks, whose hues of gold, light blue, and dark blue are compatible contrasts with the basic color scheme of the church. Their shiny texture and costly gold trim mark them off as ritual garb. Skin cloaks were the precolonial male dress first received on initiation; and valuable pelts set off the rich from the poor. But the form of the cloak is also a comment upon the Tshidi experience of colonialism, again being evocative both of high-church vestments and of Victorian military uniform. South African Zionists make widespread use of cloaks, staffs, and bishop's mitres, the ritual raiments of the Church of England, reflecting perhaps the orthodox origin of certain of its prophets but also the historical link between the Anglican mission and the imperial regime. The uniform of the Full Witness Church both recalls and scrambles the regalia of the high church by giving men cloaks and staffs but placing the mitres, transformed brilliant green, on the heads of women. This latter transformation domesticates the insignia of Protestant authority, and opposes them to the bareheaded charismatic power of the prophet and the other male leaders. The cloak in the Western context provides an obvious contrast with conventional modern male dress, invoking roles—from those of high church clergy to "superheroes"—associated with ritual and temporal power and located outside of regular productive activities.

In this manner, Zionist dress, like the *bricolages* of such protest movements as cargo cults, appropriates select signs of colonial dominance, turning historical symbols of oppression into dynamic forces of transcendence. With the same logic, the satin banners incorporate military pomp, evoking the aggressive Protestant image of "soldiers of the Lord"; the letter H affixed to them suggests perhaps a double cross, but is also emblematic of the power of literacy itself. It will be remembered that the bishop's visions were entrusted to him by a "hand writing on the wall." The apparent irony of such communication between the Holy Spirit and a semiliterate prophet makes complete sense in terms of the overall logic of the Zionist project. For literacy has been, and is, a crucial marker of the forces that subjugate the uneducated peasant-proletarian; here its potency is returned, by divine gift, to those excluded from its benefits.

The brass staff, too, condenses multiple historical allusions. Referred to as *thobane* (cudgel), it recalls the weapon given to initiates in the precolonial context, where it signified male social and physical dominance, and served as an implement of war. But the staff also evokes gleaming military dress-swords and bishops' staffs; like the Rastafarian "rod of correction" (Hebdige 1979:35), it conveys both power and defiance in a situation in which blacks are divested of military power but are frequently harassed by armed police. These staffs are used, like ritual batons of old, to punctuate the rhythms of the dance, where their vertical movements, as in the *bogwêra,* contrast with the lateral movements of the women. Kiernan (1976:343) has shown that the even more elaborate use of such "weapons" by Zulu Zionists is explicitly associated with the control of malevolent forces. For the Tshidi, the staffs act also as vertical conductors of the Spirit, that carried by the bishop being marked out from the rest. The fact that men, rather than women, carry these ritual objects, reflects the male role in the channelization of spirit force. Women are not debarred from prophecy, as the position of the bishop's elder wife (the only female staff-bearer) shows, but female charismatics are far fewer; and while women are often hosts to the Spirit, their conventionalized possession behavior expresses the passive receiving of, rather than mastery over, the intrusive power. As I showed in Chapter 3, Tswana saw the control executed by some men over others as feminizing. In the Zionist rites men dramatically reclaim a dominance lost in the degrading subjugation of the colonial encounter. In acting out this ritual superiority women serve, by and large, as submissive foils.

It is the yarn cords, however, that epitomize the logic of the whole cultural scheme. These cords evoke precolonial therapeutic practice; they were perceived as reinforcing the various thresholds to the body center—the neck, wrists, and ankles—and as stabilizing that center itself (cf. Comaroff 1980). For Tshidi Zionists, they also recall an aspect of the nineteenth-century initiation rites, in which cords (also called *dithodi*) were made from the bark of the *moshu* tree and woven into kilts that contributed to the dynamic transformation of boys into men. In that context, *dithodi* connoted the human umbilicus, and their ritual intertwining served as an icon of the construction of the social fabric, the ordered interweaving of human beings. In contrast, those of the Full Witness Church are made of brightly colored white, red, and black yarn. Thus yarn, an industrial manufacture of natural wool, is recrafted in Zionist hands, becoming an agent of social reconstruction. The cords contain the only red and black permitted in the Full Witness scheme; and they are here associated, in equal proportions, with white. Thus combined, the colors are strongly evocative of the precolonial triad, which still proclaims a notion of creative unity and cosmic balance. Hence the red and black of Protestant orthodoxy are embedded in a metaphor that seems to eclipse their sectarian significance. The *dithodi,* moreover, are overt emblems of pragmatic healing power; they bind the sufferers into a visible unity of affliction. Perhaps, like the chains of bondage in some Western youth cultures, they can be seen as a wry parody of the social predicament of the marginalized (cf. Hebdige 1979:121). But they are also the means of dynamic recreation: a mundane object is taken from its context and its meaning is reversed. Yarn, like fabric, was one of the first commodities introduced by the mission as material for female handicrafts; and knitted sweaters were among the early forms of clothing for converts, being part of everyday white dress. In the Zionist scheme, yarn is similarly used to encompass the body, particularly to secure its thresholds. Thus a familiar commodity takes on new significance by being put to work in a novel sequence of symbols.

The total Zionist costume, then, is much more than an impressionistic syncretism, an adaptive accommodation, or a retreat into romantic nativism. It is a dynamic construction whose combination of elements is governed by an implicit but palpable order—both historical and cultural. Its apparently idiosyncratic, almost poignant juxtapositions express distance both from a subordinated "traditional" world and from a neocolonial formation whose pervasive effects have deformed and devalued everyday experience. A beguiling cultural patchwork, it represents an orderly attempt—albeit not self-conscious—to encompass and reform the offending system. In its withdrawal from the dominant system and from "tradition" as an objectified scheme, Zionism mediates the two in an ingenious effort to reconcile the mutual contradictions they embody. In a sense, its costume is a "record of a people's journey" (Hebdige 1979:31). It recapitulates the process of colonialization and seeks to redress its alienating historical logic.

In sum, the Zionist protests the effects upon his personal context of articulation with the modern world system, particularly as this has been mediated through orthodox Protestantism and the coercive apparatus of the South African state. His protest is mounted from the perspective of a peripheral community whose sociocultural order has been unevenly transformed, and whose politico-economic structures have given way to the formation of classes within an embracing neocolonial system. In this community, the majority of the males and many females have been drawn into the migrant labor market, and female-headed units have come to outnumber any other type of domestic arrangement. The tension between agnation and matrilaterality, so central to the precolonial system, has increasingly been resolved by the emergence of matrilateral ties as the organizational base of much of the proletarianized population. These structural features define the point of departure for Tshidi Zionism which, making virtue of necessity, uses them as the elements of its reconstruction. The inherent individualism of the Tshidi order has been overlaid by the individualism inherent in industrial capitalist society and culture, which reduces the embeddedness of the person in ramifying webs of others, living and dead. In the wake of such retreating social networks, a universalistic deity takes center stage—although, for the most part, this deity is the pragmatic Holy Spirit rather than the more detached God of Protestantism (cf. Horton 1971). The superhuman dead, now increasingly individualized, become the refractions of this overarching Spirit.

Yet these transformations do not easily add up to a Western epistemology of any order, especially not for those Tshidi who participate both in wage labor and in peasant production but feel secure in neither. Indeed, as Zionist symbolic forms attest, the Tshidi resist the categories of colonialism from the standpoint of what remains a socially contextualized, spiritually animated universe; one which unifies the ritualized and the mundane, the domestic and the productive, the producer and the product, use and exchange. But they also no longer perceive themselves as grounded in a systematic alternative—*setswana*. On the dynamic ground of the Zionist robe, the insignia of Western and indigenous ritual, of colonial and precolonial orders, are unified and subsumed in a transcendent identity. The power relations of the established world are inverted and imprinted on the body of a community reborn.

Ritual Form

The ritual of the Full Witness Church actualizes the theme of protest and reconstruction by healing the individual and, simultaneously, incorporating him or her into the community of Zion. This process reworks indigenous initiation rites in important respects, for it is about resocialization—the reproduction of the collectivity as a product of individual rebirth. But Zionist practices differ in one fundamental respect: they stand in contrast to, rather than in harmony with, their surrounding sociocultural ground (cf. Werbner n.d.). The symbolic order they create attempts to reform rather than reinforce the "natural" qualities of the given world, and draws upon a power that is in competition with existing hegemonies. In this sense, Zionist healing reverses the logic of initiation; it seeks to move its participants from center to periphery and to disengage them from their embeddedness in prevailing centripetal forces. Rather than eclipse the house and female reproductive processes with images of masculine domination, it endeavors to resurrect shattered male control through the revitalizing metaphors of female fertility. But the composite rites, again, are no return to a precolonial Eden, for their participants have eaten from the tree of knowledge and have been irreversibly transformed by their historical experience. The ritual protests the fact that the Tshidi world has been displaced by this historical process, but it also strives to appropriate and redirect the dynamic properties of such change, constructing a system that subjects novel values and powers to the control of a precolonial social logic.

In the Zionist church, baptism is the act that initiates members into a cult of perpetual healing and reintegration. As I have noted, baptism brings the therapeutic immersions of Dowie to an Africanized Jordan, eclipsing Protestant notions of conversation and plunging the initiate into the restorative waters of the Zionist "well." This baptism lays great emphasis upon the dissolution of prior identity, the initiate vividly experiencing the death that is the cost of rebirth. Here we recall the dual metaphors of sacrifice and rejuvenation in precolonial circumcision rites, for as Sundkler (1961:202ff.) has stressed, baptism in Zion involved both terror and rejoicing. The Tswana attitude, like that of the Zulu, to large concentrations of water is one of fear and awe. Indigenous legend tells of a snake that "bleats like a kid" (*noga ya potsane;* "snake of the kid") and inhabits deep dark pools, consuming those that enter them. Precolonial Tswana ate neither fish nor aquatic creatures and seldom swam. Such attitudes still had general currency in the late 1960s and infused the act of ritual immersion with danger. As Sundkler notes, water creatures have come to personify the evils of a corrupt world that threaten the initiate even as he crosses over to the promised land. Baptisms that I observed in the Full Witness and other Zionist churches took place at a local dam, and participants were visibly terrified, most of the women having to be dragged in, crying uncontrollably. Immersion was preceded by a confession (*bolela,* "to tell," the same as to "testify"), in which initiates breathlessly recalled a string of personal misdeeds, centering around sexual "looseness" and the "eating of filth," acts which in the Zionist scheme typify defiling transactions with an alien world (cf. Sundkler 1961:211).

The pragmatic intention underlying Zionist rites is most clearly seen in the healing process itself. Here, the formal structure of the ritual sequence captures the impetus of the entire movement: in its synthetic and

creative juxtaposition of Protestant forms (*go rapela*) and those of tradition (*go bina*), it seeks to rehearse and redress essential paradoxes of
everyday experience. These rites are not explicitly routinized, nor rigidly
separated from practical events in time and space. While there is a notion
of the Sunday service, the most frequent ritual "work" is occasioned by
circumstance rather than by the objective schedule and the clock. The
term used for such "work" is the indigenous *tiro,* implying creative action upon the world. Indeed, the *tiro* of Zion sets itself up in opposition
to *bereka,* wage labor, for it seeks to return estranged dimensions of the
self, to engender a state of social and spiritual integrity.

The work of Zion has its point of departure in Methodist orthodoxy,
taking the outward form of a structured "church service," which begins
and ends with transformed versions of Protestant liturgy. The Zionist
discourse, however, systematically reworks Protestant symbols, thereby
protesting the hegemonic as it is expressed in establishment Christianity.
But its logic is less an inversion of Methodist practices than an autonomous synthesis. The point of departure, the Methodist hymn, serves
primarily to highlight the distance that Zionism has traveled from its
source: a rousing beat and urgent percussion immediately announce the
simultaneous involvement of body, mind, and spirit. Physical gesture
and intricately harmonized song orchestrate the formerly distinct participants into a single community. The pounding drum not only declares the
onset of the special "work" of ritual time and space; it also dramatizes the
gulf between the children of Zion and the followers of Wesley. The
drum is *the* aural signal of Zionist identity. As a local Methodist lay
preacher put it, trying to explain the pull exercised by the movement on
his congregants: "They hear the sound of the drum and they follow it"
(*ba latêla moropa*). Indeed, its sonorous beat infuses the air with a sense of
vibrancy, of power and control, which contrasts with the decorous, almost ethereal bell that calls the Methodists to Sunday service, its sound
not designed to elicit a physical response or to resonate with indigenous
musical forms. To the orthodox, the drum can signal a smouldering
threat, just as to the Victorian missionaries it conveyed the challenge of
pagan ritual and Satanic power (cf. Hebdige 1979:31). In the Zionist
churches, its mere beat is sufficient to induce the first signs of possession
in the congregation.[12]

The precolonial Tswana lacked the highly developed drumming tradition of other southern African peoples, such as the Zulu, for whom it
was part of the *ngoma* cult of possession, divination, and healing
(Ngubane 1977). While early observers among the southern Tswana report only the *lichâka* (reed pipe), modern Tshidi insist that the drum (*moropa*) has always been a part of their dance tradition. As stated earlier,
percussion was traditionally provided by the women, who enhanced

their clapping and stamping with foot-rattles. In Tshidi Zionist churches, rattles continue to play an important role, the wild seed pods and plant fiber having been replaced by bottle caps and wire, obsolescent industrial products being pressed into indigenous shape so as to animate the rituals of a counter-hegemony.

The Full Witness service is ordered in such a manner as to achieve the transformation of personal and collective identity contained in the metaphor of healing. The ritual itself is the kernel, recreating in condensed form the logic inherent in the practical formulations of the whole movement, that is, the unification of the community of Zion and its separation from a defiling world. Indeed, the Zionist church strives to achieve what Turner has called "permanent liminality" (1969:145), associated by him with the desire for *communitas* (p. 96). Unlike Turner, however, I do not envisage such liminality as an instance of a universal state of formless communion which would, in all societies, be the antithesis of structure, being locked with it in a perpetual dialectic of mutual reinforcement (cf. Turner 1969:96ff.). Zionist liminality exists, it is true, in dialectical opposition to the social order which spawned it, but as "counter-" rather than "anti-structure" (cf. Williams 1977:114). Furthermore, this liminality is not formless; its deconstruction of established sociocultural arrangements entails a reconstruction which both subverts and seeks permanent transformation of a historically specific system. More generally, however, it is not an all-or-none state: the transient and highly codified healing ritual of Zion effects the central metamorphosis of what is a transformative movement. Such ritual involves a heightened, fleeting sense of *communitas,* in which the boundaries between man, woman, and spirit all but dissolve. It is this fluid integration that remains behind in the symbol of the holy water. But such dissolution is merely a more intensified form of the condition that the whole movement seeks to produce in its daily practice, a condition born not so much of a universal quest for transcendence as of a particular attempt to reverse the impact of colonization; to heal the immediate sense of estrangement, the loss of self-determination that the Tshidi experience in their everyday world.

Like the poetic structure of the initiation rites, the Zionist service is composed of a set of overlapping sequences which together constitute a cumulative process: within and then between sequences, juxtaposed meanings are contrasted and transformed until the climactic metamorphosis is realized. The logic of the metamorphosis itself is laid out in the origin myth of the church—the exile from urban bondage to the site of liminal reconstruction. The rites will concretize the dislocation of the world of work and migration, and dissolve it in the unifying force of the Spirit.

In the practical context, ceremonial dress, song, and gesture all serve to frame the shift from mundane to ritual time and space. But the ritual domain remains continuous, in important respects, with the encompassing world, and the rites must continually rework the contradictions inherent in this continuity. Like the photograph of the American car on the wall, soon to be enveloped in the dust of collective dance and enthusiasm, the signs of external domination and depersonalization will be turned—for the duration of the service—into symbols of healing and reconstitution. The still recognizable forms of the Methodist hymns and the rites of *go rapela* will serve to usher in the dynamic cadence of *go bina*. Within the square cubicle, carefully sealed off from the outside world, the congregants form themselves into a closely-knit circle. Coordinated harmonies and bodily gestures begin to weld the uniformed participants into a single body, facing the prophet, the vehicle of the Spirit.

Once this framing and focusing has been achieved, the summoning of the Spirit (*go bitsa*) begins. In this sequence, a dramatic distinction will be made between the individuated quest for spiritual fulfillment and a mediated collective catharsis. The circle is broken as participants drop to the floor, each calling upon the Spirit in terms of his or her private affliction. Their voices become ever louder and their utterances less coherent. As this part of the ritual reaches its deafening crescendo, it exemplifies competitive, mutually negating effort and spiritual discord. The women are more susceptible to this uncontrolled and uncoordinated possession, and their physical movements exemplify disarticulation.

It is the men who bring this disorderly show to a halt, rising at the sign of their leader to reform the circle. The cacophany is turned into harmony, and the participants are welded into a single body of affliction. The offering of testimony (*go bolela*) now makes subjective perception into common experience, and the physical distress of individual sufferers serves to signify a more global malaise in the collective consciousness. In contrast to Protestant preaching, which is rooted in the exegesis of the written word and a rationalist conception of truth, Zionist testimonies are the immediate expression of a reality holistically perceived, of a system of meaning that does not distinguish knowledge from experience. As we have seen, such testimonies exhibit a common semantic structure: unintegrated, personalized feelings ("my heart is sore") being given increasing rhetorical reinforcement and assuming increasingly objective form. The growing intensity of the narrative is achieved through mounting speed, volume, and frequency of formulaic punctuation; the isolation of the sufferer is reduced and her distress made tangible as her utterances are subsumed into the poetic structure of the ritual text. I suggested that the stereotyped content of testimony laid out the social, spatial, and moral opposition between the experience of wage labor in the white man's world (the dairy in Mafeking; work in Randfontein) and "home" ("here

with the bishop"). Bodily affliction is countered by the promise of healing, and evil spirits with holy water and cords. For the work of Zion is to
mediate the tension framed by testimony, its symbolism reversing the
dislocations of the outside world and subsuming the person into a unifying scheme. The sample testimony cited above also voices the paradox of
the Zionist utopia, however; for, while already a participant in the
bishop's healing, the child concerned remains ill. The mother's doubts
("I hope this evil spirit will be sent away") are overlaid with the op-
timistic momentum of the rite itself; but under conditions of poverty and
malnutrition, enteritis remains a major cause of infant death and is unlikely to be responsive to prophetic intervention.

The ritual now moves to its climax, the metamorphosis to be wrought
by divine healing. This performance brings about a transference between
the prophet, the medium of spiritual abundance at the center of the ritual,
and the physically depleted congregants at the periphery. The withdrawal of the altar marks the shift to the dance form of *go bina,* which
evokes the structure of the rituals of the precolonial community, especially those of initiation. Here again the dance realizes collective integration, achieved in defiance of a world that enforces personal and social
differentiation. The whirling circle builds up a unitary momentum, like a
dynamo generating the spiritual energy increasingly manifest in the body
of its central conductor. The ever closer coordination of physical gestures
under the driving beat and the physiological effects of the circling motion
seem to dissolve the margins between individual participants, who act
and respond as one body. This unification, soon to be completed by the
infusion of spirit, dramatically reverses the state of physical and social
disarticulation that the testimonies expressed; it cuts across the fragmentation of person and community which pervades the experience of black
South Africans under apartheid. In the founded space that Zionism cre-
ates, the rites of *go bina* remove the obstacles that impede the fluidity of
social relations and personal mobility.

The spatial metaphors of the dance also contrast centrality with marginality, and verticality with laterality, vigorously asserting male control
and dominance. The movements of the men make more of an exhibition
of skilled, intricate steps and aggressive gestures than did precolonial performances, suggesting that the Zionist tradition has drawn heavily upon
the polyethnic forms synthesized in the South African mining compounds. The close and disciplined coordination and dramatic swoops and
shifts of level recall the Zulu and Swazi war dances (see Elliott 1978:164).
They are combined with the military motions—inspired directly by colonial activity—that played a central symbolic role in such movements of
protest as the Beni *ngoma* dance of east and central Africa, a dance whose
forms found their way into the Witwatersrand compounds with Nyasa

migrants (Ranger 1975; van Onselen 1976:190ff.). Echoes of this latter style are stronger in the Z.C.C. rites discussed below; but, among Zionists in general, as in the mine compound, such performances appropriate the signs of colonial might and integrate them with indigenous gestures of communal force, producing novel statements of self-asserting and belligerent defiance in the face of physical coercion.

The structure of the dance also replays the theme of Zionist gender relations already encountered in the logic of dress. Here the order inherent in the precolonial form seems relatively unchanged, since females are clearly subordinated to the collective control of males. Yet the position of women in the modern Tshidi social system has obviously been transformed in important respects: migrant labor has left them as residues in the rural reserves, or has drawn them into the market as unskilled workers or domestics at wages even lower than those of men. In the rural areas they have been catapulted into positions of responsibility, in charge of the reproduction of the household under conditions of underdevelopment. Their apparent autonomy from male authority has only meant their subjection to a more diffuse but totalized oppression. Among the petite bourgeoisie, where family structure has been less undermined by migrant labor, women are increasingly moving into the classic female occupations of their class, schoolteaching and nursing. In this population, the more explicit espousal of an ideology of liberal individualism is accompanied by an embryonic concern with female equality. For most of the Tshidi population, though, inequality is perceived in racial stratification and the ranking of status groups, not in gender relations. In Zionism, the quest for power focuses on the manipulation of diverse symbols of might, which would seem to promise the restoration of male control; the quest is predicated, in the ritual context, upon female submission. Moreover, within the congregation as a social collectivity, the inspired healer tends to function as senior male kinsman to his largely dependent female following.

The focal rite of Zionist healing is an act of ritual consummation: the prophet mediates the culminating fusion of the Spirit force and its human recipients. The thirsty "drink from the well," the "oppressed" are "entered" and "filled"; wasting, that central Tswana metaphor of depletion, is replaced by the rounded contours, the extension of the bodily space, that epitomizes well-being. The water of the spirit "washes away" (*kgophola*) the defilement that has accumulated in the person through the social and material transactions with the outside world, quenching thirst and cooling the heated blood that is incapable of smooth flow.

Those who have drunk at the well of Zion become the physical bearers of the Spirit outside the liminal confines of the ritual itself; this, indeed, is the fervent implication of the healing rite. In their own communion, the Zionists imbibe the Spirit directly. Among them, the divine intervention of Christ is almost totally ignored. In fact, for Tshidi Christians more generally there remains a structural opposition between Jesus as white ancestor and the partisan figures of the indigenous ancestors, who mediate actively with the remote deity (Comaroff 1974:272ff.). A local Anglican priest put the matter thus:

> We have been presented with a Christ with whom we have no identity at all. The Europeans [i.e. whites] draw him as a hippy, an effeminate Christ, sentimental and not a real man. That is why I usually find the Devil, the picture of him, more interesting than those of Christ. He is really a man. He has dignity and power. He's virile (Comaroff 1974:284–85).

As this statement suggests, moreover, the figure of the devil is not so easily consigned, either, to his more conventional Western niche. In fact, in the modern Tshidi cosmos, evil remains primarily social in origin: in the Zionist case, it is wrought by spirits working at human behest or by the pollution of the world beyond their reinforced boundaries; for non-Zionists, sorcery, the heat of sexual pollution, and the withdrawal of support by offended ancestors remain its more prevalent sources.

The ritualized donation of money that concludes the Full Witness service, and occurs in most southern African Zionist churches, would appear contradictory; for it seems to fetishize the archetypal sign of the system that the movement itself protests. As the "altar" is returned to the ritual space, congregants engage in, even celebrate, a prototypical Protestant ritual, making individual cash contributions in a studied and conspicuous manner. Holy collection is a central Protestant legitimation of the role of money, of the "natural," taken-for-granted quality of commoditization. Despite its obvious continuities with such orthodoxy, the Zionist rite neatly reverses the logic of the original. The mode of donation, for example, is the obverse of the Christian notion of charity, in which the "left hand knows not the action of the right," a giving that severs the bond between giver and recipient. Zionist donation is paradoxically referred to as *go koleka* ("to collect"); the Protestant term "collection," from which this term derives, has been transposed into a verb that connotes accumulation unto the self, not the alienation from the self that is implied by the Christian ideal. Of course, Zionist donations are a utilitarian accumulation in one sense; in the Full Witness Church the money goes to the support of the leader's domestic establishment, to the social and material core of the movement. But the bulk of such support is provided by congregants in labor and foodstuffs—the work of their hands. Thus the ritualized contribution of *go koleka* would seem to be freighted with other significance; the carefully individuated style of donation, the exhibition of the coin and its noisy consignment of the jar, representing an attempt to impress the identity of the donor upon the anonymous cent.

Gregory (1980:649) has argued that, in contexts of colonial articulation, the presence of money does not inevitably destroy nonmonetized systems of exchange. In fact, it may be appropriated to the logic of such exchange as a qualitative rather than a quantitative measure. Among the Tshidi Zionists, money is indeed a qualitative measure: as is the case in many black American denominations, the donation is not a subject of rivalry (Vincent Wimbush, personal communication). This contrasts with Gregory's own New Guinea example, where church contributions feed into a system of competitive status enhancement. Within the Full Witness congregation, not only is the use of money limited almost entirely to ritual contexts,[13] the size of gifts is almost always the same. Moreover, the symbolic order of the Zionists devalues the signs of commoditization, especially the red heat of "blood/money." Thus, the practice of *go koleka* inverts the usual role of money; instead of abstracting from the person the essence of himself, of separating him from the collectivity of person and spirit, its use in the church involves a personalized appropriation of its inherent power, realized by identifying the giver with the cash gift.

Rather than being a medium of self-estrangement, then, money becomes a vehicle, in the ritual context, for regaining control over the self in the gift, a personalized contribution to the fund of power of the collectivity. The carefully individuated style of donating unvarying amounts removes from money its function as an anonymous marker of quantitative value, thereby throwing into relief its role as qualitative signifier. The accentuated idiosyncracy of self-presentation in the *koleka* rite, each person dancing in a distinctive style, contrasts with the uniformalizing practice of the rest of the ritual process; it would seem to suggest a personalized control over the flow of money, a feature absent from the experience of the everyday market economy. But this individually reclaimed value does not remain with the self; for the fullest realization of the return to the self of its essence is the ability to give, especially to give a gift that binds donors together in a substantial unity. In contributing to a collectivity in whose integral circulation the donor seeks self-fulfillment, he or she reverses the loss of self associated with wage labor. The rite of *koleka* really is about "collection"; it involves the dramatization of the social bonds, the interweaving of individuals, that constitutes the community. Coming at the end of the rite, it reinforces the transient climax of spiritual integration, achieved by the healing process, with a consolidation of formerly dispersed substance; the diffusion of divine Spirit (water) in the body of Zion is replicated in the controlled circulation of money/blood.

The Zion Christian Church

I have examined the Full Witness Apostolic Church in Zion as a token of a type of social phenomenon produced by the conjuncture of a particular set of historical conditions in southern Africa. At this level, Zionism is a panethnic movement, shaped by the circumstances surrounding the rise of the neocolonial state and the emergence of a class of black peasant-proletarians. This structural predicament is in no sense unique and, in general outline, Zionism is strikingly similar to the creative responses of peoples elsewhere on the periphery of the European world. Thus the Tshidi churches, as I have already suggested, share many structural and ideological features with cults in the New World, and I shall return, in the conclusion, to the analytical significance of such similarities. But I have also argued that Dowie's movement, originally serving a population structurally akin to the Tshidi, has undergone transformation in its mutually determining relationship with South African social forms. In the ethnically segregated rural reserves, for instance, Zionism was brought face to face with the persisting cultural schemes of non-monetized, kin-based production. In the Tshidi case it was introduced into a sociocultural context whose indigenous elements were themselves undergoing realignment; it was assigned a positional value in this overall, shifting system according to which it was opposed to Protestant orthodoxy and, along with other Christian denominations, to "tradition," a relationship which then began to mediate the new cleavages arising in the rural community as a result of articulation. In due course, religious orientation became the major index of status groups—the blurred collective representation of class—with Zionism being the mode of practice that typified the illiterate poor.

The discussion thus far has been predicated upon the assumption that Tshidi Zionism is a unitary category. This is both warranted and unwarranted; in terms of the inclusive Tshidi scheme, a generalized Zionist paradigm is recognized from both within and outside the movement. It is associated with a particular conceptual and practical style and with a common socioeconomic situation. The key Zionist signs—its color scheme, the robes and flowing hair, the drum and the baptism, inspired healing and holistic separatism—are all linked to the "poor," and to a mode of everyday practice which is manifestly not that of the colonial cultural hegemony. In this sense, for the outside, Zion is a unitary category. Zionists themselves also recognize a common identity as affiliates of *dikereke tsa Moya,* the churches of the Spirit. Yet, as within all segmentary orders, this identity is based on the notion of unity amidst diversity; under the umbrella of the movement, there is an ongoing differentiation, for the essence of a Zionist identity is the membership of a small face-to-face unit, in which participants seek to realize a perpetual mediation of experiential tension, a present apocalypse. All do the "work of Zion"; but, within the overarching paradigm, a process of symbolic involution has taken place.

The Zion Christian Church represents a particular transformation of the Zionist order; one which resolves the inherent tension between charisma and routine by stressing the normative to a greater extent than any other southern African group. In so doing, it comes closest to Dowie's original organization. For this reason, and because of its indigenous identity as the Zionist church par excellence, I do not follow Sundkler's usage (1961:320ff.) which identifies this, and several others like it, as distinct "messianic" types of movement. Indeed, the sociocultural forms of the Z.C.C. may be seen to express a logic which is essentially similar to that elaborated above, protesting the same neocolonial cultural forms from a particular position within the same structural niche as that occupied by the rest of the followers of Zion.

As I have noted, the Z.C.C. is the largest indigenous religious movement in southern Africa. It is panethnic, with a membership spanning international boundaries; its constituencies run counter to the established geopolitical order, being centered on a strongly centripetal holy site in the rural Northern Transvaal. The church was built up by two Pedi brothers of the Lekhanyane lineage who together marshaled both the charismatic power and the organizational skill to hold together a quasi-bureaucratic hierarchy of hundreds of dispersed local congregations (West 1975:50). By constructing a particularly powerful central place, which administers a fund of spiritual, material, and symbolic power, the Z.C.C. has managed to counteract, for the most part, the inherent tendency toward fission and secession in such movements. Edward Lekhanyane, the elder brother, was a man of considerable creative flair and insight, and was installed as chief mediator among mediators with the Holy Spirit; in structural terms at least, a black Christ. But his was not the reign of the world-renouncer. The movement's headquarters at Morija is renowned for its size and opulence. It is located on a large estate and the leaders are equipped with a fleet of sleek American cars. Such focal symbols do not seem fortuitous; like the car on the calendar in the Full Witness Church, they connote control not only over white status symbols, but over fluid motion and space. Indeed, the demonstration of such control, exercised from the center, is an important aspect of the church's apparatus of power. At "Passover" and, to a lesser extent, the ritual New Year, buses carrying thousands of members make their way to the huge assembly ground, where the prophet addresses the uniformed multitudes over a modern electronic sound system (see plate 7).[14] The ability to will a population of such size across the country—even if for bona fide religious purposes—is perceived as extremely threatening to the state. Morija is a graphic icon of the appropriation of the material and spiritual cargo of the neocolonial system. The choice of name is itself significant: Morija (Moriah) was a biblical name for Jerusalem (2 Chron. 3:1), the place where the Temple was built. This was an appropriation by the theocratic state of the name of the *original* cult center at Mt. Moriah, somewhat to the north (Gen. 12:6; 22:2). The Morija of the Z.C.C. is on

Plate 7   The Zion Christian Church: Passover gathering at Morija (*Women's World*, 21 May 1970).

the high plateau in the north of the Transvaal province in modern South
Africa, a reestablishment of the "original" Holy Place that had been
eclipsed by the state capital (Pretoria) and economic center (Johannesburg) to the south. This iconography, then, recalls the exodus to the
periphery encountered before in the origin myth of the Full Witness
Church.

The Lekhanyane descent group has integrated ritual and temporal
power in the Z.C.C. structure in a manner which echoes precolonial
chiefly authority. A mark of this achievement is the fact that, in recent
years, despite a major secession, the leadership has twice devolved in the
direct Lekhanyane line, the dynasty having overcome the notoriously
difficult problem of establishing the hereditary legitimacy of charisma
(cf. Weber 1947:365; Sundkler 1961:117; West 1975:61). In the process of
"central place competition" (Werbner n.d.) nothing succeeds like success. Movements which accumulate such a fund of power, which establish complex and ramifying organizations, acquire a stature and an
overarching authority that rival the state's in important respects; and
their ability to do this encourages even greater centralized control and
centripetal movement.

Notwithstanding the widespread folklore about the wonders of Morija—its impressive buildings, rich farmland, and Easter collection taken
in a ten-gallon oil barrel—its magnificence remains far removed from the
realities of local Z.C.C. congregations. That of the Tshidi, for example,
meets for service each Sunday on an open lot at the fringe of the stad, in a
rough brick building with no roof. Only a handful of the hundred or so
members has ever been to Morija to sample its opulence firsthand. For
most, the more global significance of the uniform they wear may be
important, especially when traveling the migrant route, where it provides an identity beyond the local; but, in practical terms, they are participants in a bounded, face-to-face congregation which seldom meets
with other nearby branches. It is this local unit that forms the regular
ritual community, the cosmological center, the pool of general cooperative assistance, and the well of visions drawn upon by congregants in
managing their everyday experience. Thus, while the macro-structure of
the Z.C.C. provides an extensive cognitive map and a social identity to
rival the divisive categories of the apartheid system, the micro-structure
of its constituent groups tends to define the main universe of action from
a distinctly local perspective. In fact, at this level, the Z.C.C. takes its
place as one among many Zionist churches.

Edward Lekhanyane was the "archbishop" of the movement, followed by his descendants in turn. Local congregations are led by a clutch
of men, a minister (*moruti*), a prophet (*moporofeta*), a secretary (*mok-
waledi*), and a treasurer (*mmoloki ya madi*; literally "conserver of the mon-

ey)."[15] The effective division of labor between charismatic and legal authority is the same here as in most Zionist groups, except that the proliferation of offices reflects the Z.C.C.'s more extensive scale and hierarchical structure; its organizational forms are modeled, to a greater degree than those of other Zionists, upon the bureaucratic structures of the colonial order.

In fact, the balance within the Z.C.C. between local-level autonomy and centripetal power is its particular genius. Secession has been relatively contained and the proportion of men in its ranks is higher than in most black southern African churches, Zionist or other. About one-third of the Tshidi membership in 1970 was male, its large leadership cadre including several who functioned as lower-order visionaries and who, in the other Zionist groups, would probably have seceded to form their own congregations. Women did not hold office in their own right but as the spouses of male leaders. The membership in Mafeking seems to have been drawn from roughly the same socioeconomic stratum as the other Zionist groups, with one telling difference: it comprised more men and women in employment, especially female domestic workers, and contained fewer who were engaged in peasant production. Of all the local Zionist churches, it claimed the highest proportion of the local working population. Its members were also more scattered residentially than was the case with the Full Witness Church, where the overlap of ward and congregation was great. The Z.C.C., in other words, is the church of the more thoroughly proletarianized in the community: as a result, its sociocultural forms are the product of a necessarily complementary existence with the demands of wage labor; and it makes practical and iconic use of more than the snatched, disembodied signs of the neocolonial system, putting coherent features of the productive and organizational forms of the latter to work in its own interest. At the national level, the church owns farmland which it works by mechanized means, though its proceeds are used primarily in support of the cult center, and the bulk is not marketed. It also employs bureaucratic techniques of administration and accounting, although white businessmen in Johannesburg tell of shopping expeditions made by Z.C.C. leaders bearing hundreds of rands in small change taken directly from church collections. The model of the alternative Zion that shapes this movement is not the encapsulated group on the desert fringe; it is the new Jerusalem, a centered theocracy. Yet, at the local level, its congregations function like encompassed liminal societies, their regular practice being a perpetual ritual protest and a healing catharsis which repeatedly attempts to redress the contradictions of political coercion and economic dependency.

It is hardly surprising, then, that, within the Tshidi community, the organizational and symbolic scheme of the Z.C.C. should closely resemble that of the Full Witness Church. Its ritual calendar also centers, in practical terms, on the well of healing (although, in this case, the latter is clearly situated in public "religious" space, and is confined to the weekend). In addition, the Z.C.C. performs a similar range of life-crisis rites, including elaborate river baptism; it observes almost identical dietary taboos, enjoins endogamy, and discourages the consultation of both Western and "traditional" doctors.

The Z.C.C. uniform, while sharing the underlying symbolic scheme of Zionism as a whole, shows several distinctive variations. Because the congregation is more directly engaged in the money economy than most groups, its uniform tends not to be worn outside the context of ritual performance. However, the icon of the spiritual power of the movement, a metal badge, is always pinned to the clothing of members during their waking hours, prominently displaying the stamp of the church over any other apparel. The badge is a silver star on which the letters Z.C.C. are inscribed, and it is attached to a contrasting strip of black cloth. Sometimes referred to as "the star of Lekhanyane," it conflates biblical and colloquial Western usage, and serves both expressive and pragmatic ends, usually being worn "over the heart" to proclaim incorporation in the ranks of Zion; but it may also sometimes be placed next to afflicted bodily parts to effect healing. The very notion of the badge is, of course, associated with a particularly Western form of identity marking: it is the product of a proliferated set of achievable "roles" and "statuses," which may be "pinned on" to the person through a composite of external signs rather than as intrinsic capacities of his or her being. The Z.C.C. star is an emblem of commercial manufacture, but it represents a movement that seeks to retool the dominant system in its own image. For in the star, signifier and signified are inseparable; the badge both represents Lekhanyane's power and embodies it in tangible form. Attached prominently to the apparel of wage labor, it confers upon the wearer a more substantial, intrinsic identity.

Although Z.C.C. dress, particularly that of the women, makes little use of white, the men do wear conspicuous white boots, themselves an important emblem of the movement. The predominant material of male attire is khaki cotton, which emulates colonial and neocolonial uniforms, both military and bureaucratic. The lack of white in ritual clothing here may be associated with the more routinized form of charismatic power operant in this church; it may also be due to the fact that its members live more fully in the industrial world, and seek bolder appropriations of its large-scale secular structures. Its color and forms still reproduce the logic of contrast between Zion and orthodoxy, however. Thus the female Z.C.C. uniform is a standard Zionist transformation of the Protestant model: a calf-length, straight skirt, a Victorian tunic with rounded collar and a neat headscarf. The tunic is daffodil-yellow and the skirt and head-scarf are bottle-green; the wives of office-bearers are distinguished by tunics of bright blue.

The male Z.C.C. uniform (see plates 8 and 9) contrasts more strongly with usual Zionist apparel. It consists of a khaki jacket and trousers, or shorts the same color with knee-length socks, and a collar and tie. This uniform recalls both the dress of British imperial troops and the uniform of modern South African civil servants, such as administer the bureaucratic intricacies of apartheid. The jacket has the letters Z.C.C. embroidered on the left chest, above which the movement's badge tends to be displayed. Men also wear black peaked caps—like those of the modern military or of liveried servants—on the front of which the silver star appears again. Most distinguishing of all are the large, white, flat-soled boots, specially crafted within the movement itself and carefully whitened for ritual performances. These boots often exaggerate the size of the wearers' feet to almost comic proportions. They come into their own during the initial sequence of the typical Z.C.C. service, that of "praising with the feet" (*go bina ka dinao*), during which loud and rhythmical marching and stamping are prominent features. Finally, to complete the outfit, male office-bearers usually carry wooden staffs.

At face value, the Z.C.C. male garb would appear to reverse the principles of the dress code of the Full Witness Church and, by implication, of Zionists more widely. The men wear trousers which, in contrast with the colorful female tunics and skirts, seem to reproduce the key gender distinctions of Western apparel. But men here do not wear the cuts and fabrics typical of the workplace; they don suits and ties that, in the Western context, mark off military, administrative and service roles from those of material production per se. As members of an organization in which they are both the servants and the warriors of a charismatic leader, their dress is analogous to that of functionaries who, in the wider society, work both as the guardians and attendants of powerful institutions. By putting on the uniform of the military and the bureaucracy, the Z.C.C. man appropriates the insignia of those who wield the sword and pen—in his experience, the visible faces of colonial and neocolonial domination. Moreover, the khaki uniform of the service, rather than productive, sector of the modern state—those who regulate the flow of goods and people rather than produce them—is brought into juxtaposition in the male outfit with the distinctive boots and the forceful gestures of masculine control performed by them. In this way, the potency perceived in images of the state apparatus is conflated with the spiritual dynamism drummed up by the accentuated feet.

The color of the Zionist boots may connote activating spiritual power, but it also conflicts with modern Western notions of serviceability, implying conspicuous "leisure" and prestige (Veblen 1934). These are definitely not work shoes; in fact, they are often referred to, by Tshidi both in and outside the Z.C.C., as "cricket boots," evoking the sport perceived by the colonized in Africa and elsewhere as emblematic of the ceremonial pursuits of British imperial culture (as in the film *Trobriand Cricket,* which demonstrates the ritual appropriation of the game and of its subtle combative logic by peoples engaged in long-standing patterns of competitive exchange).[16] The Z.C.C. boots are large, and the vigorous male ritual dancer appears to be "all feet," his actions involving closely coordinated steps whose main feature is the pounding on the bare ground. Participants assert that, in this manner, they "stamp evil underfoot," or "tramp it down in the dust" (cf. Moore n.d.:104 on "stamping" in comparable Caribbean movements). Such dance styles again have their origin in the polyethnic cultural forms of the industrial workplace; stamping was a feature of the Zulu war dance (Elliott 1978:164), and it also echoes the marching drill of the syncretistic Beni

Plate 8   The Zion Christian Church: male ritual dress.

Plate 9   The Zion Christian Church: praising with the feet.

ngoma movements mentioned above. In the precolonial Tswana perception, the sole of the foot was permeable to pollution and sorcery concoctions on the ground. To the Tshidi at least, the thick–soled shoes were a
quest for invincibility; yet, like the exaggerated "bovver boots" of British skinheads, they also seemed to signal a protest and a gesture of frus-
tration, a means of dramatizing the desire to control a recalcitrant world.
The boots, then, invoke precolonial and colonial signs of power; the
wearer, with his oversized feet, internalizes both kinds of signs and energetically treads down the persistently threatening "evil" of his everyday
world.

The rites of the Z.C.C. differ in certain respects from those of other
Zionist groups, although their underlying structure appears very similar.
Regular collective ritual takes place each Sunday; unscheduled services
are prevented, for the most part, by work routines. Congregants gather
at midday under a tree alongside the roofless church and, when sufficient
have assembled, the "outside" portion of the service begins, men and
women forming separate, adjacent circles in a spot where two patches
have been worn bare in the scrub grass. They start to dance (*go bina*) in a
style less like the concentric form of indigenous ritual, and more eclectic
and expressive of the panethnic organization of the church itself. But
local cultural features do impress themselves on forms of movement and
song. The women commence by clapping and stamping, several wearing
Tswana foot-rattles. The hymns are from the Z.C.C. collection, *Songs of*

Zion, printed at the movement's headquarters and translated into several southern African languages. A favorite for commencing the service is:

Sione Sione	Zion! Zion!
Re kopa thata	We ask for power.
Re tlile-kwa-go wêna	We have come to you,
Wêna o botshabêlô	You are our refuge!

The tempo is sprightly and the rhythm of the chant clearly indigenous. The women begin to shuffle round in a circle and execute solo or paired maneuvers in the center. These enact long-standing gestures of female productive activity—stamping and winnowing grain—typical of the dance at *bojale* and marriage. The short hymn is repeated in several harmonic variations; individual women might dance up to others, clap their hands before them and lead them from the circle for secluded consultation. This indicates that one has received a vision offering insight into the personal circumstances of the other. While the parallel is not explicitly acknowledged, the style of interaction between visionary and recipient evokes that of Tswana divination (Comaroff 1980). But such insight is couched in terms of the Zionist cosmology, and it is a continuous feature of the life of Z.C.C. congregations; the power of reciprocal revelation thought to reside within ordinary Z.C.C. members unites them in a flow of symbolic exchanges whose common logic is the quest for a meaningful resolution to everyday suffering. The fact that anyone of either sex may be the involuntary medium of a revelation has acted as a leveling mechanism within the hierarchical framework of the church. The Spirit conveys powers of insight upon all the followers of Lekhanyane, but these gifts are hedged about by conventionalized constraints. The activities of the female circle, for instance, are usually supervised by one of the male office-bearers who, carrying his staff, might control the dancers' tempo, terminating one song, beginning another, and sanctioning the departure of visionaries from the circle.

The male circle simultaneously shuffles and sways to a distinct hymn, its movement being in no way coordinated with that of the women. Songs frequently combine biblical reference to worldly evil, expiation, and apocalypse with images of precolonial production:

Bua ka Emmanuel	Speak about Emmanuel
O utlwêla boshula	He hears tales of wickedness.
O utlwêla tlhapêlô	He hears about profanation.
Emmanuel o ichwarela	But Emmanuel forgives us.
Tsogang le bine	Wake up and sing/dance.
[a humming chorus, ending with Ja! Ja! Ja!]	
Dikgomo, o tshwanela go di disa	Cattle, you have to take care of of them.
Dikgomo, di ya kganya	Cattle will shine/be radiant!

The structure of such songs contrasts the evil of the world with the immediate, transforming redemption of Zion, a redemption to be made actual by the healing rites to follow. "Emmanuel" is a frequent invocation in the song of the Z.C.C.; it refers to the founder, Edward Lekhanyane, whose identity has been elided with that of the successive heads of the church. The Z.C.C. makes more use of the biblical lexicon than do many smaller Zionist groups; the universalizing properties of these symbols serve to unify micro-historical and cultural variation, while remaining pliable enough to speak simultaneously to local concerns. The image of Emmanuel establishes the supreme status of the leader of the Kingdom of Zion for, in the Bible, it refers to Christ (Matt. 1:23). But there is no explicit invocation of the transcendent white savior, and Emmanuel's forgiveness is realized in the present space-time world. The technique of oblique reference to established scriptural images (Morijah for the new Jerusalem; Emmanuel for Christ) serves to appropriate and revalue focal Christian symbols.

The songs also contrast spiritual deliverance from temporal evil with a seemingly different mode of transformative action, that effected through precolonial cattle rites. In fact, Z.C.C. rhetoric often associates Lekhanyane with a "great ox," recalling the multiple capacities of cattle in most Bantu-speaking societies—the "God with the wet nose." But Emmanuel's perpetual redemption is necessary because of the thoroughgoing defilement of the everyday world; this is spoken of in terms of the consumption of forbidden flesh—that is, the breach of dietary and sexual proscriptions—but echoes also the corporeal evil of the Protestant tradition. The wickedness, then, is of the world beyond Zion, continuing immersion in which is a constant source of pollution. As implied by the women's dance, the symbolism of this church plays repeatedly upon the juxtaposition of precolonial and neocolonial modes of production, seeming to express the conflict caused by the articulation of the two in the lives of peasant-proletarians. In the Z.C.C. service, the dramatizations of the dance circle and the subsequent recital of praises replace the offering of testimony; they similarly objectivize the distress that is the focus of the healing rites to follow.

The pace and excitation of the male dancers continually increase, the regular thud of boots welding the contrasting images into a single whole. By the time the minister breaks into the refrain that is the rallying call of the "Soldiers of Zion," the dancers have reached a close coordination, and the performance moves from a statement of problem to a display of collective physical resolve:

Tsogang batlhabani	Wake up soldiers.
Ntwa e simologile	The war has begun.
Morena ke Yo	Here is the Lord.

Loso ke lo	Here is death.
Ke boifa fa ke le bona	I am afraid when I see it.
Badira boshula batataêla le basia	The evil ones tremble with the cowards.
Thata le kopanyo	Strength and unity!

The song, like many others of the movement, is a call to arms. It presents images of combat and of a Spirit of deadly power in a dualistic moral universe. The dancers move to form pairs and take turns in running into the center of the circle, bringing down their feet with a resounding thud in time to the music. The rest move on the spot, swaying, swinging their arms and lifting their feet in seeming parody of a military march. Individuals break this formation intermittently by moving back and forth and leaping into the air with staffs outstretched, then sinking to their haunches. This again evokes the stylized "mine dances" of urban migrant culture on the Witwatersrand, where a famous "gum boot" routine was executed with similar aggressive energy before white audiences. This is the drill of the troops of the theocracy, a form which quite evidently also constitutes "recreation." Here Sunday "leisure" contrasts with labor; but it is shaped by a defiance of the physical regimentation of the workplace, its denial of the possibilities of resistance. These dances, performed with enthusiasm and skill, might continue for a couple of hours before the minister calls upon everyone to enter the church. Here the functional, often invisible, black laborers in the white state leap with aggressive self-assurance. Yet, while such gestures register protest against the structures of domination, they also recreate the worker, returning him, recharged, to oppressive toil.

In pragmatic terms, the Z.C.C. dance is a replication of the ritual in the Full Witness Church that has already been discussed. Closely coordinated movements and the exchange of inspired visions reconstruct the bonds of a community lost. But the songs of the Z.C.C., like the other organizational features of the movement, draw more heavily on the forms of institutionalized power, conflating Protestant images of the soldiers of the Lord with imperial and native military emblems. The significance of this in modern South Africa seems very obvious: within the "safe" and legitimate world of ritual action, a composite show of defiance is being acted out. Men demonstrate the threat of their physical strength and call for unity in countering evil with death. The boots beat out a tattoo of resistance and resolve. While there is seldom overt reference to the diffuse coercion of the neocolonial marketplace, or to the more concentrated oppressions of the apartheid state, the identity of evil is unmistakable.

The "outside" dancing summons the Spirit, the champion of the soldiers of Zion. The palpable, aggressive energy so aroused is now channeled toward the transformation not of the system at large, but of the ailing bodies of its victims, who begin to move to the church for the performance of the healing rites. Inside, the organization of space more closely approximates the structure of Protestant orthodoxy. The congregation sits on benches, men on the right and women on the left; all face the table in the front, behind which are seated a row of male office-bearers.[17] But the forms of ritual orthodoxy are here shaped to very different ends: on the table stands a large enamel bucket of water, a pile of domestic commodities, and several small bottles of water. On entering the building, the men remove their caps. The prophet, anonymous up to this point, sits quietly apart from the leaders and begins to show contained signs of possession, snorting and shaking his shoulders. The minister and other functionaries take turns in reciting prayers or, rather, praises to Lekhanyane:

> We must greet Lekhanyane. When we first became aware of things in the world, he was there. Let us praise him! He has traversed the lands of many peoples [cries of "Emmanuel!" and ululations]. They call him the big ox; he carries all our burdens. He is a man of the river and pools, he bears the multitudes. Peace be with him! ["Amen!"]. We praise you, Lekhanyane, who has grown mighty. Your cry is heard across the seas. In England and America they hear that Jerusalem has been conquered. Return to Zion and sing praises. Intercede for us, Lekhanyane, bring down the Spirit. You are the leader of Zion; now lead your lost people to the light! Amen![18]

This utterance is more like a praise poem offered to precolonial chiefs (*go boka;* Schapera 1965) than a Western prayer (*go rapela*). Spiritual and temporal power, Zion and the world system, are conflated in this set of images. The big ox, controller of the water sources, is also Baptist, Mosaic leader, and Redeemer. The potency of Lekhanyane transcends conventional boundaries; he regulates movement in space, reuniting what has been separated. His mighty kingdom eclipses the white Jerusalem and has been recognized, if not in South Africa, then by legitimating agents of the Anglo-Saxon world. But the evident power of Lekhanyane is yet to fulfill its greatest promise, the liberation of his people, who remain enveloped in a specific, South African darkness. The call for utopian deliverance, implicit in most Zionist healing, is here given unambiguous voice. And throughout the recitation of this and like praises, individuals move up to the table to "collect"—i.e. to pledge themselves to the collectivity—in the manner described earlier.

The rites thus far have been building a cumulative contrast between the worlds of darkness and light, a contrast that now moves toward a focal resolution. Again, the healing of the afflicted body serves as the metonym for the more global transformation, effecting a transfer of meaning such that darkness is flooded by light. Indeed, fire is often used to complement water in the Z.C.C. ritual. The prophet rises and stands before the table. The congregants form themselves into a long, gently swaying line, men at the fore, and approach the table one by one. The minister stands alongside, holding the bucket of water, first slapping each person smartly on the head and chest, and then sprinkling him or her with holy water. Congregants sing heartily and punctuate the prophet's inaudible muttering with shouts of "Amen!" After all have been treated, the men remove their boots and pile them on the table beside the commodities and water bottles. Those with severe ailments are given more elaborate treatment: on one occasion, the prophet produced his green membership card with its official church stamp and pressed its concentrated power against the pulsing fontanel of a sick child. He then took an old English-language newspaper from a pile under the table and formed it into a cone, which he ignited, holding it close to the child's head and allowing the smoke to play around it. Finally he crushed the ashes and rubbed them into the child's forehead. Such use of newspapers is widespread among Zionists in southern Africa (Daneel 1970:46), apparently another instance of the ritual appropriation of the power of the written word; the practice seems to transform the obsolescent waste of industrial production into a medium capable of healing the afflictions that such production generates. Indigenous Tswana healers would frequently burn carefully constructed medicinal concoctions, themselves poetic combinations of signs invoking both an affliction and its negation. The smoke permitted medicaments to permeate the sufferer and the air around him, and the ashes represented the welding of the dynamic combination into a homogenous substance. The flame is an image of the transforming power of the Spirit; in the precolonial context, as I mentioned earlier, the spirit was said to rise from the body in death "like smoke."

After everyone had received individual treatment, the prophet moved forward, raising his staff, and entreating that Lekhanyane request the Spirit to enter the accumulation of material goods. He then sprinkled water over the table, which was piled high with boots, and signalled that the congregants might come to claim their possessions. After a short benediction and a final song, the service came to an end.

The ritual of the Z.C.C. service, then, expresses certain differences from that of the Full Witness Church and, by extension, of other Zionists; but beneath these contrasts there appears to lie a similar semantic order and motivating logic. For all Zionist groups alike attempt to reform the received world by means of a syncretism of images and practices, a syncretism drawn from the local and global systems whose contradictory merger it seeks to transcend. Lekhanyane's church has constructed this *bricolage* somewhat differently than have the majority of South African

Zionist groups; it seems to challenge neocolonial orthodoxy more boldly, seeking to carry off whole institutional complexes, rather than to remove signs piecemeal, and to bend these complexes to its own defiant purpose. Like the original church of Dowie, the Z.C.C. has been able to gain access to means of production in its own right, although this has been limited to the apex of the movement and is of more symbolic than pragmatic significance to the rank and file. It has taken over techniques of production and communication from the mainstream society, embedding them within a scheme based upon opposed principles; in this manner, it strives to return to the dispossessed the values alienated by colonialism. Those principles of reconstruction, however, are shared widely among most Zionists, and among many other marginalized peoples on the fringes of the industrial capitalist domain. In what sense, therefore, may we conclude that the local-level movements examined here are unique?

Furthermore, as I noted at the very outset, while the discourse of Zion is radical in many respects, it cannot escape reproducing what it seeks to transform, perpetuating what it seeks to escape. This is especially true when such movements are locked within positions of stark dependency. Like the other Zionist churches, the Z.C.C. cannot really change the structural basis of its followers' malaise, although it might alter considerably their consciousness and modes of practice. Such reform is not historically unimportant, though, as violent confrontations between so-called utopian movements in Africa and the forces of the colonial and neocolonial state have shown (van Binsbergen 1976; Marks 1970). But how precisely are we to assess their final historical significance? Notwithstanding the need to dispense with crude, determinist notions of power and centrist theories of history when examining these movements, ought we to conclude of the Z.C.C., for instance, that the greater its success the greater its failure in relation to its own explicit goals? Despite white ambivalence toward this church—itself a significant political fact—does not the Z.C.C. ultimately mediate structural contradictions as they surface in the experience of its followers? Does its vital symbolic iconoclasm, its creative imagination, merely return its participants more efficiently to the neocolonial workplace? Do Zionists not facilitate the effective reproduction of the very circumstances they protest? These are the questions to be carried forward to my concluding assessment of the dialectics of modern Tshidi history.

8

Conclusion

Religious distress is at the same time the expression of real distress and the *protest* against real distress. Religion is the sigh of the oppressed creature, the heart of a heartless world, just as it is the spirit of spiritless conditions.

Karl Marx, On Religion

My treatment of modern religious movements has been an attempt to sustain the initial claim that such phenomena are to be understood as the product of a "dialectic in a double sense": on the one hand, the structural interplay of sociocultural order and human practice; on the other, the historical articulation of systems dominant and subordinate. These movements cogently objectify the social and symbolic realignments that mark Tshidi history; their imaginative categories, their association and dissociation of signs, provide a coherent scheme through which the world is experienced and acted upon. I have implied that, to understand these phenomena, we must view them as the outcome of a process of simultaneous reproduction and transformation, a process set in motion by the engagement of a particular indigenous system and a specific extension of European colonialism. This conjuncture was one of reciprocal determination, albeit not in like proportions. For, as Hegel (1967:234ff.) observed long ago, the relationship of lordship and bondage is inherently one of unequal but *mutual* dependence. In contrast to slavery, however, where the owner himself had to provide for the reproduction of his work force, the economic logic of modern South Africa has ensured that its peripheral peoples must sustain themselves by a complementary reliance upon subsistence production and wage labor. It is within the contradictory experience of the peasant–proletarian, whose predicament few Tshidi have escaped, that their modern cultural order has been formed.

I have suggested that the initial meeting of the Tshidi with the agencies of European imperialism was mediated by a coherent symbolic order; and that this order was itself reformed in a more sustained confrontation with the iconography and practices of colonialism. The resulting *bricolage* represented a particular instance of a universal process of symbolic construction—the repositioning of signs in sequences of practice, "texts" which both press new associations and reproduce conventional meanings. Such practice varies in its intentionality and its formal elaboration, from the implicit meanings of reformed habit to the assertive syntax of transformative rites. Its substance, in any context, is a matter of circumstance; marked efforts to signal dissent or to induce innovation often occur in situations of radical structural cleavage—such as result from conquest, proletarianization, or the sudden sharpening of contradictions within hierarchical orders. The purposive act of reconstruction, on the part of the nonelite, focuses mainly on the attempt to heal dislocations at the level of experience, dislocations which derive from the failure of the prevailing sign system to provide a model for their subjectivity, for their meaningful and material being. Their existence is increasingly dominated by generalized media of exchange—money, the written word, linear time, and the universal God—which fail to capture a recognizable self-image. These media circulate through communicative processes which themselves appear to marginalize peoples at the periphery; hence the major vehicles of value have come to elude their grasp. In these circumstances, efforts are made to restructure activity so as to regain a sense of control. Repositories of value, like the Zionists' money, are resituated within practices that promise to redirect their flow back to the impoverished, thus healing their affliction. Dissenting Christianity has often, in the Third World, offered the terms for such reformulation. Its logic seems to reverse the signs of Protestant orthodoxy and the global industrial culture; its reintegration of spirit and matter, for instance, or its insertion of the subject in a web of tightly ordered sociomoral relations, seeks to restrict the circulation of generalized media, offering to return lost value and meaning to the alienated.

South African Zionism was an enterprise of precisely this sort. In the hands of peoples like the Tshidi, it created a middle ground between a displaced "traditional" order and a modern world whose vitality was both elusive and estranging. For all its inability to reverse the brute structures of dominance, Zionism as sociocultural form has proved remarkably durable; this is testimony to the salience of its message in addressing the persisting experiential paradoxes of those at once incorporated and peripheralized by the forces of colonial capitalism. Indeed, in South Africa it served to unite a large proportion of those most marginal to established orthodoxies, its signs having become, as I noted, a "blurred collective representation of class." Together with a range of similar iconoclastic movements—the "sects" of Protestant origin in the Caribbean for instance (Simpson 1970), and the *cofradias* spawned by Catholicism in Latin America or the Philippines (Warren 1978; Ileto 1979)—Zionism is part of a second global culture; a culture, lying in the shadow of the first, whose distinct but similar symbolic orders are the imaginative constructions of the resistant periphery of the world system.

Thus, in the diffusion of the image of Zion—from English nonconformism, through American fundamentalism, to the shantytowns and rural villages of the Third World—there is a yet unwritten history of colonialism which concerns the spread of countercultural forms of Western origin, often fed directly on the bastard traditions of our civilization. Horton (1967; 1971:105f.), for instance, notes the tendency for dissenting African movements to light upon such "side-alleys" of Western culture as faith-healing and occultism. Indeed, like American Pentecostalism, European counterorthodoxies—among them, spiritualism, Rosicrucianism, and theosophy—have historically been an important source of symbols and practices for dissidents in Africa, Latin America, and the Caribbean, who find in them a rejection of the logic of rational materialism and its reified religion. Despite their diverse origins, these symbolic orders share an opposition to the categories of bourgeois liberal secularism; and all promise to subvert the divisive structures of colonial society, returning to the displaced a tangible identity and the power to impose coherence upon a disarticulated world.

The diffusion of these counterhegemonic European forms has been subtle and diverse; their spread can no more be treated in terms of gross, global generalities than can the colonialization to which they stand in symbolic opposition. Wherever they appear, they are the product of contingency, of the conjuncture between external agencies and specific local systems under particular circumstances.[1] Thus, while the history of Tshidi cultural transformation (including the ironic role of Christianity) has been replayed over and over again on the periphery of the world system, such processes never take place—as Thompson (1963:10) has noted in a similar context—in *just* the same way. Indeed, I have taken pains to show how the substance of Tshidi Zionism derives from a distinctive confluence of local and global factors; how its iconic forms and practical implications are to be understood in terms of a particular people's journey. While that journey might be similar to expeditions elsewhere in the First and Third Worlds, neither the point of departure nor the route taken are ever identical.

Zulu Zion and the Cults of the Caribbean
The Dialectic in Comparative Perspective

It follows, if this approach is valid, that the Zionism of the Tshidi should vary in telling respects from that of their counterparts, even in closely related societies. Zulu Zionism, the South African case for which the richest comparable material has been produced, provides a valuable contrast, showing distinctions that stem both from variations in the precolonial system and in its mode of engagement with colonialism. It is most effectively viewed as the product of a dialectical process similar in form to that which occurred among the Tshidi, but somewhat different in substance.

The underlying historical significance of Zionism for the Zulu, the Tshidi, and other southern African peoples is patently similar (cf. Pauw 1974:231ff.; Sundkler 1976; Kiernan 1974, 1976, 1977); that much is assured by shared sociocultural features among the southern Bantu-speaking peoples, and by their common structural predicament within the South African state. For reasons suggested below, the Zulu were unique in the subcontinent in their strong initial opposition to early European incursion, both secular and religious. In the first few decades of the century, Independent Christianity was an important collective mode of resistance to white hegemony (see Marks 1970); but, by the latter half of this century, progressive structural differentiation and the harsh realities of apartheid had led to a greater ideological polarization, vividly expressed in the religious opposition between orthodoxy and Zionism. This divide revealed the declining significance of the Independent denominations, with their revisionist message of biblically indexed nationalism; but it also marked the distance between a secularized political consciousness and the religious imagination in general (Sundkler 1976:308). Today the Zionist church is both the refuge and the emblem of the poor and uneducated, those "at the bottom of the heap" (Kiernan 1977:40); as among the Tshidi, its modes of practice are encapsulating, and they signify resistance to the institutions and categories of the dominant culture (Kiernan 1974). These practices also express the contradictions of a movement economically dependent yet ideologically separatist: there is clear evidence, especially among urban Zionists, of a necessary accommodation to the circumstances of wage labor (Kiernan 1977).[2] There is, at the same time, a strong "counteracting" association, one that serves what Sundkler (1976:319) has termed a "freedom from inner dependence on European tokens of grace"; an attempt to utilize values gleaned from the mainstream society to negate its very rationale.

While these considerations speak to the shared cultural heritage and historical role of Black Zionism in South Africa, the *bricolage* of the Zulu

church is distinct from that of the Tshidi in several respects. Most significant, perhaps, is the tendency to form large, incorporative movements,
focused upon theocratic centers. Such movements, of the sort encountered in the Z.C.C., provide a significant alternative to the small, liminal
congregations typically found among the Tshidi. Sundkler (1961:307ff.)
gives ample account of the rise of such nucleated groups around charismatic figures he describes as "prophet-kings." These men manage to
acquire control over small expanses of land, reorganizing productive relations among the faithful and establishing relatively viable collective es-
tates. Their congregations, like Zulu Zionist groups in general, tend to
develop more formally ranked leadership offices than among the
Tswana, tapping more elaborate hierarchies of spiritual power. Their
cosmology, for instance, includes the construct of "angel," which conflates Western images of personified spirit with those of the indigenous
cult of the dead (Sundkler 1961:252; Ngubane 1977:148). In fact, the persisting salience of ancestral invocation for Zulu Zionists underlines the
continuing ideological relevance of norms of agnatic authority and values
of lineage continuity in their world and in their conceptions of personhood, power, and agency (see Sundkler 1961:251).

   These distinctive characteristics of Zulu Zion are clearly related to the
nature of the indigenous social order and to its unique colonial history.
While the Tswana settlement pattern coexisted with centralized regulation of access to productive resources, the Zulu lived in scattered agnatic
hamlets, control over economic activities being vested in local-level authorities (cf. Sansom 1974[a]:135ff.). The Nguni structure involved a
more extended politico-administrative hierarchy, with a complex distribution of jurisdictions based on descent; indeed, its potential for elaboration and segmentary aggregation was realized, immediately prior to
overrule, in the mighty regime of Shaka. In contrast, the Tswana polity
was constituted in such a way as to engender a tension between chiefly
command and the exigencies of household production. This systemic
conflict, which played into the schismatic effects of agnatic endogamy,
created the ever-present possibility of the individuation and scattering of
domestic units. Moreover, there were no corporate lineages here, and
administrative divisions cut across descent group affiliations. The Zulu,
on the other hand, were organized into patrilineal corporations and exogamous clans, which coincided with territorial constituencies of authority and were objectified in an elaborate ancestor cult. Adjacent districts,
in turn, were "held in contiguity" by local leaders, whose only route to
expansion was at the expense of neighbors (Sansom 1974[b]:258). In such
a system, the exercise of control over others was embodied in physical
processes of extraction and domination. This was dramatized by the
spectacular extension of sovereignty achieved by Shaka, whose domin-

ion was symbolized both in the supreme power he wielded over life and death (Walter 1969) and in the ritualization of his person as the incarnation of extraordinary spiritual force. Shaka, we are told, dispensed with his royal rainmakers as a statement of his consummate creative capacity (Sundkler 1961:101ff.). Among the Tswana, in contrast, the power of the chief was less intrinsic to his person and more dependent upon the skilled enhancement of ritual experts; indeed, the officeholder had continual need to demonstrate his spiritual potency and political support, and stood in perpetual danger of falling victim to agnatic competition. Moreover, the very constitution of the social field and of personhood among the Tshidi—the ambiguity of rank, the stress on the strategic negotiation of relations, and the absence of corporate patrilineages—ensured that the ancestor cult was less significant and that threats to the self should be thought of in terms of the calculus of agnatic sorcery.

By virtue of their impact on Zulu colonial history, the distinguishing features of the indigenous system affected the manner in which Zionism took shape there. In the early nineteenth century, the stress on the bounded polity, inscribed in the ethos of corporate group identity, led the Zulu to resist all colonial advance and evangelization. Indeed, the predatory organization which closed this state to incursion from the outside also motivated the *defikane* that rendered the Tswana chiefdoms open and susceptible to mission penetration. This period of Zulu resistance provides the epic instance of heroic defiance in the consciousness of modern black South Africa. When the missions eventually did gain entry, in 1850, they were granted their own tracts of land, each establishing autonomous nucleated settlements. This arrangement was a function of the dispersed residential pattern and the segmentary structure of the prevailing political order, from which the evangelists were thus excluded. Under these conditions, the latter could draw converts, who, having identified with Christianity, were regarded as having been "spat out" (Guy 1979:19) by the indigenous body politic. They became incorporated into the local mission societies, which achieved a degree of spatial and cultural closure impossible among peoples like the Tshidi, with their more concentrated residential and political arrangements. In fact, the very first black congregation calling itself "Zionist" in South Africa was the product of one such nucleated mission community in Zululand (Sundkler 1976:43) and operated according to a model of autonomous theocracy.

As Sundkler (1961:102) has made clear, the ideal of heroic kingship and the incorporative, bounded polity were important in this and subsequent Zionist constructions:

> One of the most important clues to an understanding of the Independent Church is to regard it as an escape into history, into the glorious Zulu history

which was brought to an abrupt end by the Whites. . . . The kingship
pattern of Zulu society is imprinted on the leadership in *all* the independent
Churches. The leader whether "Bishop," "Overseer" or "President" is a
king, *inkosi*, and the church is his tribe. (Emphasis in original)

Such, then, were the prophet-kings of Zulu Zion, leaders whose charismatic power was inscribed in their person and the forceful underpinning
of an ancestral hierarchy. These historical figures, rather than living
members of the ruling line, have been a focus of the quest for symbolic
reconstruction on the part of the marginalized majority; for, as Marks
(1978:193) has demonstrated, modern Zulu royals, through the sharpening of class conflict, have become "a bulwark for the African petty bourgeoisie as for the ideologies of segregation."

Very different was the legacy of chiefship for the Tshidi Zionist imagination. Here the mission was initially incorporated within the orbit of
the centralized polity, seldom managing to establish spatially distinct
Christian settlements. Within the indigenous polity, inherent contradictions precluded extreme concentrations of power, and centralization never eclipsed the counter-ideal of a dispersed network of matrilaterally
linked domestic units. This latter model has survived, and serves as the
template of Zionist organization, the figure of the prophet being also a
would-be kinsman to his localized and largely female flock. The lack of
concerted political might bequeathed the Tswana chiefdoms a less heroic
confrontation with the advancing forces of colonialism; rather than capit-
ulate in an epic show of physical defiance, the Tshidi chiefship petered
out in a protracted struggle to retain power through a process of negotiation that was mediated, for the most part, by the mission and the language of Christianity. The slow, lingering death of the chiefship was
graphically exemplified by the physical spectacle of a series of rulers
overcome by political coercion, debt, and liquor. As the Tshidi Zionist
cases have shown, their search for historical renewal focuses upon prophetic figures from outside their own tradition.

The general issues raised by Tshidi Zionism, viewed in terms of the
dialectics of colonialism, are further exemplified in the very different
context of the Caribbean. What appear at first glance to be symbolic
forms very close to those of South African Zionism have here established
themselves within the varied and vibrant counterculture of an alienated
underclass—those left on the midground between a relatively settled
peasantry and a securely employed urban proletariat (Simpson 1970:227;
Forsythe 1980:81). Revival Zion is one of a range of movements whose
iconoclastic imagery seeks to recount and revalue a history of domination (Hebdige 1979:32ff.), welding the symbols of Protestant dissent
with (largely West) African icons that convey a mythic origin and destiny. Like Tshidi Zionism, such movements are attempts to recast the

commonsense forms of the orthodox culture on the part of those who most fully embody its contradictions. Their followers reject participation in formal politics or the labor unions, preferring a more radical exercise of self-realization and acting out a form of subjectivity which defies dichotomous individualism. Their imaginative constructions range from the articulate and self-conscious scheme of Rastafarianism, with its vision of Babylonian exile and Ethiopian deliverance, to the more implicit message of Revival Zion, which plays upon the familiar forms of ancestrally mediated spirit possession, the healing power of water, and the generative force of robes, drumming, and dance (Simpson 1970:172; Moore n.d.:69ff.).

The similarities between this and the signifying practices of South African Zionism illustrate yet again the dialectics of countercultural formation: shared symbolic forms are the result of a historical conjuncture not merely fortuitous. (Dowie introduced his church to the Caribbean via Cuba in 1905.) Such similarities also speak to the homologous structural predicaments of the populations concerned. Like their South African counterparts, the former slaves of the Caribbean had been ruled by the culture of the Protestant Bible and had developed an indigenous protest which prefigured the cultural logic of such later infusions from the West as fundamentalist Zionism. English evangelism had already been established in Jamaica by the beginning of the nineteenth century and had engendered an explicit opposition to its elusive god and estranged sense of person—a divinity that was accessible and assertive, and a subjectivity receptive to its intrusion (Brathwaite 1971:254). The slave populations went "into the wilderness to seek the spirit," their union with its penetrating force facilitating a regained sense of self and dignity. As Brathwaite (1971:264) suggests, mission Christianity thus unwittingly served to "recharge the batteries of the slaves' imagination," contributing a cluster of signs to the symbolic interplay that gave rise to a coherent cultural identity. Yet, for a sizable sector of this population, the subjugation of slavery has given way to a more subtle, diffuse, and intangible mode of oppression. The marginalized in the shantytowns of neocolonial modernity still seek the spirit in the wilderness, striving to appropriate its unorthodox power to their project of self-realization and resistance. They do not vent their defiance in the arenas of combat defined by the established culture but in loci diffused in the everyday world, jarring the eye of the orthodox observer with their defiant reformulations of mundane practice. Caribbean sectarians construct their own symbolically nuanced vision of the Promised Land, a vision whose similarity to that of peoples like the Tshidi must be measured primarily in terms of the reduction of their worlds to a structural uniformity by the colonial encounter. Forsythe (1980:62) has said of the Rastafarian movement what I have of

the Tshidi Zion, namely, that it is "no passing cultural fad or oddity on
the local or international landscape but a product of the intense racial and
class struggles growing out of [their] past." His analysis suggests that the
movement, far from being an idealized retreat, is a call for "an alternative
counterculture," a worldview more appropriate to the experiential reality of its followers.

Beyond the "Politics of Resistance"

This shift of emphasis from liminality to resistance brings us back to the
key analytical concern of this study. At issue is the definition of constructs basic to the social sciences—power, motivation, resistance, reproduction, and transformation. In my study of one people's history, I
have examined the manner in which symbolic schemes mediate structure
and practice; how, within a system whose parameters were themselves
being redefined in the colonial context, there was a complex interdependence of domination and resistance, change and perpetuation. I have argued that this system was a "hierarchical, coordinated cluster of relations" (Foucault 1980[a]:198), in which the exercize of centralized power
required that mechanisms of politico-ritual control impose their domination on the more diffuse domains of production, exchange, sexuality,
and nurture. The dynamics of the Tshidi order, both as precolonial and
colonized field, is to be understood in terms of the articulation of these
two domains: the formal apparatus of power and the implicit structures
of everyday practice. Just as colonialization was a process which over-
powered both indigenous institutions and the commonsense categories
of the Tshidi world, so resistance lay in the struggle to counteract the
invasion in all its aspects.

In fact, as I have implied, the process of overrule and marginalization
that has been the fate of such peoples as the Tshidi serves not only to cut
off the majority from the levers of politico-economic control; the mechanisms of migrant labor and rural dependency also construct a world
which seems invaded by alienating forces whose source and rationale
remain hidden. Under South African conditions, uprooted rural migrants are also prevented from realizing any thoroughgoing, long-term
identity with the urban workplace and an active black proletariat. Yet,
while collective action of a "political" nature is consistently thwarted,
the attempt to reassert control, to return to the world some form of
coherence and tractability, continues. The effort is pursued through accessible implements that remain at the command of the "powerless" and
that speak to the contradictory location of the person in the world—the
physical body and the practices which establish viable selfhood and a
sense of relationship with a meaningful context. Hence, in the domains

of everyday practice that escape direct control, a protest is mounted that acts upon the implications of neocolonial wage labor in its apartheid form and also upon the effects of commoditization on personal and social being. Such resistance, then, while it might not confront the concentrated forces of domination, defies the penetration of the hegemonic system into the structures of the "natural" world.

Of course, the form of such resistance is largely implicit. I have argued that, while the colonial encounter objectivized Tshidi perceptions of the dominant power-relations in their universe, this has not given rise to an explicit consciousness of class or to modes of strategic class action. They do have a sense of race, but their resistance, I have tried to show, goes far beyond a discourse about color. Yet they remain largely unselfconscious in any literal sense of the counterhegemonies they construct. Like Lévi-Strauss's *bricoleur,* they operate with signs that lie "half-way between percepts and concepts" (1966:18). Even while their practice stems from a felt desire to cast off the shackles of domination, their structural predicament condemns them to reproduce the material and symbolic forms of the neocolonial system.

How, then, do we assess such a phenomenon as Tshidi Zionism in the final analysis? Are such movements merely finely wrought self-delusions, so entrapped within the structures of domination that they unwittingly put their imaginative power at the disposal of the regime they protest? Does Zionism, in mediating but not transcending the contradictions of its context, merely return its followers as reserved, docile workers in the edifice of apartheid? Such is the view of many black intellectuals in South Africa, who see in the "sects" a form of utopian bondage to be obliterated (Ndebele 1972, as quoted by Sundkler 1976:319).

Although, from the front line of the struggle, it would seem that the assessment of practical effectiveness must of needs be all or none, the historical record raises more equivocal questions about the nature of sociocultural determination; about the emergence of collective self-consciousness, for example, or the role in this process of symbolic iconoclasm. More than this, if we confine our historical scrutiny to the zero-sum heroics of revolution successfully achieved, we discount the vast proportion of human social action which is played out, perforce, on a more humble scale. We also evade, by teleological reasoning, the real questions that remain as to what *are* the transformative motors of history.

The *realpolitik* of oppression dictates that resistance be expressed in domains seemingly apolitical, and the dynamics of resistance among oppressed people elsewhere have shown that the connection between seemingly unworldly powers and movements and the politics of liberation is subtle and various, denying simple dichotomization in terms of re-

sistance and compliance (Lanternari 1963:316). So-called utopian movements have frequently motivated violent clashes with temporal authorities whose jurisdiction they deny, and while such confrontation has seldom immediately destabilized the regimes they oppose, their aftermath
usually has significant long-term implications, both for the dominant
and the dominated (see Buijtenhuijs 1973 on the Mau Mau; van Binsbergen 1976 on the Lenshina rising). In this sense, Ileto (1979:7) reminds
us, "no uprising fails." Moreover, as van Binsbergen's analysis suggests,
the more radical "sectarian" resistance mounted by those distanced from
a thoroughgoing identification with the urban workplace and the culture
of the elite often entails a rejection of its conceptual forms—of the material individualism, and the dichotomy between religion and politics, frequently reproduced by nationalist movements in the Third World. An
overly rigid application of this same dichotomy, and of the division between the symbolic and the instrumental, and between thought and action, can serve to blind us to the interdependence between domains
which our ideology sets too definitively apart. Indeed, a growing interest
in symbolic dimensions of power formerly eclipsed in mechanical historical models has pointed to the subtle but cogent political role of ritual
practice—of dance, song, and spirit mediumship—in the struggle for
African liberation (Ranger 1975, 1977; Vail and White 1978; van Onselen
1976; Lan n.d.).

In my analysis of Tshidi Zionism I have attempted to show that its
coded forms did not spell out a mere apolitical escapism but an attempt,
under pitifully restrained circumstances, to address and redress experiential conflict. Far from being a liminal refuge, the movement was an integral part of the culture of the wider social community, drawing upon a
common stock of symbols, commenting upon relations of inequality both
local and more global, and communicating its message of defiance beyond
its own limited confines. Of course, we have yet to test Sundkler's suggestion that the regained sense of self realized through Zionism in South
Africa might render its participants "more prepared for the next phase and
stage in the struggle for the liberation of man" (1976:319). But the existing
ethnographic record offers ample evidence of the role of sectarian dissent
in the making of working-class culture and consciousness, and would
affirm his view, provided that the notion of "struggle" is not too nar-
rowly defined. In his comparative account of agrarian revolt, Scott
(1977:224) notes the significance of religion for the oppressed at the periphery, where it serves as a "cradle" of social links and moral dissent. The
symbolic opposition so fostered comes closest, he argues, to "class consciousness." At the same time, Scott stresses that the very marginalization
of such peoples radicalizes their vision, so that it is not easily assimilated to
the culture of either urban elites or of the proletariat, the latter having
"both feet" on the terrain of industrial capitalist society (p. 231). This gulf

remains, even where a certain convergence of interest might engender common struggle; indeed, as numerous Third World instances suggest, the alternative worldview may give form to a distinct and only partially integrated "revolution" within "mainstream" revolutionary processes (Ileto 1979:223).

The comparison that I have drawn between the rural South African Zion and the iconoclastic movements of other neocolonial contexts suggests that, whatever their revolutionary potential, we deal here with the culture of more than a millenarian minority; we confront the coherent response—the distinct order of value and practice—of a large sector of the population on the cultural and economic fringe. This is the universe of the marginalized of the modern world system, in some respects a latterday sequel to the making of the European working classes. The logic of this process does not reproduce the structures of proletarianization in any simple sense, however, and its hybrid product, the peasant-worker, poses a complex challenge to established sociohistorical analysis.

Neither must we be too dismissive of the creative human project that is embodied in such peripheral movements. The fact that the oppressed are frequently forced to voice their protest in domains seemingly marginal to the real exercise of power makes them "primitive" and "prepolitical" only to a vulgar, ethnocentric social science. As Bourdieu (1977:189) has noted, the failure to recognize that there exist mechanisms capable of reproducing the political order independently of direct intervention has condemned us to ignore a whole range of conduct concerned with power, defining the political only in terms of a "preconstructed object" foisted on our science by our own ideological categories. As it is with politics, so with resistance: we cannot confine our assessment of historical practice to the utilitarian operations of tangible domination or explicit opposition. As Gordon (1980:257) has argued, "the category of resistance cannot be made to exclude its (supposedly) 'primitive' or 'lumpen' forms of manifestation"; consequently, "the binary division between resistance and nonresistance is an unreal one." Indeed, the same may be said of the opposition between "symbolic" and "instrumental" practice.

As I have shown, a view of power, determination, and resistance that seeks to escape the ethnocentric categories of Western social science leads to the pursuit of a model that integrates historical process and anthropological analysis. It calls for a methodology that takes account of the interplay of subjects and objects, of the dominant and the subservient, and treats social process as a dialectic at once semantic and material. Such, at least, would seem to be the challenge of the histories of peoples like the Tshidi; histories which lie not only in the shadow of the modern world system but of the mode of social inquiry it has generated.

Notes

Chapter 1

1. I do not imply that the Tshidi themselves perceived their predicament in these terms, or that their world was one of schizoid division (cf. Field 1960). The relationship between their structural predicament and their modes of consciousness is a good deal more complex, and forms the very substance of this inquiry.

2. This construct originates in the lexicon of the Tel Quel group and their concern with the pragmatic construction and deconstruction of meaning, primarily in the context of aesthetic texts. (See also Hebdige 1979:117f.) I use the concept here to denote both the meaningful structure inherent in practice, and the practical structure inherent in meaning.

3. Broadbent (1865); Brown (1926); Burchell ([1822–24] 1953); Campbell (1815, 1822); Holub (1881); Livingstone (1857); Mackenzie (1871; 1883; 1887); Moffat (1842).

4. Brown (1921); Lemue (1854); Willoughby (1905, 1909).

5. Matthews (1945); Molema (1920, 1966, n.d.); Plaatje n.d.[a].

Chapter 2

1. Molema (1920, n.d.[a], 1966) and Matthews (1945) are the main indigenous histories that have been published; the major missionary accounts are Moffat (1842), Broadbent (1865), and Mackenzie (1871, 1883, 1887). Holub, a Czechoslovakian traveler, recorded useful observations of the Tshidi during the middle of the nineteenth century (1881, vol. 1); and Stow (1905), Wookey (1913), and Theal (1911) have written historical accounts from distinct perspectives. As regards unpublished sources, I have made use of Tshidi oral histories, especially those provided by Morara Molema, a collateral kinsman of the ruling line and sometime Chief's Representative among the Barolong in southern Botswana, and by Stephen Phetlhu, personal secretary to Chief Lotlamoreng and his heir, Kebalepile. I have also consulted unpublished historical manuscripts (e.g., "A History of Methodism among the Tshidi Barolong," by S. M. Molema) and the notes of S. T. Plaatje and Z. K. Matthews. Finally, I have drawn from the corre-

spondence on file in the Tribal Office in Mafeking, from the archives of the Methodist Missionary Society (Bechuanaland Correspondence 1838–57, Box XVII), and from the *Wesleyan Methodist Mission Society Reports,* Vol. XXIV (1888–90).

2. The viability of this conventional classification, and the more inclusive scheme of which it is a part, has been subjected to criticism by linguists and non-linguists alike (Westphal 1963; Legassick 1969).

3. Breutz (1955–56:25) provides a summary table of the main sources of genealogical data.

4. See Legassick (1969:103–4), who points to the more sustained attempt at state building among the Pedi at roughly the same time. These cases provide a useful and important comparison with the more dramatic and widely analyzed processes of incorporation among the Northern Nguni.

5. Montshiwa means "one who has been taken out" or "exiled." This reflects the Tswana naming practice according to which individuals are identified with the circumstantial events surrounding their birth (Matthews 1945:13; Molema 1966:10; Lichtenstein 1930, vol. 2:381).

6. The status of this transaction was later to be contested by South African politicians and historians. See Molema (n.d.[a]:46) for an indigenous account of this debate.

7. Lye (1969:201), one of the few historians to have examined the role of the missions among the Sotho-Tswana in the post-*defikane* period, fails to capture the complex relationship between indigenous systems and the church. He presents the Seleka, for example, as "subjects of a mission polity," and hence as totally determined by the latter. But, as I shall try to show in the Tshidi case, local communities and their leaders in fact exerted considerable control over the scope and nature of evangelical activity, which was not introduced into a cultural void. For a more subtle account of the church in Seleka history, see Molema (n.d.[a]: 143ff.).

8. See Molema (1966:35); also, Mackenzie (1883:33).

9. Correspondence from Ludorf, 1 March 1852, to the Methodist Missionary Society (Box XVII).

10. Correspondence from Ludorf, 16 October 1852, to the Methodist Missionary Society (Box XVII).

11. Ibid. Correspondence from Ludorf, 16 October 1852, to the Methodist Missionary Society (Box XVII).

12. Holub (1881, vol. 1:283).

13. See Holub (1881, vol. 1:296), who claims that women actually defended adherence to the church because "Christianity raised them to an equality with their husbands."

14. There is less evidence of the Tshidi becoming agricultural laborers for the Boers of the Western Transvaal at this point. In fact, both their residence pattern and their overt ideological antagonism to the settlers would have militated against it. But other Barolong in the troubled border zone did work as farm hands (Molema 1966:77).

15. Evidence for such consolidations was gathered from ward and household histories collected in Mafeking in 1969–70, and from records in the Tshidi Tribal Office.

16. Montshiwa had almost continual European secretarial assistance during this period: Rev. Ludorf was replaced by Rev. Webb in 1873, and two itinerant Englishmen, Henry Frazer and Christopher Bell, also provided general bureau-

cratic services (Molema 1966:104). The missionary-politician, John Mackenzie, acted as official British mediator with Montshiwa and other Tswana chiefs in the years prior to annexation.

17. See Molema (1966:157); Dachs (1975:259); Vindex (1900:117f., 367f., 371f.); Samkange (n.d.:12).

18. Bantu Commissioner, Mafeking District, File: Barolong Chiefship, letter #S.N.M. 27/3/15.

19. "Bantu" here refers to Africans; "colored," to the population of mixed racial descent.

20. In his unpublished field report Matthews (n.d.[b]:3; c. 1938–39) records that the national Voortrekker Centenary commemorating the Boer quest for self-determination caused "great apprehension. . . . All kinds of rumours were current about . . . young [Afrikaner] men making these celebrations the occasion for attacks of violence on the Natives." He adds that rural Barolong regard Afrikaners with "bitterness, hatred and suspicion." This echoes Molema's earlier comment to the effect that "racialism is the atmosphere in which the Boer breathes" (1920:271).

21. The quinquennial South African Agricultural Census is of little assistance in assessing Tshidi productivity during the first half of this century. Not only do the categories of information vary for "non-White" populations; when data are provided on the reserves, Mafeking is entered as a single district, with no differentiation being made between the Tshidi and their Ratlou and Rapulana neighbors. Breutz (1955–56: 45a) offers one of the few available breakdowns for the component groupings of this district.

22. Matthews (n.d.[a]:1–2).

23. Not all such "farms" would have been cultivated with the use of the plow. By 1970, while most smallholdings in the charge of women were plowed under sharecropping arrangements with male farmers, a proportion of female producers merely utilized hoes and digging sticks. Although only one instance was recorded of a woman plowing in her own right, women *had* begun to handle animals in the absence of men (Breutz 1955–56:48).

Chapter 3

1. See Burchell (1953, vol. 2:361), who noted the "semi-nomadic" existence of the southern Tswana and the frequent movement of their capital towns, concluding that they were thus midway on the evolutionary path from nomadic to settled existence.

2. As Legassick (1969:95ff.) has noted, the term "Sotho-Tswana" itself appears to have come into regular use toward the end of the eighteenth century.

3. For evidence of this sociocultural opposition among the Tswana in the nineteenth century, see Mackenzie (1883:227).

4. An individual was proscribed from marrying his or her own siblings, parents' siblings, and siblings' children. Wives of a man's father (other than his own mother) were marriageable (Schapera 1938:127). A few Tswana groups, such as the Tshidi, permitted half-sibling unions.

5. For a critique of one such account of Tswana consciousness, see Comaroff (1982[b]).

6. Several nineteenth-century observers attested to extensive belts of cultivated land around southern Tswana settlements. Thus, in 1820, Campbell (1822, vol. 1:181) described a town on the borders of then Barolong country as having a

population of 10,000–12,000 people, and fields that stretched "at least twenty miles in circumference."

7. Tswana burial rites underscored this contrasting gender identity: the bodies of women, buried under the floor of the secluded backyard, were sprinkled with corn and surrounded with implements used in the preparation of food; the bodies of men, interred in the cattle-byre at the margins of the household or at the central *kgotla,* were laid alongside some cow dung and an ox bone (Willoughby 1928:40).

8. Solomon (1855:62) gives a description of cooperative female labor, as does a report in the *South African Christian Recorder* (March 1831:23; quoted by Kinsman n.d.[a]:5). Such a work party (*letsema*) was recruited for labor-intensive tasks (e.g. harvesting and threshing) and was provided with corn porridge and beer (cf. Schapera 1938:254).

9. See, for example, Holub's reference to a party of women who were gathering in the veld (1881, vol. 1:252).

10. This association was visible, too, in such customary practice as the burial of the dead, in the fetal posture, in a hollowed-out niche in the ground. Moreover, an aborted fetus, disruptive to the fertility of the earth, was also held to be a prime ingredient in sorcery concoctions used to interfere with human fertility (see text).

11. The use that a caretaker might make of *mahisa* cattle was clearly specified; it excluded their alienation in exchange without the express consent of the owner (Schapera 1938:246).

12. I use this term in a specific sense here, mindful of the still unsatisfactory state of attempts to apply the concept of class to prefeudal and precapitalist formations. This category of bush clients would appear to have represented an embryonic class within the various stratified Tswana chiefdoms, their access to the means of production being through relations of patronage. Such relations, however, differed from those of the classical manorial system in that they were neither formalized contractually nor of fixed duration; in fact, these clients often transferred allegiance from one patron to another, and might even move between polities on occasion. Capable of supporting themselves in the wild for periods of time, they formed a fluctuating margin between the various chiefdoms; moreover, they lived in symbiosis with the latter, being ultimately dependent on them for their existence but rendering them valued "natural" products.

13. Such verbal capacity was epitomized in the generative power of public oratory, but it extended to the management of words in general. Kinsman (n.d.[b]:15) quotes an early mission observer among the southern Tswana (*Grahamstown Journal,* 3:122 [4.24.1834]): "by Bechuana education, a woman has nothing to do with the news and communications of men, she has to mind her work and leave *mahuku* ("words") to men alone."

14. Such transfers of allegiance were explicitly recognized in Tswana *mekgwa le melao* ("law and custom"), where conventional provision was made for granting citizenship to immigrants from other chiefdoms (Schapera 1938:118ff.).

Chapter 4

1. I have noted the difficulties involved in constructing the history of such peoples as the Tswana, at least using conventional historiographic methods. The early accounts were very uneven in their coverage of ritual and "belief": such material was simply less visible—both in a practical and an interpretive sense—to transient visitors who did not understand Setswana and viewed the natives

through a nineteenth-century consciousness. Not only were the "superstitions" of the peoples regarded with moral disdain and, if perceived at all, described perfunctorily; there was also an inability to comprehend these as aspects of inclusive cosmologies, or as the functional counterpart of religion in the West. Burchell, a traveller, concluded with unusual sensitivity in 1812 that he had neither the length of observation nor the linguistic skill to know the superstition of the Batlhaping "correctly"; still, "of religion, as shown by outward forms of worship," he saw not the least sign (1953, vol. 2:383). Nor did longer coresidence and greater linguistic competence necessarily alter this perception. Moffat, after twenty years of mission work among the Batlhaping, retained the view that he was introducing Christianity into a spiritual vacuum (see 1842:244). Yet both categories of observer provided valuable accounts of everyday life among the southern Tswana and included details of dress, gesture, interpersonal conduct, and ritual, details which are revealing of cultural categories. They also recounted observations of some taboos and "superstitions." Two more extensive bodies of missionary work, those of Willoughby and Brown, contain more scholarly and systematic descriptions of ritual and cosmology, and these could be compared for internal consistency and contrasted with earlier records and later ethnographic materials. I draw on all these sources here, and upon my own study of indigenous Tshidi cosmology (1974).

2. See Holub (1881, vol. 1:383); Brown (1926:101f.). For a fuller discussion of the Tshidi ancestral cult, see Comaroff (1974:119ff.).

3. Historical and linguistic evidence suggests that the Sotho-Tswana term for supreme being—*modimo*—was an impersonal noun, formed by adding the singular prefix *mo-* to the *-dima* stem (Moffat 1842:260–62; Smith 1950:118). In Setswana, the prefix *mo-* forms nouns both of Class 1 (personal) and of Class 3 (impersonal; Sandilands 1953:27). Contextual evidence suggests that *modimo* might have been the singular of *medimo,* the impersonal dead of the wild. In modern Setswana, the personalized supreme being is taken to be the singular of *badimo,* the ancestors.

4. The data on which this account is based are taken largely from two lengthy descriptions published by missionaries in scholarly journals (Willoughby 1909; Brown 1921; see n. 1 above). But the material has been contrasted with that available in the early sources (Kirby 1939, vol. 1:271ff.; Campbell 1822, vol. 2:172ff.; Holub 1881, vol. 1:398ff.; Mackenzie 1881:376ff.). These data were also complemented by my observations of an initiation cycle, held in one of the subdivisions of the Mafeking district in 1970.

5. These texts have been left in their original form and hence employ an outdated orthography.

6. Cf. Silverstein (n.d.:5). Aspects of this analysis of metaforces of power in traditional oratory have proven useful in examining the relationship between poetic structure and efficacy in Tswana ritual.

7. Here, however, there was a revealing difference: the placenta contained the dynamic properties of natural generation and was potentially usable for acts of powerful malevolence. It was thus carefully hidden to prevent its abuse by sorcerers (Schapera 1971[b]:209). The foreskin, on the other hand, was generatively inert, and was merely thrown in the bush, like childhood itself.

8. As I have noted above (chap. 3, n. 13), the evidence from the nineteenth century indicates that women were regarded as marginal to the verbal creativity of men.

9. While the Tswana symbolic order lacked a thoroughgoing organization

based upon bilaterality, it did associate the right hand with culturally dominant forms and forces. Thus "right," *siame,* also meant "righteous," "straight"; "left," *molema,* connoted "spoilt" (i.e. indulged) and "crooked."

10. This term is also used to refer to the stage of the marriage process in which the groom, after the exchange of some or all of the bridewealth, would sleep with the bride at her parents' house, returning to his agnatic home by day. The practice was kept up until a child was born, when virilocal residence was assumed. *Go ralala* was thus a transient mode of residence for the groom, during which he was a "visitor" in the domain of his affines (see Schapera 1938:135).

11. See Language (1943:119). I observed the same procedure among the Tshidi in 1970. Of course, both flag and horse were features of the colonial encounter. Experience of battle (especially, for the southern Tswana, the Boer War) further associated white flags with "truce." Here the mounted rider is clearly a sign of enhanced control of time and space, orchestrating the reincorporation of the "new men" into the community. The flag and the horse mark a sequence of sexual combat, the notion of "truce" as the young men flee to the bush being enhanced by indigenous connotations of "whiteness."

12. Tshidi informants in 1970 stressed the centrality of such sacrifice, but the older sources make no mention of it, except in respect of the related Sotho people (Ellenberger 1912:227–28). It would appear that the accession of young men to social maturity merited some signal of altered relationship to the collective body of dead agnates, with whom they could now engage in ritual transaction.

13. In this account I have placed less emphasis upon the power of knowledge per se since, for the Tswana at least, authority rested on a general transformative capacity that permitted no thoroughgoing distinction between "knowledge" and "practice." Initiation shaped such capacity—the essence of fully "social" being—in the initiates themselves through symbolic action upon them. But the efficacy of the rites derived ultimately from the power of the chief, who embodied an innate force to act on the world, a force which, while it clearly involved "knowledge" and "experience" in *our* view, did not rest upon such disembodied capacities in the Tswana conception.

14. *Sebilo,* it will be recalled, was a valued object of trade among the indigenous southern African communities in the early nineteenth century.

15. Although there are more individual references in the earlier sources to *bojale* than to *bogwêra*—its location within the town made it more visible to outsiders—the data on female initiation are sparse and disparate. For these rites were also secret, and nineteenth-century observers, all men, were unlikely to have learned much about their substance, even if they had wished to.

Chapter 5

1. I translate *boloi* here as "sorcery," for such malevolent practice was generally conceived to be dependent upon the manipulation of material substances. Such ministrations, however, were only successful if accompanied by the appropriate intention; material and nonmaterial forces worked in unison in Tswana magic, for good and ill. This underlines the inadequacy of the sorcery/witchcraft distinction as it has been developed in the African context, the former implying the use of malevolent substances, the latter entailing immanent spiritual capacity alone (see Turner 1967:112ff.). Indeed, it is a distinction that derives from, and perpetuates, an ethnocentric segregation of matter from spirit.

2. Calvinist denominations were not to enter the field until later; the doctrine of predestination posed obvious problems for their mission enterprise and served

as a legitimating ideology for the permanently inferior status, both spiritual and social, of the "children of Ham."

3. This was, of course, a more widely shared Protestant conception. Moffat, of the London Missionary Society, put the matter in even more militantly imperialistic terms (1842:255): "whoever goes to preach the unsearchable riches of Christ among the heathen, goes on a warfare which requires all prayer and supplication, to keep his armor bright, and in active operation, to wrestle and struggle, and toil, in pulling down the strongholds of Satan, whether in Africa, India or the islands of the Pacific."

4. Several reports of the period tell of attempts on the part of peoples in the interior to prevent missionaries from going on to other neighboring groups, who were invariably represented as "hostile" and "dangerous" (Broadbent 1865:25; Moffat 1842:341).

5. "Transparency" must be understood in relation to the Western empirical ideal of "true definitional precision," a state only approached but never achieved in natural language (see Silverstein n.d.:3). Despite our own prevalent assumption that "signals" can be clearly distinguished from "symbols," and that at least technical discourse is free from metaphoric allusion, this reflects our own reductionist ideology rather than a more complex, ever-proliferating semiotic reality.

6. In the Tshidi case, a history of particularly strong opposition to Boer encroachment excluded this area of the market, at least until overrule (see Molema 1966:109).

7. See, for example, the sources used by Kinsman (n.d.[b]), and the data drawn upon in more general accounts of the period, such as Crisp (1896). In part, the Batlhaping were simply closer to the colonial borders and hence more accessible to observation. Also, the L.M.S. station established by Moffat at Kuruman (see map, p. 19) had become widely known, and was an obvious focus for white visitors. The L.M.S. had had an unbroken tenure of this mission field and their records are far richer than those left by Methodists working among the Barolong. Moreover, the dispersed residence pattern of the Tshidi during this period militated against contact by outsiders, except at the increasingly well-known settlement of Mafikeng.

8. For a concise overview of this debate, see Foster–Carter (1978).

Chapter 6

1. This usage is derived from the Dutch *stadt* and Afrikaans *stad,* meaning "town."

2. This department has undergone several changes of name under the present regime in the attempt to ameliorate its image. Formerly the "Department of Native Affairs," it is now the "Department of Cooperation and Development."

3. In the attempt to channel Tshidi settlement from the stad to the new township, the local Department of Bantu Affairs tried to limit the granting of residential sites in the former, or to make them conditional upon the fulfillment of irksome requirements such as the erection of costly fencing.

4. "Baas" is Afrikaans for "boss," the term of address that white Afrikaans-speaking males conventionally expect of Africans, and that the latter view as a mark of their subjugation.

5. At the time, R1 = $1.12.

6. From the Afrikaans *kerk* ("church"), this term connotes a "religious" institution, spatially and organizationally distinct, such as was introduced by the mission.

7. For a fuller discussion of the problems presented by this theory of meaning and mode of analysis, see Chapter 1.

8. A specific instance illustrates this continuous process: the Morians Episcopal Apostolic Church in Zion was introduced into the stad in the late 1950s. In 1969, while attempting to trace the connections between Zionist churches in the area, I learned that no fewer than seventeen offshoots were operating in private homes within a radius of half a mile of the original site. The founder of the parent organization asked me whether there were any national laws to compel his former followers to reunite under his leadership.

9. See, for example, *Wesleyan Methodist Mission Reports,* vol. XXIV, 1888–90: "Our gold fields, offering opportunities for obtaining constant employment and good wages, are drawing great numbers of heathens from regions which are at present beyond our reach."

10. There had, in fact, been earlier sporadic attempts by black converts to emancipate themselves from mission authority. One of the first of these occurred among the southern Tswana when the head of a Tlhaping section played an active role in the secession from the London Missionary Society that led to the founding of the Native Independent Church in 1885 (see Pauw 1960:52ff.; Sundkler 1961:38). These early breakaways took place within particular chiefdoms or localized rural areas, expressing the desire to form "national churches," to unite Christian leadership with the ritual authority of chiefs, or to weld denominational identity with that of particular ethnic groups (Sundkler 1961:39). This was by and large a transient development; it was in the mining compounds around *Gauteng* (literally "Golden City," Johannesburg), that secessionary movements really gained momentum.

11. See Sundkler (1961:56ff.), who uses the term "Ethiopian" to describe the category of churches here typed "Independent"—i.e. those which originated in the Protestant missions or in secessions from them, and which retained the latter's sociocultural forms, but combined them with a liberal black nationalist charter. Ethiopia, mentioned in the Psalms and in the Acts of the Apostles, gave biblical legitimacy to a "primitive" African church, and this was conflated with the image of Ethiopia as the seat of a long-reigning African Christian dynasty. Sundkler suggests that this was further reinforced by knowledge among South African secessionists of the Abyssinian victory over the whites at Adowa in 1896, and of the Italo-Abyssinian War of 1935 (1961:57). There was also a contribution from Marcus Garvey's ideology, which depicted blacks more generally as the "down-trodden children of Ethiopia that might rise to be a great power among the nations" (Sundkler 1961:58). This linked the cultural scheme of these Independent churches with contemporary developments in black self-consciousness in North America, and with subsequent movements such as Jamaican Rastafarianism.

12. The following that was to develop in southern Africa was to outnumber and outlast the parent church and all of its offshoots; but this following was soon to secede from the original movement.

13. Dowie not only talked of founding an "immense industrial movement" (Harlan 1906:55), he elaborated a "theocratic platform," the basis of a "new party in [the] political affairs of the U.S. of America." The rationale of this venture was to contrast explicitly with the "democratic ideal," which "had been in vogue" in the world in which members of his movement had been "born and raised" (Harlan 1906:6–7).

14. There is, of course, variation among the many Zionist churches in South

Africa with respect to such features; and a number of groups, which lie on the margins between the Zionist and the Independent categories, exhibit some but not all of these variations (cf. West 1975:18). As West notes, healing practices are invariably present if a church is to be regarded as Zionist, as are rites of purification and some form of spirit possession (usually accompanied by such manifestations as glossolalia). Taboos vary in content, generally proscribing dietary items such as pork and alcohol, and often forbidding the consultation of both "traditional" and Western doctors. Many groups are also endogamous by preference (Kiernan 1974).

15. See also Berglund (1967); Kiernan (1974, 1976, and 1977); Mayer (1961); and West (1975). Pauw (1960) describes the range of religious movements among the Tlhaping in the fifties, including their Zionist churches.

16. Chief Lotlamoreng, who had been continuously challenged by the Molemas from within the ranks of the Methodist church, opened the capital to other denominations as soon as he took office. He joined the Roman Catholic church shortly after its founding, sending his elder son, the future Chief Kebalepile, to a Catholic boarding school. None of the chiefly line were more than nominal church members, however.

17. Locally gathered information about the entry of Independent and Zionist groups into the Tshidi area was complemented by material contained in the records of "Applications for Recognition by Bantu Churches," Department of Bantu Administration and Development, Pretoria. Government policy between 1925 and 1963 made significant rights and privileges available to leaders of those African churches "recognized" by the Department of Bantu Administration (see Sundkler 1961:77ff.). When the policy was discontinued, only 10 of the approximately 2,500 churches that had made application had been accorded official status. Petitions for recognition gave details of the size and distribution of the membership of each denomination. The files of this correspondence thus provide a historical record of Independent and Zionist proliferation all over the country, although the desire to impress officialdom probably served to exaggerate the scale of the congregations.

18. Records of application for church sites, Office of the Bantu Affairs Commissioner, Mafeking, F6 No. 11/5/2.

19. Formal statistics cannot give definitive evidence of these dynamic processes, for we are dealing with general sociocultural realignments, not merely shifts in the formal "membership" of institutions. Moreover, membership figures are themselves difficult to compile because of the nature of the churches: Zionist groups, for instance, are constantly proliferating and have fluctuating bodies of participants. Such groups seldom keep written records, and verbal estimates reflect the desire, at times, to impress with the size of their followings (cf. West 1975:44). Orthodox and Independent churches do keep records, but they vary in scope and accuracy. Biographical and survey materials are more valuable sources, especially as regards shifts in allegiance. Thus, in a sample of 100 adult Tshidi with orthodox church affiliations, 80 were found to have remained in the church of first baptism; in a similar sample of Zionists, only 12 had not changed denominations. Of the Zionists, 80 had originated in orthodox or Independent churches. There were only five cases of movement from Zionist to more orthodox ranks (all to the Methodist church).

20. Of the non-Protestant Western denominations, the largest was the Roman Catholic church, with a membership of 800 in 1970. Others, such as the Baptist and the Pentecostal Holiness Church were affiliated to similar white

groups in South Africa, and had small local followings. The latter tended to retain the forms of their white fundamentalist parent groups, with only minimal signs of indigenization.

21. The largest of the Independent churches among the Tshidi was the African Methodist Episcopal, which had affiliated with the black North American church of the same name after seceding from the Methodist church in South Africa. This link rendered its status more like that of the orthodox churches in the modern Tshidi view. Many smaller Independent groups have disintegrated, or have become conflated with churches of the Zionist category (cf. West 1975:19).

Chapter 7

1. See *Report of the Commission for Native Affairs* for 1903 and 1905 (South Africa, Department of Native Affairs). See also Sundkler (1961:73).

2. As this suggests, the widespread association of spirit and water probably stems from universal human perceptions of primary physical substances and processes; the particular connection between the two in churches which counter established orthodoxy seems to be part of the attempt to make concrete the reified God of modern Protestantism, part, that is, of a wider reaction to the dualistic epistemology of the establishment. (See, for instance, the role of holy water in the "Revival" churches of Jamaica, whose parallels with South African Zionism are considered below; Simpson 1970:171.)

3. The Zulu counterpart, which expresses a distinction rooted in ecological differences, is the "pool," a naturally dammed spot in otherwise flowing water (Sundkler 1961:201ff.).

4. Cf. West (1975), who reports a clear division of labor between "bishop" and "prophet" as normative and charismatic leaders respectively. The more complex, overlapping role-structure that has developed among Tshidi Zionists is illustrated by the fact that the prophetic leader of the Full Witness Church bore the title "bishop." (See Daneel 1973, who suggests the same phenomenon among Shona Zionists.)

5. In keeping with the more self-conscious notion of system and orthodoxy among the local Protestant elite, its members regarded such Zionist consultations as a breach of proper conduct, and tended to keep their visits to the "prophets" a secret.

6. This may indeed not be true of all Zulu Zionists. Kiernan (1976), for instance, describes preaching in an urban Zulu Zionist church in 1976. However, the very notion of preaching and biblical exegesis was foreign to the ritual structure of most Tshidi Zionist groups (cf. Sundkler 1961:191). For a depiction of Tshidi Zionist practice, see *Heal the Whole Man,* a film made by Paul Robinson.

7. A mining town on the western Witwatersrand in the Transvaal.

8. The nutritional level of much of the modern Tshidi population is low, especially among the stratum found in the Zionist churches. This, plus the rigors of heavy industrial work, the physical circumstances of the migrant, and the dearth of local medical facilities, ensures that life expectancy is relatively depressed. While no statistics of any order are available, general observation and private practitioners' accounts suggested in 1970 that kwashiokor, pellagra, tuberculosis, and bronchial disease were quite common, and that the infant mortality rate was high (at least 150 per 1,000 live births, a local doctor suggested). Moreover, local hospital facilities for blacks were very limited, insufficient even to cope with extreme emergencies. Six white general practitioners worked in the district, but their fees were out of reach of most of the black community.

9. West (1975) also notes that overt opposition between members of the two church types in Soweto was expressed in the reciprocal appellations of "tick birds" (i.e. Zionists) and "black sheep" (i.e. "Ethiopian-type" churches). This choice of images suggests that the contrast between churches of "spirit" and "law" among Tshidi is more widespread: for the tick bird connotes an undisciplined white predator, swooping down on its prey at will, while the black sheep is the lackluster, hidebound follower.

10. In this sense, even orthodox Tshidi live morally from "hand to mouth" (Weber 1958:116) in that breaches can be rectified in life; they are not elements in a cumulative "moral career."

11. As I have already stressed, such "orthodoxy" might represent continuity with Western hegemonies for the Tshidi; but it has in fact involved a transformation of Protestant forms in response to indigenous practice—just as Zionism's manifest "innovation" also embodies certain continuities.

12. The psychophysiological effects of such "sonic driving" have been the subject of systematic study in comparable contexts of possession (Neher 1962; Sturtevant 1968).

13. Of course, most members remain involved in monetized exchange to some degree, paying taxes and being dependent on the labor and commodity markets; however, within the congregation, monetary transactions are limited almost entirely to such ritualized gifts.

14. This large-scale movement of Z.C.C. members to the Northern Transvaal is widely covered in the existing black media (see, for instance, plate 6). The Afrikaans and English media also carry reports of the annual event, one that is unusual, for there are strict laws governing black assemblies in modern South Africa.

15. The numerous Zion Christian congregations operate everywhere in the local vernacular. Grand assemblies at Morija make use of simultaneous translations from Sepedi (the language of the founder) into all the major southern African languages. But local ritual at times incorporates Sepedi, and local leaders have usually mastered some of the language (cf. Sundkler 1961:320).

16. *Trobriand Cricket*, a film by Jeremy Leach.

17. Such gender segregation within the spatial organization of church activities is widespread in southern Africa, and represents early mission attempts to accommodate indigenous gender-based divisions in domestic and communal life. This contrasts, of course, with Western churches, both orthodox and other, in which participants tend to assemble in nuclear family units.

18. *Re lothsa Lekhanyane. Pele re bona lefatse le tsa lefatseng le, Lekhanyane e ne e setse e le kgale a le teng. A re mo tumiseng! O sepetse le naga tse dintši, mo letseng mekgolokwane Emmanuel. Ke Kgomo ye kgolo Lekhanyane le kganya mmele, ya rweleng mathata a 'kgomo tsa gagwe. Ke kubu ya dinoka le madiba, o rwele mashaba. Khotso ga e ate! Amen! Re ya go rêta Lekhanyane, senatla sa dinatla. Mokgosi wa gago o kwetse mose wa mawatle. Engelane le Amerika bare Jerusalem e thupilwe. Boya Sion o opele ditumiso. Re ete pele Lekhanyane, o re rapêlêlê. Bitša Moya wo o halalelang o tle. Ke wena moetapele wa Sione; isha batho bago ba ba timetseng leseding! Amen!*

Chapter 8

1. This diffusion often has its self-conscious agents. As Horton (1971:105ff.) suggests, however, such cultural forms have frequently been sought out by their would-be recipients at source. (Dowie's emissary to Johannesburg was sent in response to a request from South Africa; see above, chap. 6.) The lack of "fit"

between these unorthodox movements and the sociocultural forms of the colonial and neocolonial establishment has meant that the former have typically lacked
the coherent mission organizations of the orthodox churches. But their inter-
nalization, driven by the relevance of their symbolic forms to indigenous experience, usually had a vigorous momentum of its own.

2. In fact, for both the Zulu Zionist and his Tshidi counterpart, there is little
prospect, under current political conditions, of enrichment or mobility. Nor is
his puritanical dedication to the "work" of the church likely to gain him entry to
the petite bourgeoisie, as appears to have been more possible in Zimbabwe
(Daneel 1973:177; cf. Aquina 1969); even there, a dedication to accumulation did
not permit the embourgeoisement that was characteristic of the history of less
oppressed Puritan groups in the First World (cf. Kiernan 1977:40). Of course, it is
the very impossibility of melioration or mobility for the Zulu or Tshidi masses,
their structural entrapment, that ensures the stereotypical reproduction of the
Zionist churches. Kiernan's materials reinforce the message of Tshidi Zionist ritual, that such small surpluses as are realized by members are "reinvested" in the
collective resources of the organization itself (1977:40).

Bibliography

Agar-Hamilton, J. A. I. 1928. *The Native Policy of the Voortrekkers*. Cape Town: Maskew Miller.

———. 1937. *The Road to the North: South Africa, 1852–86*. London: Longmans, Green.

Althusser, L. 1971. Ideology and Ideological State Apparatuses. In *Lenin and Philosophy and Other Essays*. Trans. B. Brewster. London: New Left Books.

Alverson, H. 1978. *Mind in the Heart of Darkness: Value and Self-Identity among the Tswana of Southern Africa*. New Haven: Yale University Press.

Amselle, J.-L. 1976. *Les migrations africaines*. Paris: Maspero.

Aquina, Sister M. 1969. Zionists in Rhodesia. *Africa*, 39(2):114–36.

Ardener, E. 1977. The "Problem" Revisited. In *Perceiving Women*, ed. S. Ardener. London: Dent.

Armytage, W. H. G. 1961. *Heavens Below: Utopian Experiments in England*. Toronto: University of Toronto Press.

Asad, T., ed. 1973. *Anthropology and the Colonial Encounter*. London: Ithaca Press.

Ashton, E. H. 1937. Notes on the Political and Judicial Organization of the Tawana. *Bantu Studies*, 11(2):67–83.

Barolong boo Ratshidi N.d. Files of the Tribal Office.

Barrow, J. 1806. *A Voyage to Cochinchina*. London: Cadell & Davies.

Barth, F. 1973. Descent and Marriage Reconsidered. In *The Character of Kinship*, ed. J. Goody. Cambridge: Cambridge University Press.

Barthes, R. 1973. *Mythologies*. Trans. A. Davis. London: Paladin.

Bastide, R. 1971. *African Civilizations in the New World*. London: C. Hurst & Co.

Baudrillard, J. 1981. *For a Critique of the Political Economy of the Sign*. St. Louis: Telos Press.

Berglund, A. I. 1967. *Rituals of an African Zionist Church*. University of the Witwatersrand: African Studies Program, Occasional Paper No. 3.

Bettelheim, C. 1972. Theoretical Comments, Appendix I. Trans. B. Pearce. In *Unequal Exchange*, ed. A. Emmanuel. New York: Monthly Review Press.

Borcherds, P. B. 1861. *An Autobiographical Memoir*. Cape Town: A. S. Robert and Son.

Bourdieu, P. 1977. *Outline of a Theory of Practice*. Trans. R. Nice. Cambridge: Cambridge University Press.

Brathwaite, E. 1971. *The Development of Creole Society in Jamaica, 1770–1820.* Oxford: Clarendon Press.

Braudel, F. 1980. History and Sociology. In *On History.* Chicago: University of Chicago Press.

———. 1958. Histoire et sciences sociales: la longue durée. *Annales: Économies, Sociétés, Civilisations,* 13(4):725–53.

Breutz, P. L. 1955–56. *The Tribes of the Mafeking District.* Pretoria: The Government Printer.

Broadbent, S. 1865. *A Narrative of the First Introduction of Christianity amongst the Barolong Tribe of Bechuanas, South Africa.* London: Wesleyan Mission House.

Brown, J. T. 1921. Circumcision Rites of the Becwana Tribes. *Journal of the Royal Anthropological Institute,* 51:419–27.

———. 1926. *Among the Bantu Nomads: A Record of Forty Years Spent among the Bechuana.* London: Seeley Service.

———. 1931. *Secwana Dictionary.* Tiger Kloof: London Missionary Society.

Buijtenhuijs, R. 1973. *Mau-Mau Twenty Years After: The Myth and the Survivors.* The Hague: Mouton.

Bundy, C. 1979. *The Rise and Fall of the South African Peasantry.* London: Heinemann.

Burchell, W. J. 1953. *Travels in the Interior of Southern Africa,* 2 vols. London: Batchworth Press.

Campbell, J. n.d. *John Campbell Papers.* Cape Town: South African Library.

———. 1815. *Travels in South Africa.* London: Black, Parry.

———. 1822. *Travels in South Africa . . . Being a Narrative of a Second Journey,* 2 vols. London: Westley.

Clarke, J. 1976. The Skinheads and the Magical Recovery of Working Class Community. In *Resistance through Rituals,* ed. S. Hall, T. Jefferson, and B. Roberts. London: Hutchinson.

Cohen, S. 1980. *Folk Devils and Moral Panics.* New York: St. Martin's Press.

Cohn, N. 1957. *The Pursuit of the Millennium.* London: Secker & Warburg.

Comaroff, J. 1974. Barolong Cosmology: A Study of Religious Pluralism in a Tswana Town. Ph.D. dissertation, University of London.

———. 1980. Healing and the Cultural Order: The Case of the Barolong boo Ratshidi. *American Ethnologist,* 7(4):637–57.

———. 1981. Healing and Cultural Transformation: The Case of the Tswana of Southern Africa. *Social Science and Medicine,* 15(B): 367–78.

———. 1982(a) Medicine: Symbol and Ideology. In *The Problem of Medical Knowledge,* ed. P. Wright and A. Treacher. Edinburgh: Edinburgh University Press.

———. 1982(b) Review of *Mind in the Heart of Darkness,* by H. Alverson. *American Journal of Sociology,* 87(6):1439–40.

———. 1983. Bodily Reform as Historical Practice: The Semantics of Resistance in Modern South Africa. *International Journal of Psychology,* 18(3). Special issue on "Symbol and Symptom."

Comaroff, J. L. 1973. Competition for Office and Political Processes among the Barolong boo Ratshidi of the South Africa-Botswana Borderland. Ph.D. dissertation, University of London.

———. ed. 1973. *The Boer War Diary of Sol T. Plaatje: An African at Mafeking.* London: Macmillan.

———. 1974. Chiefship in a South African Homeland. *Journal of Southern African Studies,* 1(1):36–51.

———. 1975. Talking Politics: Oratory and Authority in a Tswana Chiefdom. In *Political Language and Oratory in Traditional Society*, ed. M. Bloch. London: Academic Press.

———. 1978. Rules and Rulers: Political Processes in a Tswana Chiefdom. *Man*, n.s., 13(1):1–20.

———. 1982. Dialectical Systems, History and Anthropology: Units of Study and Questions of Theory. *Journal of Southern African Studies*, 8(2):143–72.

———. *Class, Culture and the Rise of Capitalism in an African Chiefdom*. Forthcoming.

Comaroff, J. L., and Comaroff, J. 1981. The Management of Marriage in a Tswana Chiefdom. In *Essays on African Marriage in Southern Africa*, ed. E. J. Krige and J. L. Comaroff. Cape Town: Juta.

Comaroff, J. L., and Roberts, S. A. 1981. *Rules and Processes: The Cultural Logic of Dispute in an African Context*. Chicago: University of Chicago Press.

Crisp, W. 1896. *The Bechuana of South Africa*. London: SPCK.

Dachs, A. J. 1972. Missionary Imperialism: The Case of Bechuanaland. *Journal of African History* 13(4):647–58.

———, ed. 1975. *Papers of John Mackenzie*. Johannesburg: Witwatersrand University Press for the African Studies Institute.

Daneel, M. L. 1970. *Zionism and Faith-Healing in Rhodesia*. The Hague: Mouton.

———. 1973. Shona Independent Churches in a Rural Society. In *Christianity South of the Zambezi*, ed. A. J. Dachs. Salisbury: Mambo Press.

Douglas, M. T. 1966. *Purity and Danger: An Analysis of Concepts of Pollution and Taboo*. Washington: Frederick Praeger.

———. 1970. *Natural Symbols: Explorations in Cosmology*. New York: Vintage Books.

Durkheim, E., and Mauss, M. 1963. *Primitive Classification*. Trans. R. Needham. London: Cohen & West.

Eco, U. 1972. Towards a Semiotic Enquiry into the Television Message. *Working Papers in Cultural Studies*, no. 3. Birmingham: University of Birmingham.

Edwards, J. 1883. *Reminiscences of the Early Life and Missionary Labours of the Rev. John Edwards*, ed. Rev. W. Clifford Holden. Grahamstown: T. H. Grocott.

Ellen, R. F. 1977. Anatomical Classification and the Semiotics of the Body. In *The Anthropology of the Body*, ed. J. Blacking. London: Academic Press.

Ellenberger, D. F. 1912. *History of the Basuto*. London: Caxton.

Elliott, A. 1978. *Sons of Zulu*. London: Collins.

Evans-Pritchard, E. E. 1956. *Nuer Religion*. Oxford: Oxford University Press.

Feierman, S. 1979. Change in African Therapeutic Systems. *Social Science and Medicine*, 13(B):277–84.

Fernandez, J. 1978. African Religious Movements. *Annual Review of Anthropology*, 7:198–234.

———. 1982. *Bwiti: An Ethnography of the Religious Imagination in Africa*. Princeton: Princeton University Press.

Field, M. 1960. *Search for Security: An Ethno-Psychiatric Study of Rural Ghana*. London: Faber & Faber.

Figlio, K. M. 1976. The Metaphor of Organization: An Historiographical Perspective on the Biomedical Sciences in the Early Nineteenth Century. *History of Science*, 15:17–35.

Forsythe, D. 1980. West Indian Culture through the Prism of Rastafarianism. *Caribbean Quarterly*, 26(4):62–81.

Fortes, M. 1953. The Structure of Unilineal Descent Groups. *American Anthropologist,* 55(1):17–41.

Foster-Carter, A. 1978. The Modes of Production Controversy. *New Left Review,* 107:47–77.

Foucault, M. 1972. *The Archeology of Knowledge.* Trans. A. M. Sheridan Smith. London: Tavistock.

———. 1975. *The Birth of the Clinic.* New York: Vintage Books.

———. 1980(a). *Power/Knowledge: Selected Interviews and Other Writings, 1972–77,* ed. C. Gordon. Trans. C. Gordon et al. New York: Pantheon Books.

———. 1980(b). *The History of Sexuality.* Trans. R. Hurley. New York: Vintage Books.

Frank, A. G. 1967. *Capitalism and Underdevelopment in Latin America.* New York: Monthly Review Press.

Gell, A. 1975. *Metamorphosis of the Cassowaries: Umeda Society, Language and Ritual.* London: Athlone Press.

Gerhart, G. M. 1978. *Black Power in South Africa.* Berkeley: University of California Press.

Giddens, A. 1976. *New Rules of Sociological Method.* New York: Basic Books.

———. 1979. *Central Problems in Social Theory: Action, Structure and Contradiction in Social Analysis.* Berkeley: University of California Press.

Goody, J. 1977. *The Domestication of the Savage Mind.* Cambridge: Cambridge University Press.

———. 1980. Thought and Writing. In *Soviet and Western Anthropology,* ed. E. Gellner. New York: Columbia University Press.

Gordon, C. 1980. Afterword. In *Power/Knowledge, Selected Interviews and Other Writings, 1972–1977,* Michel Foucault, ed. C. Gordon. New York: Pantheon.

Gregory, C. 1980. Gifts to Men and Gifts to God: Gift Exchange and Capital Accumulation in Contemporary Papua. *Man,* n.s., 15(4):626–56.

Griaule, M. 1965. *Conversations with Ogotemmêli: An Introduction to Dogon Religious Ideas.* London: Oxford University Press.

Grinnell-Milne, D. 1957. *Baden-Powell at Mafeking.* London: Bodley Head.

Guy, J. 1979. *The Destruction of the Zulu Kingdom: The Civil War in Zululand, 1879–1884.* London: Longman.

Hall, S. 1977. Culture, the Media, and the "Ideological Effect." In *Mass Communication and Society,* ed. J. Curran et al. London: E. Arnold.

Hall, S., Jefferson, T., and Roberts, B., eds. 1976. *Resistance through Rituals.* London: Hutchinson.

Harlan, R. 1906. *John Alexander Dowie and His Christian Catholic Apostolic Church in Zion.* Evansville, Wis.: Press of R. M. Antes.

Hebdige, D. 1979. *Subculture: The Meaning of Style.* New York: Methuen.

Hegel, G. W. F. 1967. *The Phenomenology of Mind.* Trans. J. B. Baillie. New York: Harper & Row.

Hindess, B. 1972. The "Phenomenological" Sociology of Alfred Schutz. *Economy and Society,* 1(1):1–27.

Hobsbawm, E. J. 1957. Methodism and the Threat of Revolution in Britain. *History Today,* 7:115–24.

———. 1959. *Primitive Rebels.* New York: W. W. Norton.

———. 1962. *The Age of Revolution, 1789–1848.* Cleveland: World Publishing.

Holub, E. 1881. *Seven Years in South Africa: Travels, Researches, and Hunting Adventures, between the Diamond-Fields and the Zambesi (1872–79),* 2 vols. Trans. E. E. Frewer. Boston: Houghton Mifflin.

Horton, R. 1967. African Traditional Thought and Western Science. *Africa*, 37(1):50–71; (2):155–87.
———. 1971. African Conversion. *Africa*, 41(2):85–108.
Hugh-Jones, C. 1979. *From the Milk River*. Cambridge: Cambridge University Press.
Hutchinson, B. 1957. Some Social Consequences of 19th Century Mission Activity among the South African Bantu. *Africa*, 27(2):160–77.
Ileto, R. C. 1979. *Pasyon and Revolution: Popular Movements in the Philippines, 1840–1910*. Manila: Ateneo de Manila University Press.
Inskeep, R. R. 1979. *The Peopling of South Africa*. New York: Barnes & Noble.
Isaacman, A., and Isaacman, B. 1977. Resistance and Collaboration in Southern and Central Africa, ca 1850–1920. *International Journal of African Historical Studies*, 10(1):31–62.
Jennings, A. E. 1933. *Bogadi: A Study of the Marriage Laws and Customs of the Bechuana Tribes of South Africa*. Tiger Kloof: London Missionary Society.
Kahn, J. S. 1978. Ideology and Social Structure in Indonesia. *Comparative Studies in Society and History*, 20(1):103–22.
Kiernan, J. P. 1974. Where Zionists Draw the Line: A Study of Religious Exclusiveness in an African Township. *African Studies*, 33(2):79–90.
———. 1976. The Work of Zion: An Analysis of an African Zionist Ritual. *Africa*, 46(4):340–55.
———. 1977. Poor and Puritan: An Attempt to View Zionism as a Collective Response to Urban Poverty. *African Studies*, 36(1):31–43.
Kinsman, M. n.d.(a). Notes on the Southern Tswana Social Formation. Paper read to the Africa Seminar, University of Cape Town, 1980.
———. n.d.(b). Beasts of Burden: Women in Southern Tswana Production, 1800–1840. Paper read to the Africa Seminar, University of Cape Town, 1981.
Kirby, P. R., ed. 1939; 1940. *The Diary of Dr. Andrew Smith, 1834–1836*, 2 vols. Cape Town: Van Riebeeck Society.
Kuper, A. 1975. The Social Structure of the Sotho-Speaking Peoples of Southern Africa. *Africa*, 45(1):67–81; (2):139–49.
La Fontaine, J. 1977. The Power of Rights. *Man*, n.s., 12 (3/4):421–37.
Lan, D. n.d. *Guns and Rain*. Forthcoming. London: Heinemann.
Language, F. J. 1943. Die bogwêra van die Tlhaping. *Tydskrif vir Wetenskap en Kuns*, 4:110–34.
Lanternari, V. 1963. *Religions of the Oppressed*. New York: Alfred Knopf.
Lea, A. 1928. Native Separatist Churches. In *Christianity and the Natives of South Africa*, ed. J. D. Taylor. Lovedale: A Yearbook of South African Missions.
Legassick, M. 1969. The Sotho-Tswana Peoples before 1800. In *African Societies in Southern Africa*, ed. L. Thompson. London: Heinemann.
Lemue, P. 1854. La circoncision chez les Africains du sud. *Journal de Missions évangéliques*, 29:208–13.
Lévi-Strauss, C. 1966. *The Savage Mind*. London: Weidenfeld & Nicolson.
Lewis, I. M. 1971. *Ecstatic Religion*. Harmondsworth: Penguin Books.
Lichtenstein, M. 1930. *Travels in South Africa*, vol. 2. Trans. A. Plumptre. Cape Town: Van Riebeeck Society.
Lienhardt, G. 1961. *Divinity and Experience: The Religion of the Dinka*. Oxford: Clarendon Press.
Lipset, S. M., and Raab, E. 1970. *The Politics of Unreason: Right-wing Extremism in America, 1790–1970*. New York: Harper & Row.

Livingstone, D. 1857. *Missionary Travels and Researches in South Africa*. London: Murray.

Lye, W. 1969. The Distribution of the Sotho Peoples after the Difaqane. In *African Societies in Southern Africa*, ed. L. Thompson. London: Heinemann.

Mackenzie, J. 1871. *Ten Years North of the Orange River*. Edinburgh: Edmonston & Douglas.

———. 1883. *Day Dawn in Dark Places: A Story of Wandering and Work in Bechuanaland*. London: Cassell.

———. 1887. *Austral Africa: Losing It or Ruling It*. 2 vols. London: Sampson Low.

Macknight, J. D. 1967. Extra-Descent Group Ancestor Cults in African Societies. *Africa*, 37(1):1–21.

Maggs, T. M. 1976. Iron-Age Patterns and Sotho History in the Southern Highveld: South Africa. *World Archaeology*, 7(3):318–32.

Marks, S. 1970. *Reluctant Rebellion: An Assessment of the 1906–08 Disturbance in Natal*. Oxford: Clarendon Press.

———. 1978. Natal, the Zulu Royal Family and the Ideology of Segregation. *Journal of Southern African Studies*, 4(2):172–94.

———. n.d. Industrialization and Social Change: Some Thoughts on Class Formation and Political Consciousness in South Africa, c. 1870–1920. Paper read to the Boston University African Studies Center. The Walter Rodney Studies Seminar, April 1982.

Marks, S., and Rathbone, R., eds. 1982. *Industrialization and Social Change in South Africa: African Class Formation, Culture and Consciousness, 1870–1930*. London: Longman.

Marx, K. 1959. *Economic and Political Manuscripts of 1844*. Trans. M. Milligan. Moscow: Progress Publishers.

———. 1967. *Capital: A Critique of Political Economy*, 3 vols. New York: International Publishers.

———. 1976. Contribution to the Critique of Hegel's Philosophy of Law. In *On Religion*, K. Marx and F. Engels. Moscow: Progress Publishers.

Marx, K., and Engels, F. 1970. *The German Ideology*. New York: International Publishers.

Matthews, Z. K. 1945. A Short History of the Tshidi Barolong. *Fort Hare Papers*, 1:9–28.

———. n.d.(a) Unpublished second fieldwork report. Botswana National Archives.

———. n.d.(b) Unpublished third fieldwork report. Botswana National Archives.

Mauss, M. 1973. Techniques of the Body. Trans. B. Brewster. *Economy and Society*, 2(1):70–88.

———. 1966. *The Gift*. Trans. I. Cunnison. London: Cohen & West.

Mayer, P. 1961. *Townsmen or Tribesmen*. Cape Town: Oxford University Press.

———. 1963. Some Forms of Religious Organization among Africans in a South African City. In *Urbanization in African Social Change*, ed. K. Little. Edinburgh: University of Edinburgh, Centre of African Studies.

Mbiti, J. S. 1969. *African Religion and Philosophy*. London: Heinemann.

McCracken, J. M. 1979. Rethinking Rural Poverty. *Journal of African History*, 19(4):614–15.

McDougall, L. 1977. Symbols and Somatic Structures. In *The Anthropology of the Body*, ed. J. Blacking. London: Academic Press.

Meillassoux, C. 1972. From Reproduction to Production. *Economy and Society,* 1(1):93–105.

———. 1975. *Femmes, greniers et capitaux.* Paris: Maspero.

Methodist Missionary Society [Wesleyan Methodist Missionary Society] n.d.(a). Bechuanaland Correspondence, 1838–57, Box XVII. Methodist Missionary Archives, University of London.

———. n.d.(b). Reports, Vol. XXIV (1888–90). Methodist Missionary Archives, University of London.

Moffat, R. 1842. *Missionary Labours and Scenes in Southern Africa.* London: Snow.

Molema, S. M. 1920. *The Bantu, Past and Present.* Edinburgh: Green.

———. 1966. *Montshiwa, Barolong Chief and Patriot, 1815–1896.* Cape Town: Struik.

———. n.d.(a). *Chief Moroka: His Life, His Times, His Country and His People.* Cape Town: Methodist Publishing House.

———. n.d.(b). A History of Methodism among the Tshidi Barolong. Manuscript.

Moore, J. G. n.d. Religion of Jamaican Negroes: A Study of Afro-Jamaican Acculturation. Ph.D. dissertation, Northwestern University.

Munn, N. D. 1974. Symbolism in a Ritual Context: Aspects of Symbolic Action. In *Handbook of Social and Cultural Anthropology,* ed. J. J. Honigmann. New York: Rand McNally.

Murphree, M. 1969. *Christianity and the Shona.* London: Academic Press.

Needham, R. 1967. Percussion and Transition. *Man,* n.s., 2(4):606–14.

———, ed. 1973. *Right and Left: Essays on Dual Symbolic Classifications.* Chicago: University of Chicago Press.

Neher, A. 1962. A Physiological Explanation of Unusual Behavior in Ceremonies Involving Drumming. *Human Biology,* 34(2):151–60.

Ngubane, H. 1977. *Body and Mind in Zulu Medicine.* Cambridge: Cambridge University Press.

Ollman, B. 1971. *Alienation.* Cambridge: Cambridge University Press.

Oosthuizen, G. C. 1968. *Post-Christianity in Africa: A Theological and Anthropological Study.* Stellenbosch: T. Wever.

Palmer, R., and Parsons, N., eds. 1977. *The Roots of Rural Poverty in Central and Southern Africa.* London: Heinemann.

Parkin, D. 1978. *The Cultural Definition of Political Response: Lineal Destiny among the Luo.* London: Academic Press.

Parson, J. 1980. *The "Labor-Reserve" in Historical Perspective: A Political Economy of the Bechuanaland Protectorate.* Paper read to the 23d Annual Meeting of the African Studies Association (U.S.A.), Philadelphia, Penn. Waltham, Mass.: Crossroads Press.

Parsons, N. 1977. The Economic History of Khama's Country in Botswana, 1844–1930. In *The Roots of Rural Poverty in Central and Southern Africa,* ed. R. Palmer and N. Parsons. London: Heinemann.

Pauw, B. A. 1960. *Religion in a Tswana Chiefdom.* London: Oxford University Press for the International African Institute.

———. 1974. The Influence of Christianity. In *The Bantu-Speaking Peoples of Southern Africa,* ed. W. D. Hammond-Tooke. London: Routledge & Kegan Paul.

Peel, J. D. Y. 1968. *Aladura: A Religious Movement among the Yoruba.* Oxford: Oxford University Press.

Phimister, I., and van Onselen, C. 1979. The Political Economy of Tribal Animosity: A Case Study of the 1929 Bulawayo Location "Faction Fight." *Journal of Southern African Studies*, 6(1):1–43.

Plaatje, S. T. n.d.(a). Unpublished notes.

————. n.d.(b). *Native Life in South Africa*. New York: The Crisis.

————. 1957. *Mhudi: An Epic of South African Native Life a Hundred Years Ago*. Alice: Lovedale Press.

Post, K. W. J. 1978. *Arise Ye Starvelings: The Jamaican Labour Rebellion of 1938 and Its Aftermath*. The Hague, Boston: Martinus Nijhoff.

Powles, J. 1973. On the Limitations of Modern Medicine. *Science, Medicine and Man*, 1:1–30.

Prins, G. 1980. *The Hidden Hippopotamus*. Cambridge: Cambridge University Press.

Radcliffe-Brown, A. R. 1950. Introduction. In *African Systems of Kinship and Marriage*, ed. A. R. Radcliffe-Brown and D. Forde. London: Oxford University Press for the International African Institute.

Radin, P. 1957. *Primitive Man as Philosopher*. New York: Dover Publications.

Ranger, T. O. 1975. *Dance and Society in Eastern Africa*. Berkeley: University of California Press.

————. 1977. The People in African Resistance: A Review. *Journal of Southern African Studies*, 4(1):125–46.

————. 1978. Growing from the Roots: Reflections on Peasant Research in Central and Southern Africa. *Journal of Southern African Studies*, 5(1):99–133.

Rey, P.-P. 1973. *Les alliances des classes: sur l'articulation des modes de production*. Paris: Maspero.

Sahlins, M. 1976. *Culture and Practical Reason*. Chicago: University of Chicago Press.

————. 1977. Colors and Cultures. *Semiotica*, 16:1–22. Reprinted in *Symbolic Anthropology*, ed. J. L. Dolgin, D. S. Kemnitzer, and D. M. Schneider. New York: Columbia University Press, 1977.

————. 1981. *Historical Metaphors and Mythical Realities: Structure in the Early History of the Sandwich Islands Kingdom*. Ann Arbor: University of Michigan Press.

Samkange, S. J. n.d. Rhodes and Africans. Paper read to the History Workshop Conference, University of Botswana, Lesotho, and Swaziland, Gaborone, 1973.

Sandilands, A. 1953. *Introduction to Tswana*. Tiger Kloof: London Missionary Society.

Sansom, B. 1974(a). Traditional Economic Systems. In *The Bantu-Speaking Peoples of Southern Africa*, ed. W. D. Hammond-Tooke. London: Routledge & Kegan Paul.

————. 1974(b). Traditional Rulers and their Realms. In *The Bantu-Speaking Peoples of Southern Africa*, ed. W. D. Hammond-Tooke.

Schapera, I. 1935. The Social Structure of the Tswana Ward. *Bantu Studies*, 9:203–24.

————. 1938. *A Handbook of Tswana Law and Custom*. London: Oxford University Press for the International Institute of African Languages and Cultures.

————. 1940. The Political Organization of the Ngwato in Bechuanaland Protectorate. In *African Political Systems*, ed. M. Fortes and E. E. Evans-Pritchard. London: Oxford University Press for the International Institute of African Languages and Cultures.

————. 1943. *Native Land Tenure in the Bechuanaland Protectorate*. Alice: The Lovedale Press.

————. 1947. *Migrant Labour and Tribal Life: A Study of Conditions in the Bechuanaland Protectorate*. London: Oxford University Press.

————. 1950. Kinship and Marriage among the Tswana. In *African Systems of Kinship and Marriage*, ed. A. R. Radcliffe-Brown and D. Forde. London: Oxford University Press for the International African Institute.

————. 1952. *The Ethnic Composition of Tswana Tribes*. London: London School of Economics Monographs, no. 11.

————. 1953. *The Tswana*. Ethnographic Survey of Africa, Part III. London: International African Institute.

————. 1957. Marriage of Near Kin among the Tswana. *Africa*, 27(2):139–59.

————. 1958. Christianity and the Tswana. *Journal of the Royal Anthropological Institute*, 83:1–9.

————. 1963. Agnatic Marriage in Tswana Royal Families. In *Studies in Kinship and Marriage*, ed. I. Schapera. London: Royal Anthropological Institute, Occasional Paper, no. 16.

————. 1965. *Praise-Poems of Tswana Chiefs*. Oxford: Oxford University Press.

————. 1970. The Crime of Sorcery. *Proceedings of the Royal Anthropological Institute, 1969*, 15–23.

————. 1971(a). *Rainmaking Rites of Tswana Tribes*. Leiden: Afrika-Studiecentrum.

————. 1971(b). *Married Life in an African Tribe*. Harmondsworth: Penguin.

Schneider, H. 1979. *Livestock and Equality in East Africa: The Economic Basis for Social Structure*. Bloomington: Indiana University Press.

Schoon, H., ed. 1972. *The Diary of Erasmus Smit*. Trans. W. Mears. Cape Town: Struik.

Scott, J. C. 1977. Protest and Profanation: Agrarian Revolt and the Little Tradition. *Theory and Society*, 5(1):1–38; (2):211–46.

Shaw, W. 1860. *The Story of My Mission in South Eastern Africa*. London: Hamilton Adams.

Shillington, K. 1981. Land Loss, Labour and Dependence: The Impact of Colonialism on the Southern Tswana. Ph.D. dissertation, University of London.

Silverstein, M. n.d. Metaforces of Power in Traditional Oratory. Lecture read to the Department of Anthropology, Yale University, February 1981.

Simpson, G. E. 1970. *Religious Cults of the Caribbean*. Rio Piedras: Institute of Caribbean Studies.

Smith, E. W. 1950. *African Ideas of God*. London: Edinburgh House Press.

Solomon, E. S. 1855. *Two Lectures on the Native Tribes of the Interior*. Cape Town: Saul Solomon.

Sontag, S. 1977. *Illness as Metaphor*. New York: Farrar, Straus and Giroux.

South Africa, Dept. of Native Affairs 1903; 1905. *Report of the Commissioner for Native Affairs*.

South Africa, Union of 1913. *Natives' Land Act*, no. 27.

————. 1951. *Bantu Authorities Act*, no. 68.

————. 1959. *Bantu Self-Government Act*, no. 46.

South Africa. n.d.(a) Applications for Recognition by Bantu Churches. Department of Bantu Administration and Development, Pretoria.

————. n.d.(b). Records. Office of the Bantu Affairs Commissioner, Mafeking.

Sperling, L., and Hart, K. n.d. Economic Categories and Anthropological Analysis: Labor in an East African Society. Manuscript.

Spohr, O. H., ed. 1973. *Foundation of the Cape (1811)* and *About the Bechuanas (1807)*, M. H. K. Lichtenstein. Trans. O. H. Spohr. Cape Town: Balkema.

Starr, P. 1982. *The Social Transformation of American Medicine*. New York: Basic Books.

Stow, G. W. 1905. *The Native Races of South Africa*. London: Sonnenschein.

Sturtevant, W. 1968. Categories, Percussion and Physiology, *Man*, n.s., 3(1):133–34.

Sundkler, B. 1961. *Bantu Prophets in South Africa*. London: Oxford University Press for the International African Institute.

———. 1976. *Zulu Zion and Some Swazi Zionists*. London: Oxford University Press.

Taussig, M. 1980. *The Devil and Commodity Fetishism in South America*. Chapel Hill: University of North Carolina Press.

Tawney, R. H. 1926. *Religion and the Rise of Capitalism*. London: J. Murray.

Taylor, J. G. 1979. *From Modernization to Modes of Production*. Atlantic Highlands, N.J.: Humanities Press.

Theal, G. M. 1911. *History of South Africa since September 1795*. London: Sonnenschein.

———. 1926. *History of South Africa from 1795–1872*, Vol. 2. London: George Allen and Unwin.

Thomas, K. V. 1971. *Religion and the Decline of Magic*. New York: Scribner's.

Thompson, E. P. 1963. *The Making of the English Working Class*. London: Gollancz.

———. 1967. Time, Work-Discipline and Industrial Capitalism. *Past and Present*, 38:56–97.

Treacher, A., and Wright, P., eds. 1982. *The Problem of Medical Knowledge*. Edinburgh: University of Edinburgh Press.

Troeltsch, E. 1912. *Protestantism and Progress*. Trans. W. Montgomery. New York: G. P. Putnam's Sons.

———. 1949. *The Social Teaching of the Christian Churches*. 2 vols. Trans. O. Wyan. London: George Allen and Unwin.

Turner, T. S. 1977. Transformation, Hierarchy and Transcendance: A Reformulation of Van Gennep's Model of the Structure of Rites De Passage. In *Secular Ritual*, ed. S. F. Moore and B. Myerhoff. Assen: Van Gorcum.

———. N.d.(a). The Social Skin. Manuscript. Published in abridged version in *Not Work Alone*, ed. J. Cherfas and R. Lewin. London: Temple Smith, 1980.

———. N.d.(b). Dual Opposition, Hierarchy and Value: Moiety Structure and Symbolic Polarity in Central Brazil and Elsewhere. Manuscript.

Turner, V. W. 1967. *The Forest of Symbols*. Ithaca: Cornell University Press.

———. 1969. *The Ritual Process*. London: Routledge & Kegan Paul.

Vail, L., and White, L. 1978. Plantation Protest: The History of a Mozambican Song. *Journal of Southern African Studies*, 5(1):1–25.

van Binsbergen, W. 1976. Religious Innovation and Political Conflict in Zambia: A Contribution to the Interpretation of the Lumpa Rising. *African Perspectives*, 2:101–35.

van Gennep, A. 1960. *The Rites of Passage*. Trans. M. B. Vizedom and G. L. Caffee. Chicago: University of Chicago Press.

van Onselen, C. 1972. Reactions to Rinderpest in Southern Africa, 1896–97. *Journal of African History*, 13:473–88.

———. 1976. *Chibaro: African Mine Labour in Southern Rhodesia, 1900–1933*. Johannesburg: Ravan Press.

———. 1982. *Studies in the Social and Economic History of the Witwatersrand, 1886–1914*. Vol. 1: *New Babylon*. New York: Longman.

Veblen, T. 1934. *The Theory of the Leisure Class*. New York: Modern Library.

Vilakazi, A. 1962. *Zulu Transformations*. Pietermaritzburg: University of Natal Press.

Vindex [*pseud.*]. 1900. *Cecil Rhodes: His Political Life and Speeches, 1881–1900.* London: Chapman & Hall.

Vlahos, O. 1979. *Body: The Ultimate Symbol.* New York: Lippincott.

Voigt, J. C. 1899. *Fifty Years of the History of the Republic in South Africa (1795–1845).* 2 Vols. London: T. Fisher Unwin.

Volosinov, V. N. 1973. *Marxism and the Philosophy of Language.* Trans. L. Matejka. New York: Seminar Press.

Vosloo, W. B., Kotzé, D. A., and Jeppe, W. J. O. 1974. *Local Government in Southern Africa.* Cape Town: Academica.

Wallerstein, I. 1974. *The Modern World System.* New York: Academic Press.

———. 1979. The Inequalities of Class, Race and Ethnicity. In *The Capitalist World. Economy.* Cambridge: Cambridge University Press.

Walter, E. V. 1969. *Terror and Resistance: A Study of Political Violence.* New York: Oxford University Press.

Warner, W. J. 1930. *The Wesleyan Movement in the Industrial Revolution.* London: Longmans, Green.

Warren, K. B. 1978. *The Symbolism of Subordination: Indian Identity in a Guatemalan Town.* Austin and London: University of Texas Press.

Weber, M. 1947. *The Theory of Economic and Social Organization,* ed. T. Parsons. New York: Oxford University Press.

———. 1958. *The Protestant Ethic and the Spirit of Capitalism.* Trans. T. Parsons. New York: Scribner's.

Welbourn, F. B., and Ogot, B. A. 1966. *A Place to Feel at Home.* London: Oxford University Press.

Werbner, R. P. n.d. The Argument of Images: From Zion to the Wilderness in African Churches. Forthcoming in *Theoretical Explorations in African Religion,* ed. W. M. J. van Binsbergen and M. Schoffeleers. London: Kegan Paul International.

West, M. 1975. *Bishops and Prophets in a Black City.* Cape Town: David Philip.

Westphal, E. O. J. 1963. The Linguistic Prehistory of South Africa. *Africa,* 33(3):253–56.

Whiteside, J. 1906. *History of the Wesleyan Methodist Church of South Africa.* London: Elliott Stock.

Williams, R. 1977. *Marxism and Literature.* Oxford: Oxford University Press.

Willoughby, W. C. 1905. Notes on the Totemism of the Becwana. *Journal of the Royal Anthropological Institute,* 35:295–314.

———. 1909. Notes on the Initiation Ceremonies of the Becwana. *Journal of the Royal Anthropological Institute,* 39:228–45.

———. 1928. *The Soul of the Bantu.* New York: Doubleday.

———. 1932. *Nature-Worship and Taboo.* Hartford: Hartford Seminary Press.

Wilson, M. 1976. Missionaries: Conquerors or Servants of God? Address given on the occasion of the official opening of the South African Missionary Museum. Lovedale: South African Missionary Museum.

Wilson, M., and Thompson, L. 1969; 1971. *The Oxford History of South Africa.* Vol. 1: *South Africa in 1870;* Vol. 2: *South Africa, 1870–1966.* Oxford: Oxford University Press.

Wolf, E. 1982. *Europe and the People without History.* Berkeley: University of California Press.

Wookey, A. J. 1951. *Diñwao leha e le dipolèlò kaga dicò tsa Secwana.* Tiger Kloof: London Missionary Society.

Worsley, P. M. 1968. *The Trumpet Shall Sound.* New York: Schocken.

Zola, I. K. 1972. Medicine as an Institution of Social Control. *Sociological Review,* 20(4):487–504.

Index

explanation or
...tion of a text or
...o t text?